SEVEN SEAS ENTERTAINMENT PRESENTS

Generation WITCH

story and art by UTA ISAKI   VOLUME 4

TRANSLATION
Timothy MacKenzie

ADAPTATION
Janet Houck

LETTERING
Mike Rickaby

COVER DESIGN
KC Fabellon

PROOFREADER
Danielle King
Kurestin Armada

EDITOR
Jenn Grunigen

PRODUCTION MANAGER
Lissa Pattillo

MANAGING EDITOR
Julie Davis

EDITOR-IN-CHIEF
Adam Arnold

PUBLISHER
Jason DeAngelis

GENDAI MAJYO ZUKAN VOL. 4
© Isaki Uta 2015
First published in Japan in 2015 by ICHIJINSHA Inc., Tokyo.
English translation rights arranged with ICHIJINSHA Inc., Tokyo, Japan.

Seven Seas press and purchase enquiries can be sent to Marketing Manager Lianne Sentar at press@gomanga.com. Information regarding the distribution and purchase of digital editions is available from Digital Manager CK Russell at digital@gomanga.com.

Seven Seas and the Seven Seas logo are trademarks of Seven Seas Entertainment. All rights reserved.

ISBN: 978-1-626928-08-4

Printed in Canada

First Printi

10 9 8 7

P9-ASJ-818

FOLLOW US ONLINE: *www.sevenseasentertainment.com*

READING DIRECTIONS

This book reads from *right to left*, Japanese style. If this is your first time reading manga, you start reading from the top right panel on each page and take it from there. If you get lost, just follow the numbered diagram here. It may seem backwards at first, but you'll get the hang of it! Have fun!!

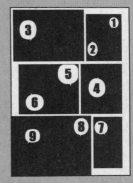

GRANDMA (SETSU-CHAN) AND GRANDPA (TAKA-SAN) DURING THEIR YOUTH.

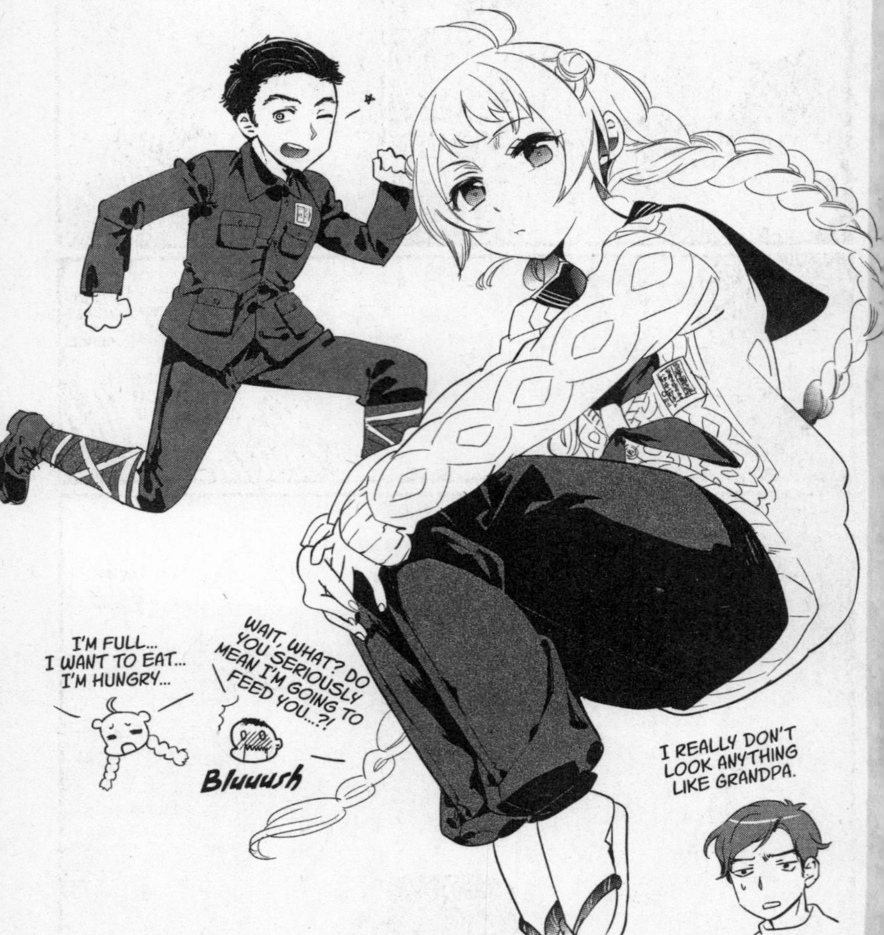
I REALLY DON'T LOOK ANYTHING LIKE GRANDPA.
WAIT, WHAT? DO YOU SERIOUSLY MEAN I'M GOING TO FEED YOU...?!
Bluuush
I'M FULL... I WANT TO EAT... I'M HUNGRY...

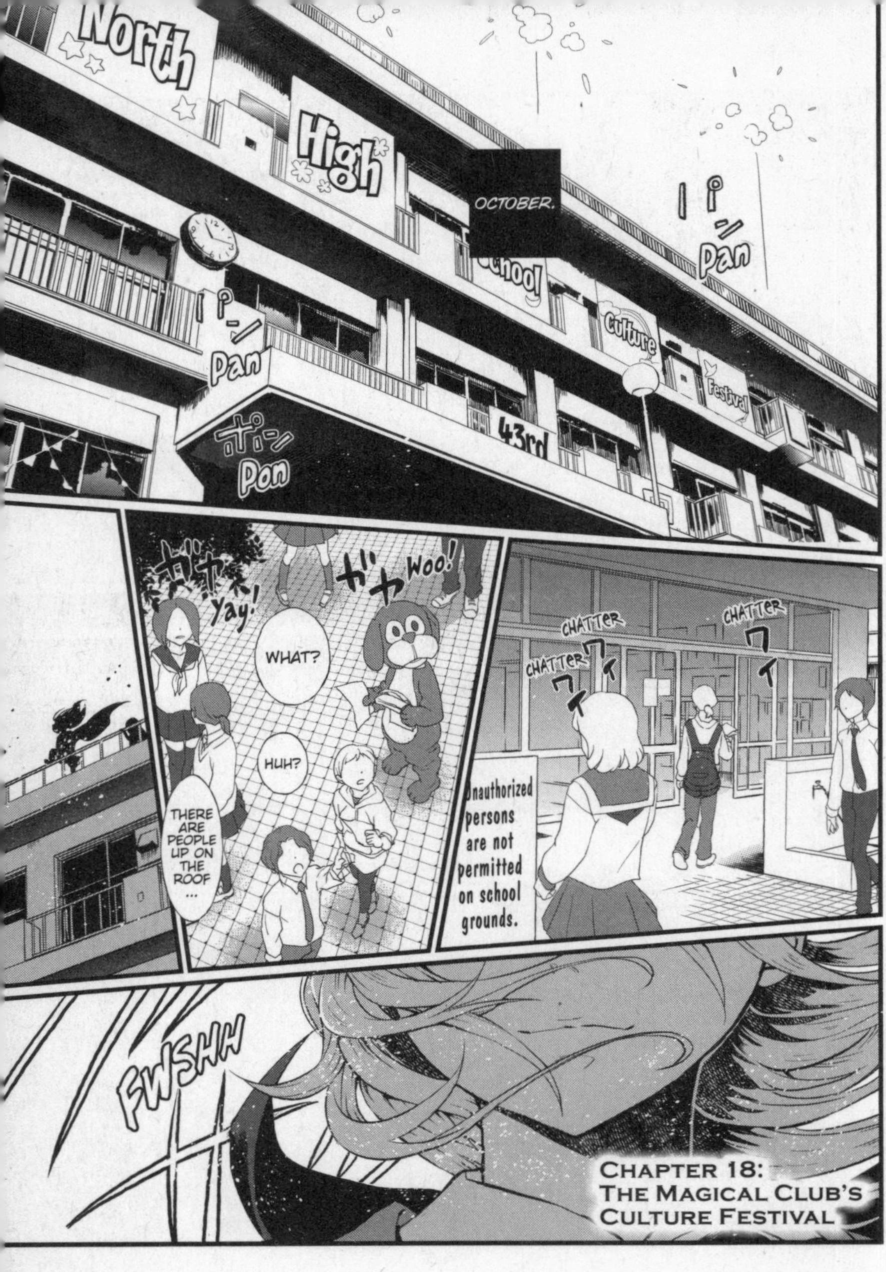

North
High
School
43rd
Culture
Festival
OCTOBER.
Pan
Pan
Pon
CHATTER
CHATTER
CHATTER
Unauthorized persons are not permitted on school grounds.
Woo!
Yay!
WHAT?
HUH?
THERE ARE PEOPLE UP ON THE ROOF ...
FWSHH
Chapter 18: The Magical Club's Culture Festival

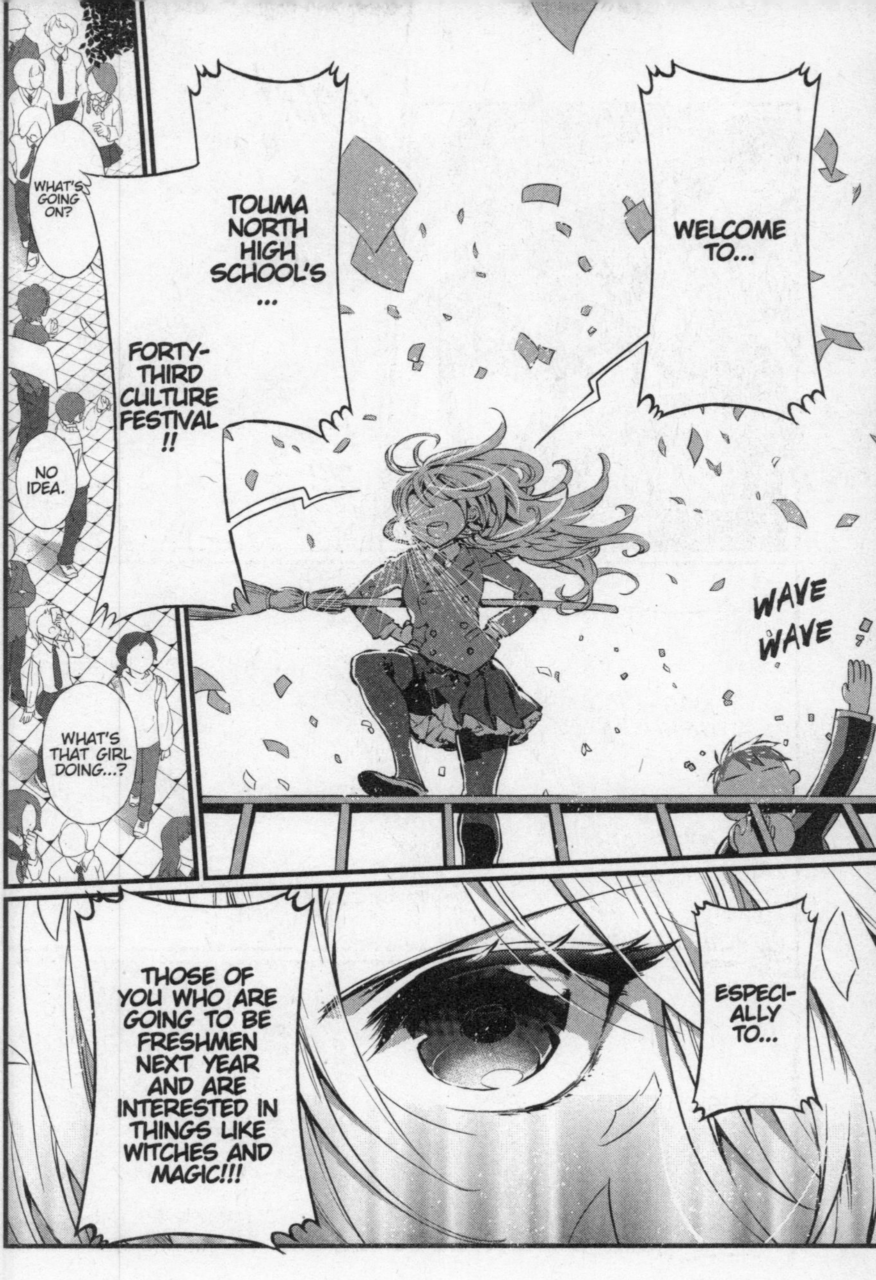
WELCOME TO...
TOUMA NORTH HIGH SCHOOL'S ... FORTY-THIRD CULTURE FESTIVAL!!
WAVE WAVE
WHAT'S GOING ON?
NO IDEA.
WHAT'S THAT GIRL DOING...?
ESPECI-ALLY TO...
THOSE OF YOU WHO ARE GOING TO BE FRESHMEN NEXT YEAR AND ARE INTERESTED IN THINGS LIKE WITCHES AND MAGIC!!!

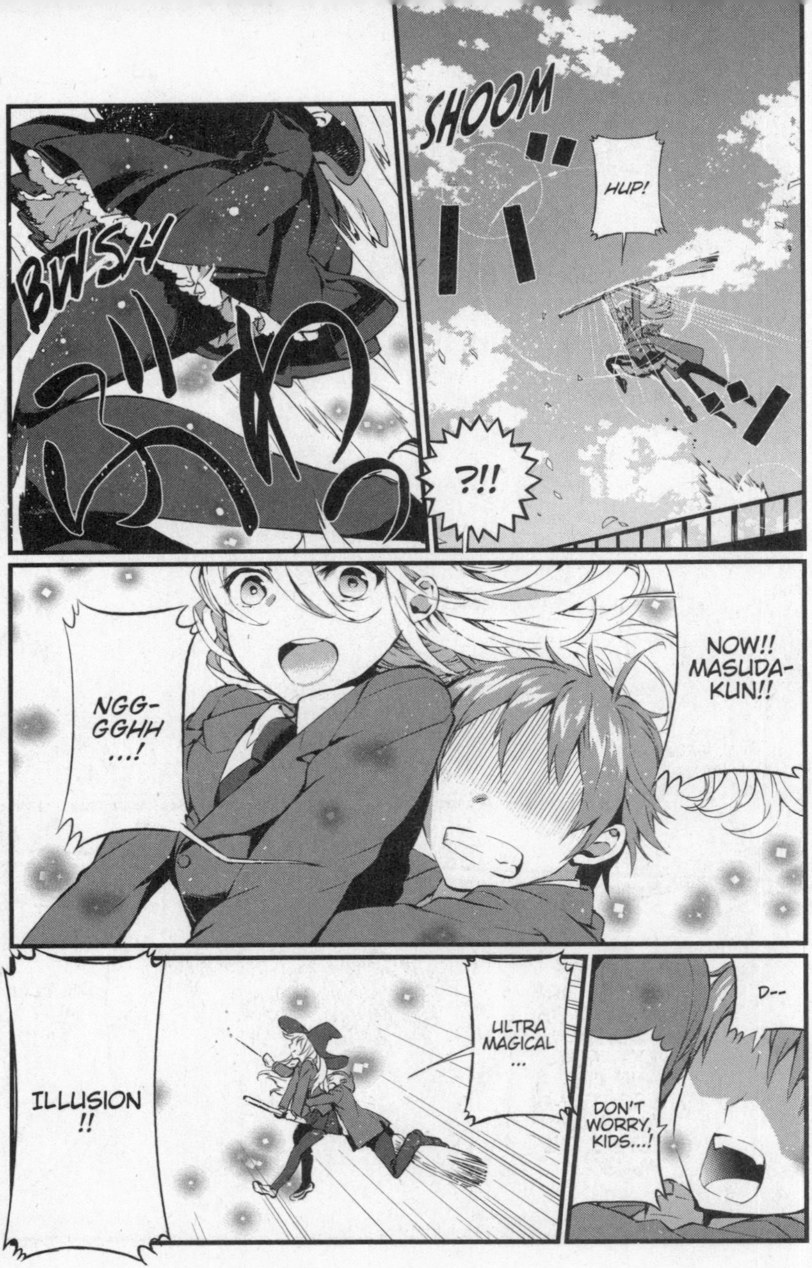
SHOOM
HUP!
?!!
BWSH
NOW!! MASUDA-KUN!!
NGG-GGHH ...!
D--
DON'T WORRY, KIDS...!
ULTRA MAGICAL ...
ILLUSION !!

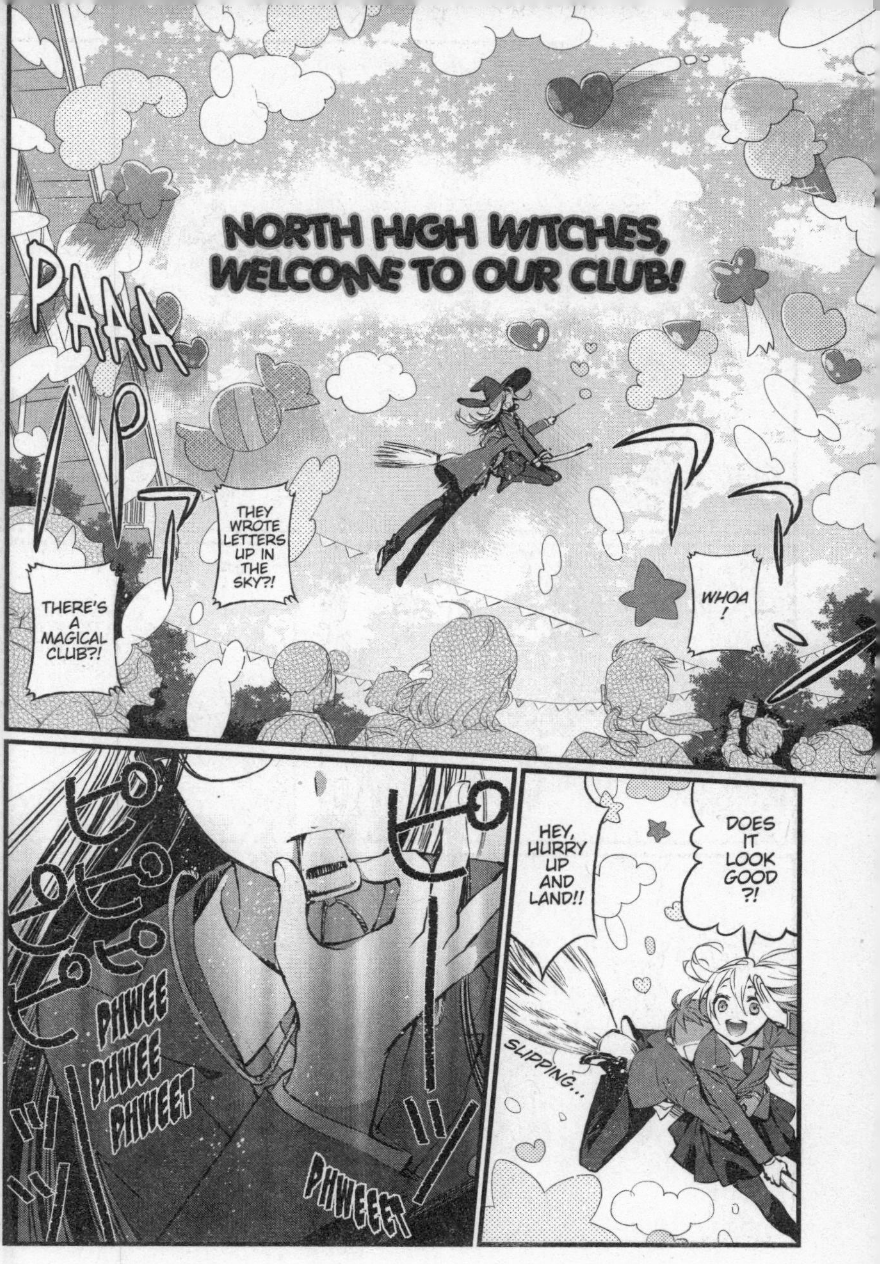
NORTH HIGH WITCHES, WELCOME TO OUR CLUB!
PAAAA
WHOA!
THEY WROTE LETTERS UP IN THE SKY?!
THERE'S A MAGICAL CLUB?!
DOES IT LOOK GOOD?!
HEY, HURRY UP AND LAND!!
SLIPPING...
PHWEE PHWEE PHWEET
PHWEEET

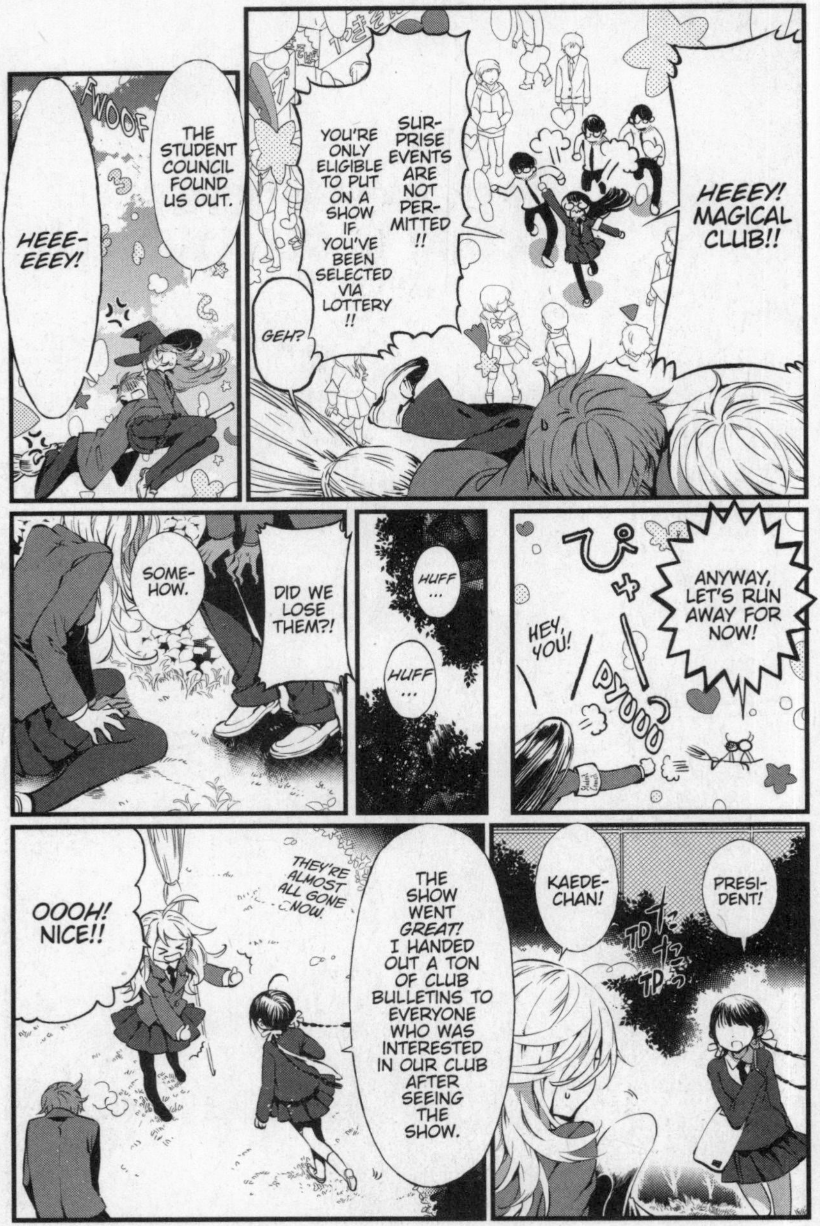
HEEEY! MAGICAL CLUB!!
SUR-PRISE EVENTS ARE NOT PER-MITTED!!
YOU'RE ONLY ELIGIBLE TO PUT ON A SHOW IF YOU'VE BEEN SELECTED VIA LOTTERY!!
GEH?
THE STUDENT COUNCIL FOUND US OUT.
AWOOF
HEEE-EEEY!
ANYWAY, LET'S RUN AWAY FOR NOW!
HEY, YOU!
PYUUU
HUFF...
HUFF...
DID WE LOSE THEM?!
SOME-HOW.
PRESI-DENT!
KAEDE-CHAN!
TP TP
THE SHOW WENT GREAT! I HANDED OUT A TON OF CLUB BULLETINS TO EVERYONE WHO WAS INTERESTED IN OUR CLUB AFTER SEEING THE SHOW.
THEY'RE ALMOST ALL GONE NOW.
OOOH! NICE!!

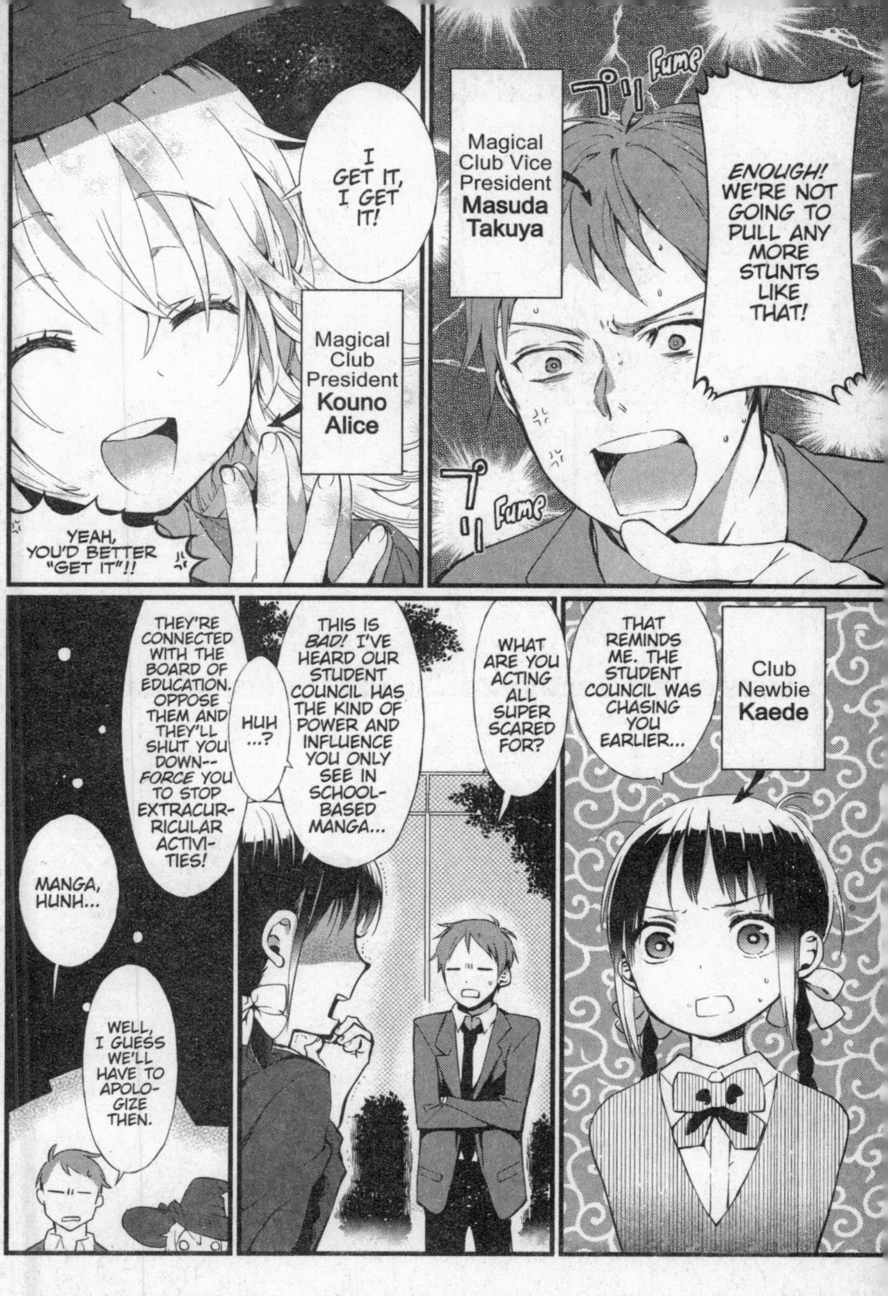
Fume
ENOUGH! WE'RE NOT GOING TO PULL ANY MORE STUNTS LIKE THAT!
Magical Club Vice President **Masuda Takuya**
Fume
I GET IT, I GET IT!
Magical Club President **Kouno Alice**
YEAH, YOU'D BETTER "GET IT"!!
Club Newbie **Kaede**
THAT REMINDS ME. THE STUDENT COUNCIL WAS CHASING YOU EARLIER...
WHAT ARE YOU ACTING ALL SUPER SCARED FOR?
THIS IS *BAD!* I'VE HEARD OUR STUDENT COUNCIL HAS THE KIND OF POWER AND INFLUENCE YOU ONLY SEE IN SCHOOL-BASED MANGA...
HUH ...?
THEY'RE CONNECTED WITH THE BOARD OF EDUCATION. OPPOSE THEM AND THEY'LL SHUT YOU DOWN-- *FORCE* YOU TO STOP EXTRACURRICULAR ACTIVITIES!
MANGA, HUNH...
WELL, I GUESS WE'LL HAVE TO APOLOGIZE THEN.

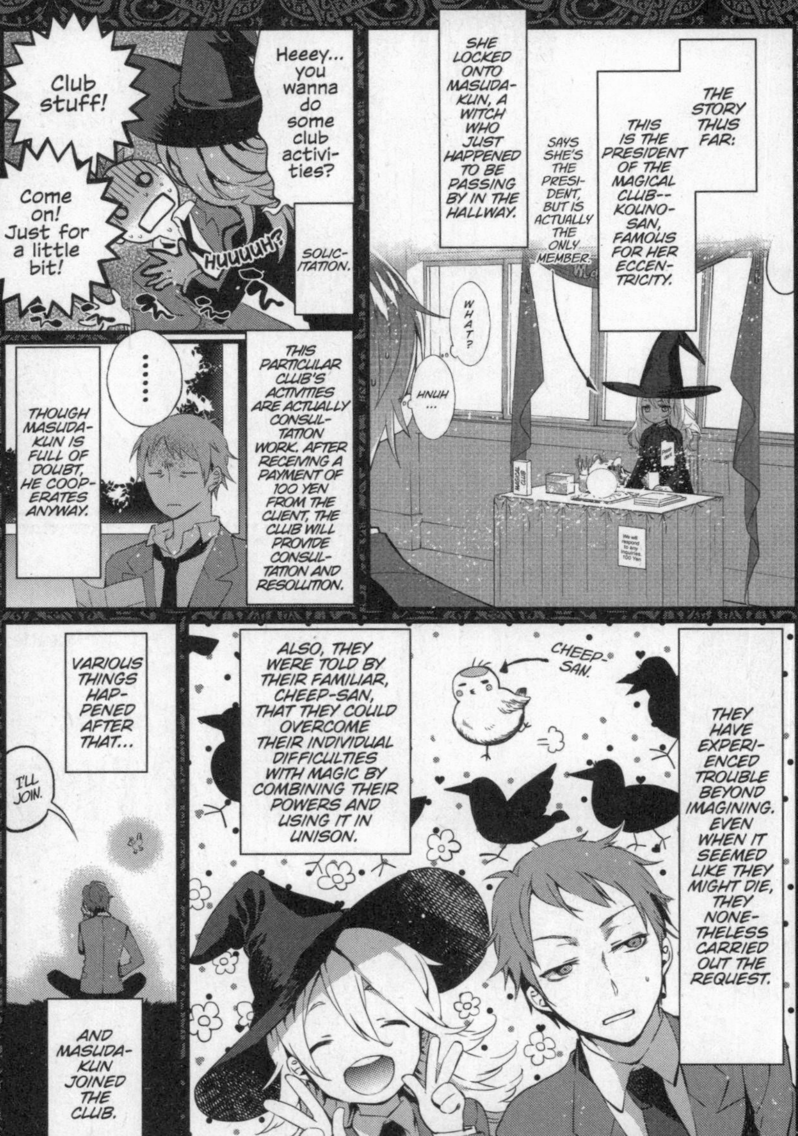
THE STORY THUS FAR:
THIS IS THE PRESIDENT OF THE MAGICAL CLUB--KOUNO-SAN, FAMOUS FOR HER ECCENTRICITY.
SAYS SHE'S THE PRESIDENT, BUT IS ACTUALLY THE ONLY MEMBER.
SHE LOCKED ONTO MASUDA-KUN, A WITCH WHO JUST HAPPENED TO BE PASSING BY IN THE HALLWAY.
WHAT?
HNUH...
MAGICAL CLUB
We will respond to any inquiries. 100 Yen
Heeey... you wanna do some club activities?
Club stuff!
Come on! Just for a little bit!
HUUUUH?
SOLICITATION.
THIS PARTICULAR CLUB'S ACTIVITIES ARE ACTUALLY CONSULTATION WORK. AFTER RECEIVING A PAYMENT OF 100 YEN FROM THE CLIENT, THE CLUB WILL PROVIDE CONSULTATION AND RESOLUTION.
......
THOUGH MASUDA-KUN IS FULL OF DOUBT, HE COOPERATES ANYWAY.
THEY HAVE EXPERIENCED TROUBLE BEYOND IMAGINING. EVEN WHEN IT SEEMED LIKE THEY MIGHT DIE, THEY NONETHELESS CARRIED OUT THE REQUEST.
CHEEP-SAN.
ALSO, THEY WERE TOLD BY THEIR FAMILIAR, CHEEP-SAN, THAT THEY COULD OVERCOME THEIR INDIVIDUAL DIFFICULTIES WITH MAGIC BY COMBINING THEIR POWERS AND USING IT IN UNISON.
VARIOUS THINGS HAPPENED AFTER THAT...
I'LL JOIN.
AND MASUDA-KUN JOINED THE CLUB.

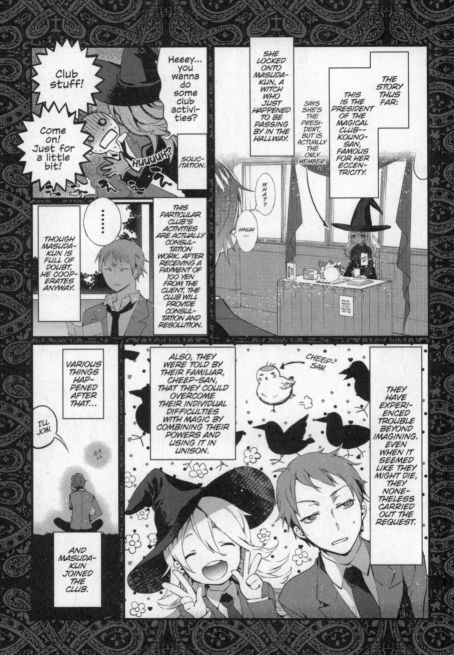

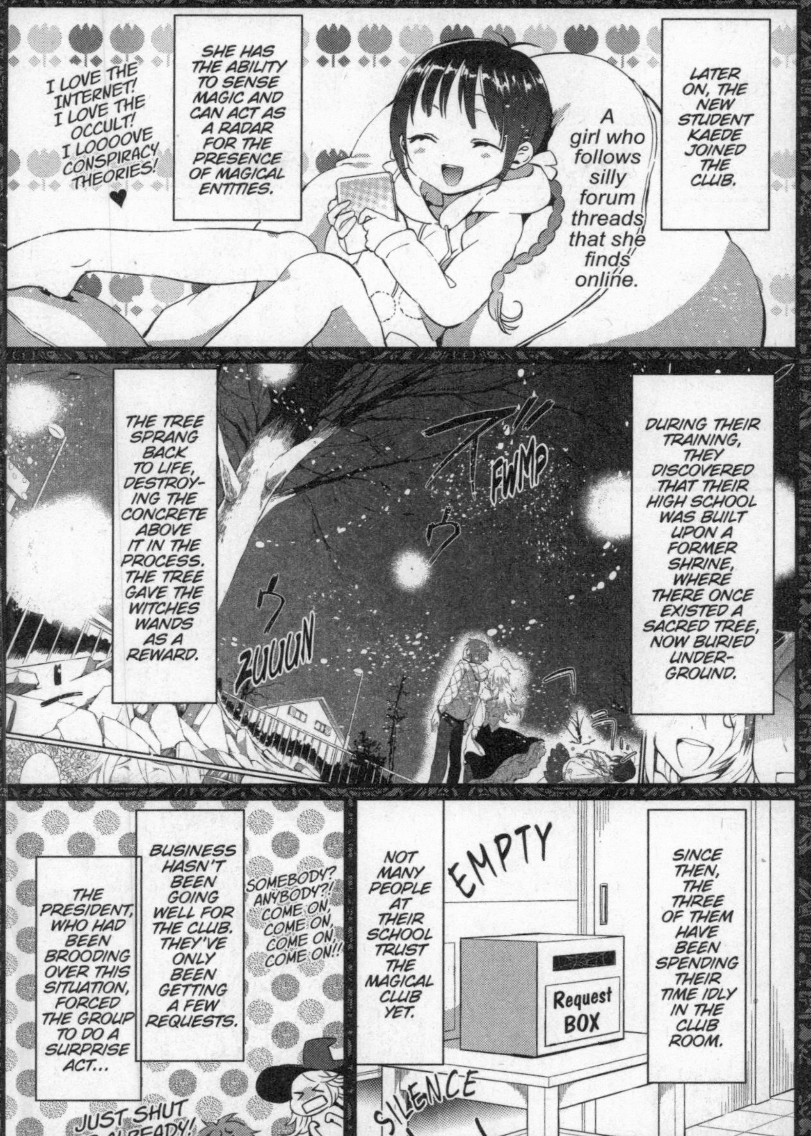
LATER ON, THE NEW STUDENT KAEDE JOINED THE CLUB.
A girl who follows silly forum threads that she finds online.
SHE HAS THE ABILITY TO SENSE MAGIC AND CAN ACT AS A RADAR FOR THE PRESENCE OF MAGICAL ENTITIES.
I LOVE THE INTERNET! I LOVE THE OCCULT! I LOOOOVE CONSPIRACY THEORIES! ♥
DURING THEIR TRAINING, THEY DISCOVERED THAT THEIR HIGH SCHOOL WAS BUILT UPON A FORMER SHRINE, WHERE THERE ONCE EXISTED A SACRED TREE, NOW BURIED UNDER-GROUND.
FWMP
ZUUUN
THE TREE SPRANG BACK TO LIFE, DESTROY-ING THE CONCRETE ABOVE IT IN THE PROCESS. THE TREE GAVE THE WITCHES WANDS AS A REWARD.
SINCE THEN, THE THREE OF THEM HAVE BEEN SPENDING THEIR TIME IDLY IN THE CLUB ROOM.
EMPTY
NOT MANY PEOPLE AT THEIR SCHOOL TRUST THE MAGICAL CLUB YET.
Request BOX
SILENCE
BUSINESS HASN'T BEEN GOING WELL FOR THE CLUB. THEY'VE ONLY BEEN GETTING A FEW REQUESTS.
SOMEBODY? ANYBODY?! COME ON, COME ON, COME ON, COME ON!!
THE PRESIDENT, WHO HAD BEEN BROODING OVER THIS SITUATION, FORCED THE GROUP TO DO A SURPRISE ACT...
JUST SHUT UP ALREADY!

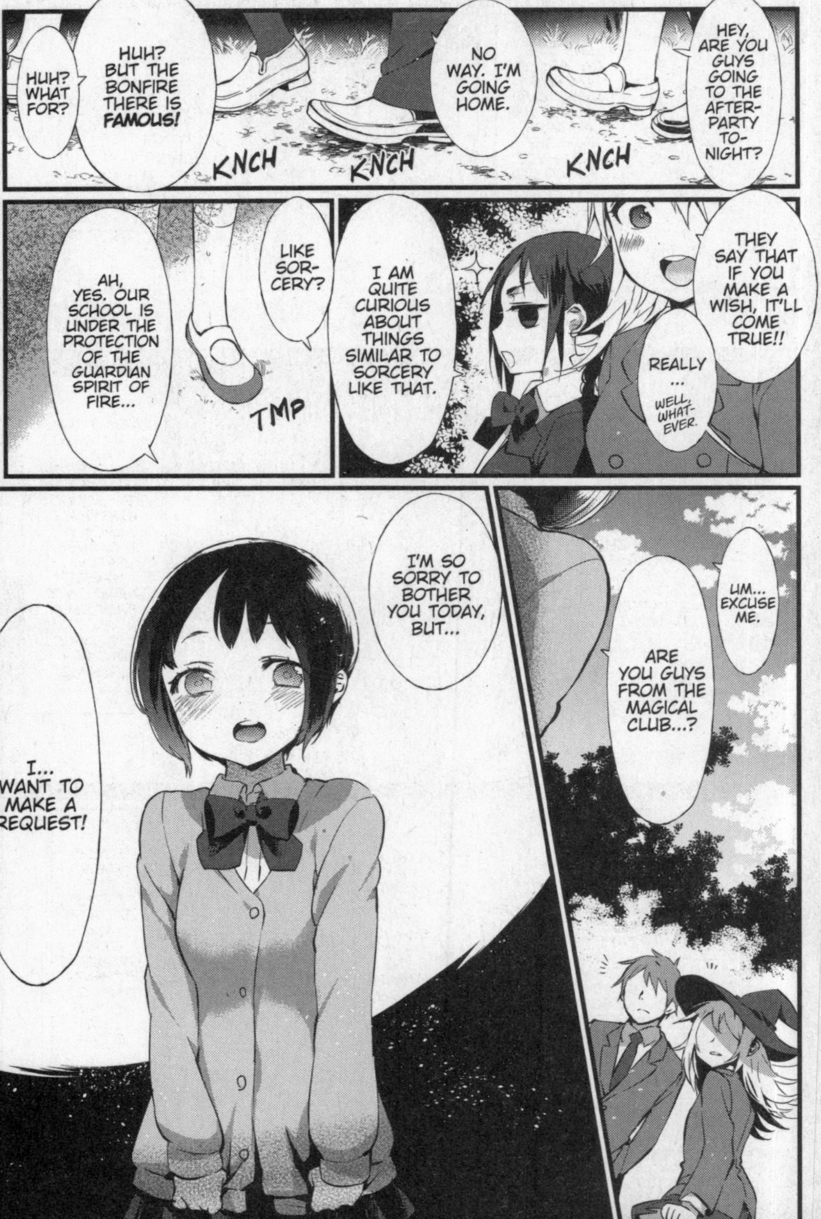
HEY, ARE YOU GUYS GOING TO THE AFTER-PARTY TO-NIGHT?
KNCH
NO WAY. I'M GOING HOME.
KNCH
HUH? BUT THE BONFIRE THERE IS **FAMOUS!**
KNCH
HUH? WHAT FOR?
THEY SAY THAT IF YOU MAKE A WISH, IT'LL COME TRUE!!
REALLY...
WELL, WHAT-EVER.
I AM QUITE CURIOUS ABOUT THINGS SIMILAR TO SORCERY LIKE THAT.
LIKE SOR-CERY?
AH, YES. OUR SCHOOL IS UNDER THE PROTECTION OF THE GUARDIAN SPIRIT OF FIRE...
TMP
UM... EXCUSE ME.
ARE YOU GUYS FROM THE MAGICAL CLUB...?
I'M SO SORRY TO BOTHER YOU TODAY, BUT...
I... WANT TO MAKE A REQUEST!

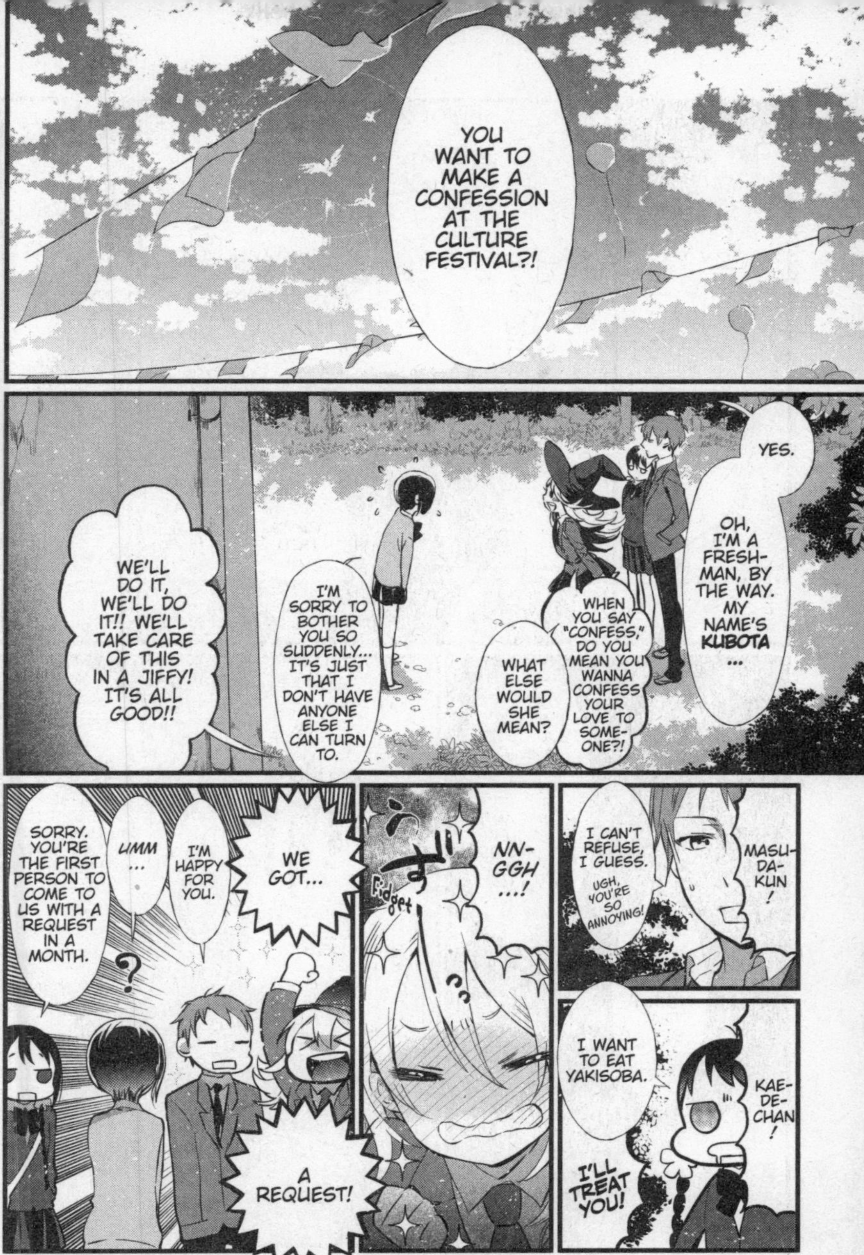
YOU WANT TO MAKE A CONFESSION AT THE CULTURE FESTIVAL?!
YES.
OH, I'M A FRESHMAN, BY THE WAY. MY NAME'S **KUBOTA**...
WHEN YOU SAY "CONFESS," DO YOU MEAN YOU WANNA CONFESS YOUR LOVE TO SOMEONE?!
WHAT ELSE WOULD SHE MEAN?
I'M SORRY TO BOTHER YOU SO SUDDENLY... IT'S JUST THAT I DON'T HAVE ANYONE ELSE I CAN TURN TO.
WE'LL DO IT, WE'LL DO IT!! WE'LL TAKE CARE OF THIS IN A JIFFY! IT'S ALL GOOD!!
MASUDA-KUN!
I CAN'T REFUSE, I GUESS.
UGH, YOU'RE SO ANNOYING!
KAEDE-CHAN!
I WANT TO EAT YAKISOBA.
I'LL TREAT YOU!
NN-GGH...!
Fidget
WE GOT...
A REQUEST!
I'M HAPPY FOR YOU.
UMM...
SORRY. YOU'RE THE FIRST PERSON TO COME TO US WITH A REQUEST IN A MONTH.
?

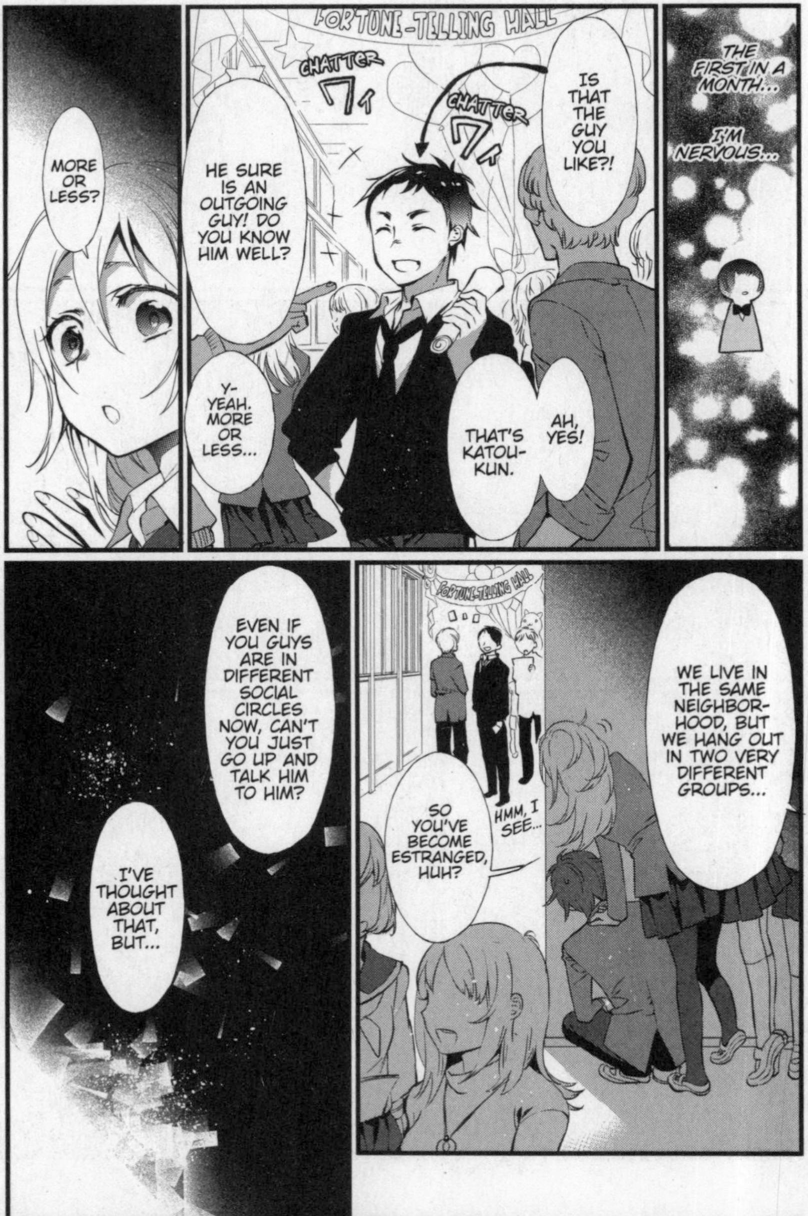
THE FIRST IN A MONTH...
I'M NERVOUS...
FORTUNE-TELLING HALL
IS THAT THE GUY YOU LIKE?!
CHATTER
CHATTER
AH, YES!
THAT'S KATOU-KUN.
HE SURE IS AN OUTGOING GUY! DO YOU KNOW HIM WELL?
Y-YEAH. MORE OR LESS...
MORE OR LESS?
WE LIVE IN THE SAME NEIGHBOR-HOOD, BUT WE HANG OUT IN TWO VERY DIFFERENT GROUPS...
FORTUNE-TELLING HALL
HMM, I SEE...
SO YOU'VE BECOME ESTRANGED, HUH?
EVEN IF YOU GUYS ARE IN DIFFERENT SOCIAL CIRCLES NOW, CAN'T YOU JUST GO UP AND TALK HIM TO HIM?
I'VE THOUGHT ABOUT THAT, BUT...

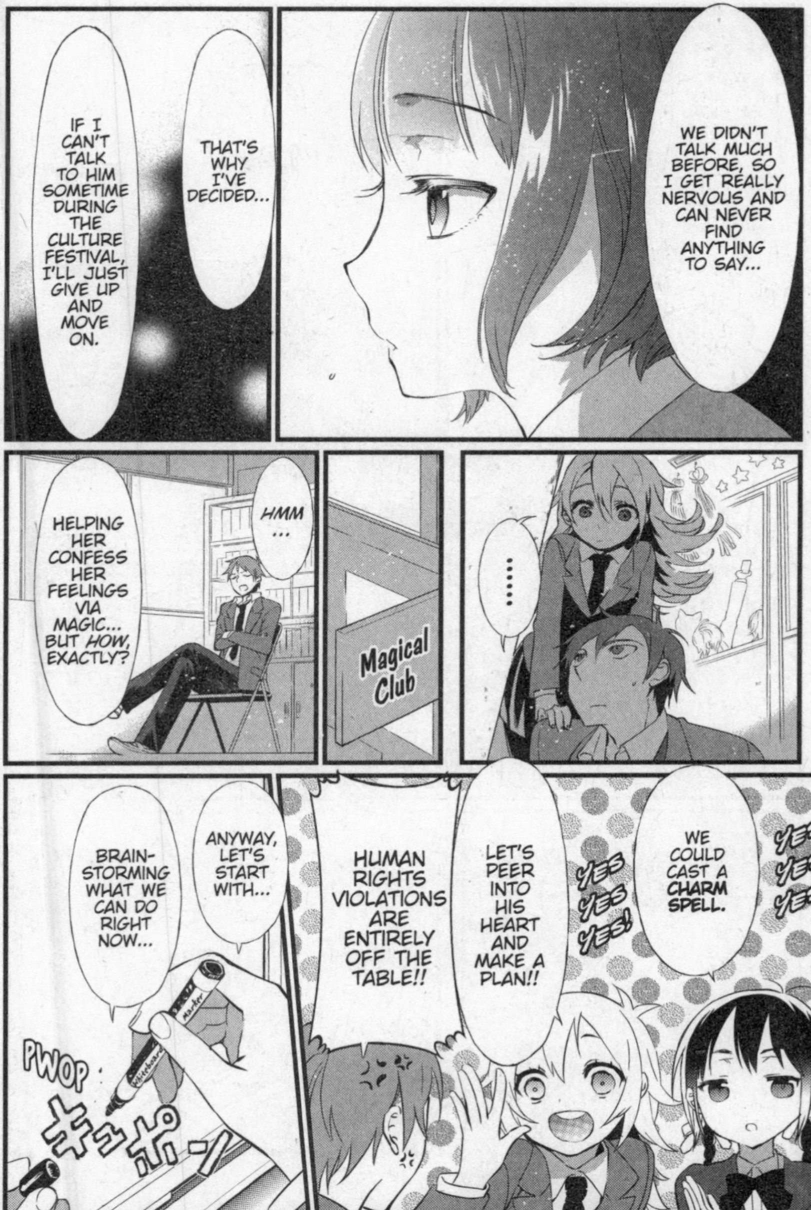
WE DIDN'T TALK MUCH BEFORE, SO I GET REALLY NERVOUS AND CAN NEVER FIND ANYTHING TO SAY...
THAT'S WHY I'VE DECIDED...
IF I CAN'T TALK TO HIM SOMETIME DURING THE CULTURE FESTIVAL, I'LL JUST GIVE UP AND MOVE ON.
......
Magical Club
HMM ...
HELPING HER CONFESS HER FEELINGS VIA MAGIC... BUT *HOW*, EXACTLY?
YES YES YES!
WE COULD CAST A **CHARM** SPELL.
YES YES YES!
LET'S PEER INTO HIS HEART AND MAKE A PLAN!!
HUMAN RIGHTS VIOLATIONS ARE ENTIRELY OFF THE TABLE!!
ANYWAY, LET'S START WITH...
BRAIN-STORMING WHAT WE CAN DO RIGHT NOW...
PWOP
キュポー!

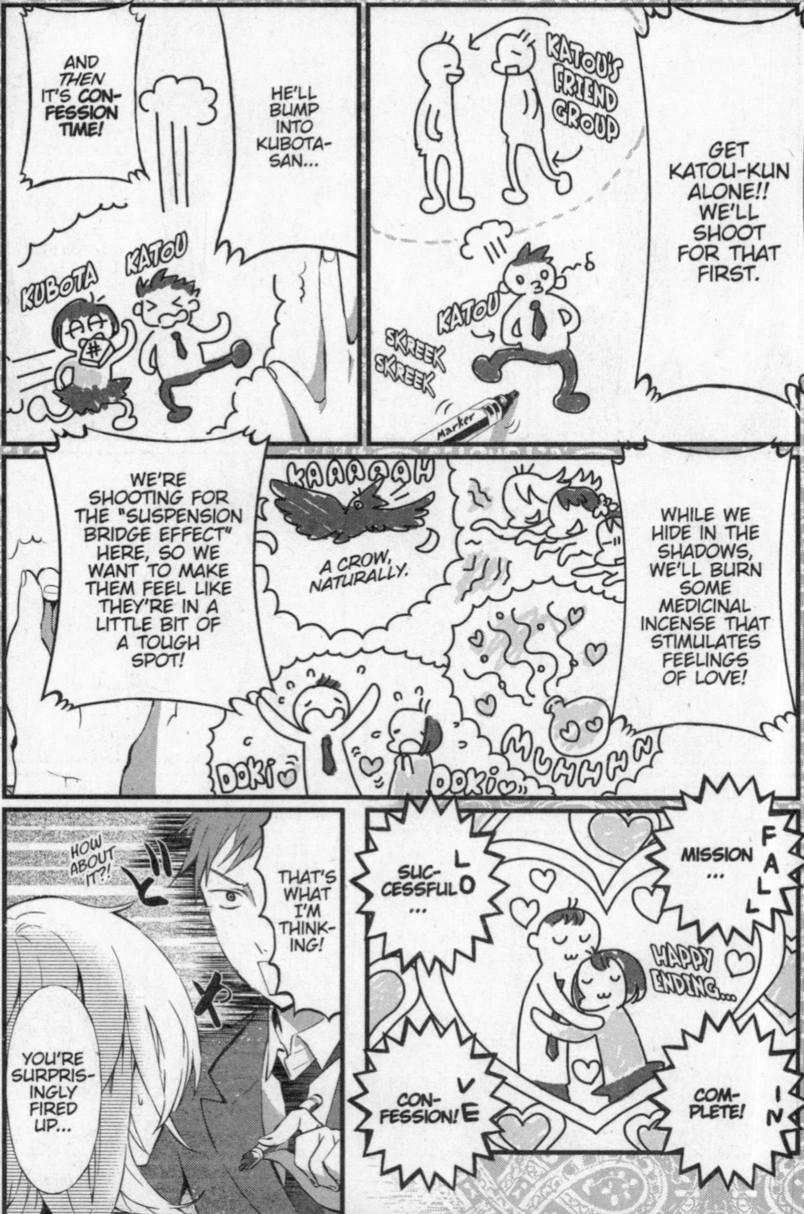
GET KATOU-KUN ALONE!! WE'LL SHOOT FOR THAT FIRST.
KATOU'S FRIEND GROUP
KATOU
SKREEK SKREEK
Marker
HE'LL BUMP INTO KUBOTA-SAN...
AND THEN IT'S CONFESSION TIME!
KATOU
KUBOTA
WHILE WE HIDE IN THE SHADOWS, WE'LL BURN SOME MEDICINAL INCENSE THAT STIMULATES FEELINGS OF LOVE!
MUHHHN
DOKI
KAAAAAH
A CROW, NATURALLY.
WE'RE SHOOTING FOR THE "SUSPENSION BRIDGE EFFECT" HERE, SO WE WANT TO MAKE THEM FEEL LIKE THEY'RE IN A LITTLE BIT OF A TOUGH SPOT!
DOKI
FALL IN LOVE
MISSION...
SUCCESSFUL...
HAPPY ENDING...
COMPLETE!
CONFESSION!
THAT'S WHAT I'M THINKING!
HOW ABOUT IT?!
YOU'RE SURPRISINGLY FIRED UP...

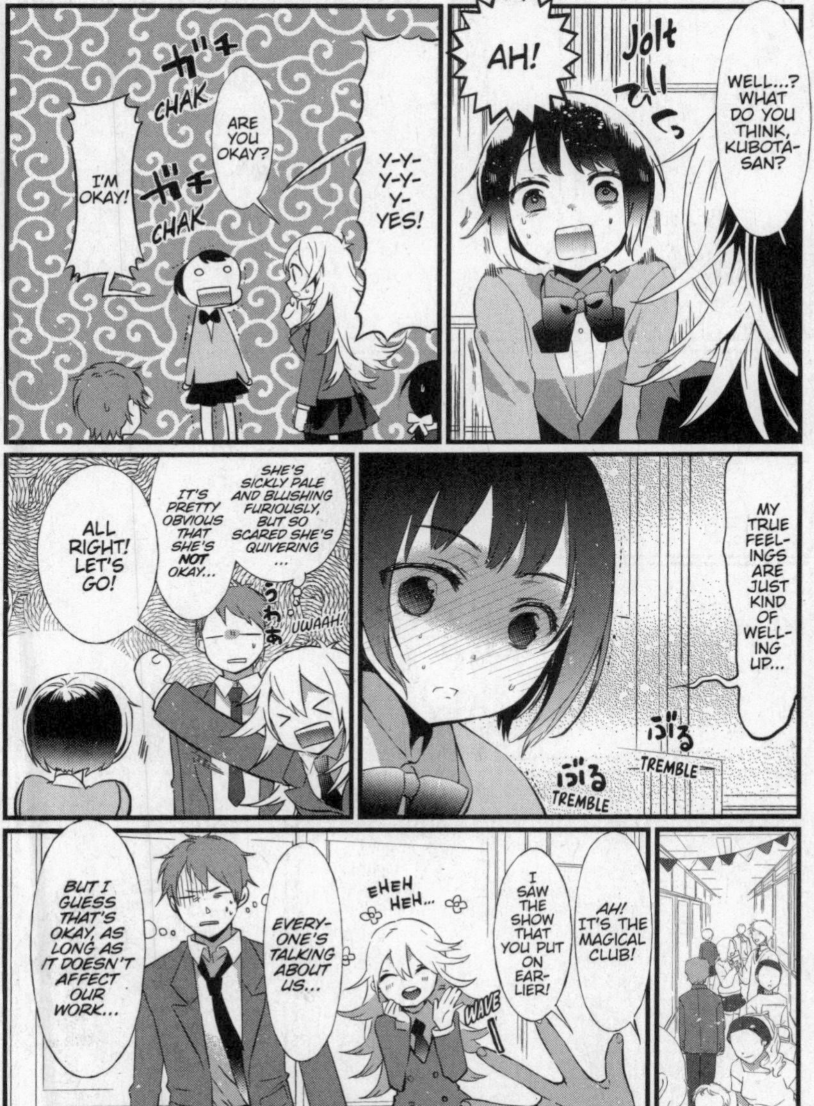
WELL...? WHAT DO YOU THINK, KUBOTA-SAN?
Jolt
びくっ
AH!
Y-Y-Y-Y-Y-Y-YES!
ARE YOU OKAY?
ガチ
CHAK
I'M OKAY!
ガチ
CHAK
MY TRUE FEELINGS ARE JUST KIND OF WELLING UP...
ぶる
TREMBLE
ぶる
TREMBLE
SHE'S SICKLY PALE AND BLUSHING FURIOUSLY, BUT SO SCARED SHE'S QUIVERING...
IT'S PRETTY OBVIOUS THAT SHE'S NOT OKAY...
ALL RIGHT! LET'S GO!
うわあ
UWAAH!
AH! IT'S THE MAGICAL CLUB!
I SAW THE SHOW THAT YOU PUT ON EARLIER!
WAVE
EHEH HEH...
EVERYONE'S TALKING ABOUT US...
BUT I GUESS THAT'S OKAY, AS LONG AS IT DOESN'T AFFECT OUR WORK...

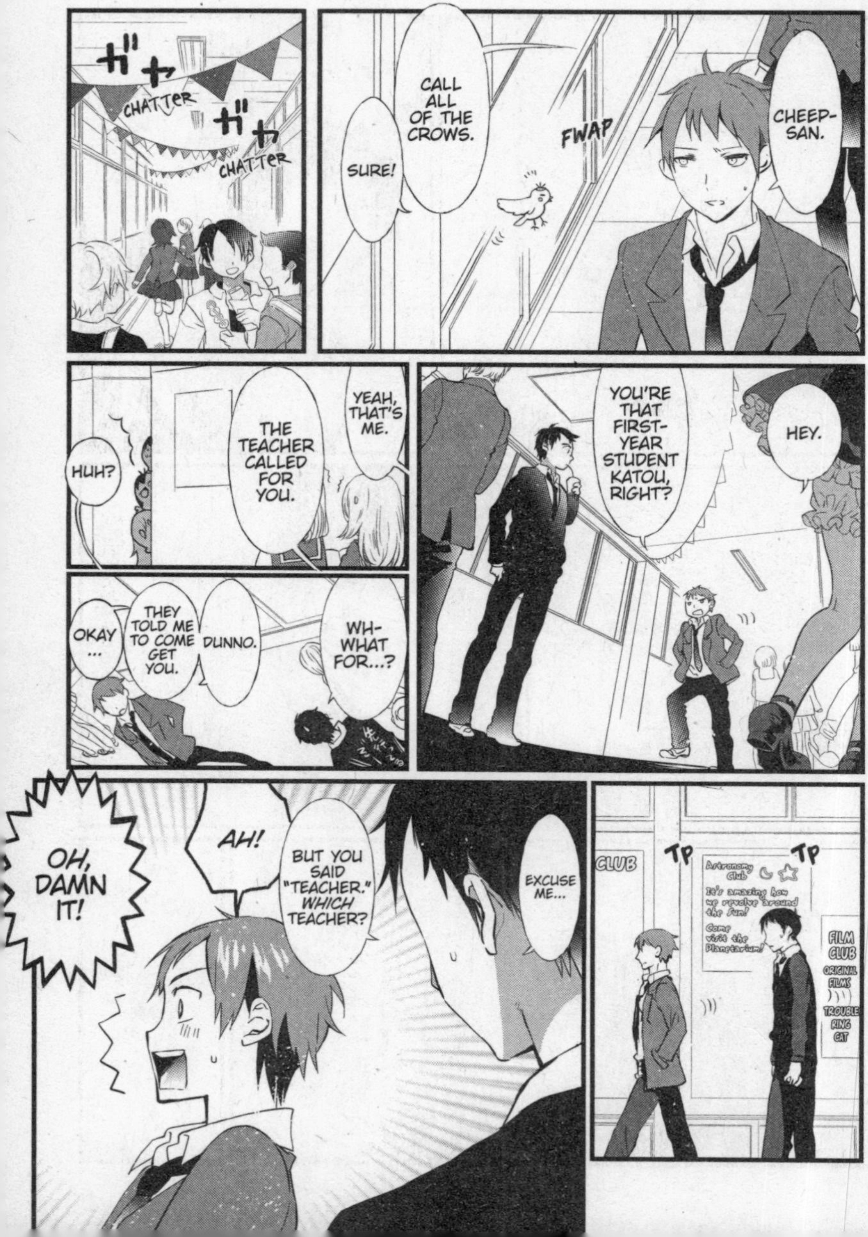
CHEEP-SAN.
FWAP
CALL ALL OF THE CROWS.
SURE!
ガヤ
CHATTER
ガヤ
CHATTER
HEY.
YOU'RE THAT FIRST-YEAR STUDENT KATOU, RIGHT?
YEAH, THAT'S ME.
THE TEACHER CALLED FOR YOU.
HUH?
WH-WHAT FOR...?
DUNNO.
THEY TOLD ME TO COME GET YOU.
OKAY...
CLUB
TP
TP
Astronomy Club
It's amazing how we revolve around the Sun!
Come visit the Planetarium!
FILM CLUB
ORIGINAL FILMS
TROUBLE RING CAT
EXCUSE ME...
BUT YOU SAID "TEACHER." WHICH TEACHER?
AH!
OH, DAMN IT!

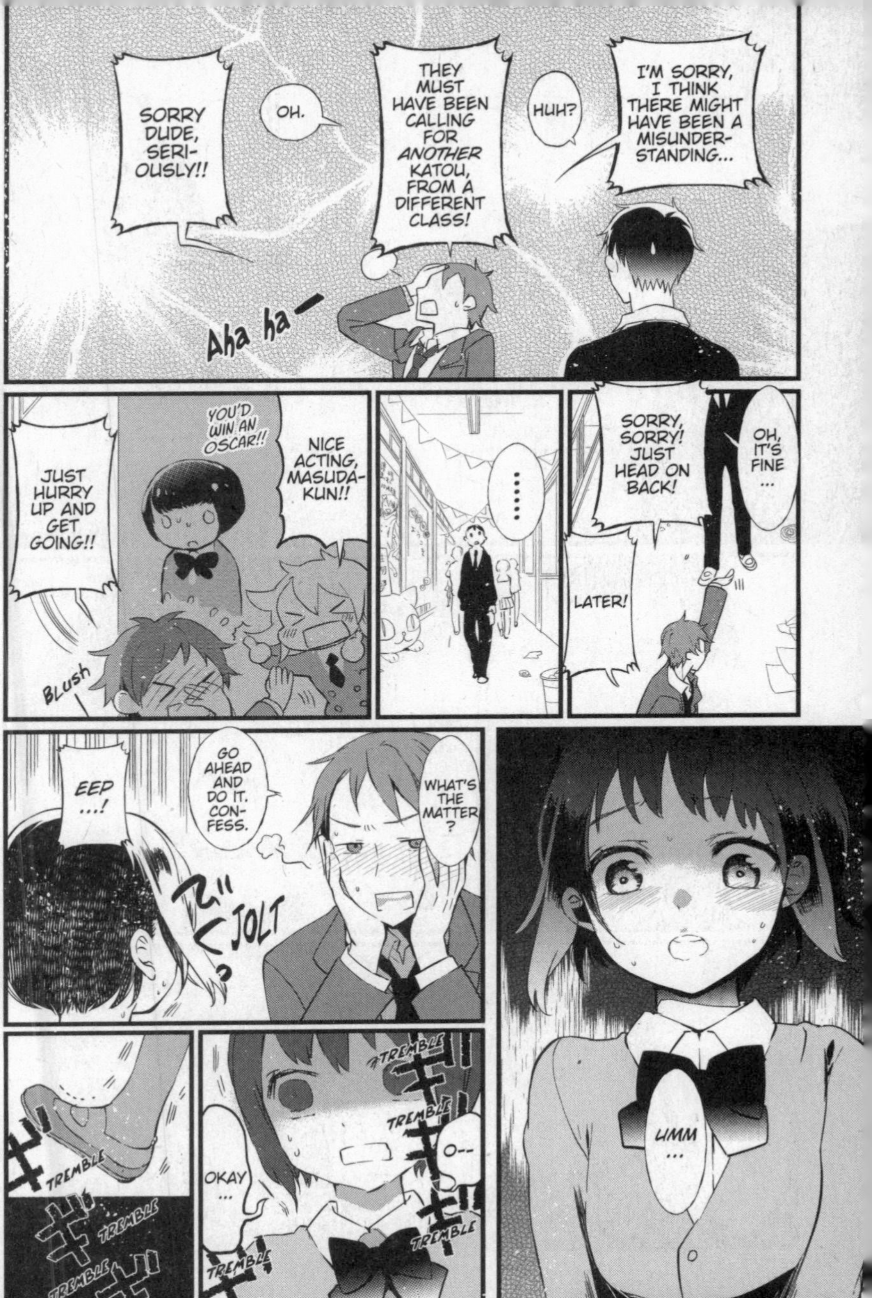
I'M SORRY, I THINK THERE MIGHT HAVE BEEN A MISUNDERSTANDING...
HUH?
THEY MUST HAVE BEEN CALLING FOR ANOTHER KATOU, FROM A DIFFERENT CLASS!
OH.
SORRY DUDE, SERIOUSLY!!
Aha ha—
OH, IT'S FINE ...
SORRY, SORRY! JUST HEAD ON BACK!
LATER!
......
NICE ACTING, MASUDA-KUN!!
YOU'D WIN AN OSCAR!!
JUST HURRY UP AND GET GOING!!
BLUSH
UMM ...
WHAT'S THE MATTER?
GO AHEAD AND DO IT. CONFESS.
EEP ...!
JOLT
TREMBLE
TREMBLE
O--
OKAY ...
TREMBLE
TREMBLE
TREMBLE
TREMBLE
TREMBLE
TREMBLE

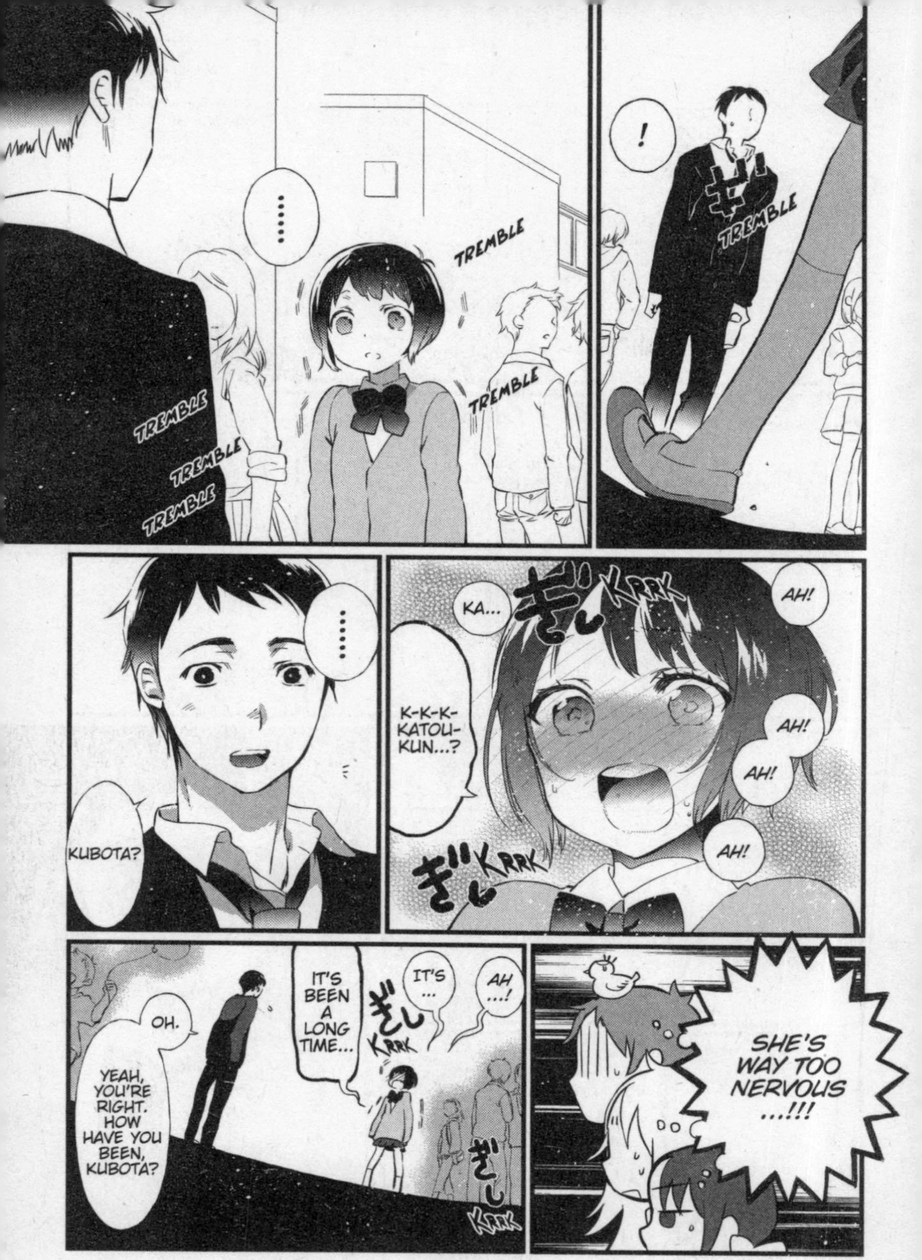
!
TREMBLE
......
TREMBLE
TREMBLE
TREMBLE
TREMBLE
TREMBLE
AH!
ぎし KRRK
KA...
K-K-K-KATOU-KUN...?
AH!
AH!
AH!
ぎし KRRK
......
KUBOTA?
SHE'S WAY TOO NERVOUS ...!!!
AH ...!
IT'S ...
IT'S BEEN A LONG TIME...
ぎし KRRK
OH.
YEAH, YOU'RE RIGHT. HOW HAVE YOU BEEN, KUBOTA?
ぎし KRRK

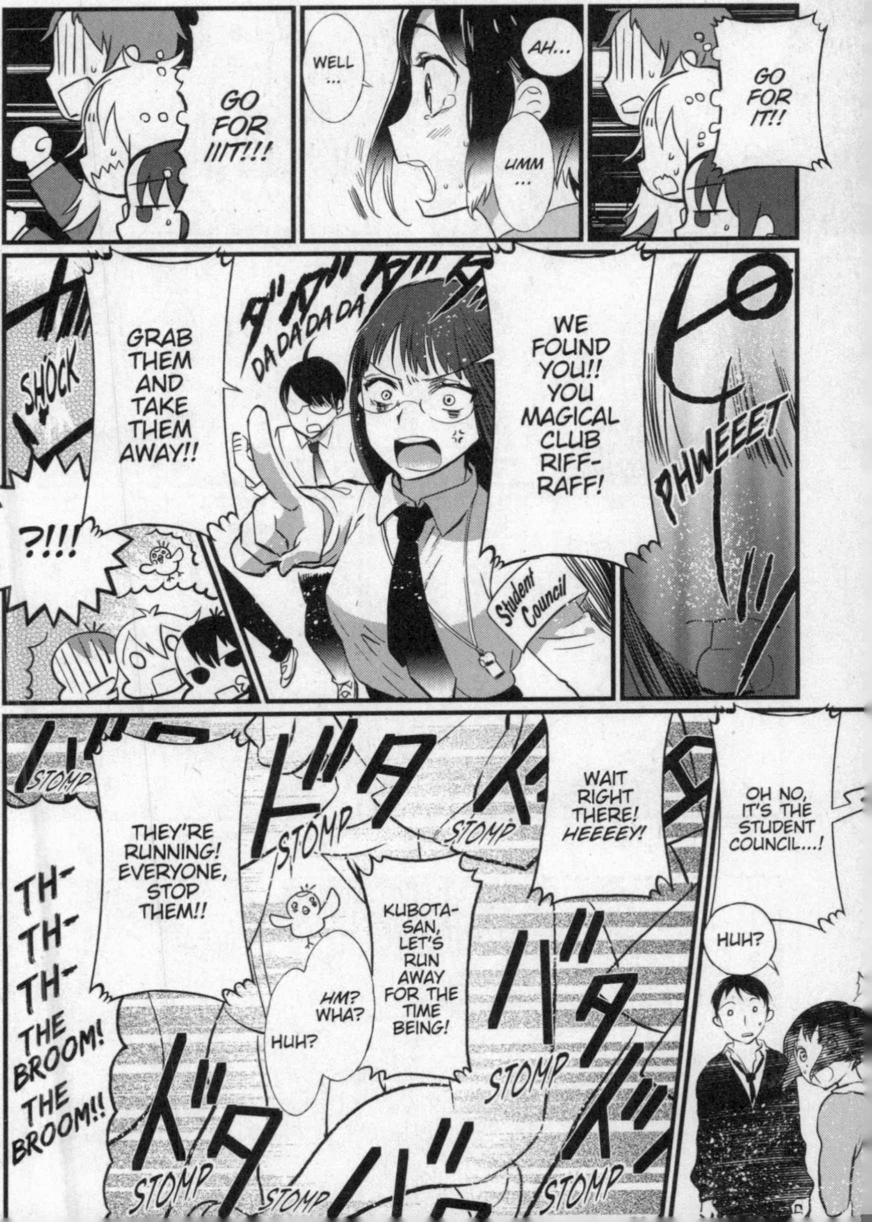
GO FOR IT!!
AH...
WELL ...
UMM ...
GO FOR IIIIT!!!
PHWEEEET
WE FOUND YOU!! YOU MAGICAL CLUB RIFF-RAFF!
DA DA DA DA
GRAB THEM AND TAKE THEM AWAY!!
SHOCK
?!!!
Student Council
OH NO, IT'S THE STUDENT COUNCIL...!
WAIT RIGHT THERE! HEEEEY!
STOMP
STOMP
STOMP
THEY'RE RUNNING! EVERYONE, STOP THEM!!
HUH?
KUBOTA-SAN, LET'S RUN AWAY FOR THE TIME BEING!
HM? WHA?
HUH?
TH-TH-TH-THE BROOM! THE BROOM!!
STOMP
STOMP
STOMP
STOMP

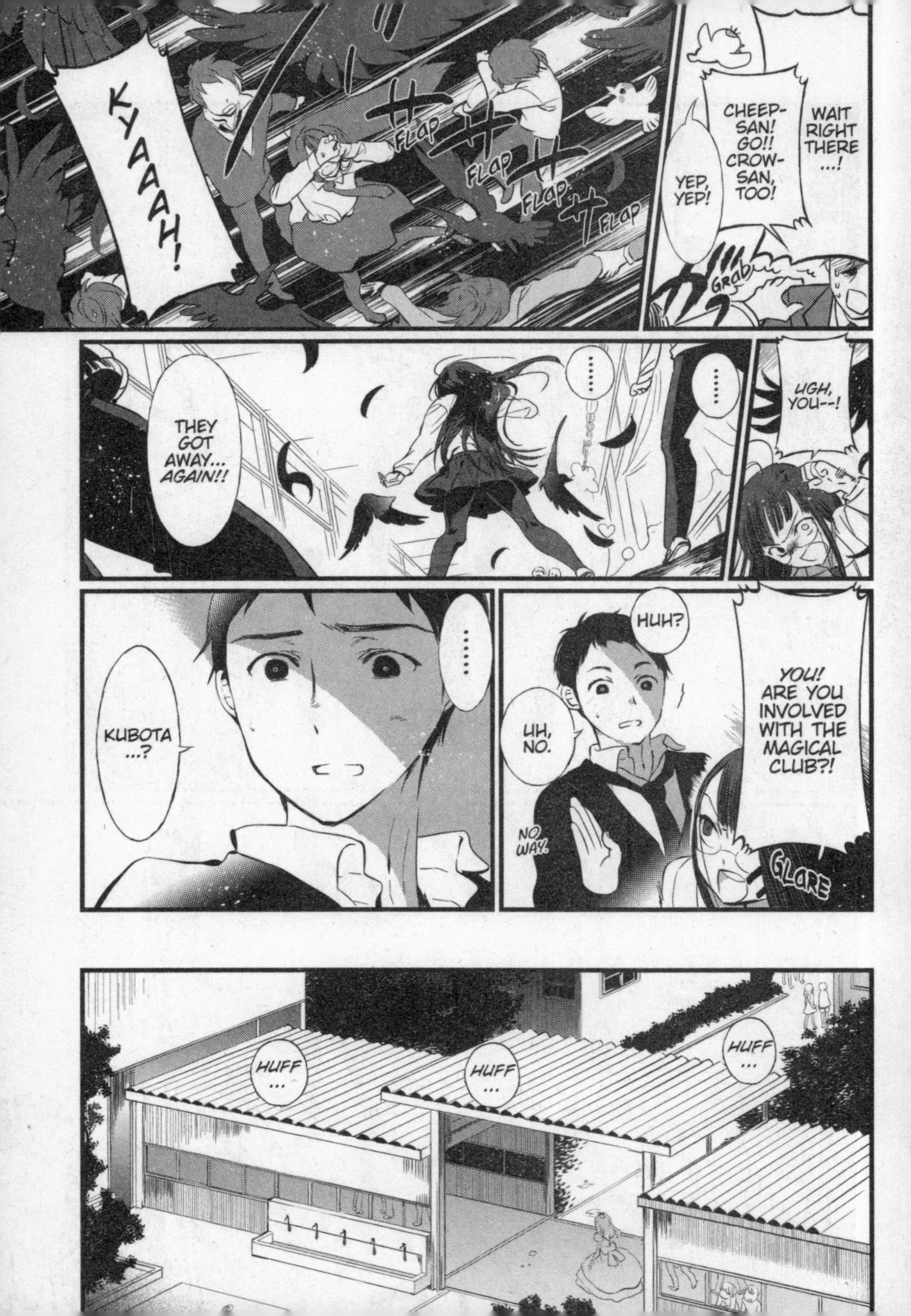
WAIT RIGHT THERE...!
CHEEP-SAN! GO!! CROW-SAN, TOO!
YEP, YEP!
GRAB
FLAP
FLAP
FLAP
FLAP
KYAAAAH!
UGH, YOU--!
......
......
THEY GOT AWAY... AGAIN!!
YOU! ARE YOU INVOLVED WITH THE MAGICAL CLUB?!
GLARE
HUH?
UH, NO.
NO WAY.
......
KUBOTA ...?
HUFF ...
HUFF ...
HUFF ...

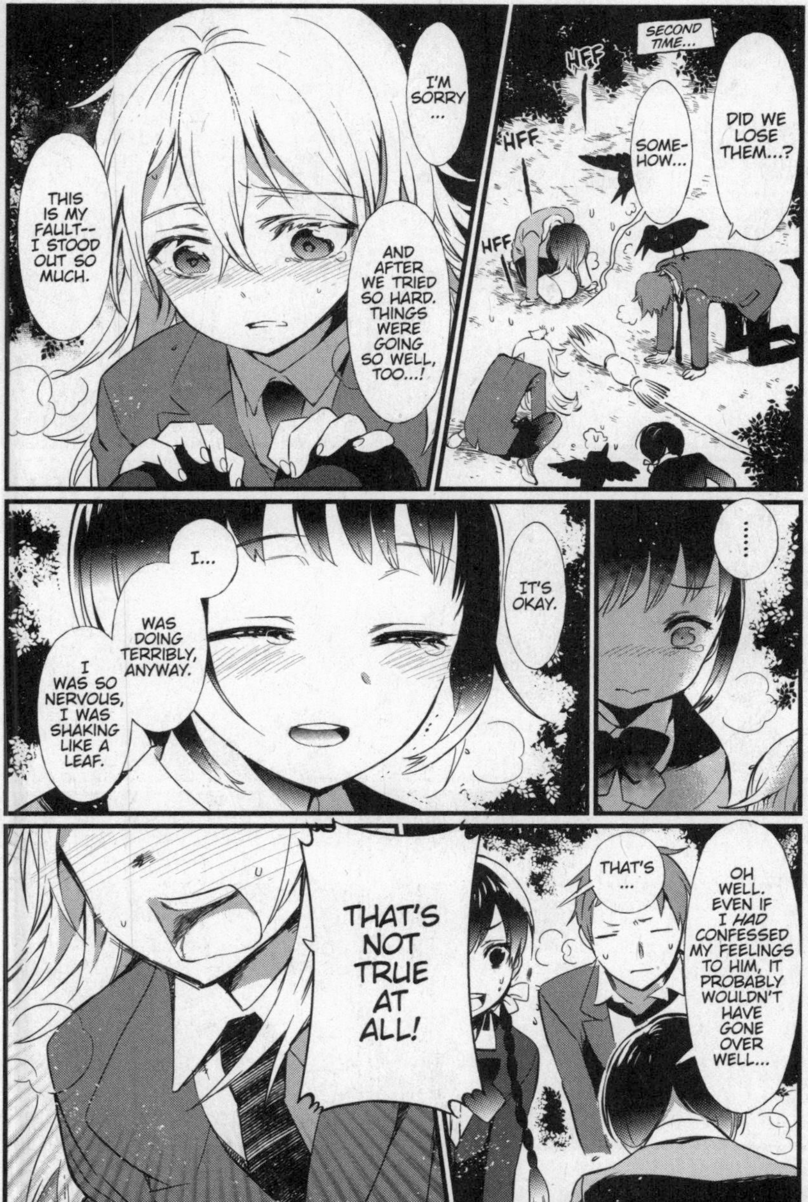
SECOND TIME...
HFF
HFF
HFF
DID WE LOSE THEM...?
SOME-HOW...
I'M SORRY...
AND AFTER WE TRIED SO HARD. THINGS WERE GOING SO WELL, TOO...!
THIS IS MY FAULT-- I STOOD OUT SO MUCH.
......
IT'S OKAY.
I...
WAS DOING TERRIBLY, ANYWAY.
I WAS SO NERVOUS, I WAS SHAKING LIKE A LEAF.
OH WELL. EVEN IF I *HAD* CONFESSED MY FEELINGS TO HIM, IT PROBABLY WOULDN'T HAVE GONE OVER WELL...
THAT'S...
THAT'S NOT TRUE AT ALL!

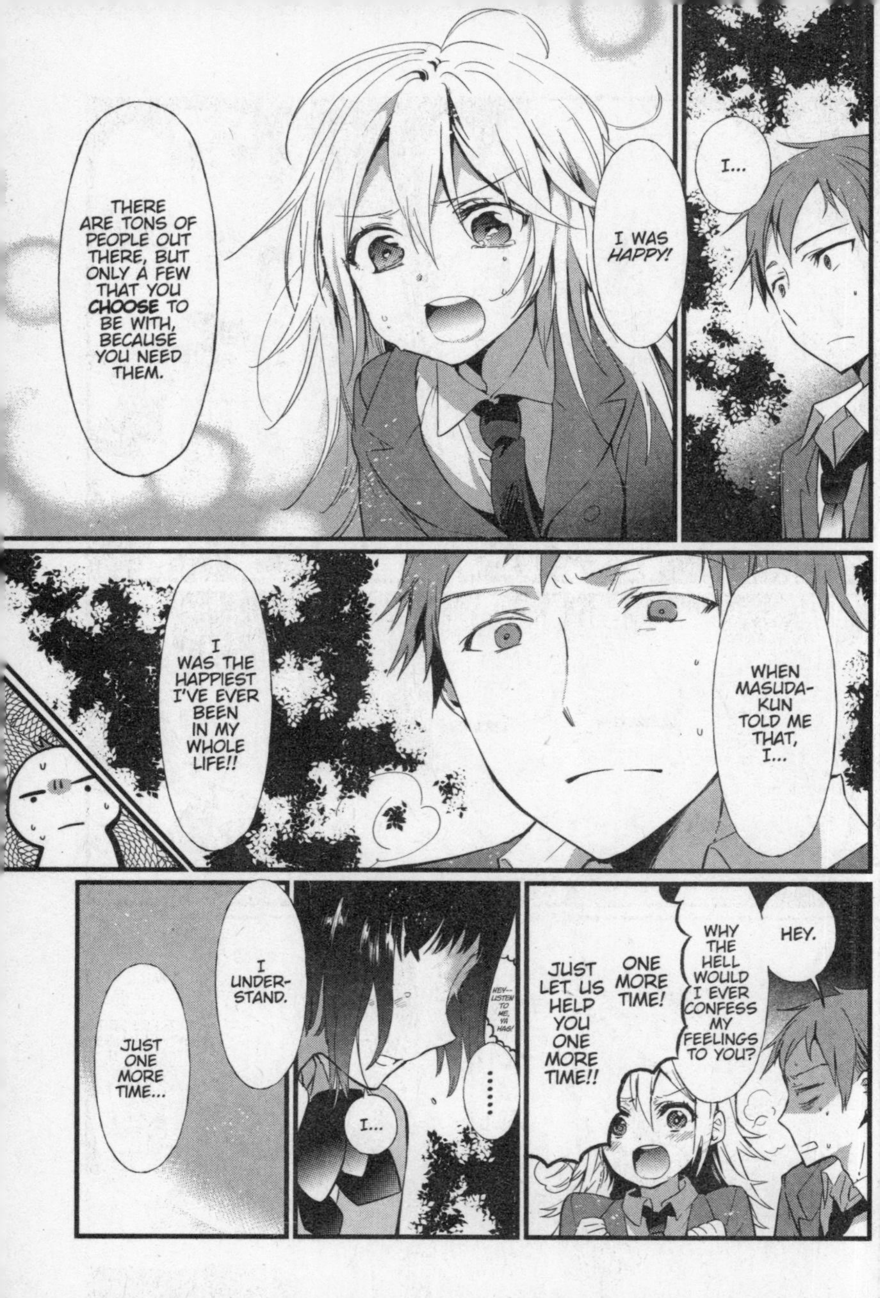
I...
I WAS HAPPY!
THERE ARE TONS OF PEOPLE OUT THERE, BUT ONLY A FEW THAT YOU CHOOSE TO BE WITH, BECAUSE YOU NEED THEM.
WHEN MASUDA-KUN TOLD ME THAT, I...
I WAS THE HAPPIEST I'VE EVER BEEN IN MY WHOLE LIFE!!
HEY.
WHY THE HELL WOULD I EVER CONFESS MY FEELINGS TO YOU?
ONE MORE TIME!
JUST LET US HELP YOU ONE MORE TIME!!
......
HEY-- LISTEN TO ME, YA HAG!
I...
I UNDER-STAND.
JUST ONE MORE TIME...

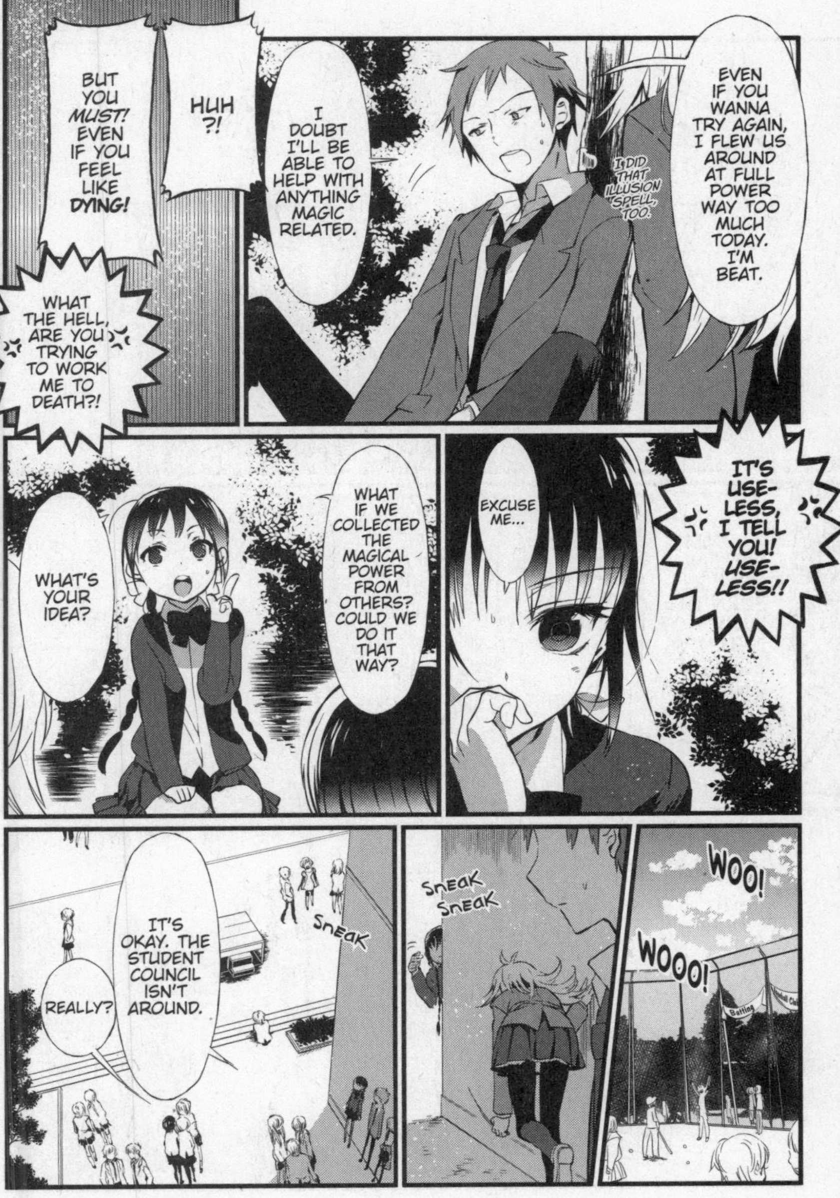
EVEN IF YOU WANNA TRY AGAIN, I FLEW US AROUND AT FULL POWER WAY TOO MUCH TODAY. I'M BEAT.
I DID THAT ILLUSION SPELL, TOO.
I DOUBT I'LL BE ABLE TO HELP WITH ANYTHING MAGIC RELATED.
HUH?!
BUT YOU MUST! EVEN IF YOU FEEL LIKE DYING!
WHAT THE HELL, ARE YOU TRYING TO WORK ME TO DEATH?!
IT'S USE-LESS, I TELL YOU! USE-LESS!!
EXCUSE ME...
WHAT IF WE COLLECTED THE MAGICAL POWER FROM OTHERS? COULD WE DO IT THAT WAY?
WHAT'S YOUR IDEA?
WOO!
WOOO!
Batting
Sneak Sneak
Sneak
IT'S OKAY. THE STUDENT COUNCIL ISN'T AROUND.
REALLY?

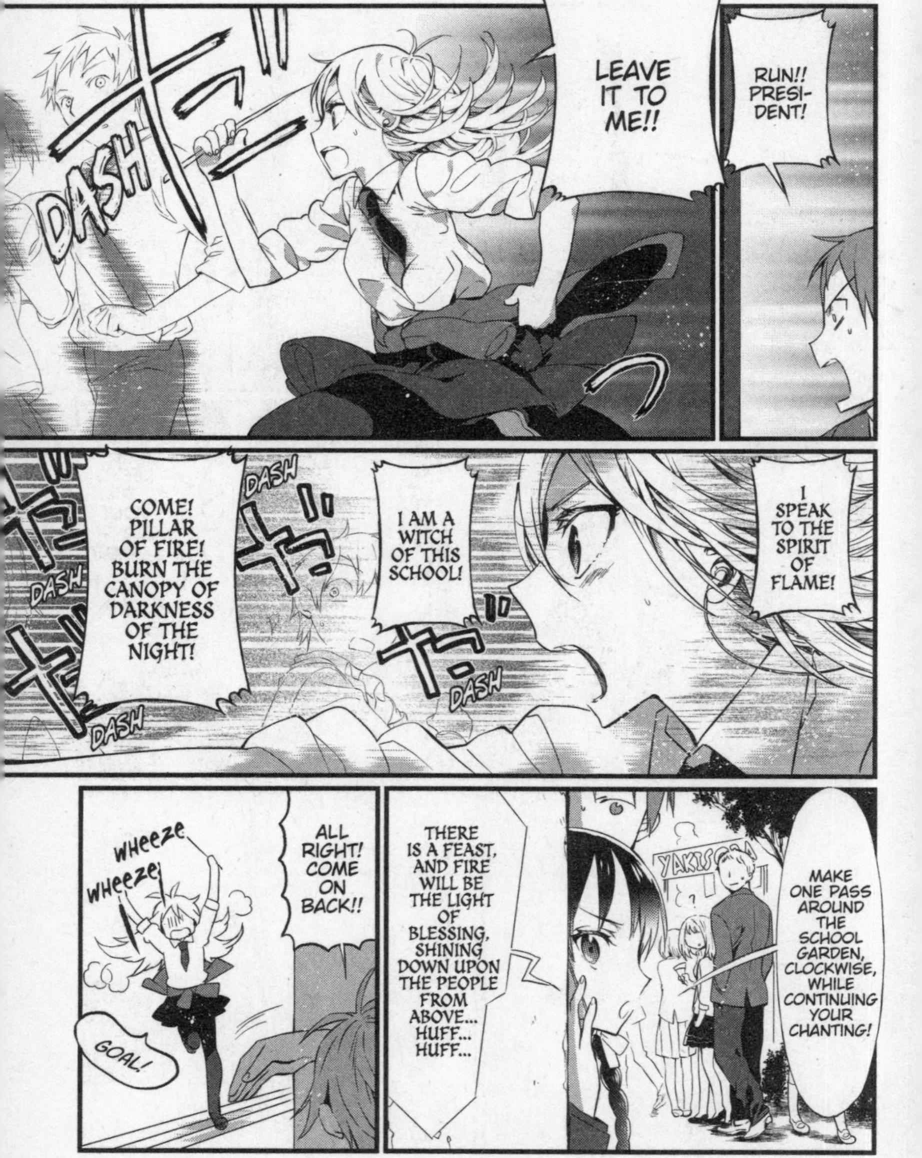
RUN!! PRESIDENT!
LEAVE IT TO ME!!
DASH
I SPEAK TO THE SPIRIT OF FLAME!
I AM A WITCH OF THIS SCHOOL!
DASH
DASH
COME! PILLAR OF FIRE! BURN THE CANOPY OF DARKNESS OF THE NIGHT!
DASH
DASH
MAKE ONE PASS AROUND THE SCHOOL GARDEN, CLOCKWISE, WHILE CONTINUING YOUR CHANTING!
YAKISOBA
THERE IS A FEAST, AND FIRE WILL BE THE LIGHT OF BLESSING, SHINING DOWN UPON THE PEOPLE FROM ABOVE... HUFF... HUFF...
ALL RIGHT! COME ON BACK!!
WHEEZE
WHEEZE
GOAL!

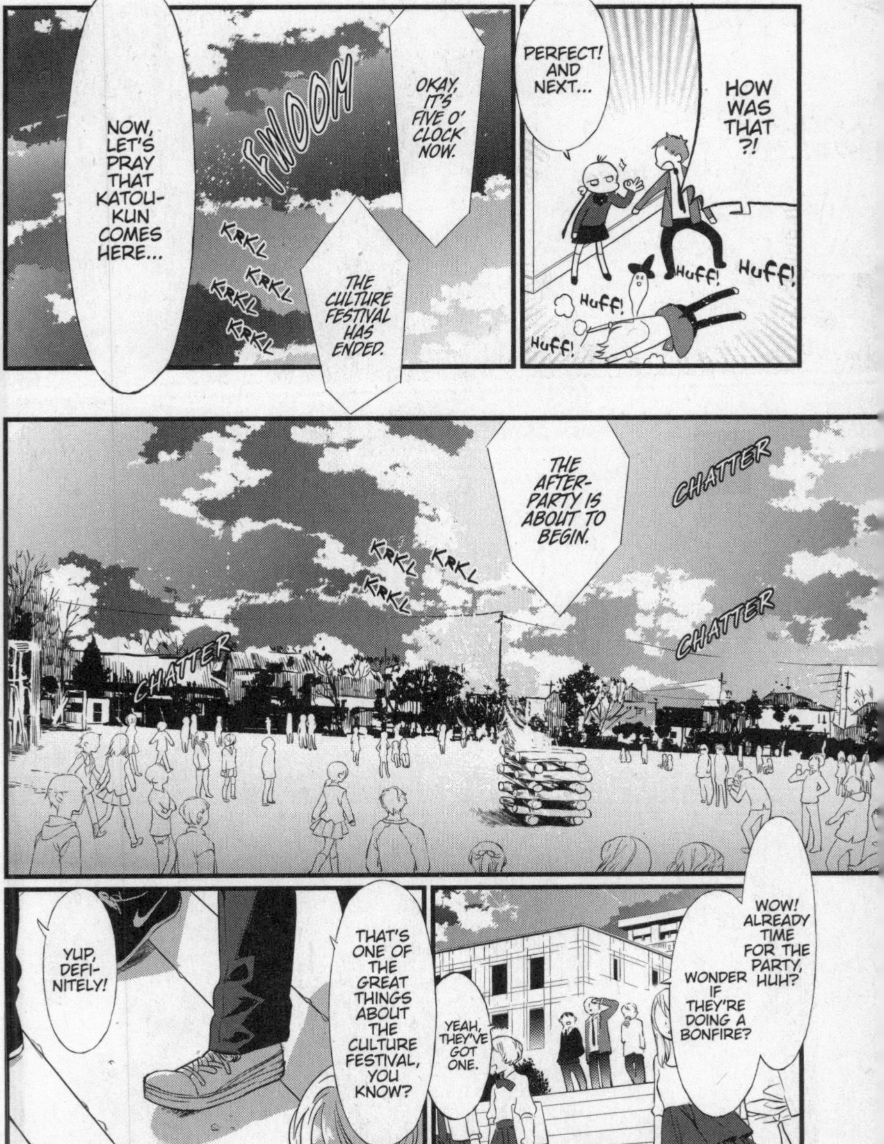
HOW WAS THAT ?!
PERFECT! AND NEXT...
Huff! Huff!
Huff!
Huff!
OKAY, IT'S FIVE O' CLOCK NOW.
FWOOM
THE CULTURE FESTIVAL HAS ENDED.
KRKL KRKL KRKL KRKL
NOW, LET'S PRAY THAT KATOU-KUN COMES HERE...
THE AFTER-PARTY IS ABOUT TO BEGIN.
CHATTER
CHATTER
KRKL KRKL KRKL
CHATTER
WOW! ALREADY TIME FOR THE PARTY, HUH?
WONDER IF THEY'RE DOING A BONFIRE?
YEAH, THEY'VE GOT ONE.
THAT'S ONE OF THE GREAT THINGS ABOUT THE CULTURE FESTIVAL, YOU KNOW?
YUP, DEFINITELY!

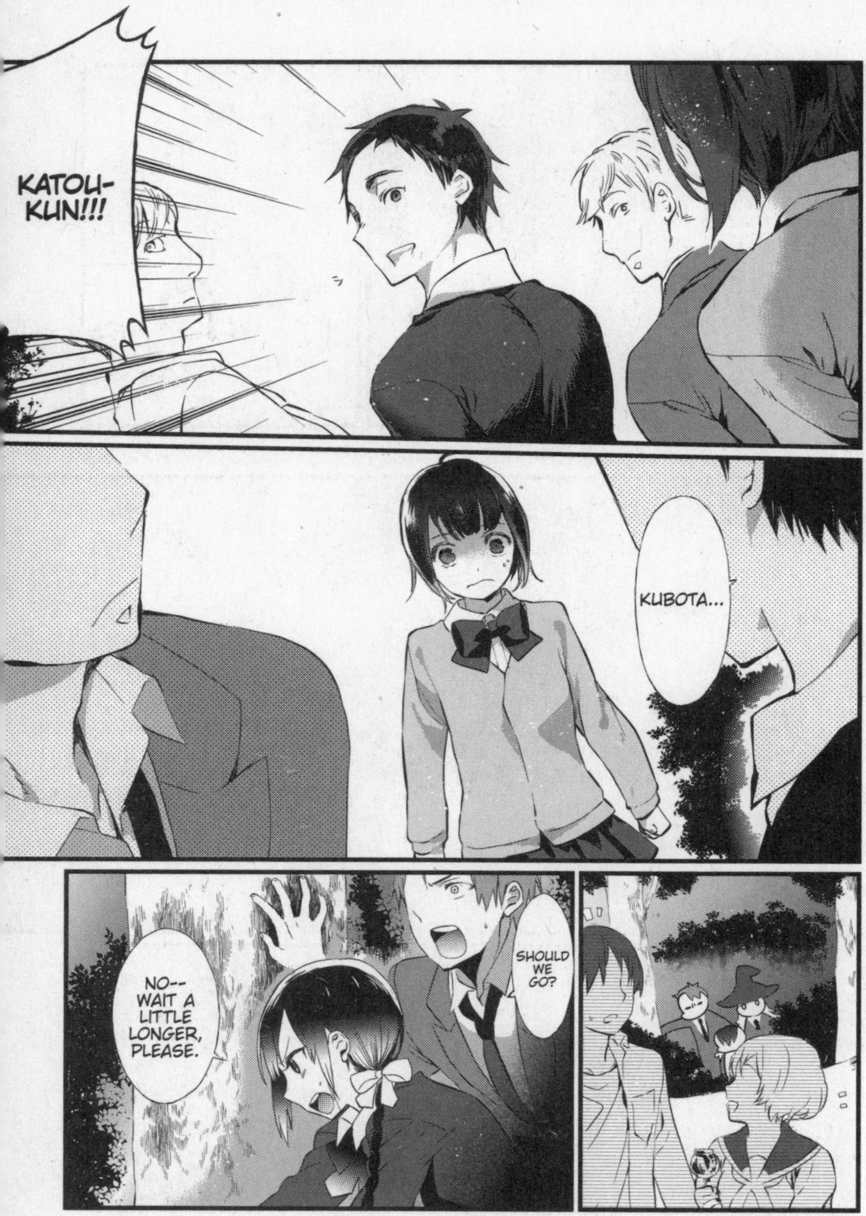
KATOU-KUN!!!
KUBOTA...
SHOULD WE GO?
NO-- WAIT A LITTLE LONGER, PLEASE.

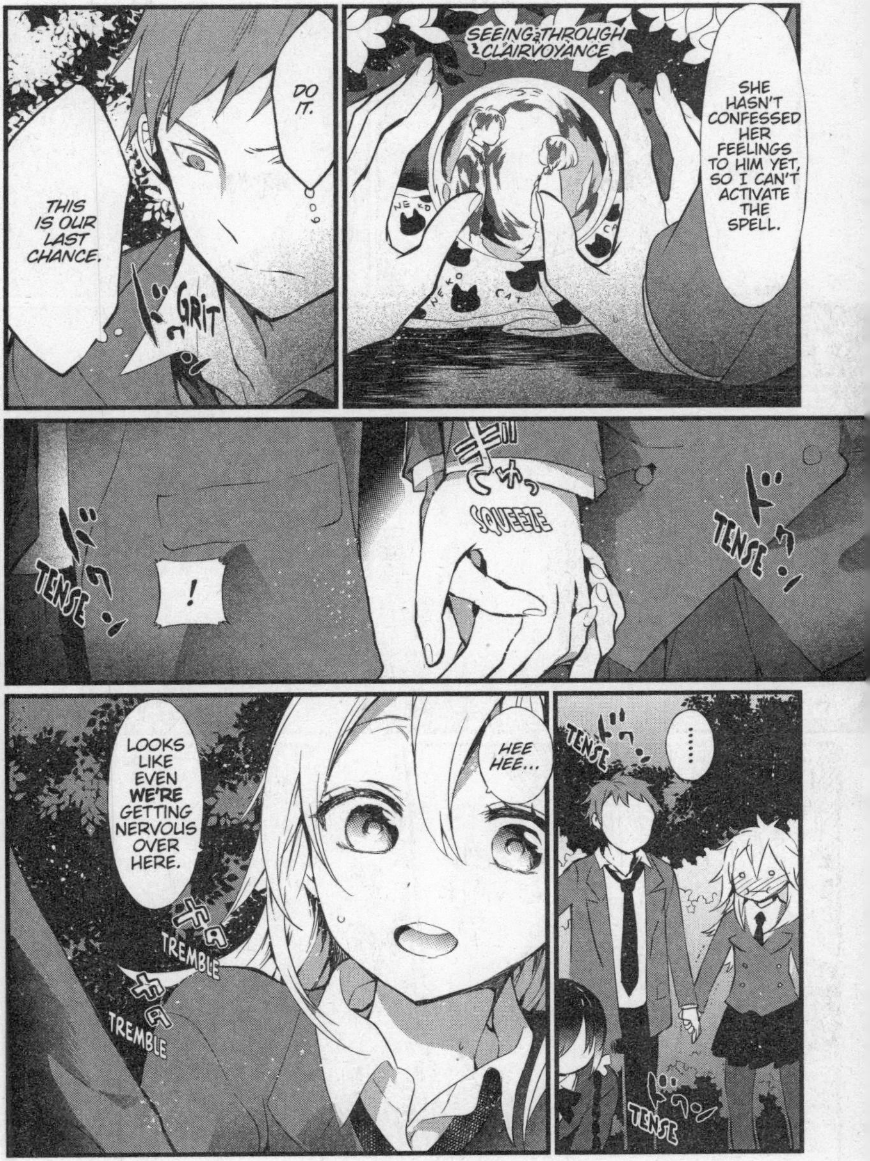
SEEING THROUGH CLAIRVOYANCE
SHE HASN'T CONFESSED HER FEELINGS TO HIM YET, SO I CAN'T ACTIVATE THE SPELL.
DO IT.
THIS IS OUR LAST CHANCE.
GRIT
TENSE
SQUEEZE
!
TENSE
......
TENSE
TENSE
HEE HEE...
LOOKS LIKE EVEN WE'RE GETTING NERVOUS OVER HERE.
TREMBLE
TREMBLE

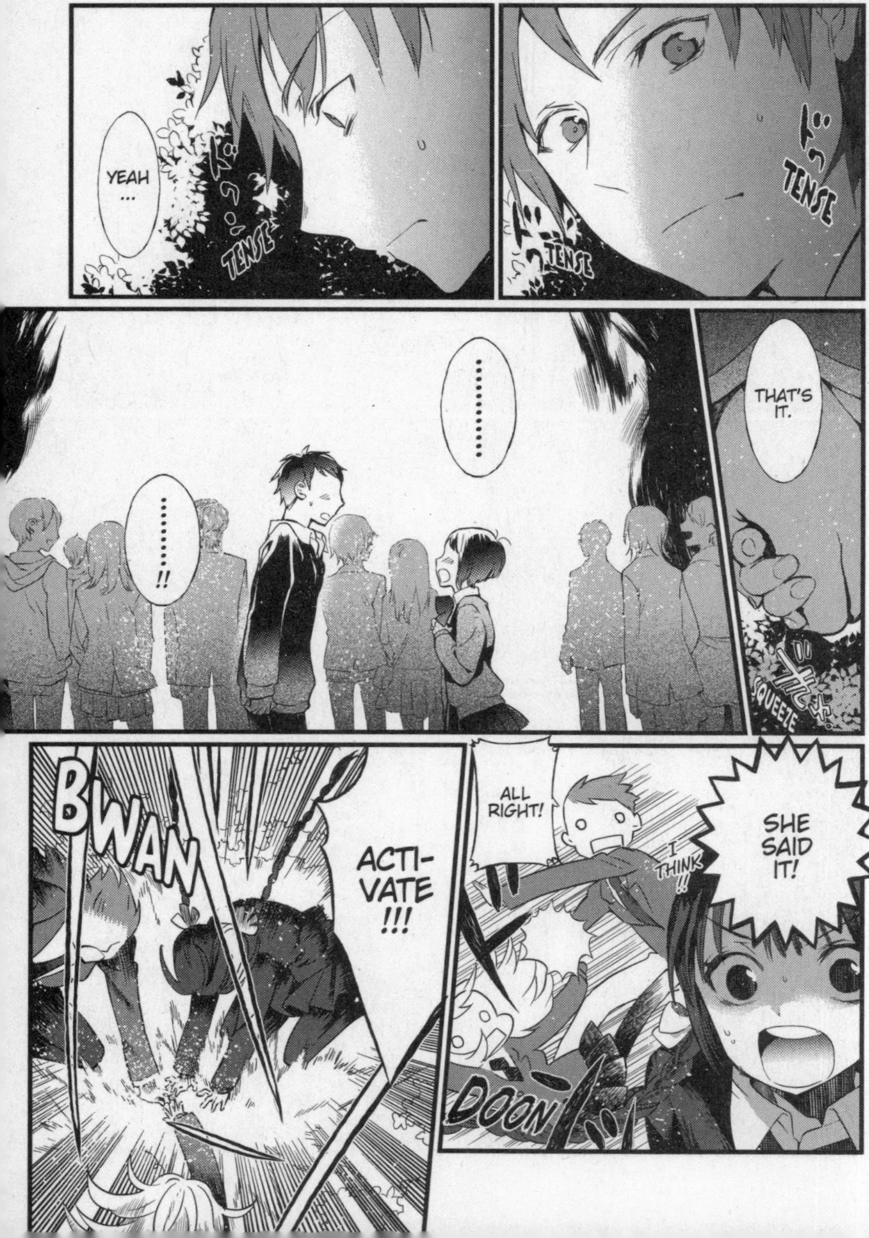
TENSE
TENSE
YEAH ...
TENSE
THAT'S IT.
SQUEEZE
....
......!!
SHE SAID IT!
ALL RIGHT!
I THINK!!
DOON
BWAN
ACTI-VATE !!!

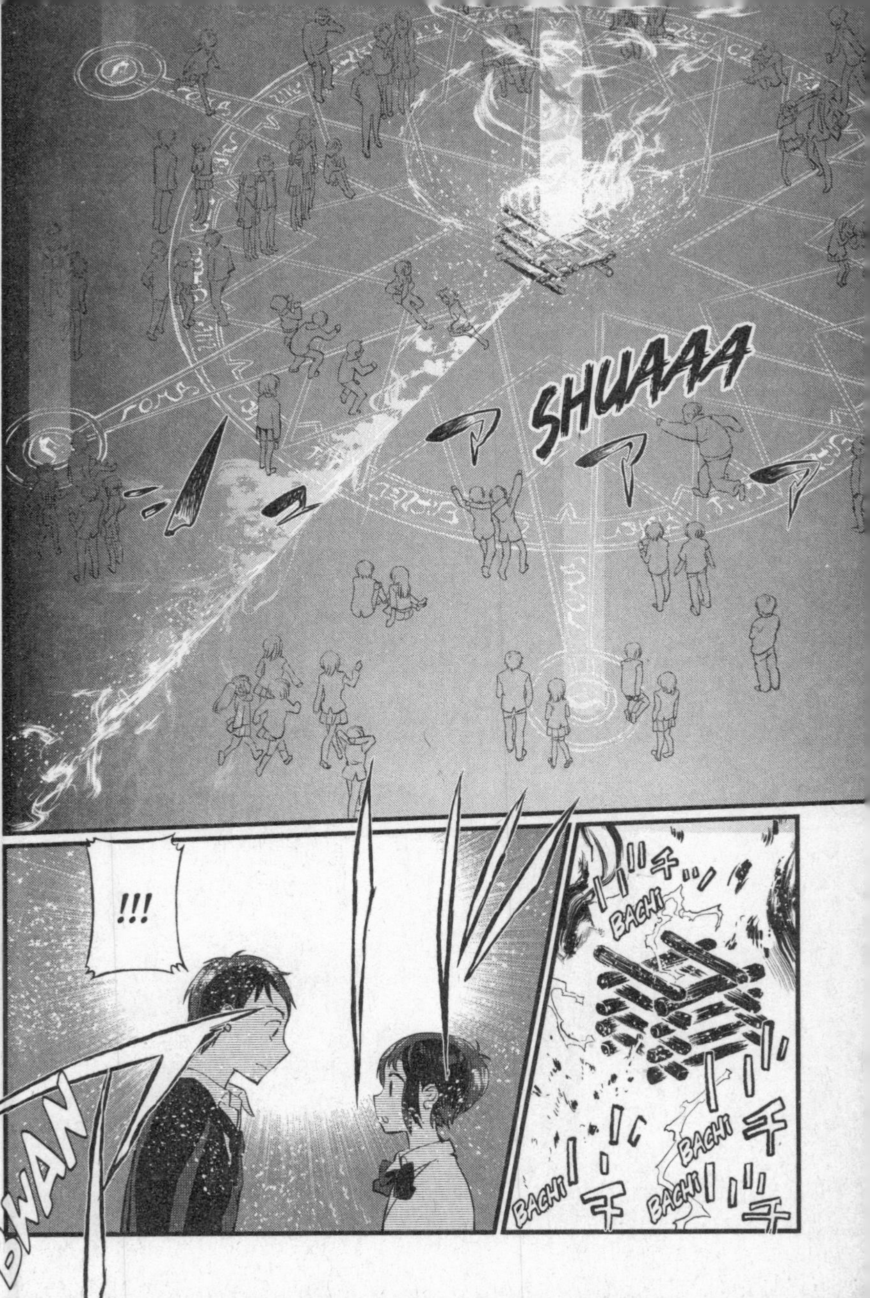
SHUAAA
BACHI
BACHI
BACHI
BACHI
!!!
BWAN

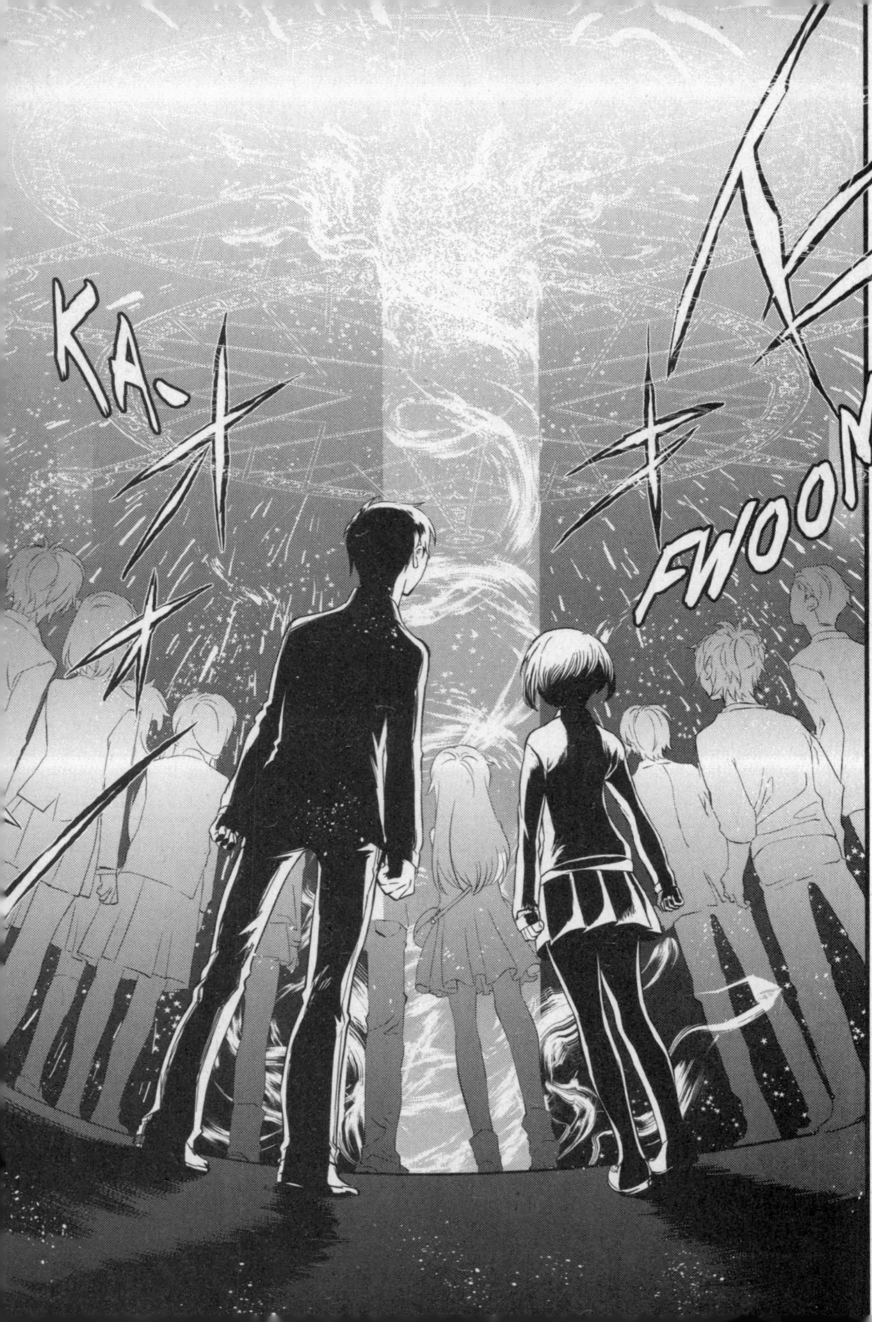

FWOOM
KA-

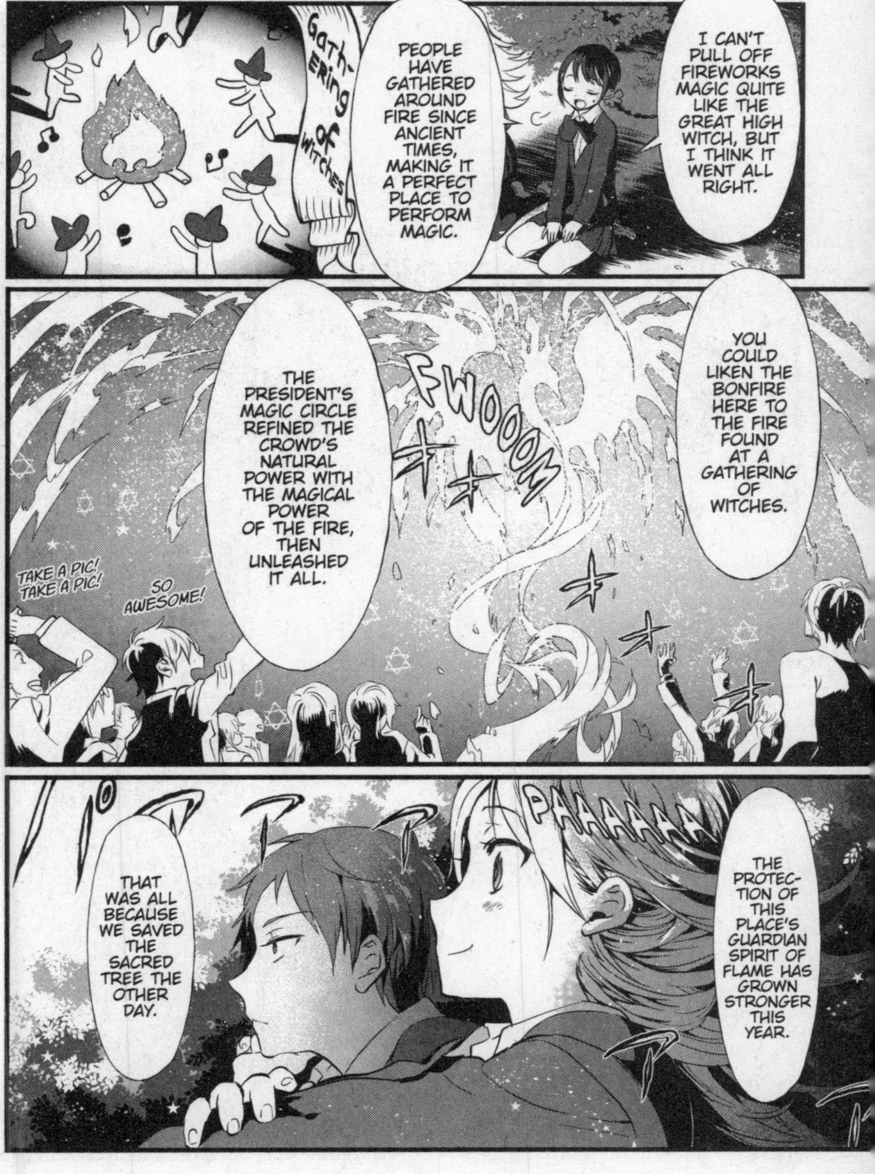
I CAN'T PULL OFF FIREWORKS MAGIC QUITE LIKE THE GREAT HIGH WITCH, BUT I THINK IT WENT ALL RIGHT.
PEOPLE HAVE GATHERED AROUND FIRE SINCE ANCIENT TIMES, MAKING IT A PERFECT PLACE TO PERFORM MAGIC.
Gath-ERing of Witches
YOU COULD LIKEN THE BONFIRE HERE TO THE FIRE FOUND AT A GATHERING OF WITCHES.
FWOOOM
THE PRESIDENT'S MAGIC CIRCLE REFINED THE CROWD'S NATURAL POWER WITH THE MAGICAL POWER OF THE FIRE, THEN UNLEASHED IT ALL.
SO AWESOME!
TAKE A PIC! TAKE A PIC!
PAAAAAA
THE PROTECTION OF THIS PLACE'S GUARDIAN SPIRIT OF FLAME HAS GROWN STRONGER THIS YEAR.
THAT WAS ALL BECAUSE WE SAVED THE SACRED TREE THE OTHER DAY.

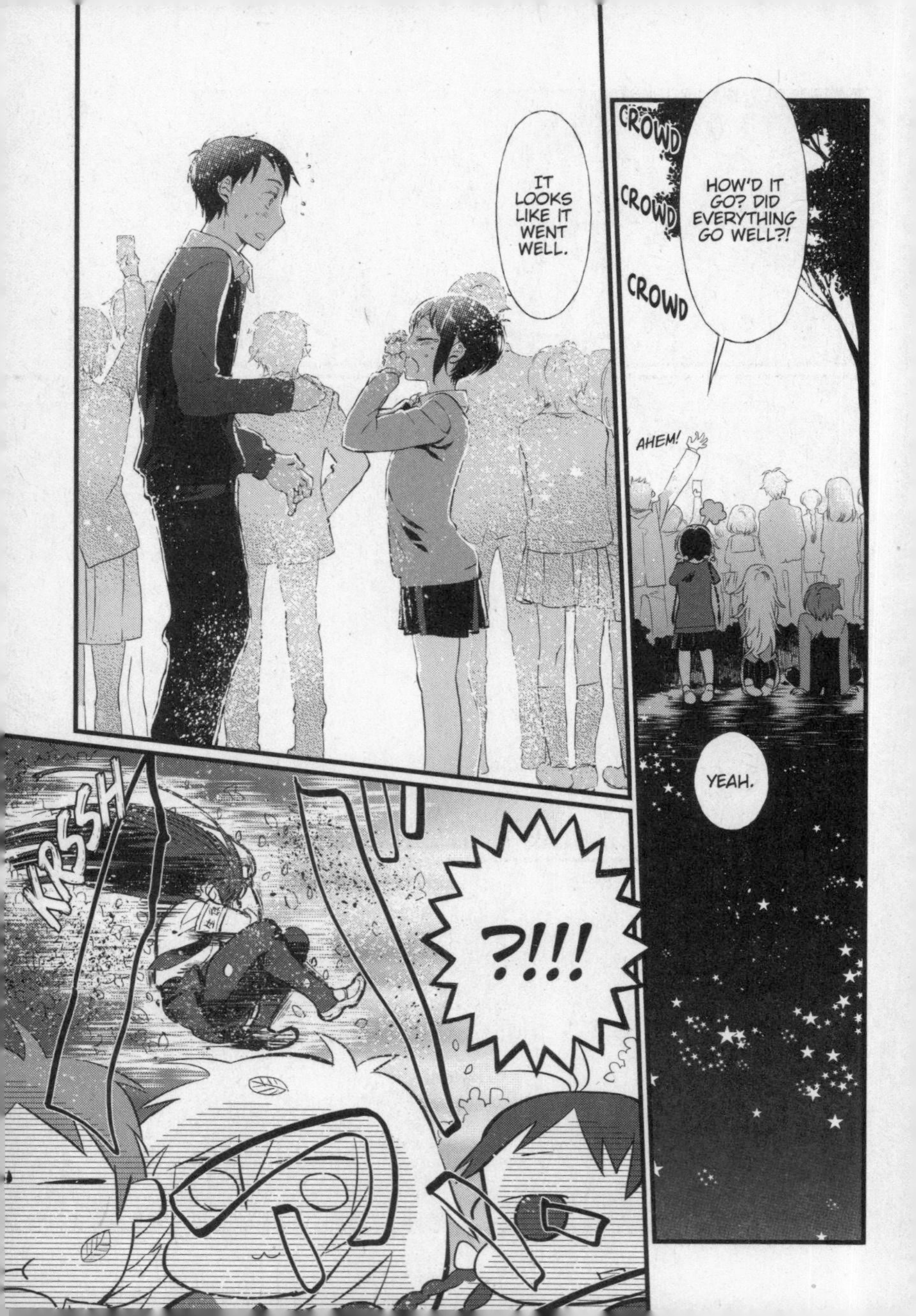
CROWD
CROWD
CROWD
HOW'D IT GO? DID EVERYTHING GO WELL?!
AHEM!
YEAH.
IT LOOKS LIKE IT WENT WELL.
KRSSH
?!!!

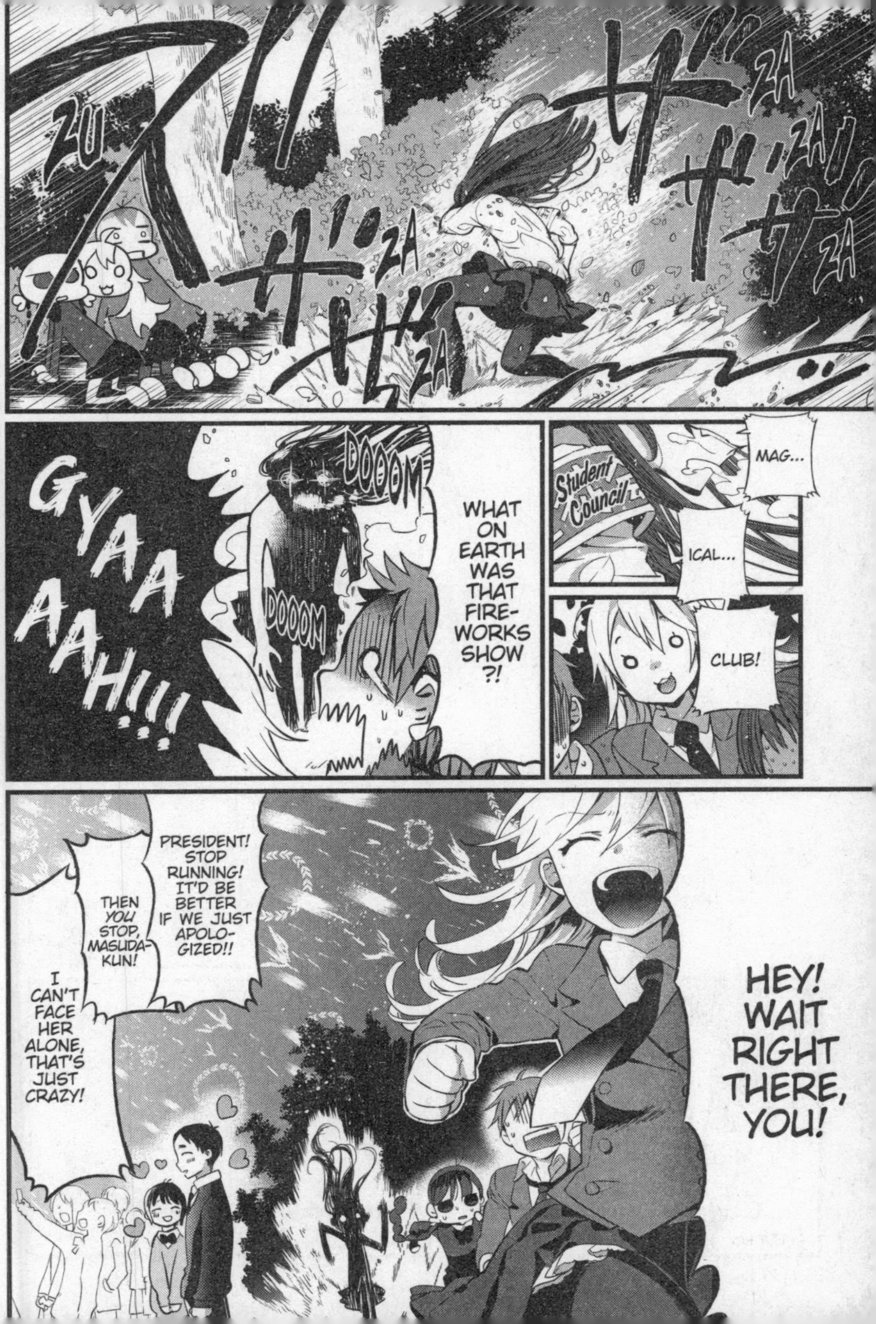

ZA
ZA
ZA
ZA
ZA
ZU
MAG...
ICAL...
CLUB!
Student Council
DOOOM
DOOOM
WHAT ON EARTH WAS THAT FIRE-WORKS SHOW?!
GYAAAAAH!!!
HEY! WAIT RIGHT THERE, YOU!
PRESIDENT! STOP RUNNING! IT'D BE BETTER IF WE JUST APOLO-GIZED!!
THEN *YOU* STOP, MASUDA-KUN!
I CAN'T FACE HER ALONE, THAT'S JUST CRAZY!

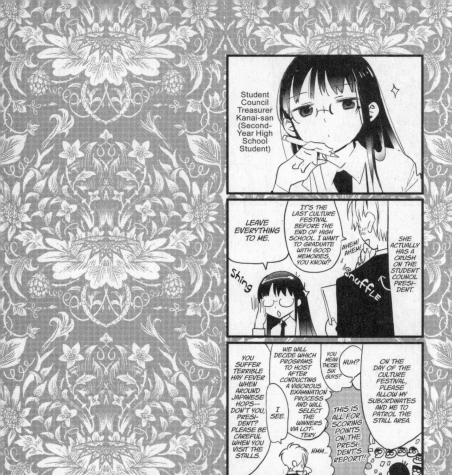

Student Council Treasurer Kanai-san (Second-Year High School Student)
SHE ACTUALLY HAS A CRUSH ON THE STUDENT COUNCIL PRESIDENT.
AHEM! AHEM!
Snuffle
IT'S THE LAST CULTURE FESTIVAL BEFORE THE END OF HIGH SCHOOL. I WANT TO GRADUATE WITH GOOD MEMORIES, YOU KNOW?
LEAVE EVERYTHING TO ME.
Shing
ON THE DAY OF THE CULTURE FESTIVAL, PLEASE ALLOW MY SUBORDINATES AND ME TO PATROL THE STALL AREA.
HUH?
YOU MEAN THOSE SIX GUYS?
THIS IS ALL FOR SCORING POINTS ON THE PRESIDENT'S REPORT!!
WE WILL DECIDE WHICH PROGRAMS TO HOST AFTER CONDUCTING A VIGOROUS EXAMINATION PROCESS AND WILL SELECT THE WINNERS VIA LOTTERY.
I SEE.
HMM...
YOU SUFFER TERRIBLE HAY FEVER WHEN AROUND JAPANESE HOPS--DON'T YOU, PRESIDENT? PLEASE BE CAREFUL WHEN YOU VISIT THE STALLS.
SLURP
SHE PUT THE MAGICAL CLUB ON HER BLACKLIST AT THE VERY BEGINNING.

AT A FAMILY RESTAURANT, AFTER THE CULTURE FESTIVAL HAS CONCLUDED.
PLEASE, NO SLEEPING IN THE RESTAURANT.
Snrrrr

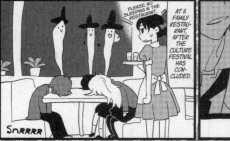

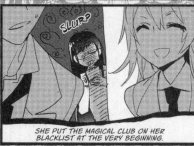

Generation WITCH

Chapter 19: The Terms of a Witch's Contract, Part 1

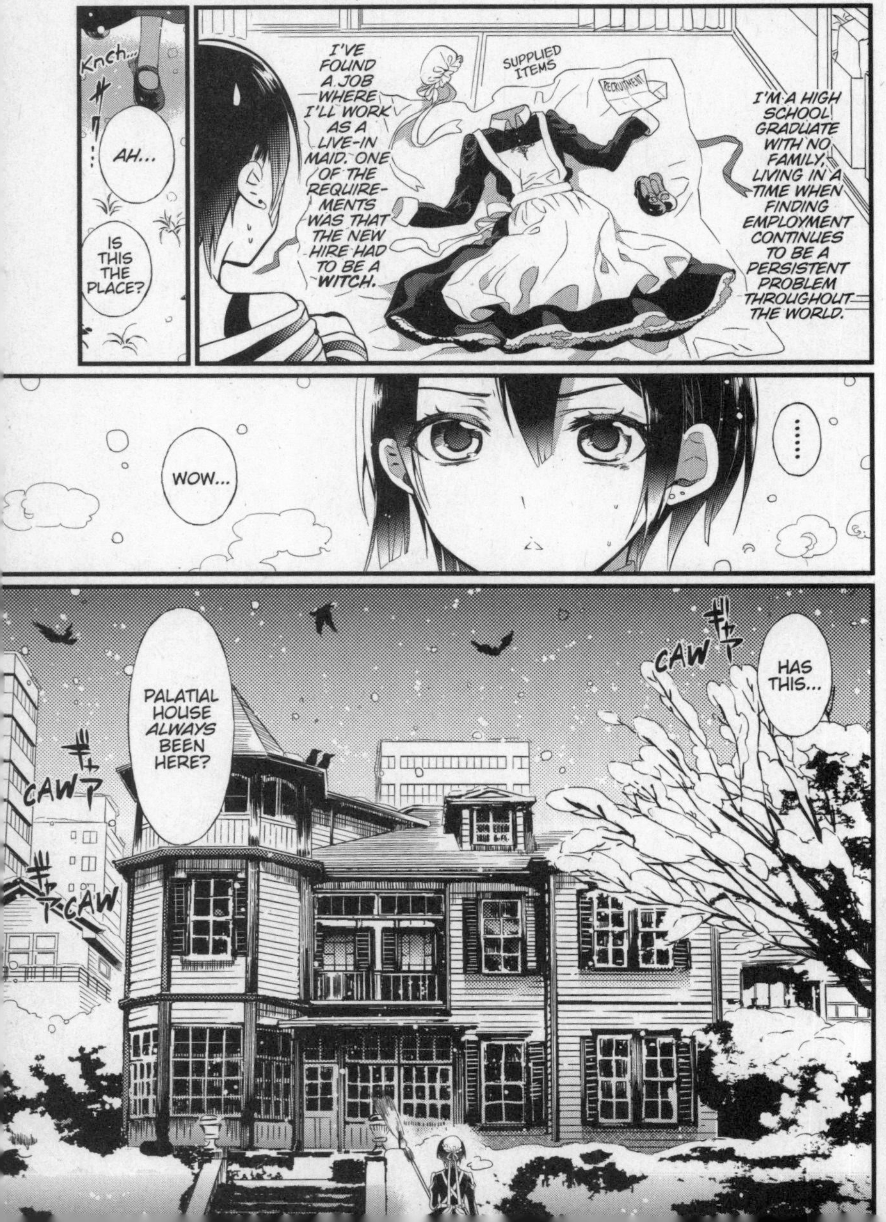

I'M A HIGH SCHOOL GRADUATE WITH NO FAMILY, LIVING IN A TIME WHEN FINDING EMPLOYMENT CONTINUES TO BE A PERSISTENT PROBLEM THROUGHOUT THE WORLD.
RECRUITMENT
SUPPLIED ITEMS
I'VE FOUND A JOB WHERE I'LL WORK AS A LIVE-IN MAID. ONE OF THE REQUIREMENTS WAS THAT THE NEW HIRE HAD TO BE A WITCH.
Knch...
AH...
IS THIS THE PLACE?
......
WOW...
CAW
HAS THIS...
PALATIAL HOUSE ALWAYS BEEN HERE?
CAW
CAW

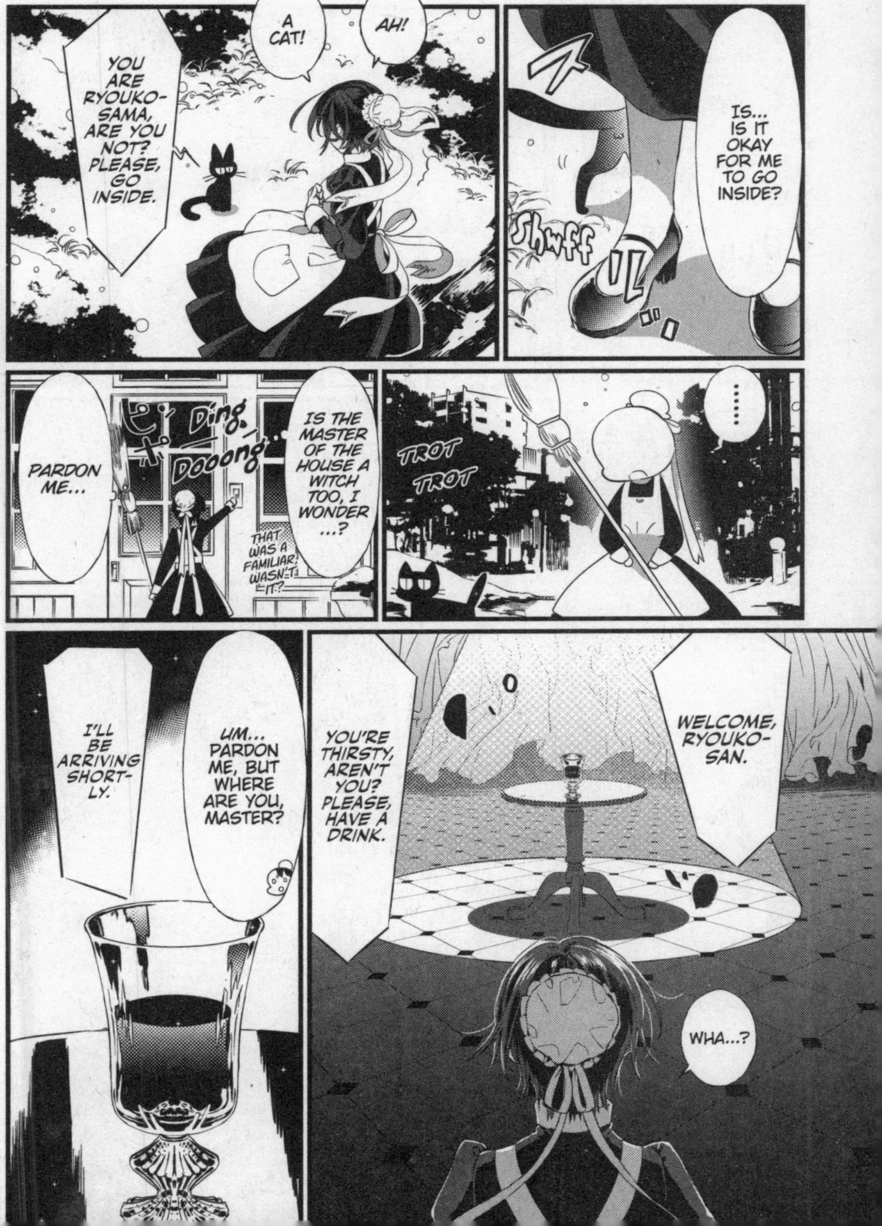
IS... IS IT OKAY FOR ME TO GO INSIDE?
Shwff
AH!
A CAT!
YOU ARE RYOUKO-SAMA, ARE YOU NOT? PLEASE, GO INSIDE.
......
TROT TROT
IS THE MASTER OF THE HOUSE A WITCH TOO, I WONDER...?
THAT WAS A FAMILIAR, WASN'T IT?
Ding Dooong
PARDON ME...
WELCOME, RYOUKO-SAN.
YOU'RE THIRSTY, AREN'T YOU? PLEASE, HAVE A DRINK.
WHA...?
UM... PARDON ME, BUT WHERE ARE YOU, MASTER?
I'LL BE ARRIVING SHORTLY.

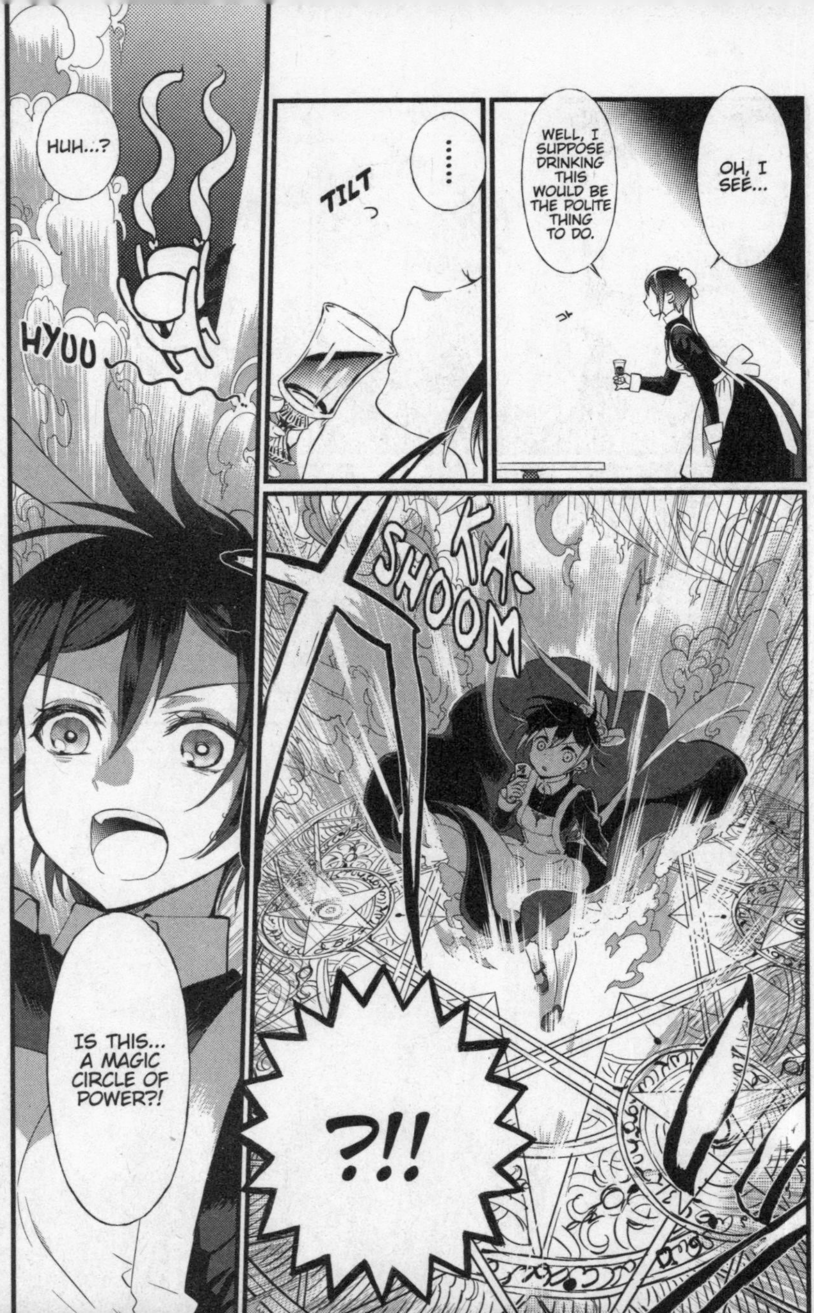
OH, I SEE...
WELL, I SUPPOSE DRINKING THIS WOULD BE THE POLITE THING TO DO.
......
TILT
HUH...?
HYUU
KA-SHOOM
?!!
IS THIS... A MAGIC CIRCLE OF POWER?!

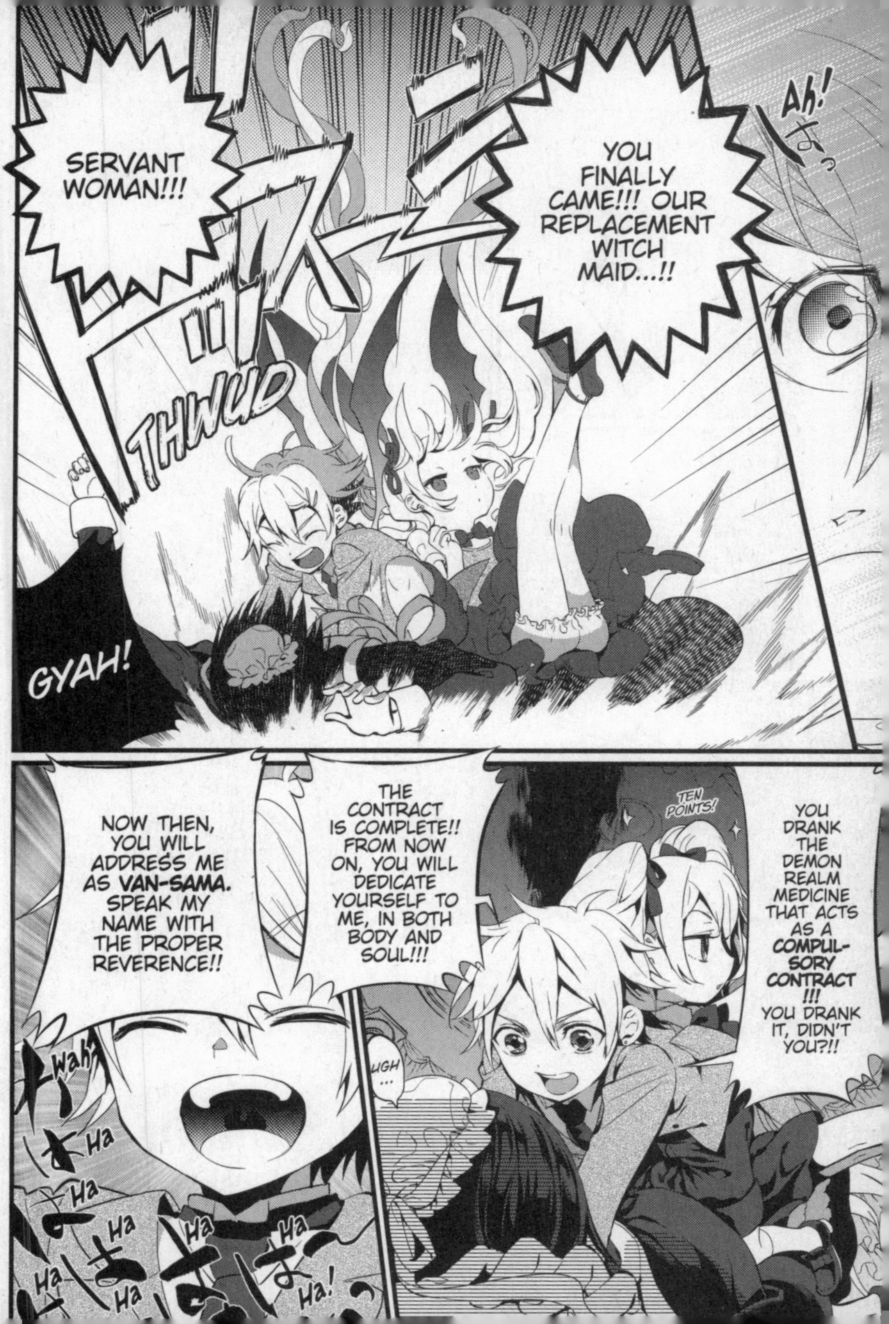
Ah!
YOU FINALLY CAME!!! OUR REPLACEMENT WITCH MAID...!!
SERVANT WOMAN!!!
THWUD
GYAH!
YOU DRANK THE DEMON REALM MEDICINE THAT ACTS AS A COMPULSORY CONTRACT!!! YOU DRANK IT, DIDN'T YOU?!!
TEN POINTS!
UGH...
THE CONTRACT IS COMPLETE!! FROM NOW ON, YOU WILL DEDICATE YOURSELF TO ME, IN BOTH BODY AND SOUL!!!
NOW THEN, YOU WILL ADDRESS ME AS VAN-SAMA. SPEAK MY NAME WITH THE PROPER REVERENCE!!
Wah
Ha
Ha
Ha
Ha
Ha
Ha
Ha
Ha!

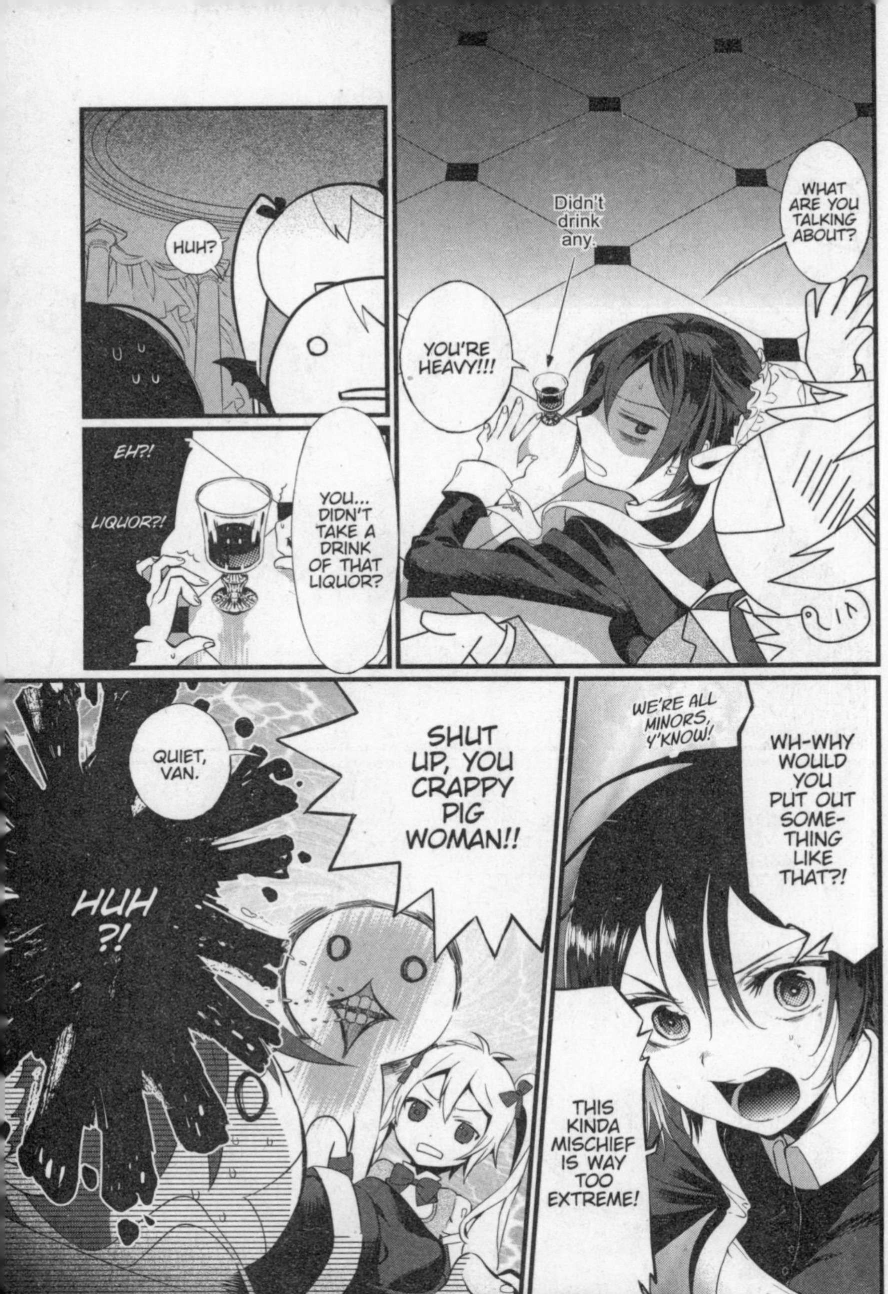
WHAT ARE YOU TALKING ABOUT?
Didn't drink any.
YOU'RE HEAVY!!!
HUH?
YOU... DIDN'T TAKE A DRINK OF THAT LIQUOR?
EH?!
LIQUOR?!
WH-WHY WOULD YOU PUT OUT SOME-THING LIKE THAT?!
WE'RE ALL MINORS, Y'KNOW!
THIS KINDA MISCHIEF IS WAY TOO EXTREME!
SHUT UP, YOU CRAPPY PIG WOMAN!!
QUIET, VAN.
HUH ?!

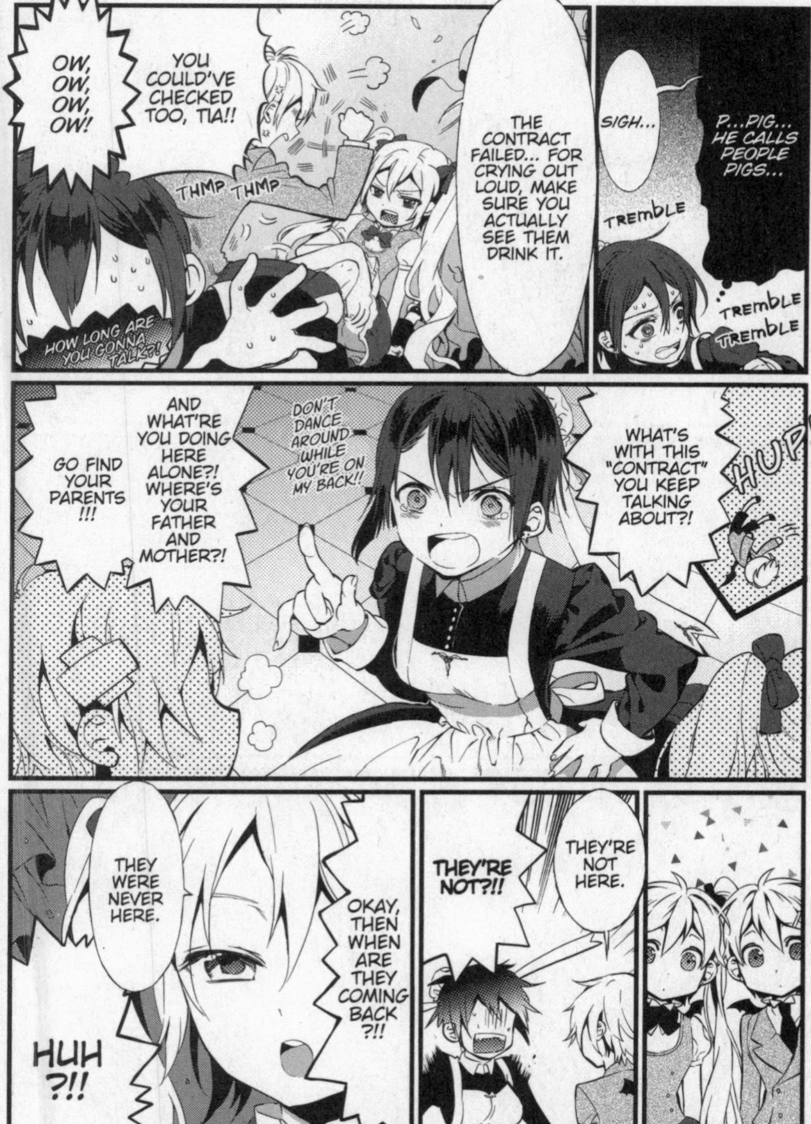
SIGH...
P...PIG... HE CALLS PEOPLE PIGS...
TREMBLE
TREMBLE TREMBLE
THE CONTRACT FAILED... FOR CRYING OUT LOUD, MAKE SURE YOU ACTUALLY SEE THEM DRINK IT.
YOU COULD'VE CHECKED TOO, TIA!!
OW, OW, OW, OW!
THMP THMP
HOW LONG ARE YOU GONNA TALK?!
HUP!
WHAT'S WITH THIS "CONTRACT" YOU KEEP TALKING ABOUT?!
DON'T DANCE AROUND WHILE YOU'RE ON MY BACK!!
AND WHAT'RE YOU DOING HERE ALONE?! WHERE'S YOUR FATHER AND MOTHER?!
GO FIND YOUR PARENTS!!!
THEY'RE NOT HERE.
THEY'RE NOT?!!
OKAY, THEN WHEN ARE THEY COMING BACK?!!
THEY WERE NEVER HERE.
HUH?!!

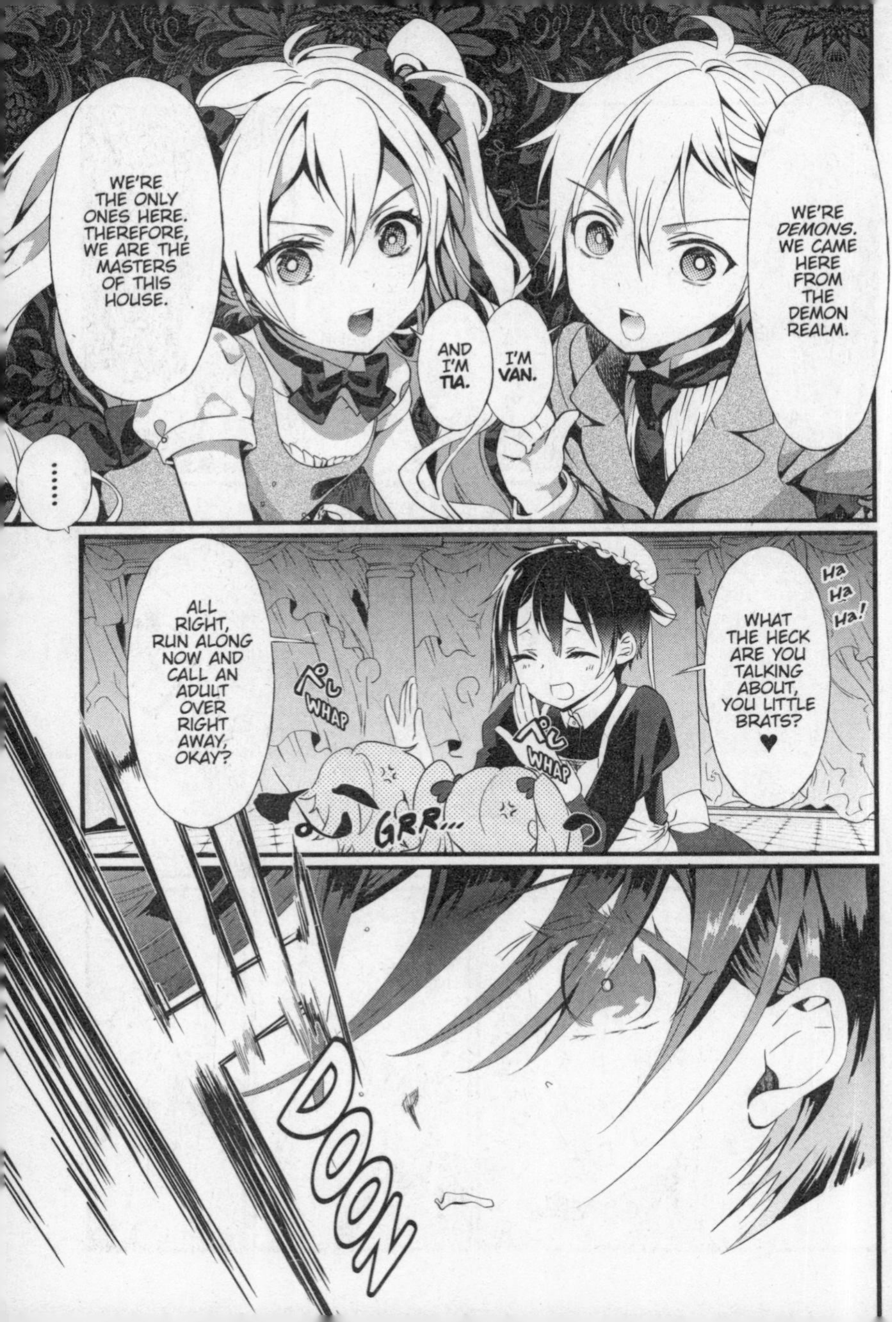
WE'RE *DEMONS*. WE CAME HERE FROM THE DEMON REALM.
I'M VAN.
AND I'M TIA.
WE'RE THE ONLY ONES HERE. THEREFORE, WE ARE THE MASTERS OF THIS HOUSE.
......
Ha Ha Ha!
WHAT THE HECK ARE YOU TALKING ABOUT, YOU LITTLE BRATS? ♥
WHAP
GRR...
WHAP
ALL RIGHT, RUN ALONG NOW AND CALL AN ADULT OVER RIGHT AWAY, OKAY?
DOOON

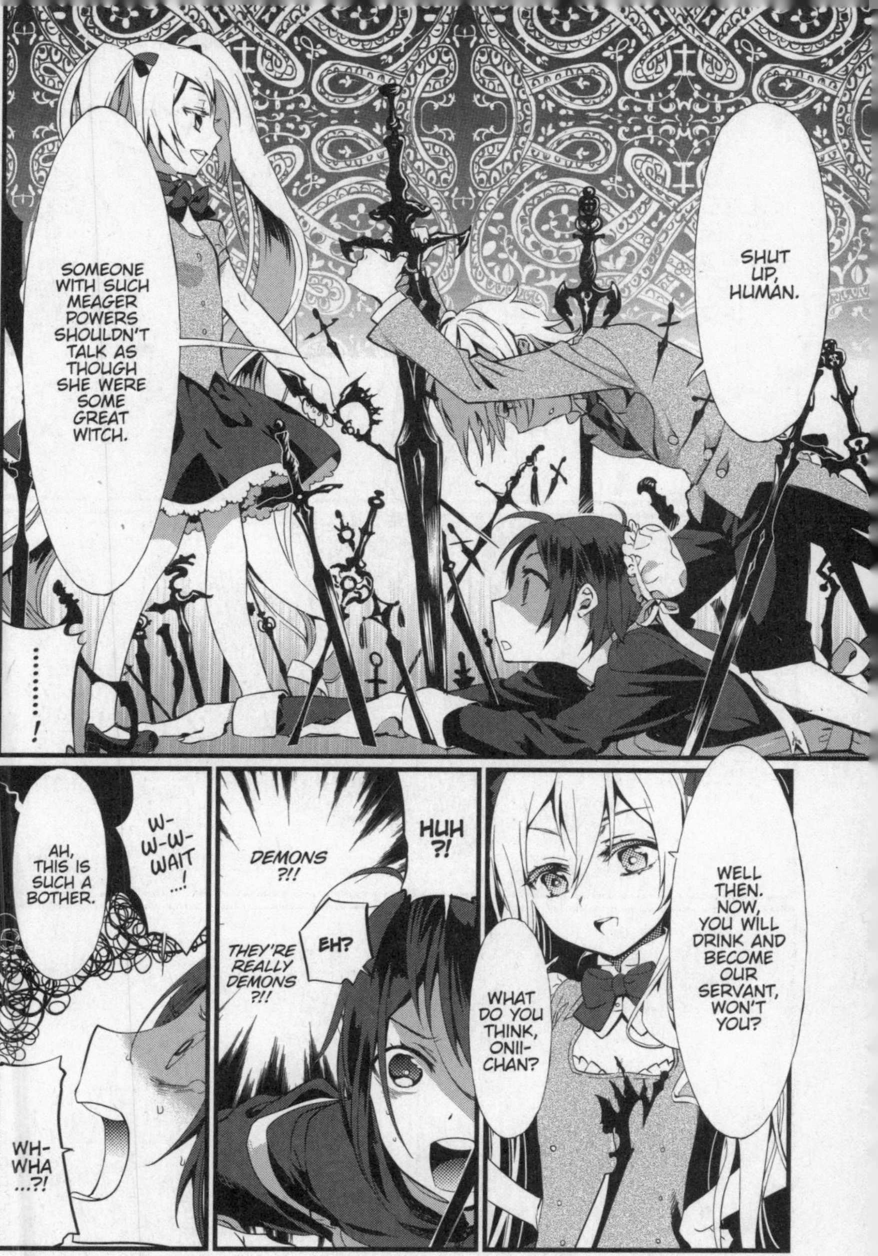
SHUT UP, HUMAN.
SOMEONE WITH SUCH MEAGER POWERS SHOULDN'T TALK AS THOUGH SHE WERE SOME GREAT WITCH.
......!
WELL THEN. NOW, YOU WILL DRINK AND BECOME OUR SERVANT, WON'T YOU?
WHAT DO YOU THINK, ONII-CHAN?
HUH ?!
DEMONS ?!!
EH?
THEY'RE REALLY DEMONS ?!!
W-W-W-WAIT ...!
AH, THIS IS SUCH A BOTHER.
WH-WHA ...?!

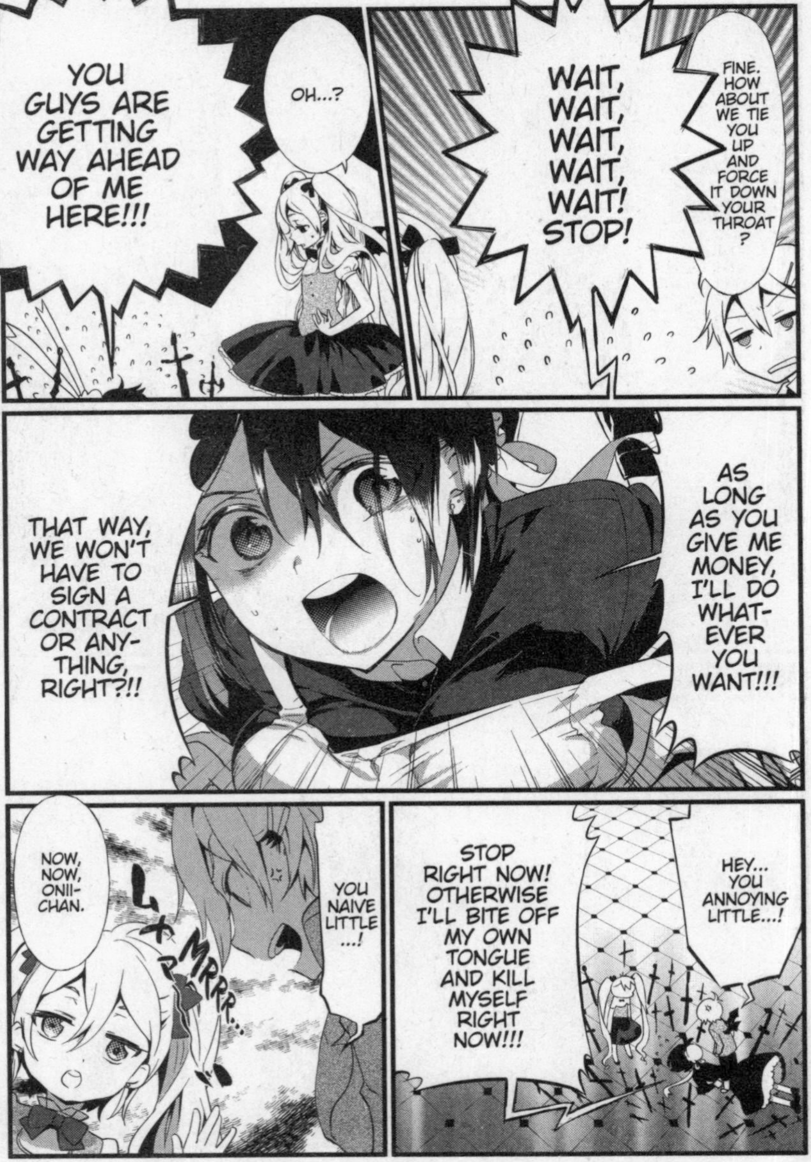
FINE. HOW ABOUT WE TIE YOU UP AND FORCE IT DOWN YOUR THROAT?
WAIT, WAIT, WAIT, WAIT, WAIT! STOP!
OH...?
YOU GUYS ARE GETTING WAY AHEAD OF ME HERE!!!
AS LONG AS YOU GIVE ME MONEY, I'LL DO WHAT-EVER YOU WANT!!!
THAT WAY, WE WON'T HAVE TO SIGN A CONTRACT OR ANY-THING, RIGHT?!!
HEY... YOU ANNOYING LITTLE...!
STOP RIGHT NOW! OTHERWISE I'LL BITE OFF MY OWN TONGUE AND KILL MYSELF RIGHT NOW!!!
YOU NAIVE LITTLE ...!
MRRRR...
NOW, NOW, ONII-CHAN.

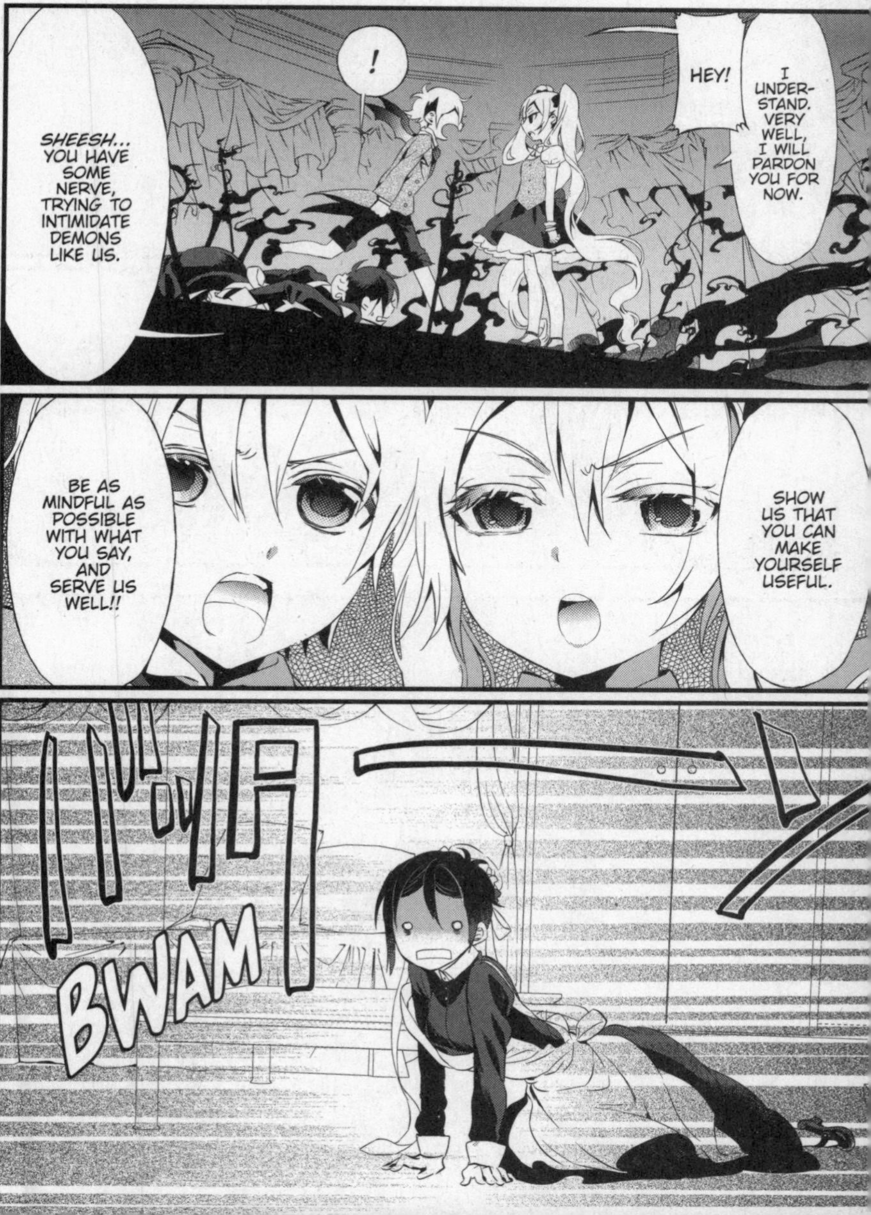
I UNDER-STAND. VERY WELL, I WILL PARDON YOU FOR NOW.
HEY!
!
SHEESH... YOU HAVE SOME NERVE, TRYING TO INTIMIDATE DEMONS LIKE US.
SHOW US THAT YOU CAN MAKE YOURSELF USEFUL.
BE AS MINDFUL AS POSSIBLE WITH WHAT YOU SAY, AND SERVE US WELL!!
BWAM

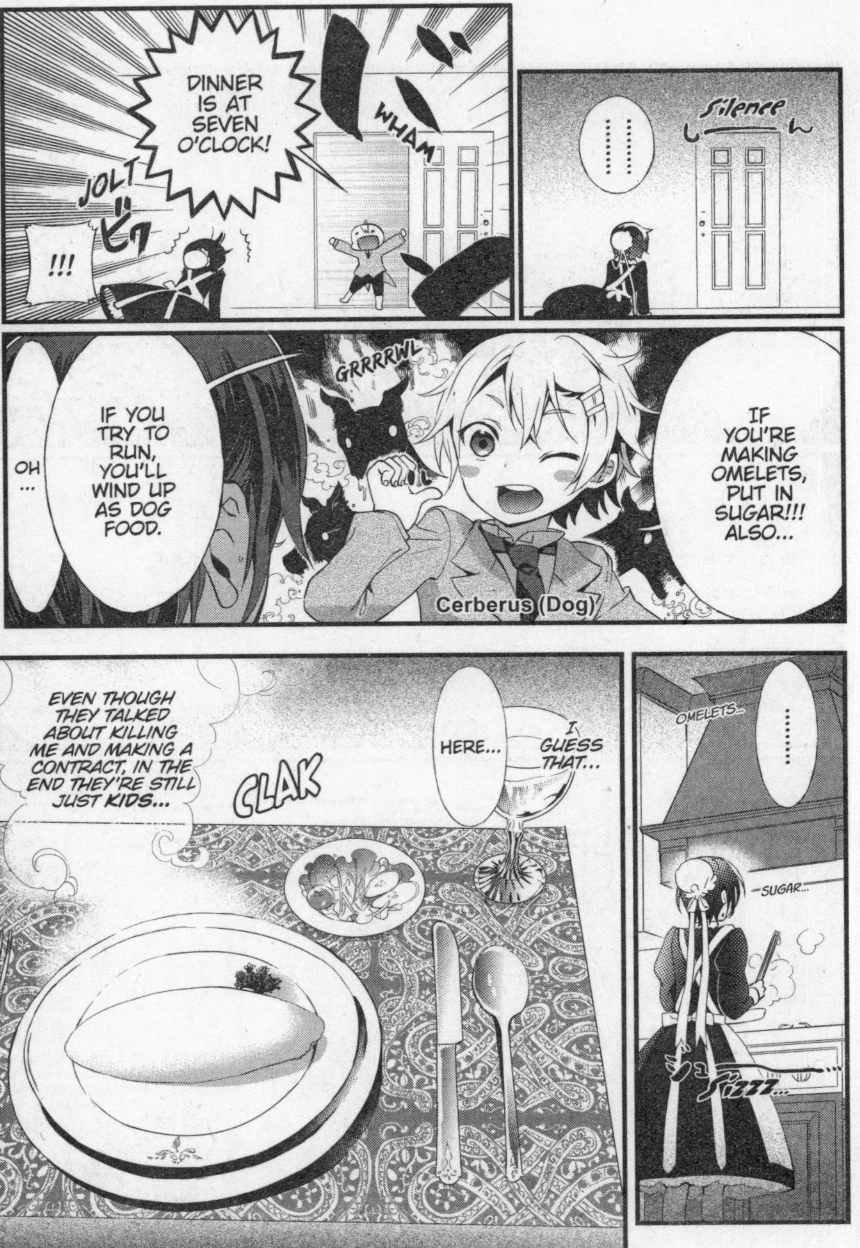
……
Silence
DINNER IS AT SEVEN O'CLOCK!
WHAM
JOLT
!!!
IF YOU'RE MAKING OMELETS, PUT IN SUGAR!!! ALSO...
GRRRRWL
IF YOU TRY TO RUN, YOU'LL WIND UP AS DOG FOOD.
OH ...
Cerberus (Dog)
……
OMELETS...
—SUGAR...
Sizzz...
I GUESS THAT...
HERE...
CLAK
EVEN THOUGH THEY TALKED ABOUT KILLING ME AND MAKING A CONTRACT, IN THE END THEY'RE STILL JUST KIDS...

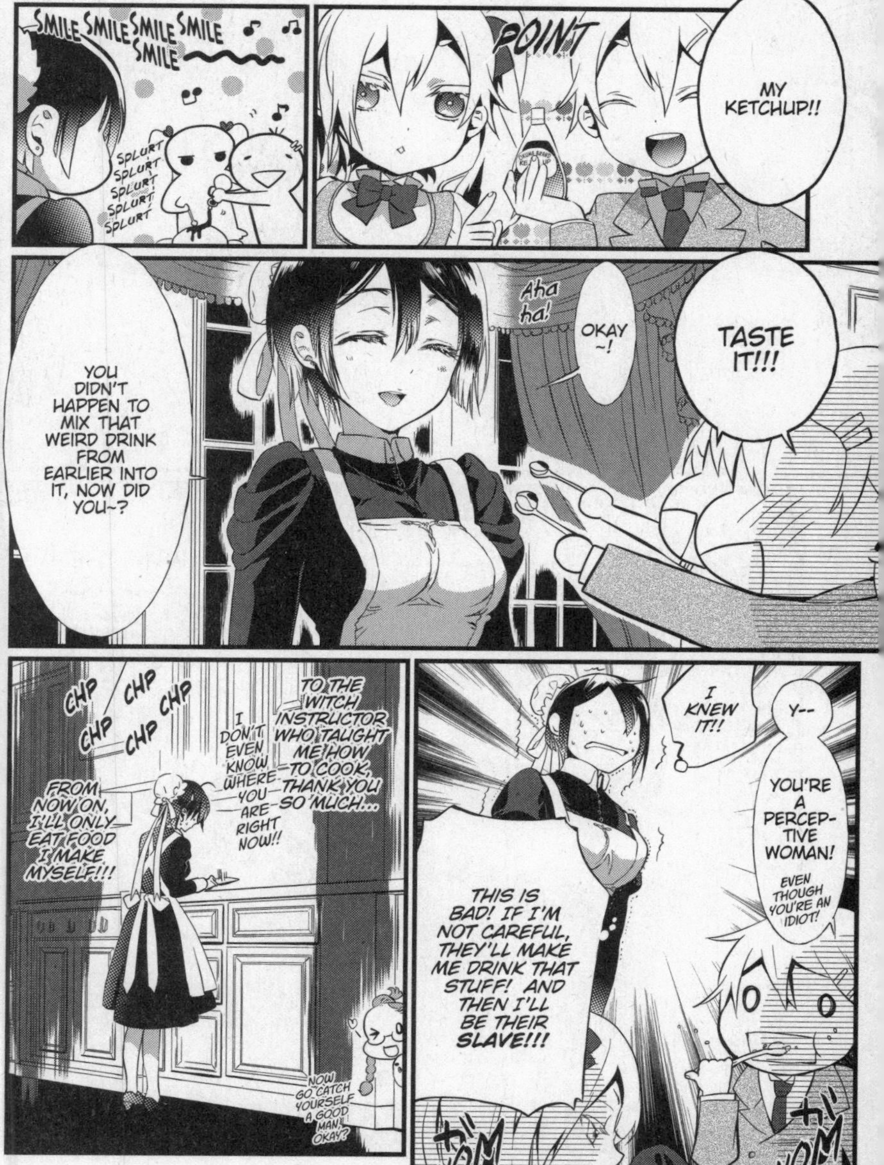
POINT
MY KETCHUP!!
SMILE SMILE SMILE SMILE SMILE
SPLURT SPLURT SPLURT SPLURT SPLURT
TASTE IT!!!
OKAY ~!
Aha ha!
YOU DIDN'T HAPPEN TO MIX THAT WEIRD DRINK FROM EARLIER INTO IT, NOW DID YOU~?
Y--
I KNEW IT!!
YOU'RE A PERCEPTIVE WOMAN!
EVEN THOUGH YOU'RE AN IDIOT!
THIS IS BAD! IF I'M NOT CAREFUL, THEY'LL MAKE ME DRINK THAT STUFF! AND THEN I'LL BE THEIR SLAVE!!!
NOM
NOM
TO THE WITCH INSTRUCTOR WHO TAUGHT ME HOW TO COOK, THANK YOU SO MUCH...
I DON'T EVEN KNOW WHERE YOU ARE RIGHT NOW!!
CHP CHP CHP CHP
FROM NOW ON, I'LL ONLY EAT FOOD I MAKE MYSELF!!!
NOW GO CATCH YOURSELF A GOOD MAN, OKAY?

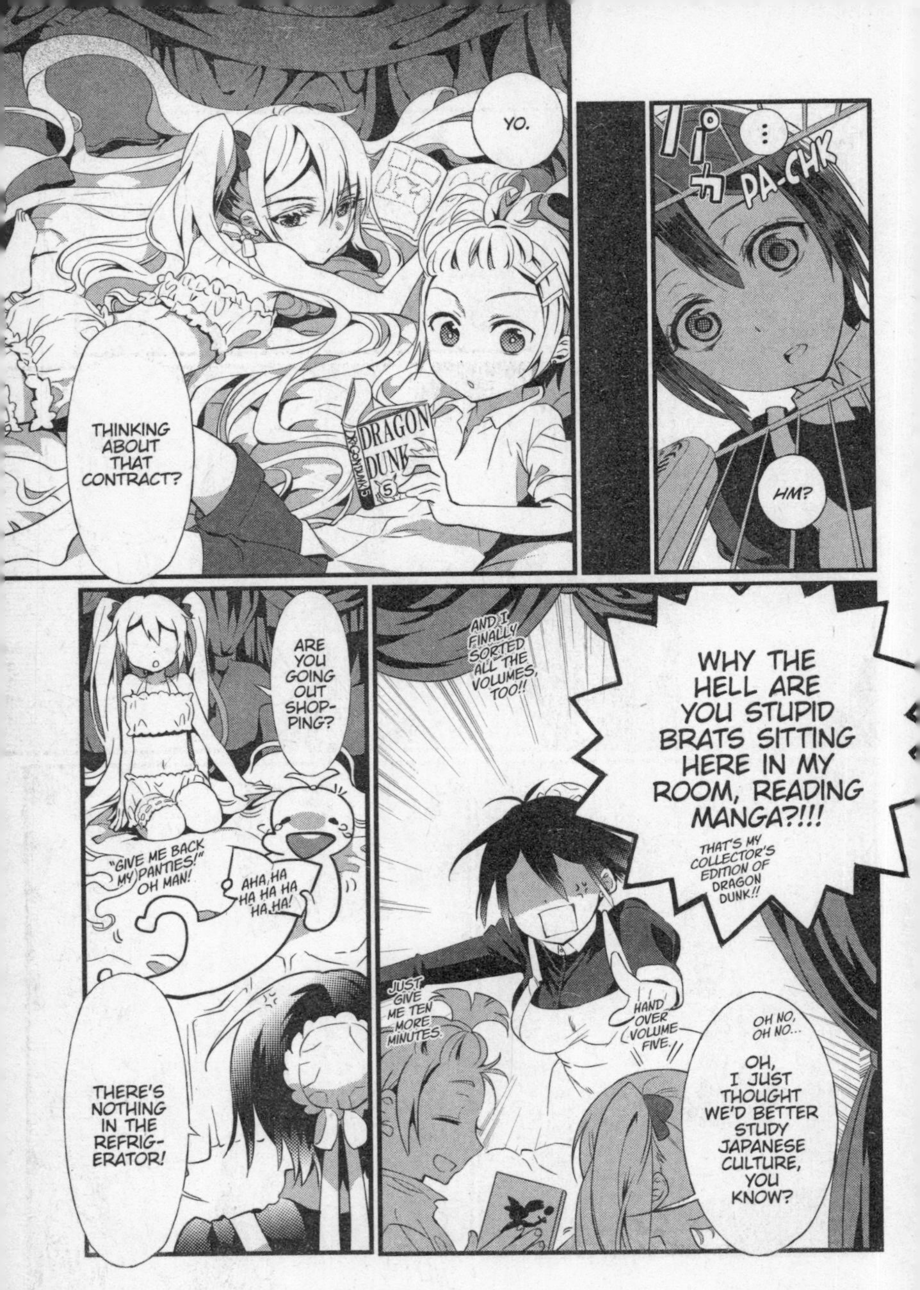

パカ
PA-CHK
...
HM?
YO.
DRAGON DUNK 5
THINKING ABOUT THAT CONTRACT?
WHY THE HELL ARE YOU STUPID BRATS SITTING HERE IN MY ROOM, READING MANGA?!!!
AND I FINALLY SORTED ALL THE VOLUMES, TOO!!
THAT'S MY COLLECTOR'S EDITION OF DRAGON DUNK!!
HAND OVER VOLUME FIVE.
JUST GIVE ME TEN MORE MINUTES.
OH NO, OH NO...
OH, I JUST THOUGHT WE'D BETTER STUDY JAPANESE CULTURE, YOU KNOW?
ARE YOU GOING OUT SHOP-PING?
"GIVE ME BACK MY PANTIES!" OH MAN!
AHA, HA HA HA HA HA HA!
THERE'S NOTHING IN THE REFRIG-ERATOR!

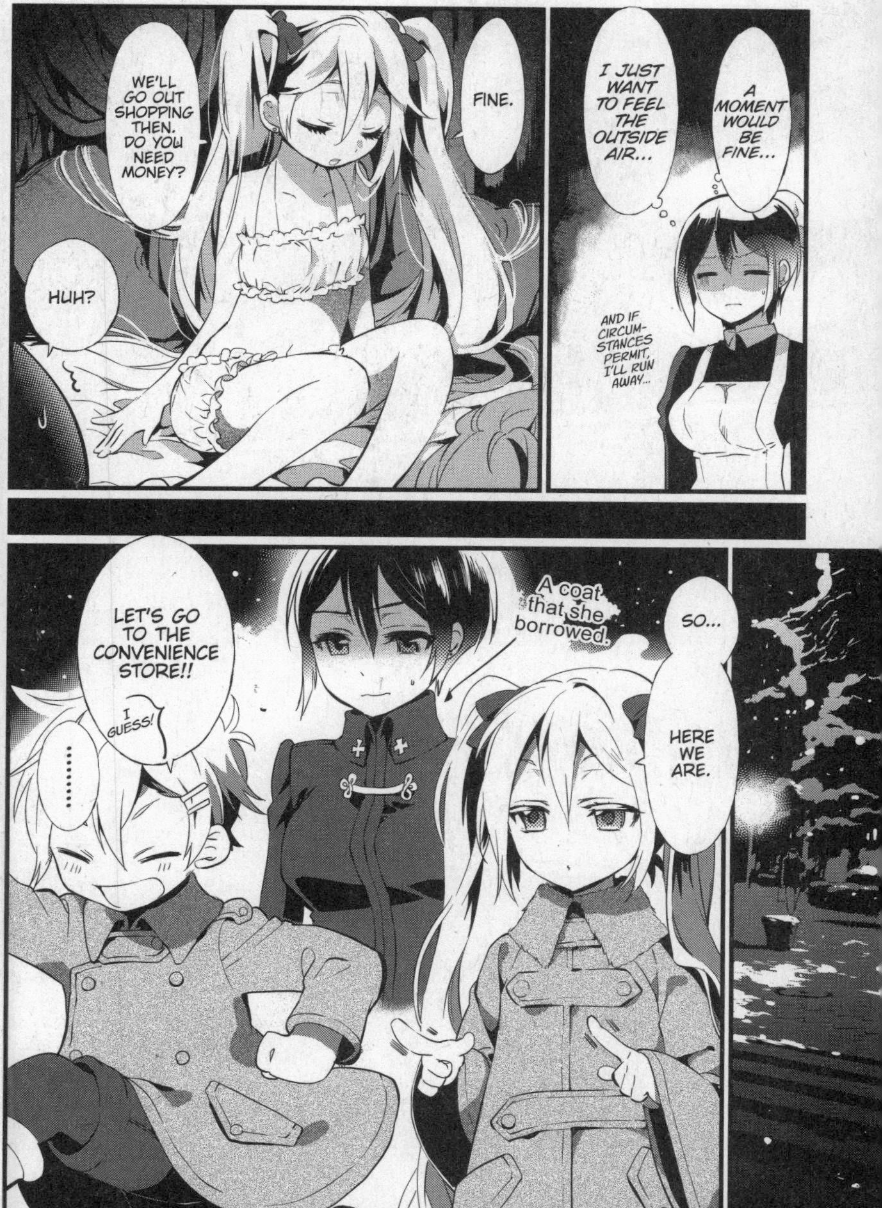
A MOMENT WOULD BE FINE...
I JUST WANT TO FEEL THE OUTSIDE AIR...
AND IF CIRCUMSTANCES PERMIT, I'LL RUN AWAY...
FINE.
WE'LL GO OUT SHOPPING THEN. DO YOU NEED MONEY?
HUH?
SO... HERE WE ARE.
A coat that she borrowed.
LET'S GO TO THE CONVENIENCE STORE!!
I GUESS!
......

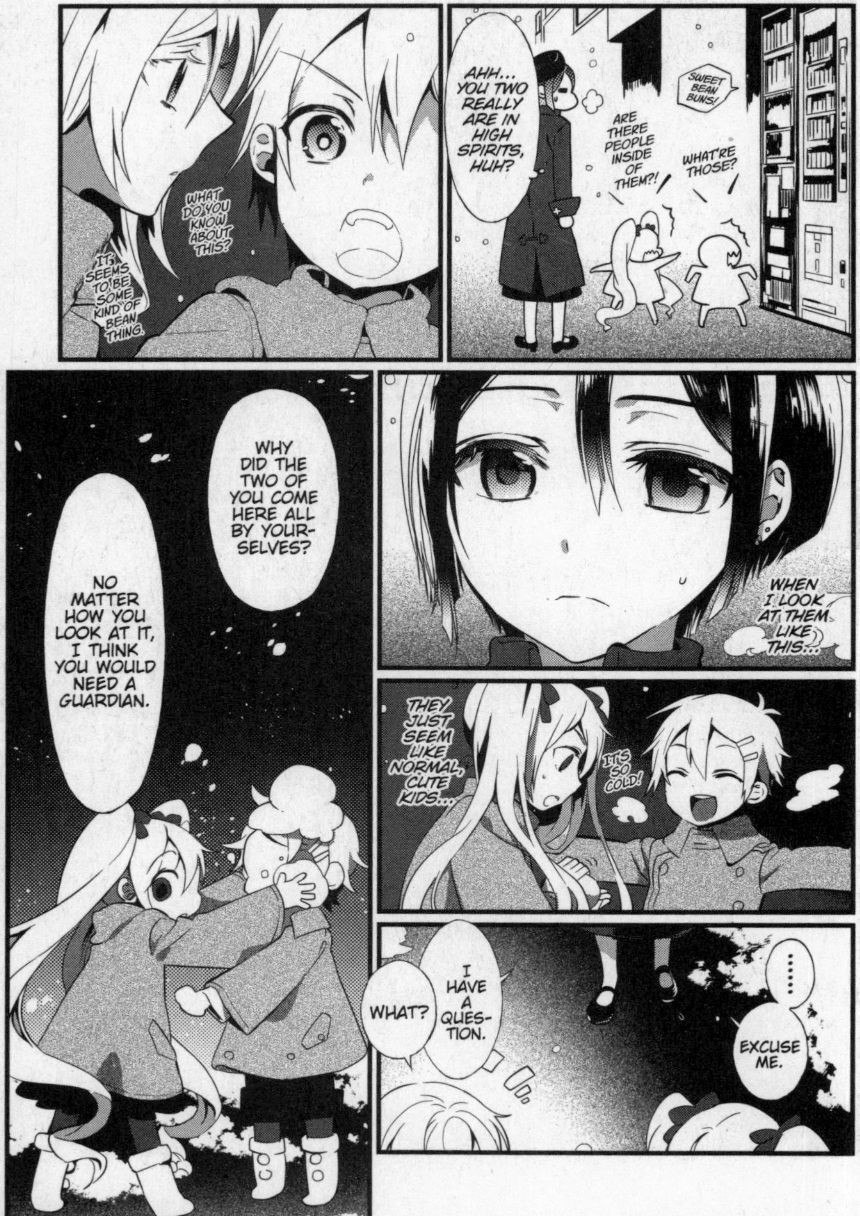
SWEET BEAN BUNS!
WHAT'RE THOSE?
ARE THERE PEOPLE INSIDE OF THEM?!
AHH... YOU TWO REALLY ARE IN HIGH SPIRITS, HUH?
WHAT DO YOU KNOW ABOUT THIS?
IT SEEMS TO BE SOME KIND OF BEAN THING.
WHEN I LOOK AT THEM LIKE THIS...
IT'S SO COLD!
THEY JUST SEEM LIKE NORMAL, CUTE KIDS...
......
EXCUSE ME.
I HAVE A QUESTION.
WHAT?
WHY DID THE TWO OF YOU COME HERE ALL BY YOURSELVES?
NO MATTER HOW YOU LOOK AT IT, I THINK YOU WOULD NEED A GUARDIAN.

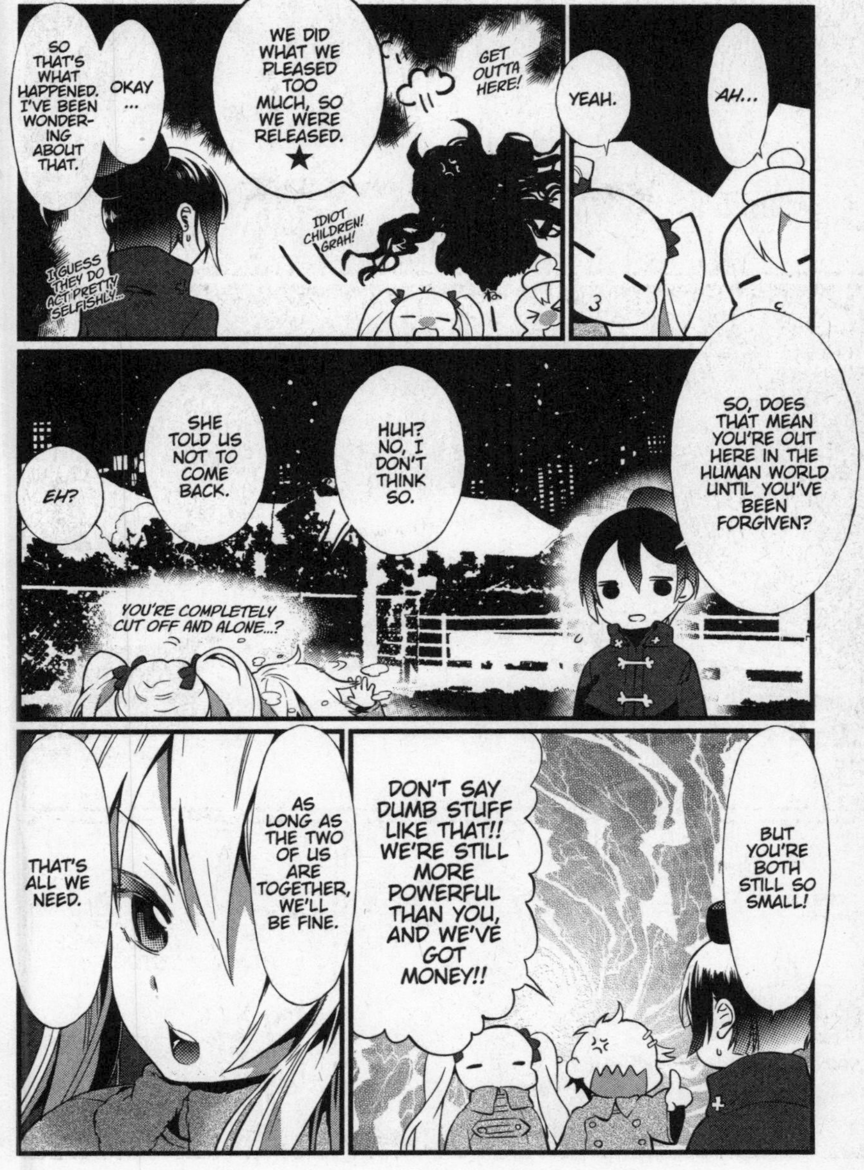
AH...
YEAH.
GET OUTTA HERE!
WE DID WHAT WE PLEASED TOO MUCH, SO WE WERE RELEASED. ★
IDIOT CHILDREN! GRAH!
OKAY ...
SO THAT'S WHAT HAPPENED. I'VE BEEN WONDERING ABOUT THAT.
I GUESS THEY DO ACT PRETTY SELFISHLY...
SO, DOES THAT MEAN YOU'RE OUT HERE IN THE HUMAN WORLD UNTIL YOU'VE BEEN FORGIVEN?
HUH? NO, I DON'T THINK SO.
SHE TOLD US NOT TO COME BACK.
EH?
YOU'RE COMPLETELY CUT OFF AND ALONE...?
BUT YOU'RE BOTH STILL SO SMALL!
DON'T SAY DUMB STUFF LIKE THAT!! WE'RE STILL MORE POWERFUL THAN YOU, AND WE'VE GOT MONEY!!
AS LONG AS THE TWO OF US ARE TOGETHER, WE'LL BE FINE.
THAT'S ALL WE NEED.

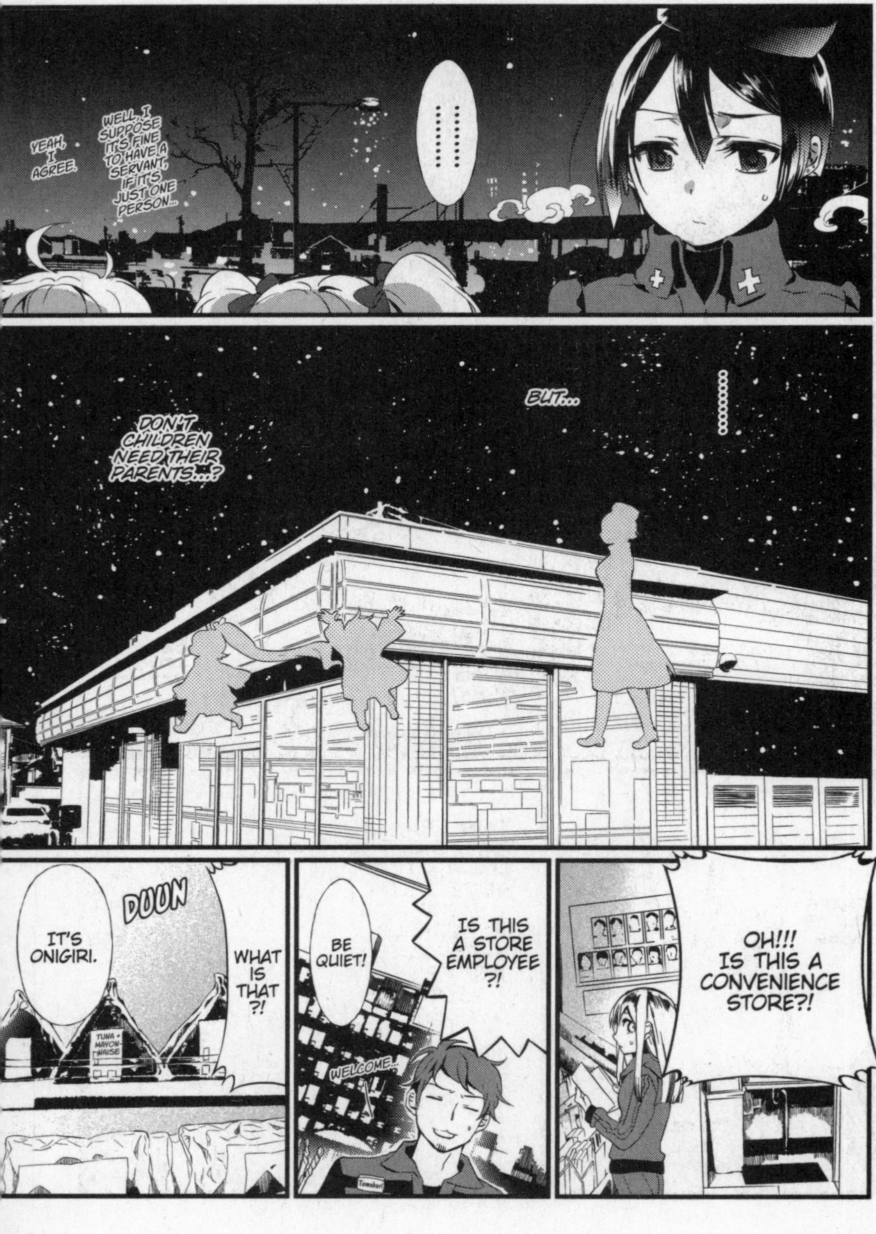
......
WELL, I SUPPOSE IT'S FINE TO HAVE A SERVANT, IF IT'S JUST ONE PERSON...
YEAH, I AGREE.
......
BUT...
DON'T CHILDREN NEED THEIR PARENTS...?
OH!!! IS THIS A CONVENIENCE STORE?!
IS THIS A STORE EMPLOYEE?!
BE QUIET!
WELCOME...
WHAT IS THAT?!
DUUN
IT'S ONIGIRI.
TUNA + MAYON-NAISE

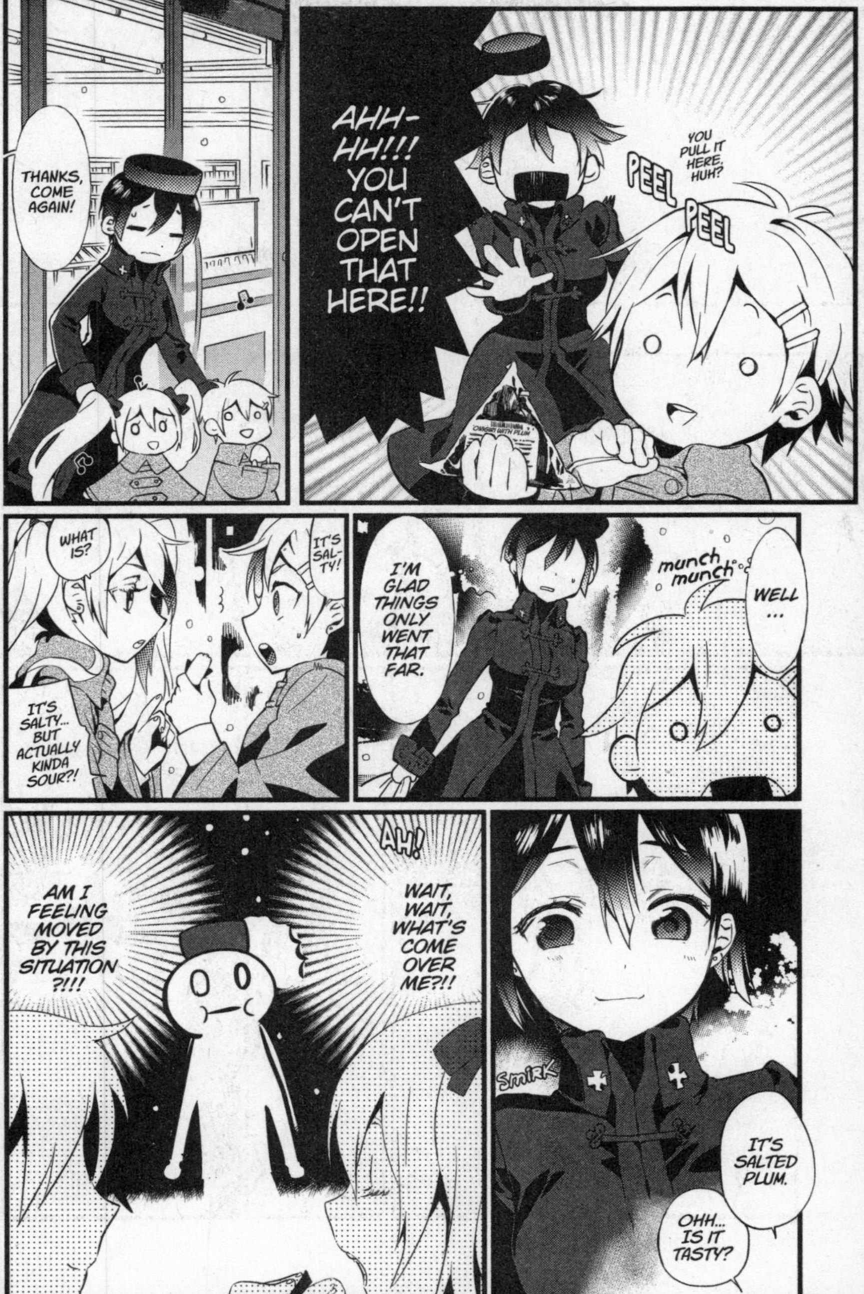
YOU PULL IT HERE, HUH?
PEEL PEEL
AHH-HH!!! YOU CAN'T OPEN THAT HERE!!
ONIGIRI WITH PLUM
THANKS, COME AGAIN!
munch munch
WELL...
I'M GLAD THINGS ONLY WENT THAT FAR.
IT'S SALTY!
WHAT IS?
IT'S SALTY... BUT ACTUALLY KINDA SOUR?!
Smirk
IT'S SALTED PLUM.
OHH... IS IT TASTY?
AH!
WAIT, WAIT, WHAT'S COME OVER ME?!!
AM I FEELING MOVED BY THIS SITUATION?!!!

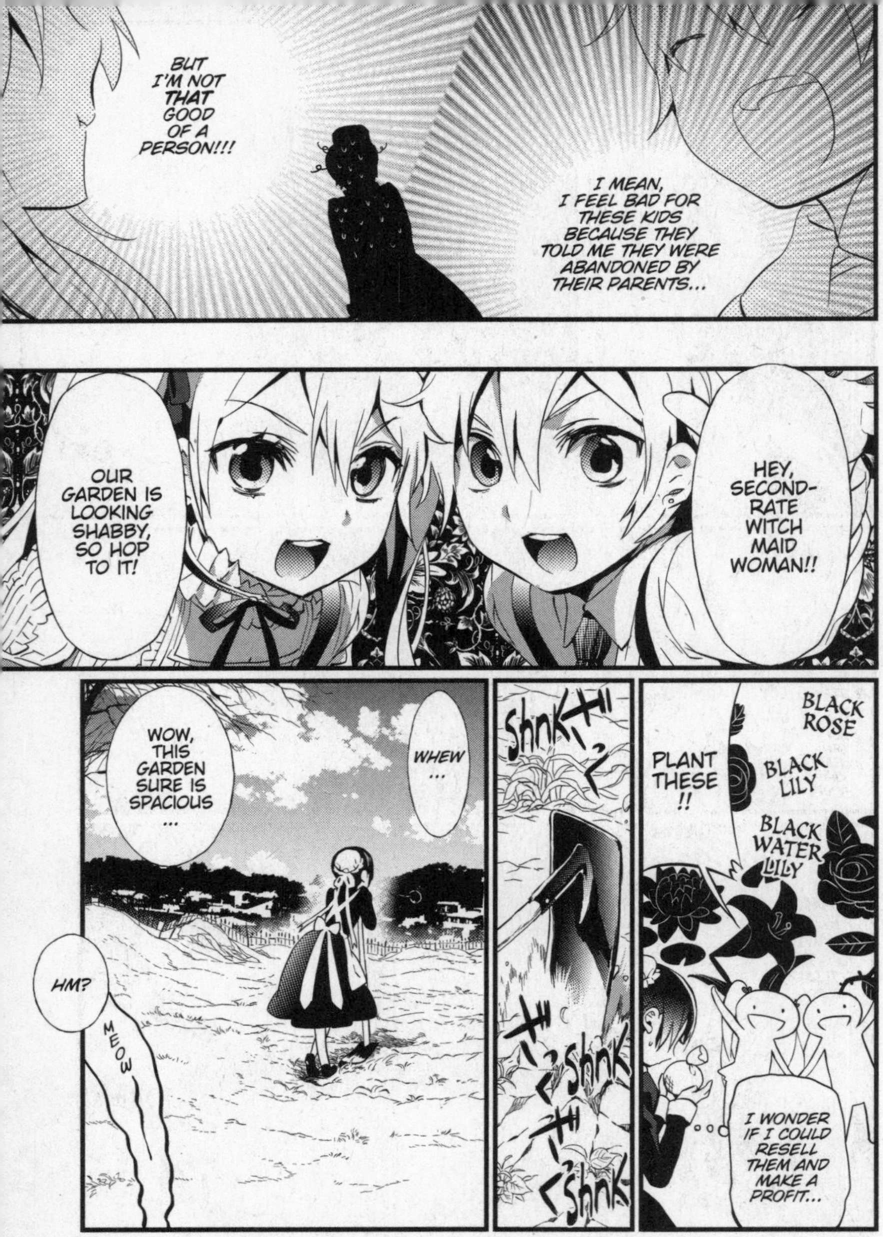
I MEAN, I FEEL BAD FOR THESE KIDS BECAUSE THEY TOLD ME THEY WERE ABANDONED BY THEIR PARENTS...
BUT I'M NOT THAT GOOD OF A PERSON!!!
HEY, SECOND-RATE WITCH MAID WOMAN!!
OUR GARDEN IS LOOKING SHABBY, SO HOP TO IT!
BLACK ROSE
PLANT THESE!!
BLACK LILY
BLACK WATER LILLY
I WONDER IF I COULD RESELL THEM AND MAKE A PROFIT...
...
Shnk
Shnk
Shnk
WHEW...
WOW, THIS GARDEN SURE IS SPACIOUS...
HM?
MEOW

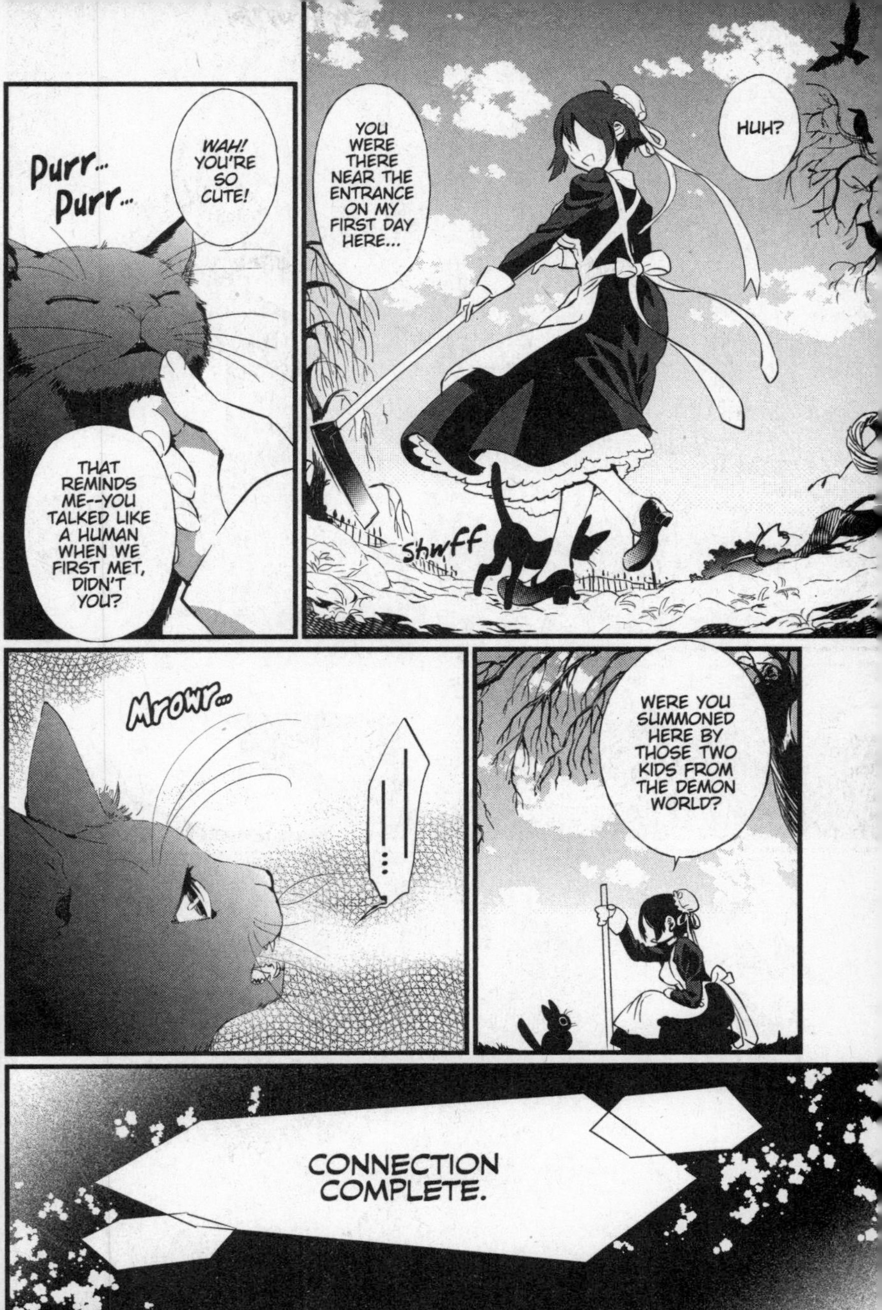
HUH?
YOU WERE THERE NEAR THE ENTRANCE ON MY FIRST DAY HERE...
Shwff
Purr... Purr...
WAH! YOU'RE SO CUTE!
THAT REMINDS ME--YOU TALKED LIKE A HUMAN WHEN WE FIRST MET, DIDN'T YOU?
WERE YOU SUMMONED HERE BY THOSE TWO KIDS FROM THE DEMON WORLD?
Mrowr...
......!
CONNECTION COMPLETE.

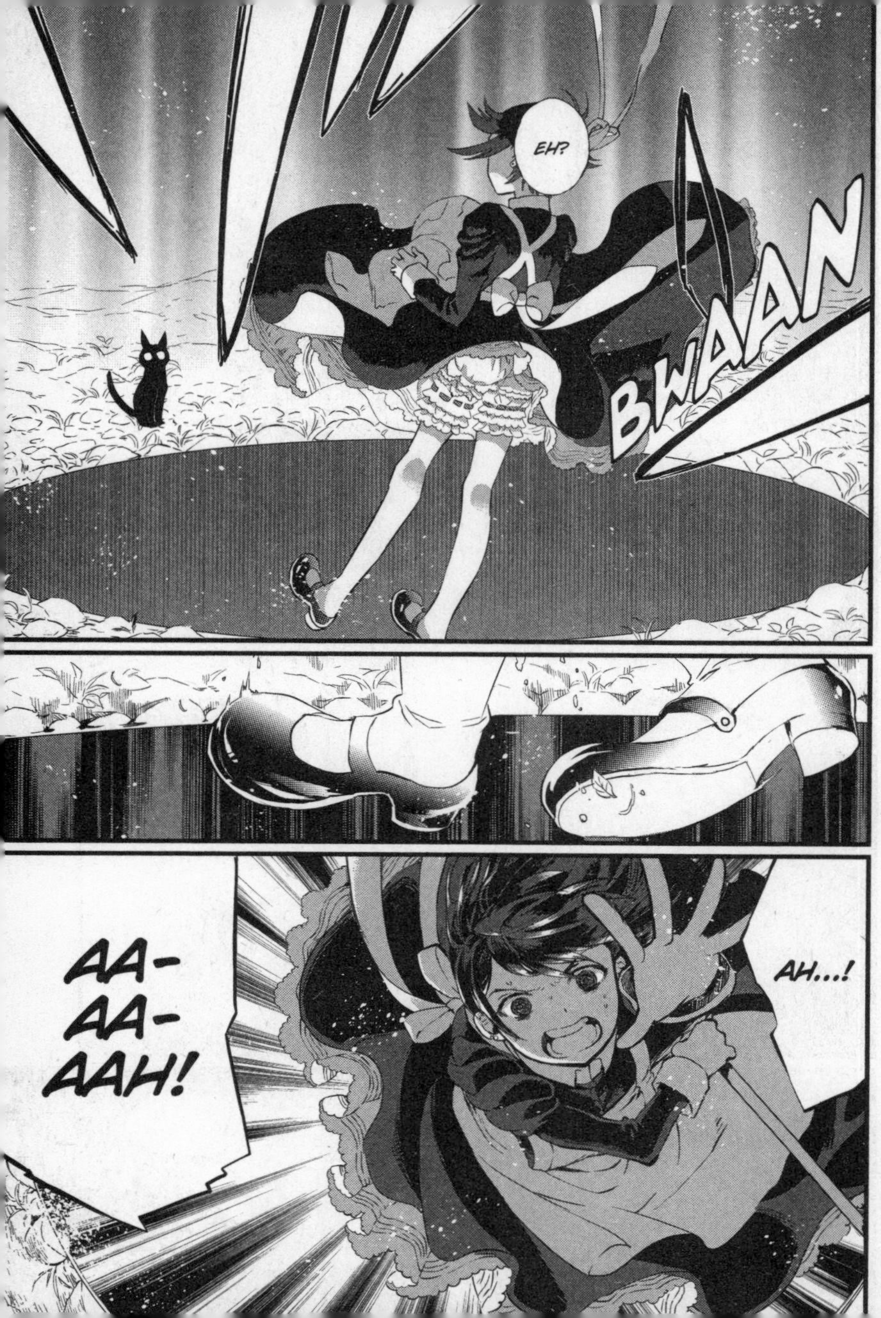
EH?
BWAAN
AH...!
AA-
AA-
AAH!

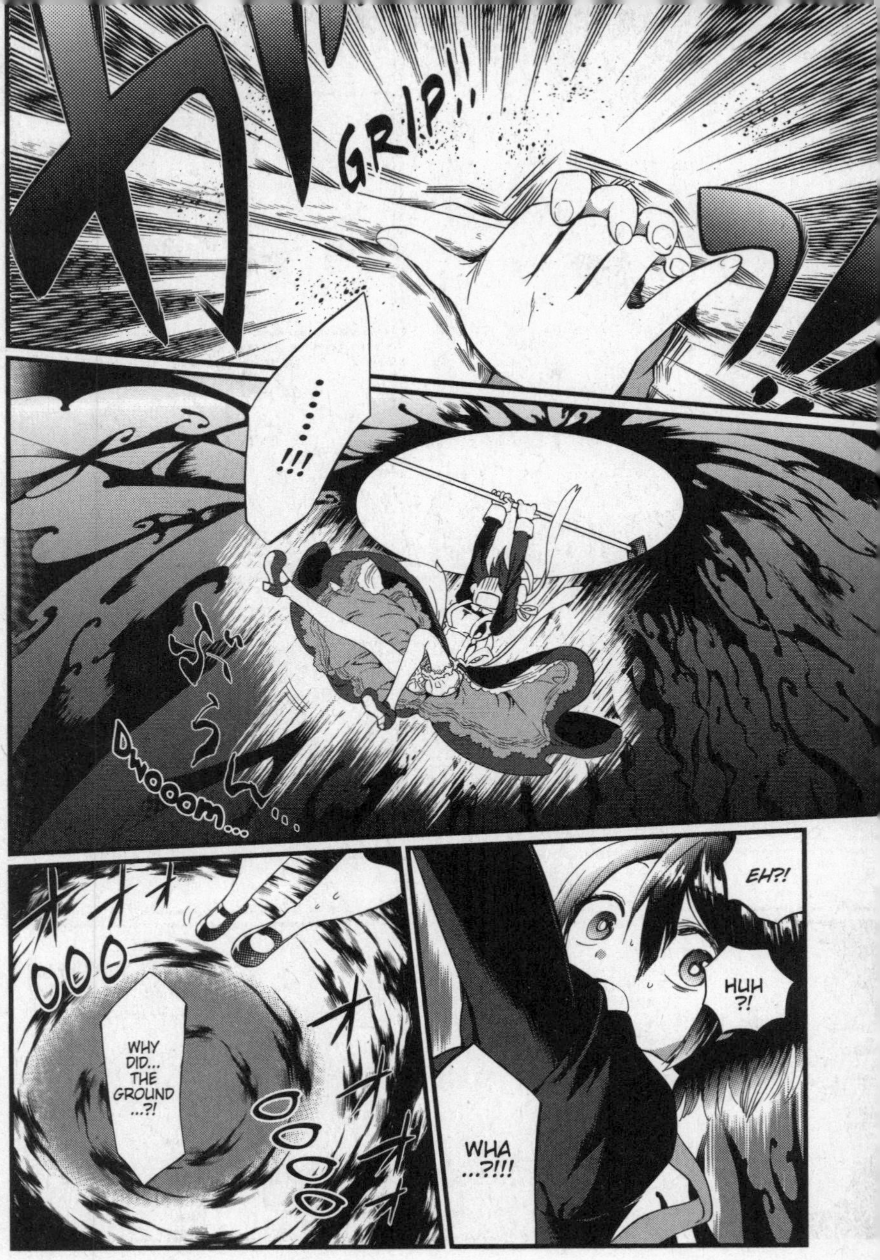
GRIP!!
......!!!
ぶらん
Dwooom...
EH?!
HUH?!
WHA...?!!!
WHY DID... THE GROUND ...?!

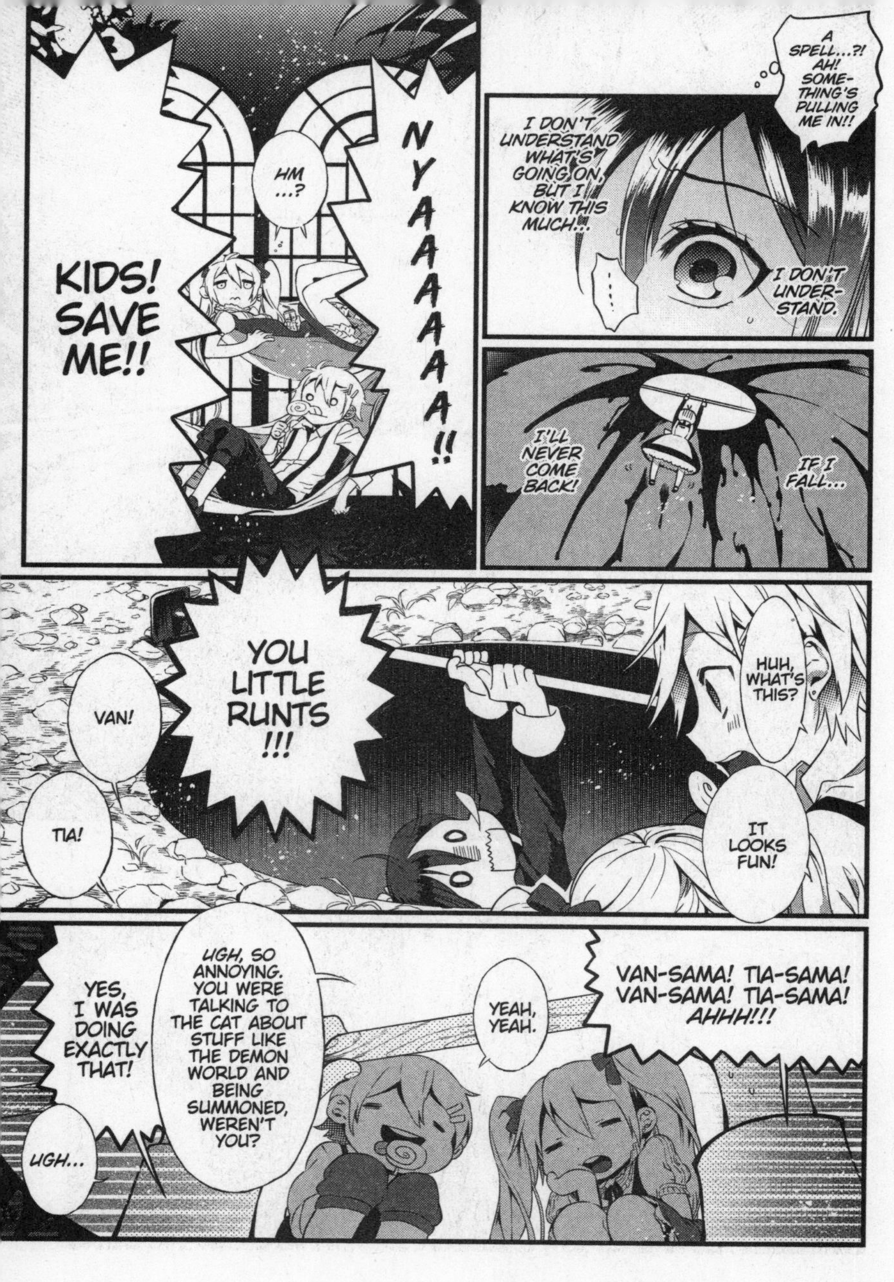
A SPELL...?! AH! SOMETHING'S PULLING ME IN!!
I DON'T UNDERSTAND WHAT'S GOING ON, BUT I KNOW THIS MUCH...
I DON'T UNDERSTAND.
......
IF I FALL...
I'LL NEVER COME BACK!
NYAAAAAA!!
HM ...?
KIDS! SAVE ME!!
HUH, WHAT'S THIS?
IT LOOKS FUN!
YOU LITTLE RUNTS!!!
VAN!
TIA!
VAN-SAMA! TIA-SAMA! VAN-SAMA! TIA-SAMA! AHHH!!!
YEAH, YEAH.
UGH, SO ANNOYING. YOU WERE TALKING TO THE CAT ABOUT STUFF LIKE THE DEMON WORLD AND BEING SUMMONED, WEREN'T YOU?
YES, I WAS DOING EXACTLY THAT!
UGH...

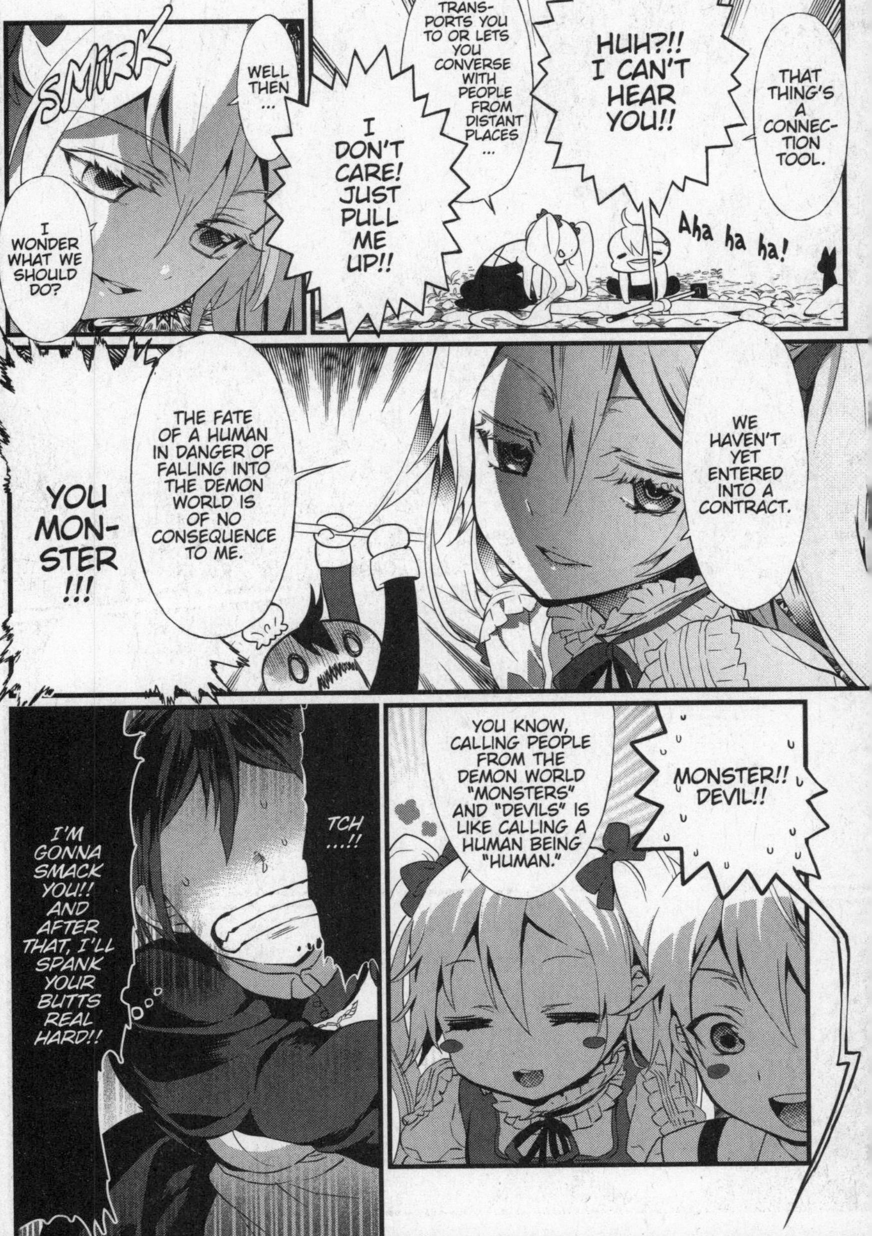
THAT THING'S A CONNECTION TOOL.
HUH?!! I CAN'T HEAR YOU!!
IT TRANSPORTS YOU TO OR LETS YOU CONVERSE WITH PEOPLE FROM DISTANT PLACES...
I DON'T CARE! JUST PULL ME UP!!
Aha ha ha!
SMIRK
WELL THEN...
I WONDER WHAT WE SHOULD DO?
WE HAVEN'T YET ENTERED INTO A CONTRACT.
THE FATE OF A HUMAN IN DANGER OF FALLING INTO THE DEMON WORLD IS OF NO CONSEQUENCE TO ME.
YOU MONSTER!!!
MONSTER!! DEVIL!!
YOU KNOW, CALLING PEOPLE FROM THE DEMON WORLD "MONSTERS" AND "DEVILS" IS LIKE CALLING A HUMAN BEING "HUMAN."
TCH...!!
I'M GONNA SMACK YOU!! AND AFTER THAT, I'LL SPANK YOUR BUTTS REAL HARD!!

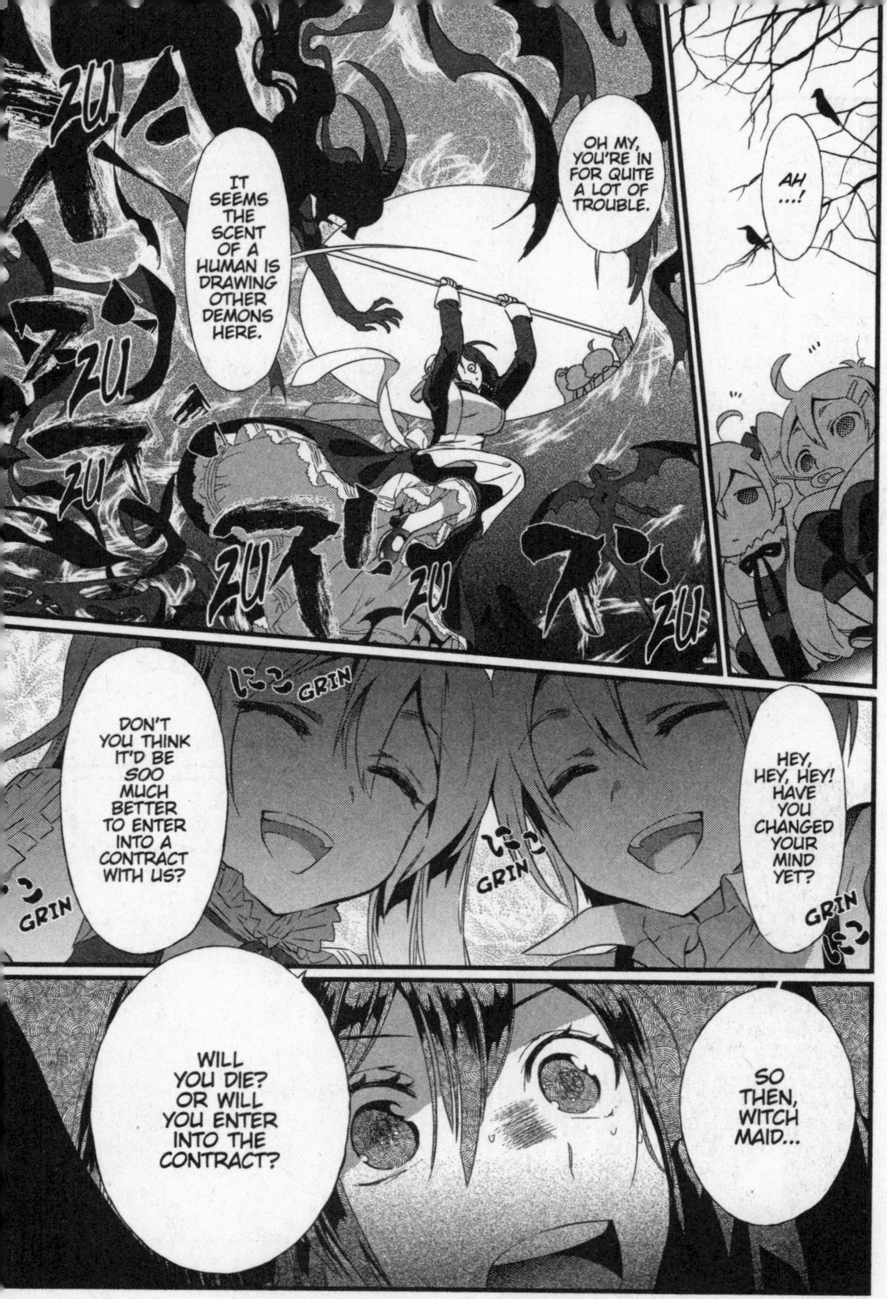
AH ...!
...
OH MY, YOU'RE IN FOR QUITE A LOT OF TROUBLE.
IT SEEMS THE SCENT OF A HUMAN IS DRAWING OTHER DEMONS HERE.
ZU ZU ZU ZU ZU ZU ZU
HEY, HEY, HEY! HAVE YOU CHANGED YOUR MIND YET?
GRIN
GRIN
DON'T YOU THINK IT'D BE SOO MUCH BETTER TO ENTER INTO A CONTRACT WITH US?
GRIN
GRIN
SO THEN, WITCH MAID...
WILL YOU DIE? OR WILL YOU ENTER INTO THE CONTRACT?

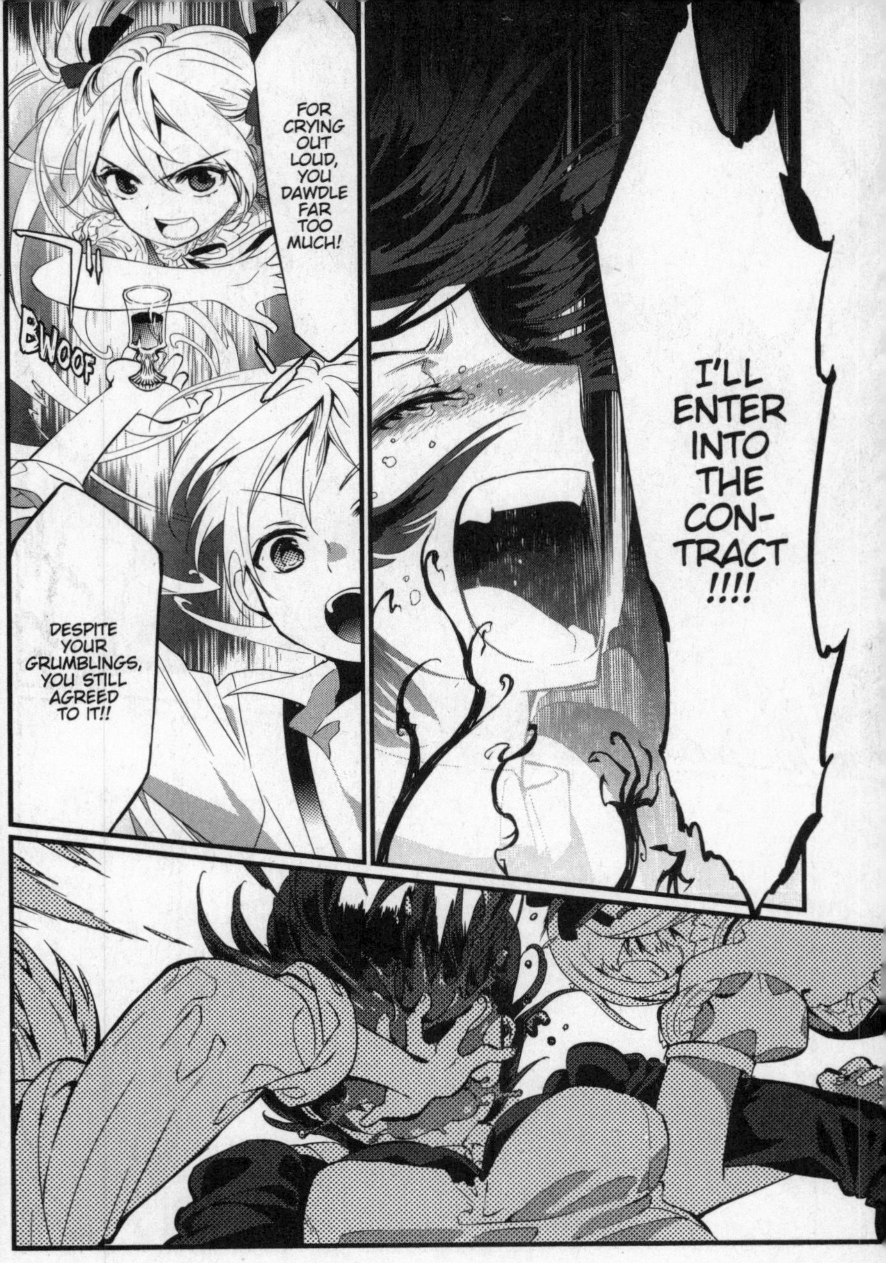
I'LL ENTER INTO THE CON-TRACT !!!!
FOR CRYING OUT LOUD, YOU DAWDLE FAR TOO MUCH!
BWOOF
DESPITE YOUR GRUMBLINGS, YOU STILL AGREED TO IT!!

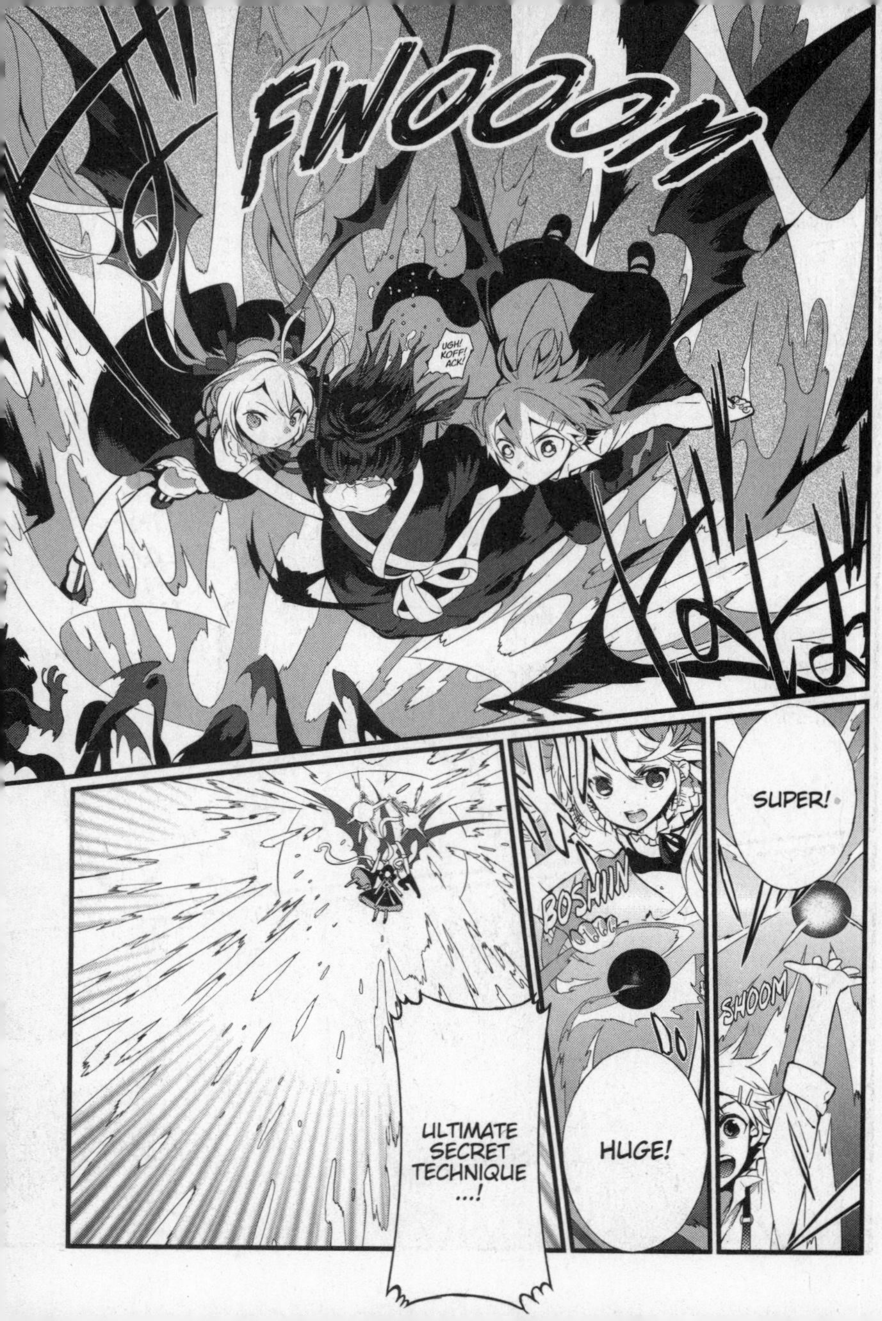
FWOOOM
UGH! KOFF! ACK!
SUPER!
SHOOM
BOSHIIN
HUGE!
ULTIMATE SECRET TECHNIQUE ...!

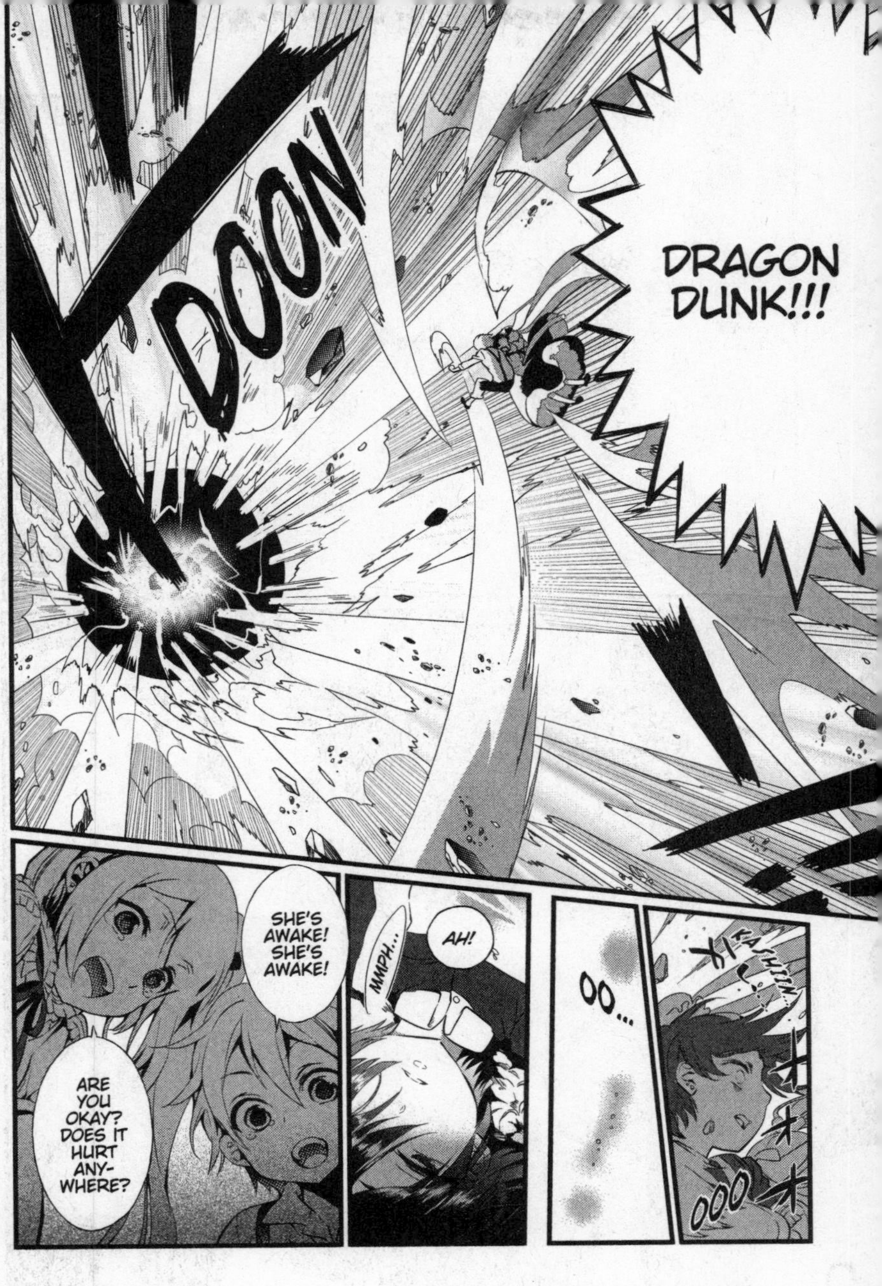
DRAGON DUNK!!!
DOON
KASHIIN...
OOO
OO...
AH!
MMPH...
SHE'S AWAKE! SHE'S AWAKE!
ARE YOU OKAY? DOES IT HURT ANY-WHERE?

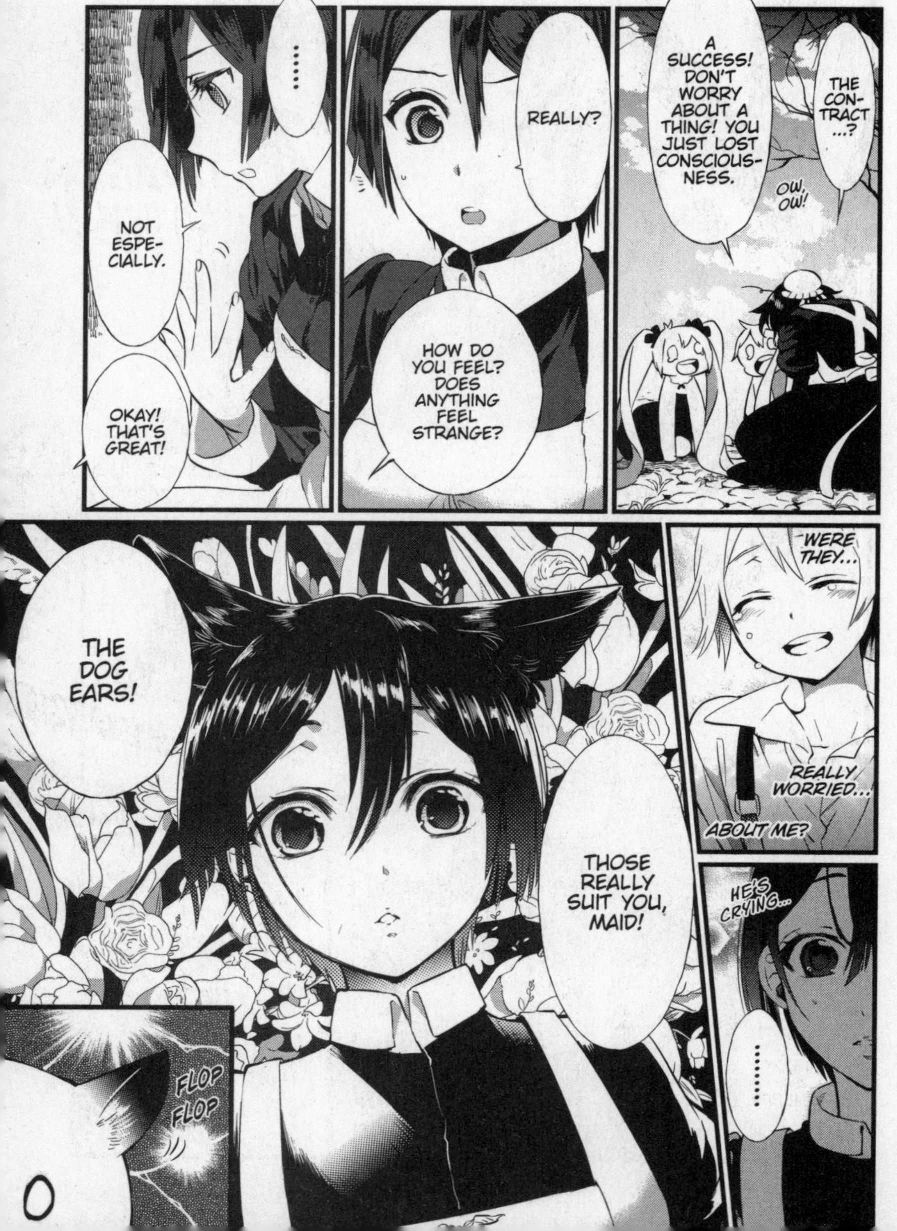
THE CONTRACT...?
A SUCCESS! DON'T WORRY ABOUT A THING! YOU JUST LOST CONSCIOUSNESS.
OW, OW!
REALLY?
HOW DO YOU FEEL? DOES ANYTHING FEEL STRANGE?
......
NOT ESPECIALLY.
OKAY! THAT'S GREAT!
WERE THEY...
REALLY WORRIED...
ABOUT ME?
HE'S CRYING...
......
THE DOG EARS!
THOSE REALLY SUIT YOU, MAID!
FLOP FLOP

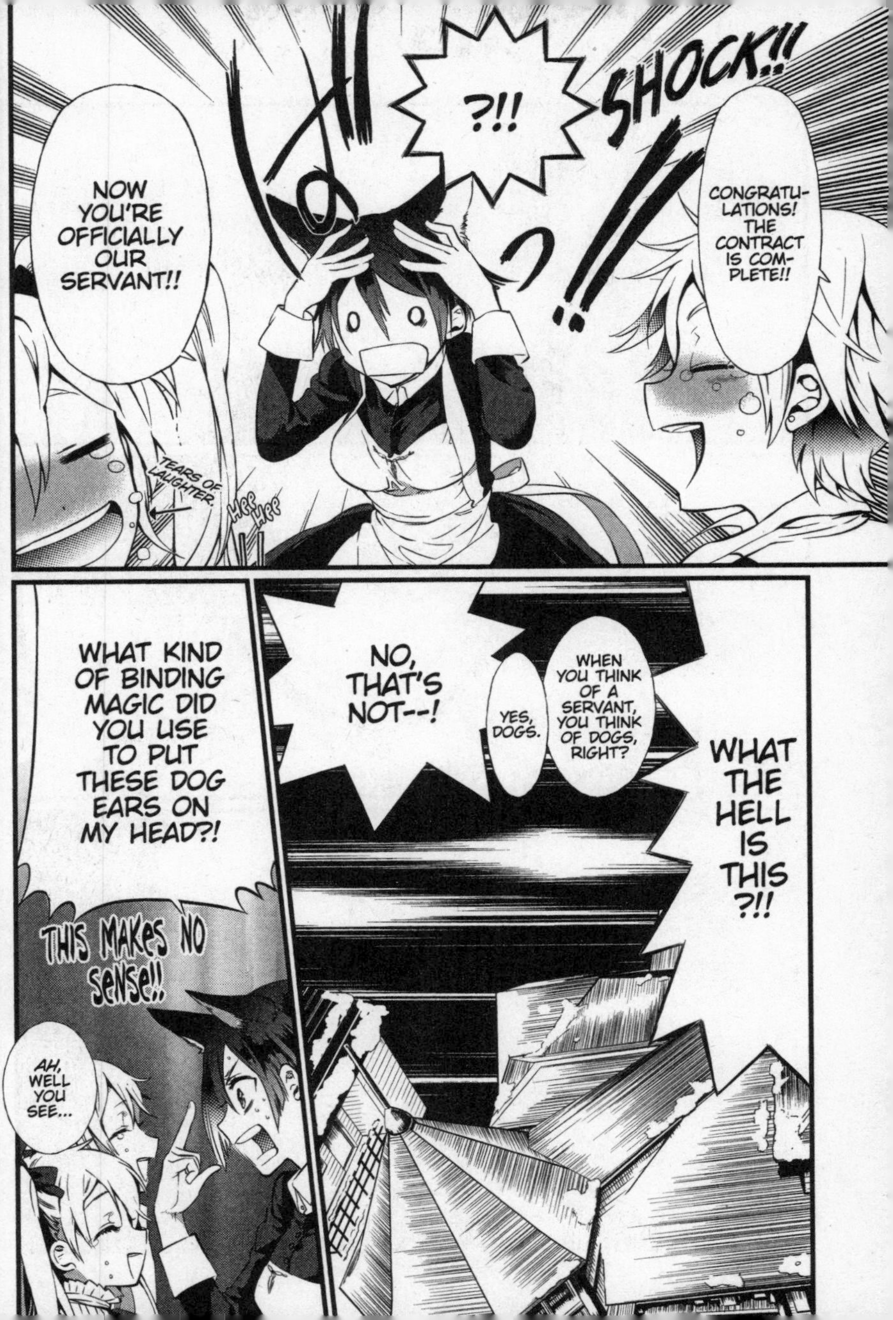
CONGRATULATIONS! THE CONTRACT IS COMPLETE!!
SHOCK!!
?!!
NOW YOU'RE OFFICIALLY OUR SERVANT!!
TEARS OF LAUGHTER.
Hee Hee
WHEN YOU THINK OF A SERVANT, YOU THINK OF DOGS, RIGHT?
YES, DOGS.
NO, THAT'S NOT--!
WHAT THE HELL IS THIS?!!
WHAT KIND OF BINDING MAGIC DID YOU USE TO PUT THESE DOG EARS ON MY HEAD?!
THIS MAKES NO SENSE!!
AH, WELL YOU SEE...

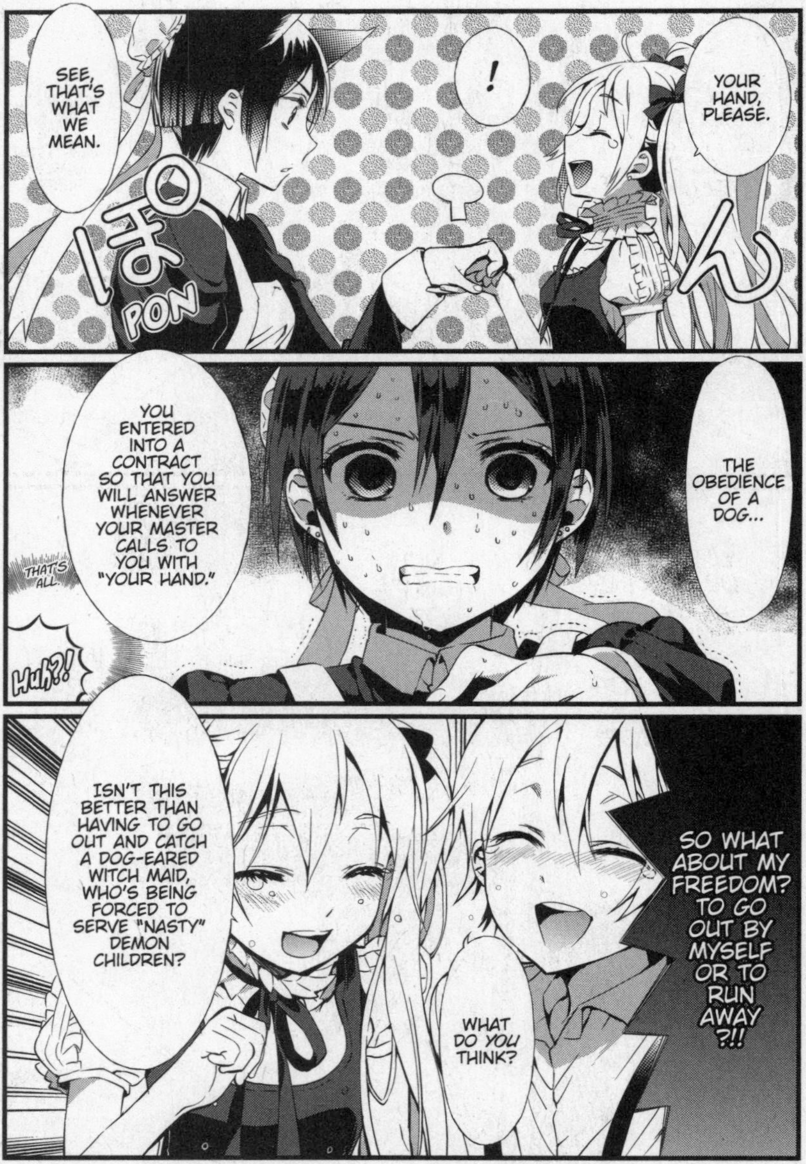
YOUR HAND, PLEASE.
!
ん
SEE, THAT'S WHAT WE MEAN.
ぽ
PON
THE OBEDIENCE OF A DOG...
YOU ENTERED INTO A CONTRACT SO THAT YOU WILL ANSWER WHENEVER YOUR MASTER CALLS TO YOU WITH "YOUR HAND."
THAT'S ALL.
Huh?!
ISN'T THIS BETTER THAN HAVING TO GO OUT AND CATCH A DOG-EARED WITCH MAID, WHO'S BEING FORCED TO SERVE "NASTY" DEMON CHILDREN?
WHAT DO YOU THINK?
SO WHAT ABOUT MY FREEDOM? TO GO OUT BY MYSELF OR TO RUN AWAY?!!

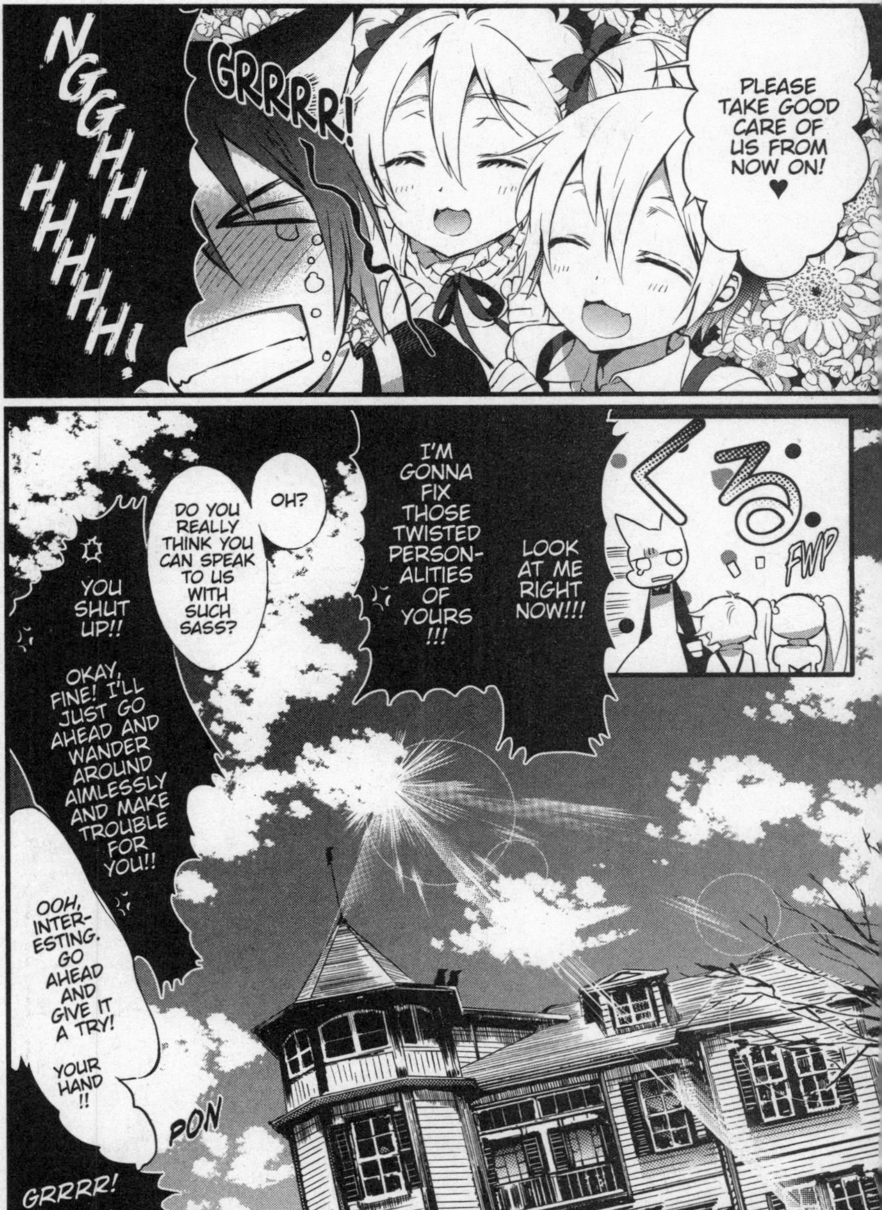
PLEASE TAKE GOOD CARE OF US FROM NOW ON! ♥
GRRRRR!
NGGHHHHHHHH!
くる
FWIP
LOOK AT ME RIGHT NOW!!!
I'M GONNA FIX THOSE TWISTED PERSONALITIES OF YOURS!!!
OH?
DO YOU REALLY THINK YOU CAN SPEAK TO US WITH SUCH SASS?
YOU SHUT UP!!
OKAY, FINE! I'LL JUST GO AHEAD AND WANDER AROUND AIMLESSLY AND MAKE TROUBLE FOR YOU!!
OOH, INTERESTING. GO AHEAD AND GIVE IT A TRY!
YOUR HAND!!
PON
GRRRR!

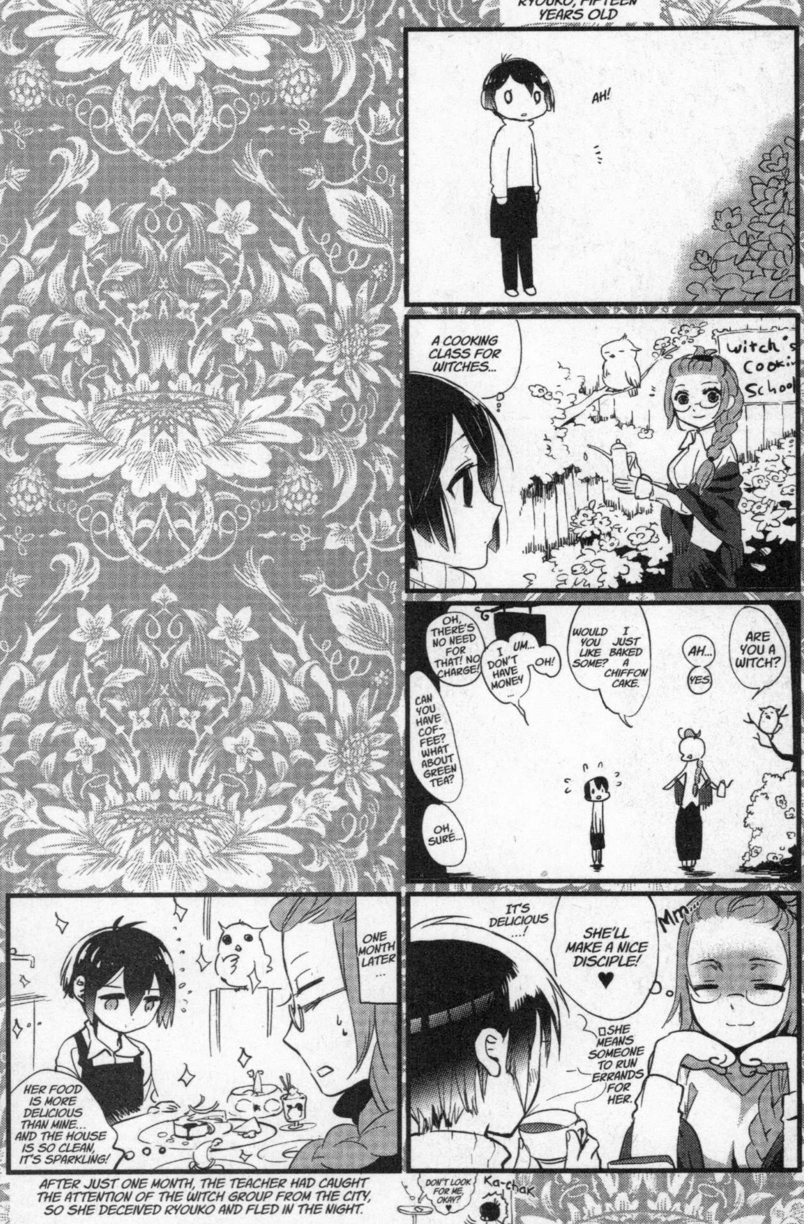
RYOUKO, FIFTEEN YEARS OLD
AH!
A COOKING CLASS FOR WITCHES...
Witch's Cooking School
ARE YOU A WITCH?
AH... YES.
I JUST BAKED A CHIFFON CAKE.
WOULD YOU LIKE SOME?
OH!
UM... I DON'T HAVE MONEY...
OH, THERE'S NO NEED FOR THAT! NO CHARGE!
CAN YOU HAVE COFFEE? WHAT ABOUT GREEN TEA?
OH, SURE...
Mm...
IT'S DELICIOUS...!
SHE'LL MAKE A NICE DISCIPLE! ♥
SHE MEANS SOMEONE TO RUN ERRANDS FOR HER.
ONE MONTH LATER...
HER FOOD IS MORE DELICIOUS THAN MINE... AND THE HOUSE IS SO CLEAN, IT'S SPARKLING!
AFTER JUST ONE MONTH, THE TEACHER HAD CAUGHT THE ATTENTION OF THE WITCH GROUP FROM THE CITY, SO SHE DECEIVED RYOUKO AND FLED IN THE NIGHT.
DON'T LOOK FOR ME, OKAY? ♥
Ka-chak

Generation
WITCH

CHAPTER 20

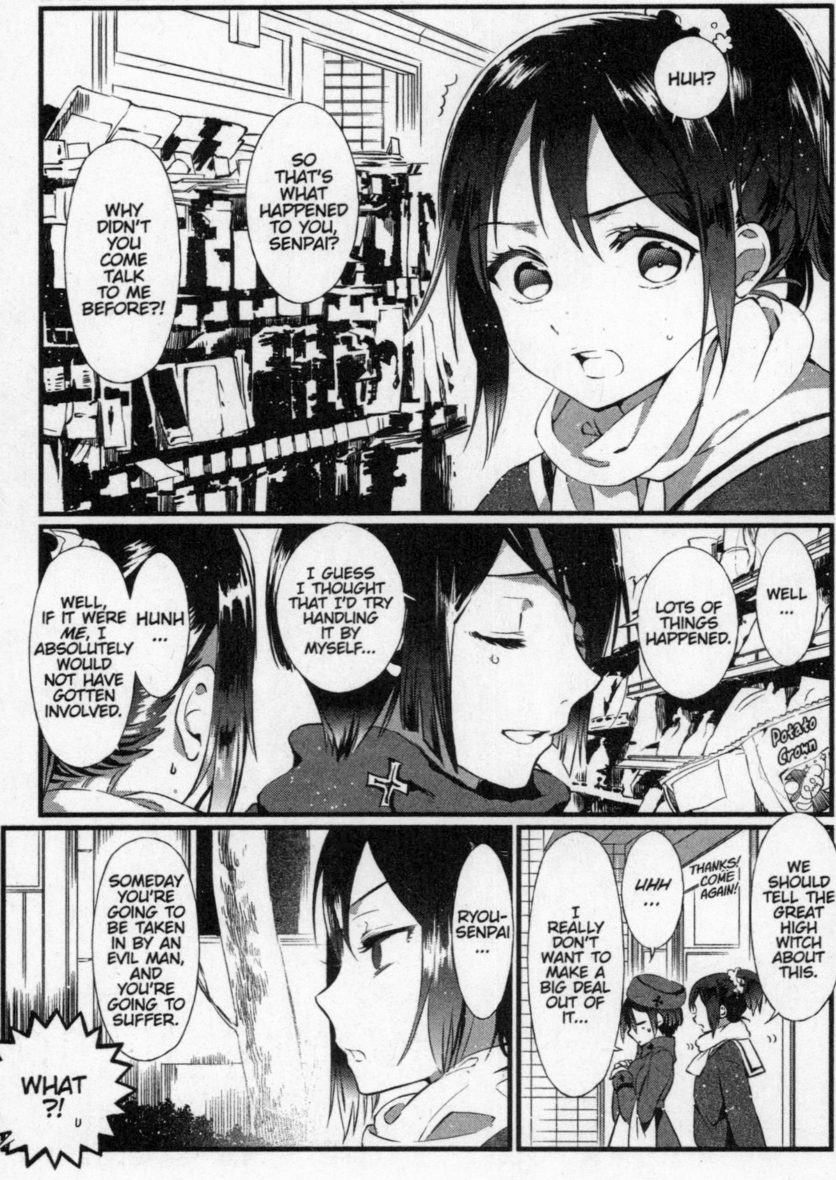
HUH?
SO THAT'S WHAT HAPPENED TO YOU, SENPAI?
WHY DIDN'T YOU COME TALK TO ME BEFORE?!
WELL ...
LOTS OF THINGS HAPPENED.
I GUESS I THOUGHT THAT I'D TRY HANDLING IT BY MYSELF...
HUNH ...
WELL, IF IT WERE *ME*, I ABSOLUTELY WOULD NOT HAVE GOTTEN INVOLVED.
Potato Crown
WE SHOULD TELL THE GREAT HIGH WITCH ABOUT THIS.
THANKS! COME AGAIN!
UHH ...
I REALLY DON'T WANT TO MAKE A BIG DEAL OUT OF IT...
RYOU-SENPAI ...
SOMEDAY YOU'RE GOING TO BE TAKEN IN BY AN EVIL MAN, AND YOU'RE GOING TO SUFFER.
WHAT ?!

Chapter 20: The Terms of a Witch's Contract, Part 2

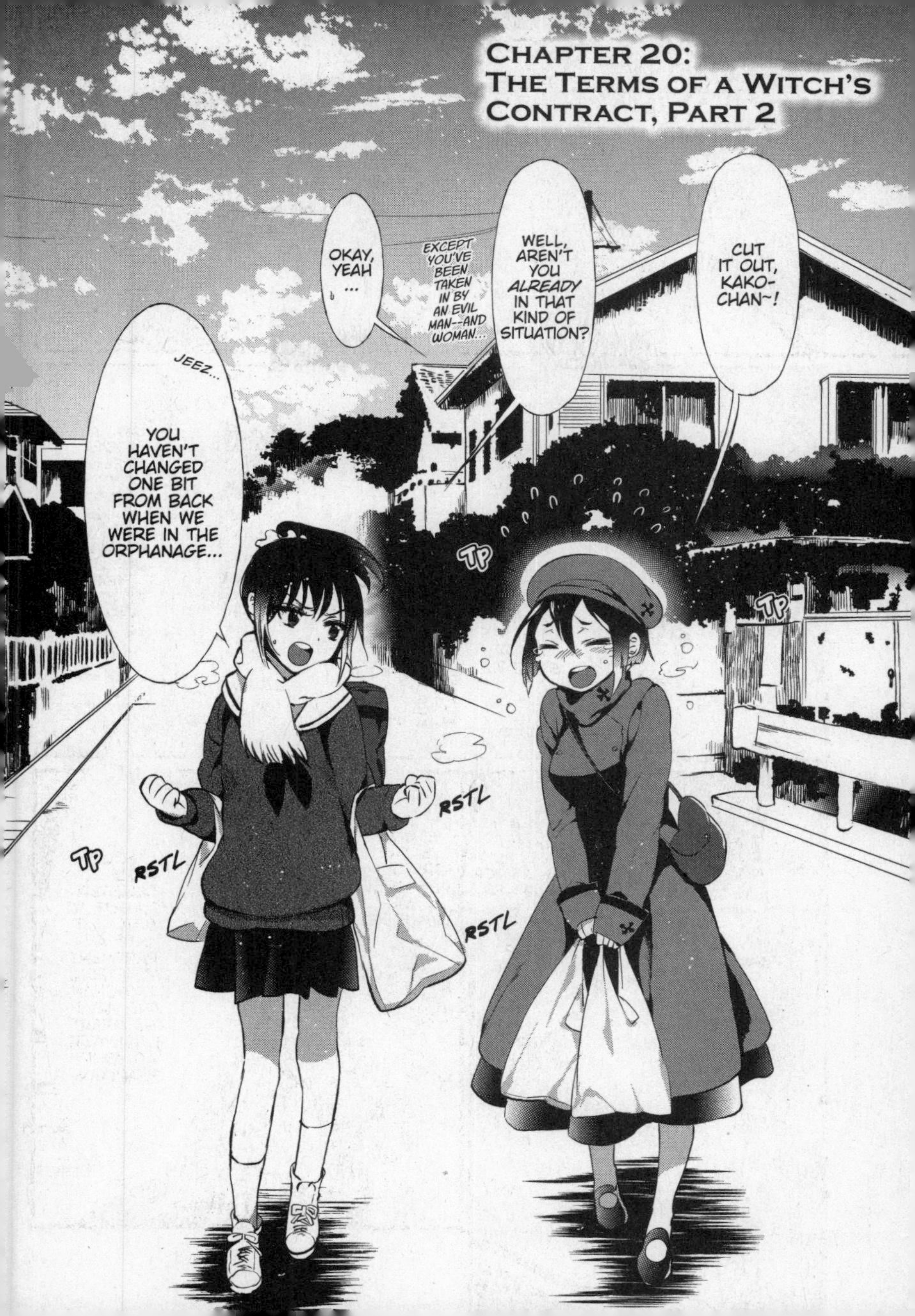
CUT IT OUT, KAKO-CHAN~!
WELL, AREN'T YOU *ALREADY* IN THAT KIND OF SITUATION?
EXCEPT YOU'VE BEEN TAKEN IN BY AN EVIL MAN--AND WOMAN...
OKAY, YEAH ...
JEEZ...
YOU HAVEN'T CHANGED ONE BIT FROM BACK WHEN WE WERE IN THE ORPHANAGE...
TP
TP
RSTL
RSTL
RSTL
TP

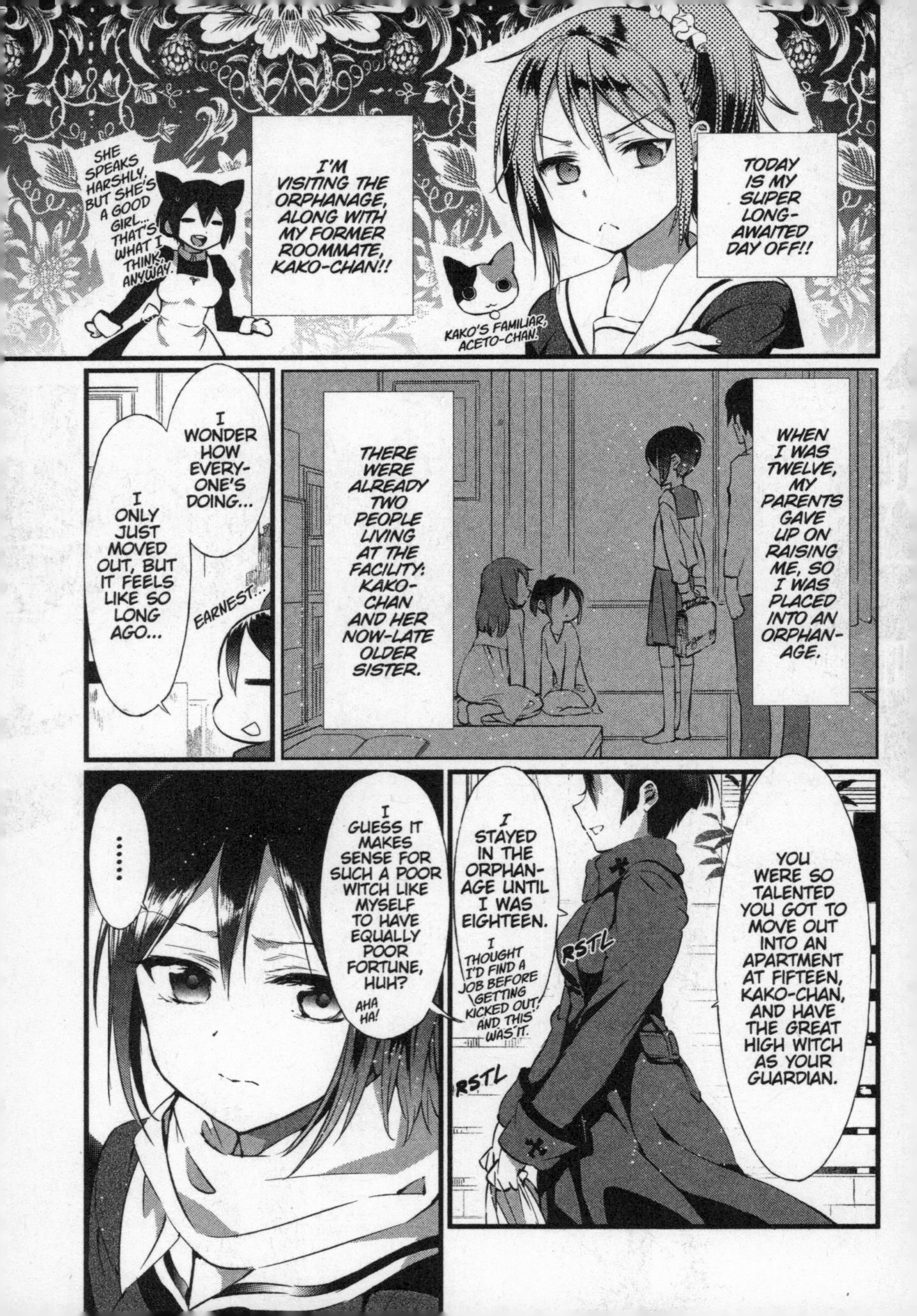

TODAY IS MY SUPER LONG-AWAITED DAY OFF!!
I'M VISITING THE ORPHANAGE, ALONG WITH MY FORMER ROOMMATE, KAKO-CHAN!!
KAKO'S FAMILIAR, ACETO-CHAN!
SHE SPEAKS HARSHLY, BUT SHE'S A GOOD GIRL... THAT'S WHAT I THINK, ANYWAY.
WHEN I WAS TWELVE, MY PARENTS GAVE UP ON RAISING ME, SO I WAS PLACED INTO AN ORPHANAGE.
THERE WERE ALREADY TWO PEOPLE LIVING AT THE FACILITY: KAKO-CHAN AND HER NOW-LATE OLDER SISTER.
I WONDER HOW EVERYONE'S DOING...
I ONLY JUST MOVED OUT, BUT IT FEELS LIKE SO LONG AGO...
EARNEST...
YOU WERE SO TALENTED YOU GOT TO MOVE OUT INTO AN APARTMENT AT FIFTEEN, KAKO-CHAN, AND HAVE THE GREAT HIGH WITCH AS YOUR GUARDIAN.
I STAYED IN THE ORPHANAGE UNTIL I WAS EIGHTEEN.
I THOUGHT I'D FIND A JOB BEFORE GETTING KICKED OUT, AND THIS WAS IT.
RSTL
RSTL
I GUESS IT MAKES SENSE FOR SUCH A POOR WITCH LIKE MYSELF TO HAVE EQUALLY POOR FORTUNE, HUH?
AHA HA!
......

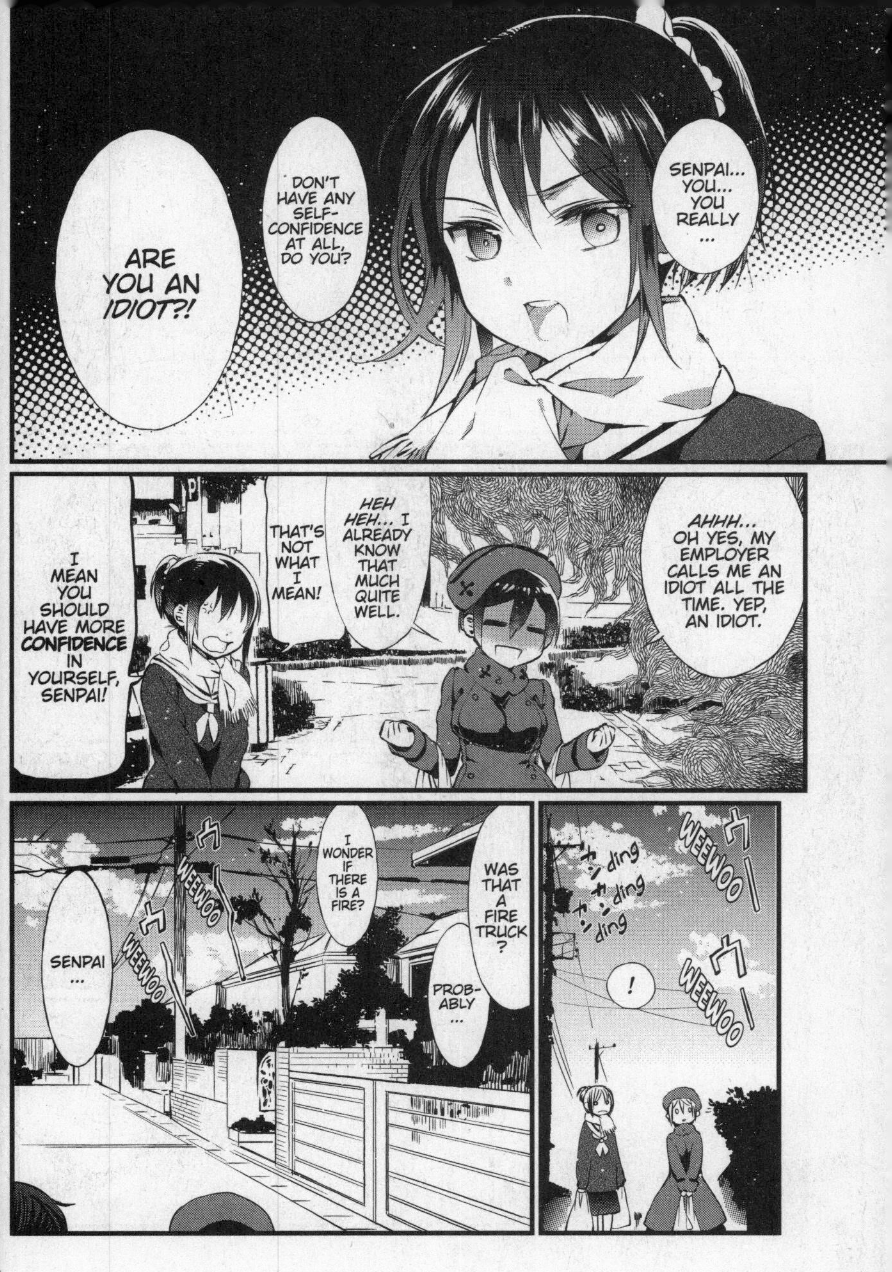
SENPAI... YOU... YOU REALLY ...
DON'T HAVE ANY SELF-CONFIDENCE AT ALL, DO YOU?
ARE YOU AN IDIOT?!
AHHH... OH YES, MY EMPLOYER CALLS ME AN IDIOT ALL THE TIME. YEP, AN IDIOT.
HEH HEH... I ALREADY KNOW THAT MUCH QUITE WELL.
THAT'S NOT WHAT I MEAN!
I MEAN YOU SHOULD HAVE MORE CONFIDENCE IN YOURSELF, SENPAI!
WEEWOO
ding ding ding
WEEWOO
!
WAS THAT A FIRE TRUCK?
I WONDER IF THERE IS A FIRE?
PROBABLY ...
WEEWOO
WEEWOO
SENPAI ...

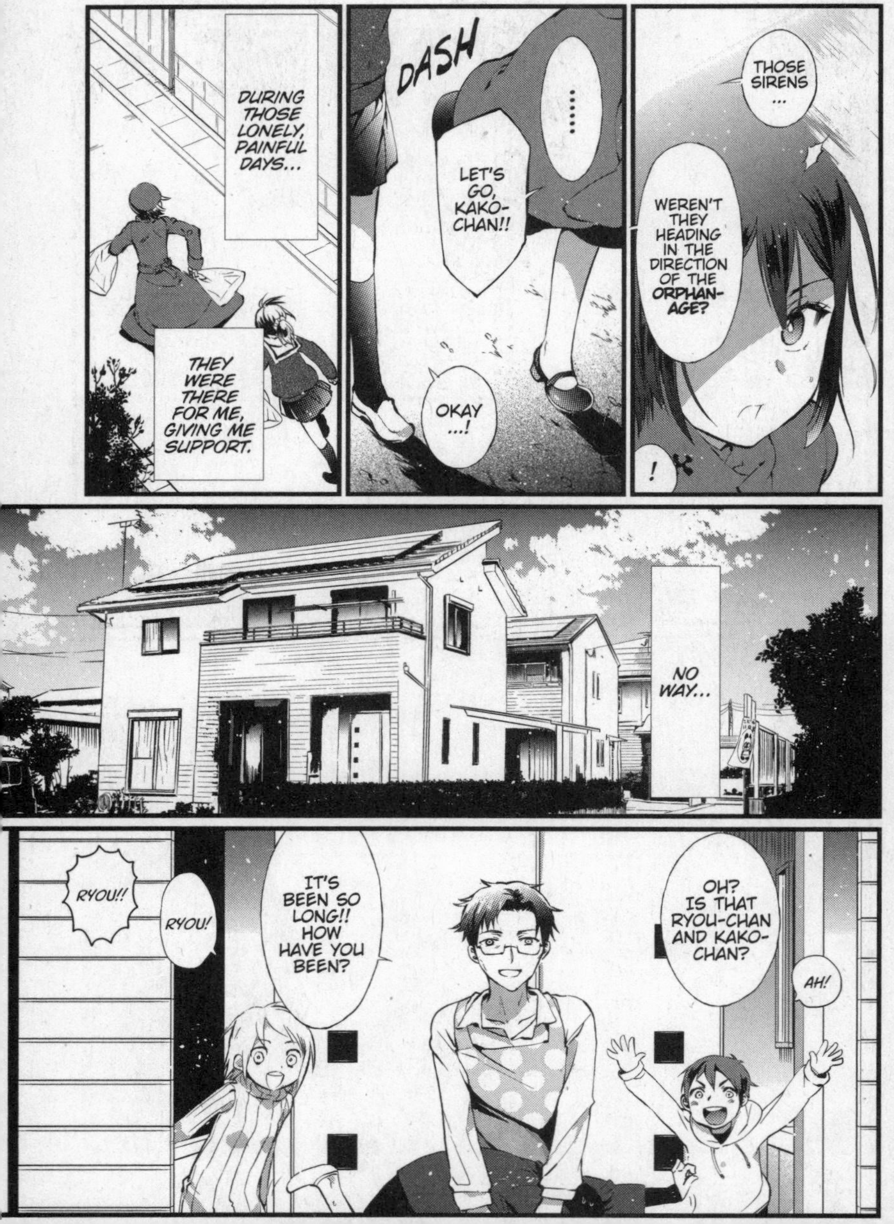
THOSE SIRENS ...
WEREN'T THEY HEADING IN THE DIRECTION OF THE ORPHANAGE?
!
DASH
......
LET'S GO, KAKO-CHAN!!
OKAY ...!
DURING THOSE LONELY, PAINFUL DAYS...
THEY WERE THERE FOR ME, GIVING ME SUPPORT.
NO WAY...
OH? IS THAT RYOU-CHAN AND KAKO-CHAN?
AH!
IT'S BEEN SO LONG!! HOW HAVE YOU BEEN?
RYOU!
RYOU!!

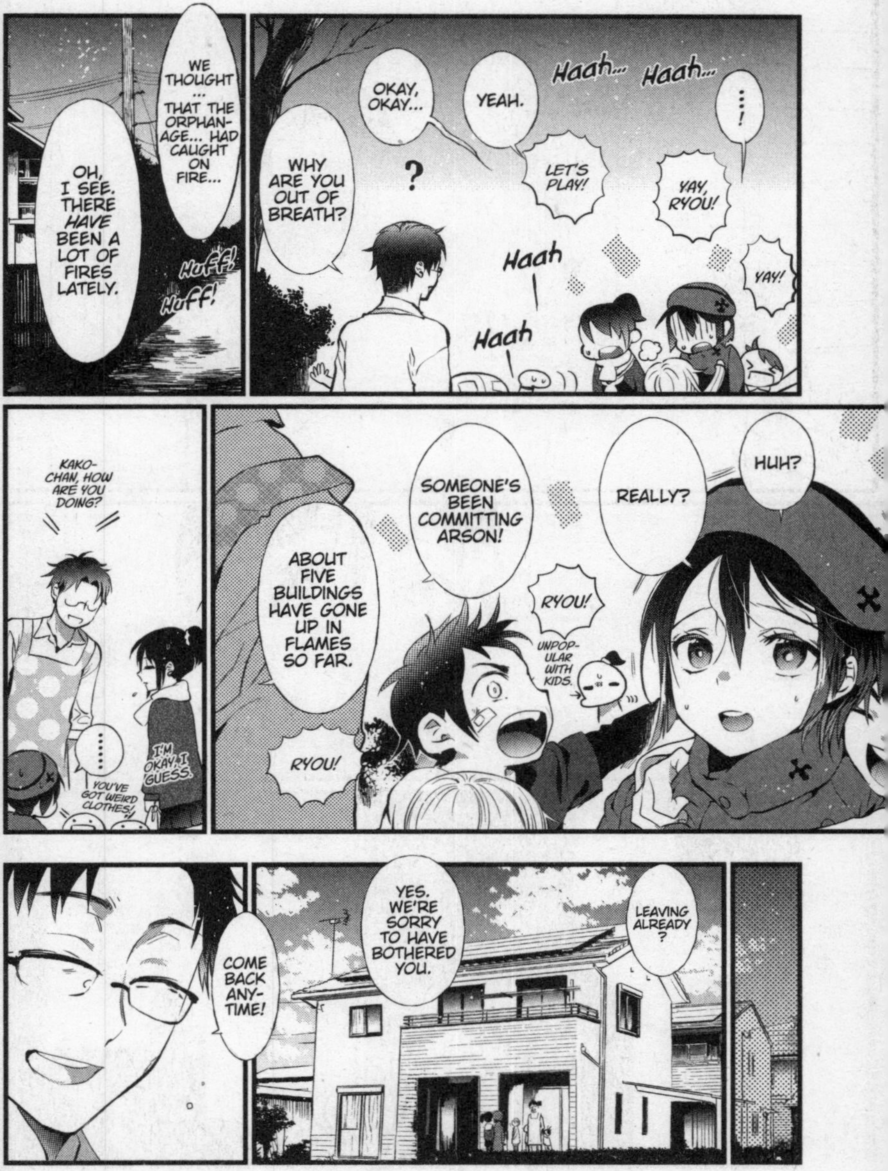

...!
Haah... Haah...
YAY, RYOU!
YAY!
LET'S PLAY!
YEAH.
OKAY, OKAY...
?
WHY ARE YOU OUT OF BREATH?
Haah
Haah
WE THOUGHT ... THAT THE ORPHANAGE... HAD CAUGHT ON FIRE...
Huff! Huff!
OH, I SEE. THERE *HAVE* BEEN A LOT OF FIRES LATELY.
HUH?
REALLY?
SOMEONE'S BEEN COMMITTING ARSON!
RYOU!
UNPOPULAR WITH KIDS.
ABOUT FIVE BUILDINGS HAVE GONE UP IN FLAMES SO FAR.
RYOU!
KAKO-CHAN, HOW ARE YOU DOING?
I'M OKAY, I GUESS.
......
YOU'VE GOT WEIRD CLOTHES!
LEAVING ALREADY?
YES. WE'RE SORRY TO HAVE BOTHERED YOU.
COME BACK ANYTIME!

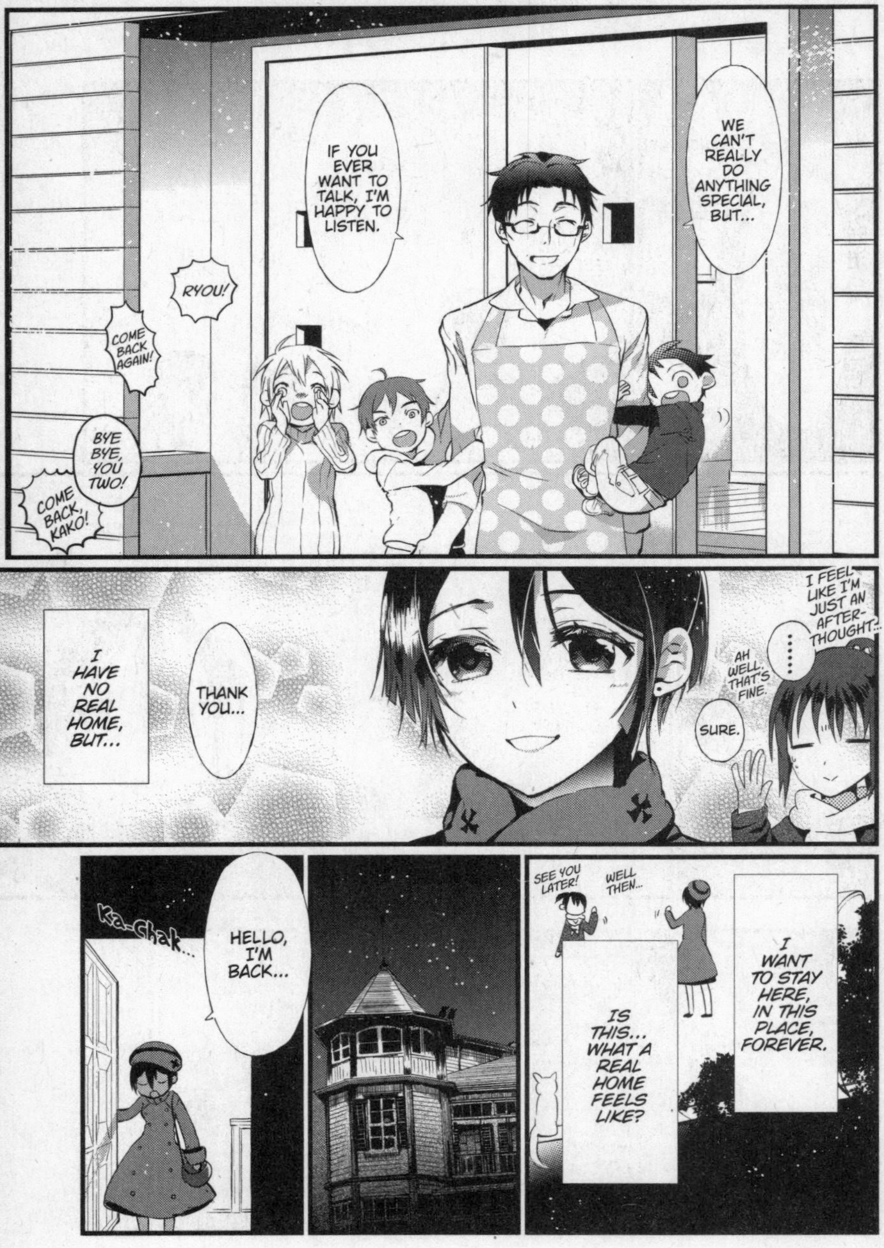
WE CAN'T REALLY DO ANYTHING SPECIAL, BUT...
IF YOU EVER WANT TO TALK, I'M HAPPY TO LISTEN.
RYOU!
COME BACK AGAIN!
BYE BYE, YOU TWO!
COME BACK, KAKO!
I FEEL LIKE I'M JUST AN AFTER-THOUGHT...
......
AH WELL. THAT'S FINE.
SURE.
THANK YOU...
I HAVE NO REAL HOME, BUT...
I WANT TO STAY HERE, IN THIS PLACE, FOREVER.
WELL THEN...
SEE YOU LATER!
IS THIS... WHAT A REAL HOME FEELS LIKE?
HELLO, I'M BACK...
Ka-Chak...

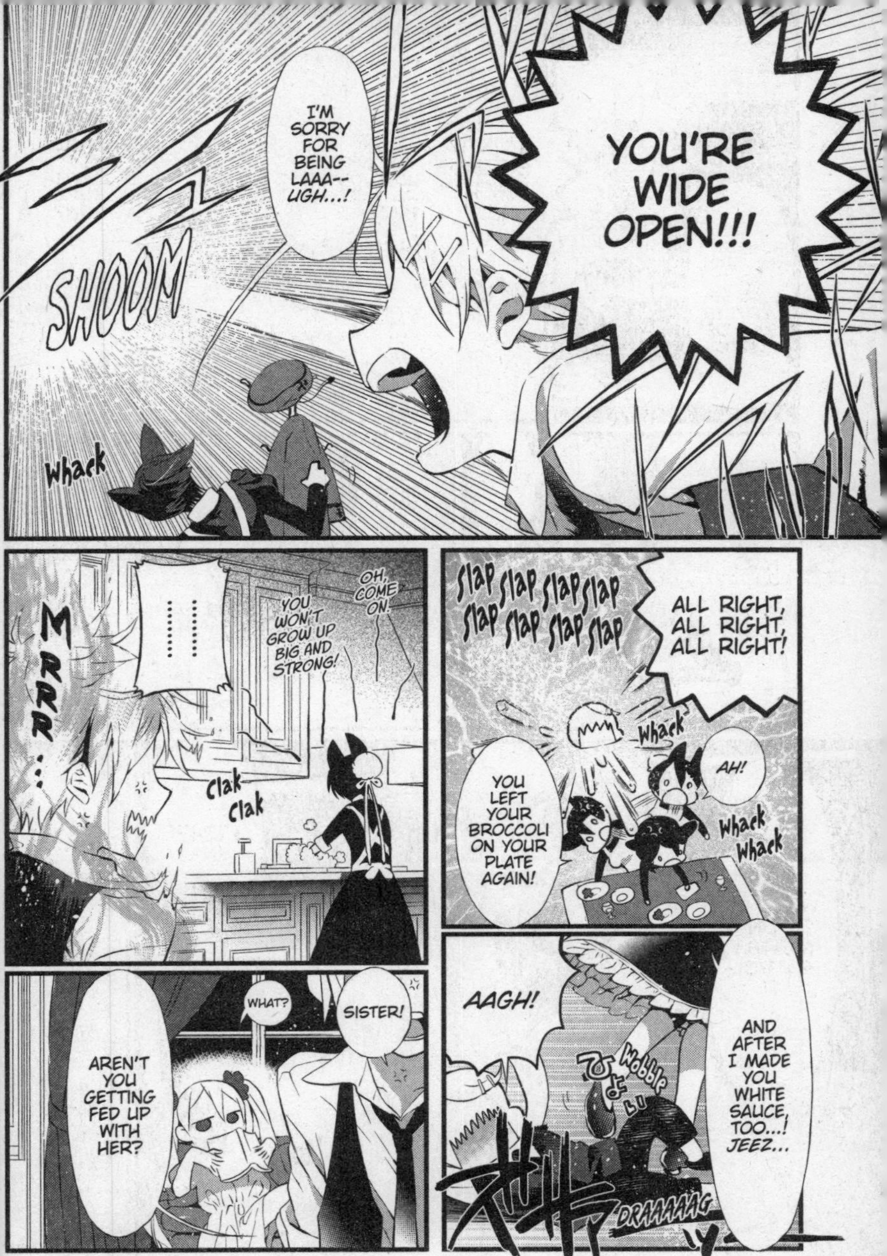
YOU'RE WIDE OPEN!!!
I'M SORRY FOR BEING LAAA--UGH...!
SHOOM
Whack
Slap Slap Slap Slap Slap Slap Slap Slap
ALL RIGHT, ALL RIGHT, ALL RIGHT!
Whack
AH!
YOU LEFT YOUR BROCCOLI ON YOUR PLATE AGAIN!
Whack Whack
OH, COME ON.
YOU WON'T GROW UP BIG AND STRONG!
......
MRRR...
Clak Clak
AND AFTER I MADE YOU WHITE SAUCE, TOO...! JEEZ...
AAGH!
Wobble
DRAAAAAG
SISTER!
WHAT?
AREN'T YOU GETTING FED UP WITH HER?

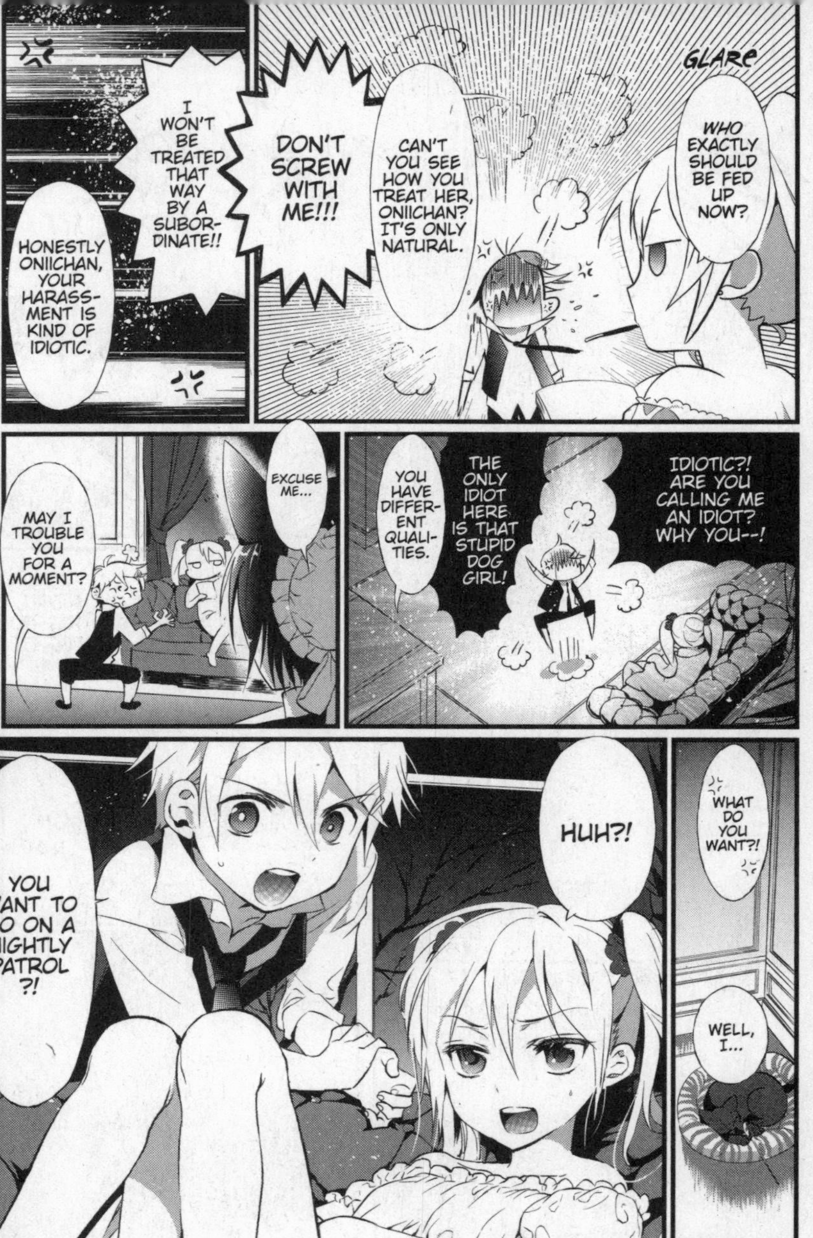
GLARE
WHO EXACTLY SHOULD BE FED UP NOW?
CAN'T YOU SEE HOW YOU TREAT HER, ONIICHAN? IT'S ONLY NATURAL.
DON'T SCREW WITH ME!!!
I WON'T BE TREATED THAT WAY BY A SUBOR-DINATE!!
HONESTLY ONIICHAN, YOUR HARASS-MENT IS KIND OF IDIOTIC.
IDIOTIC?! ARE YOU CALLING ME AN IDIOT? WHY YOU--!
THE ONLY IDIOT HERE IS THAT STUPID DOG GIRL!
YOU HAVE DIFFER-ENT QUALI-TIES.
EXCUSE ME...
MAY I TROUBLE YOU FOR A MOMENT?
WHAT DO YOU WANT?!
WELL, I...
HUH?!
YOU WANT TO GO ON A NIGHTLY PATROL ?!

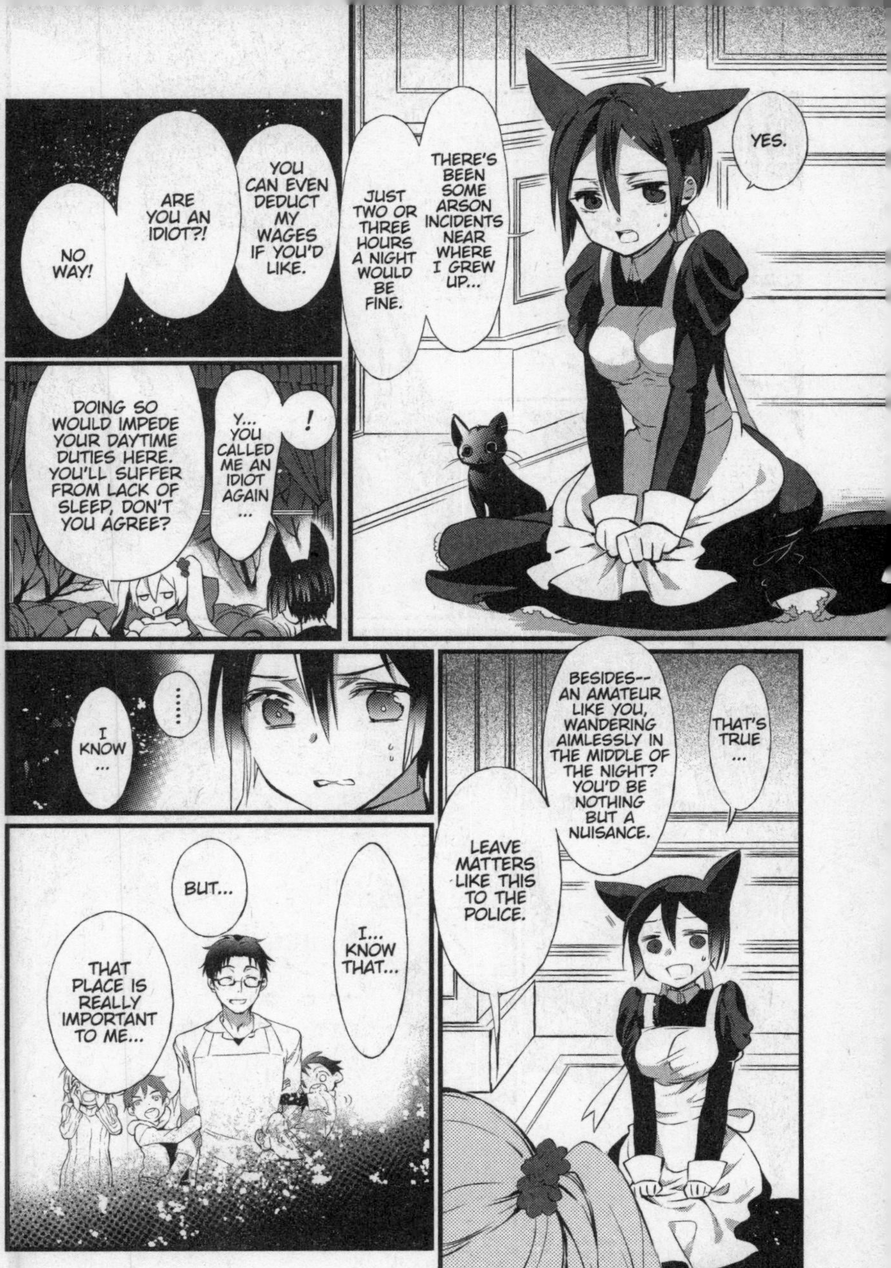
YES.
THERE'S BEEN SOME ARSON INCIDENTS NEAR WHERE I GREW UP...
JUST TWO OR THREE HOURS A NIGHT WOULD BE FINE.
YOU CAN EVEN DEDUCT MY WAGES IF YOU'D LIKE.
ARE YOU AN IDIOT?!
NO WAY!
!
Y... YOU CALLED ME AN IDIOT AGAIN...
DOING SO WOULD IMPEDE YOUR DAYTIME DUTIES HERE. YOU'LL SUFFER FROM LACK OF SLEEP, DON'T YOU AGREE?
THAT'S TRUE...
BESIDES-- AN AMATEUR LIKE YOU, WANDERING AIMLESSLY IN THE MIDDLE OF THE NIGHT? YOU'D BE NOTHING BUT A NUISANCE.
LEAVE MATTERS LIKE THIS TO THE POLICE.
......
I KNOW...
I... KNOW THAT...
BUT...
THAT PLACE IS REALLY IMPORTANT TO ME...

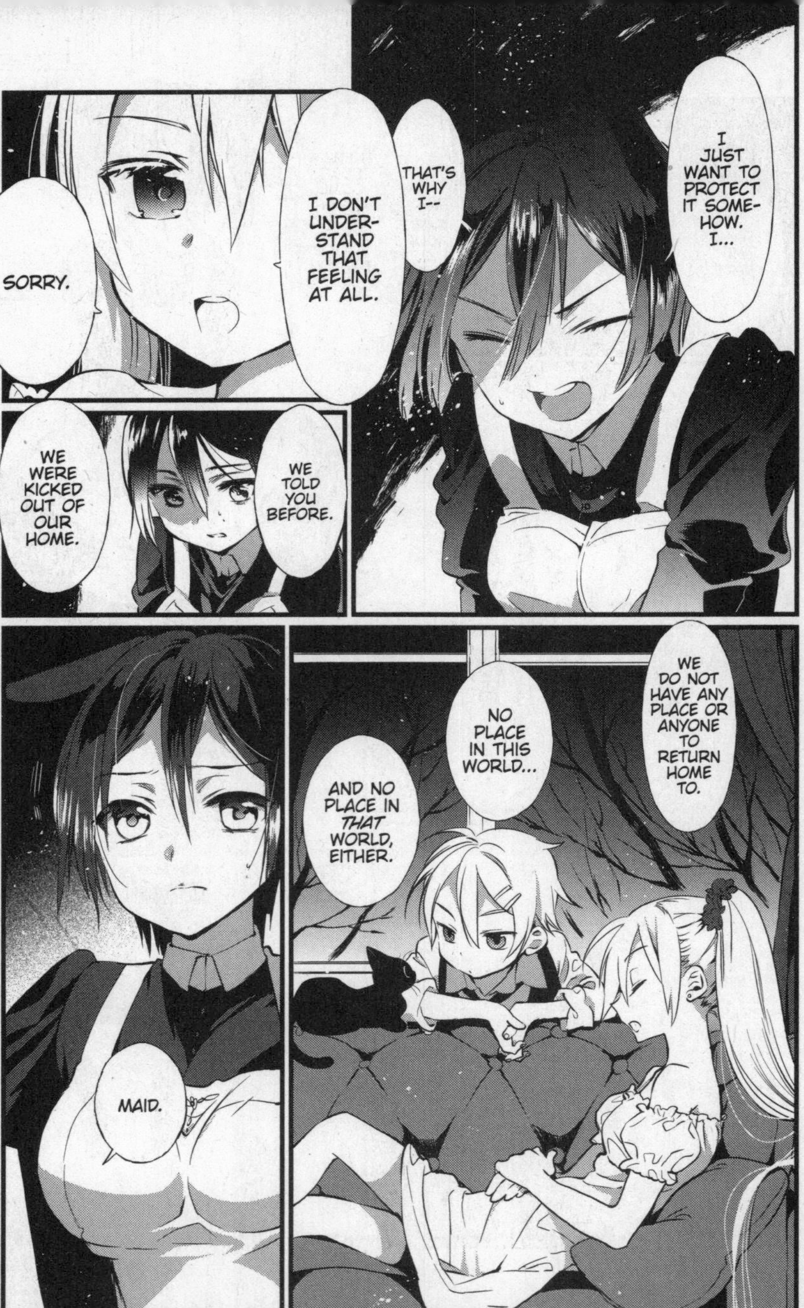
I JUST WANT TO PROTECT IT SOME-HOW. I...
THAT'S WHY I--
I DON'T UNDER-STAND THAT FEELING AT ALL.
SORRY.
WE TOLD YOU BEFORE.
WE WERE KICKED OUT OF OUR HOME.
WE DO NOT HAVE ANY PLACE OR ANYONE TO RETURN HOME TO.
NO PLACE IN THIS WORLD...
AND NO PLACE IN *THAT* WORLD, EITHER.
MAID.

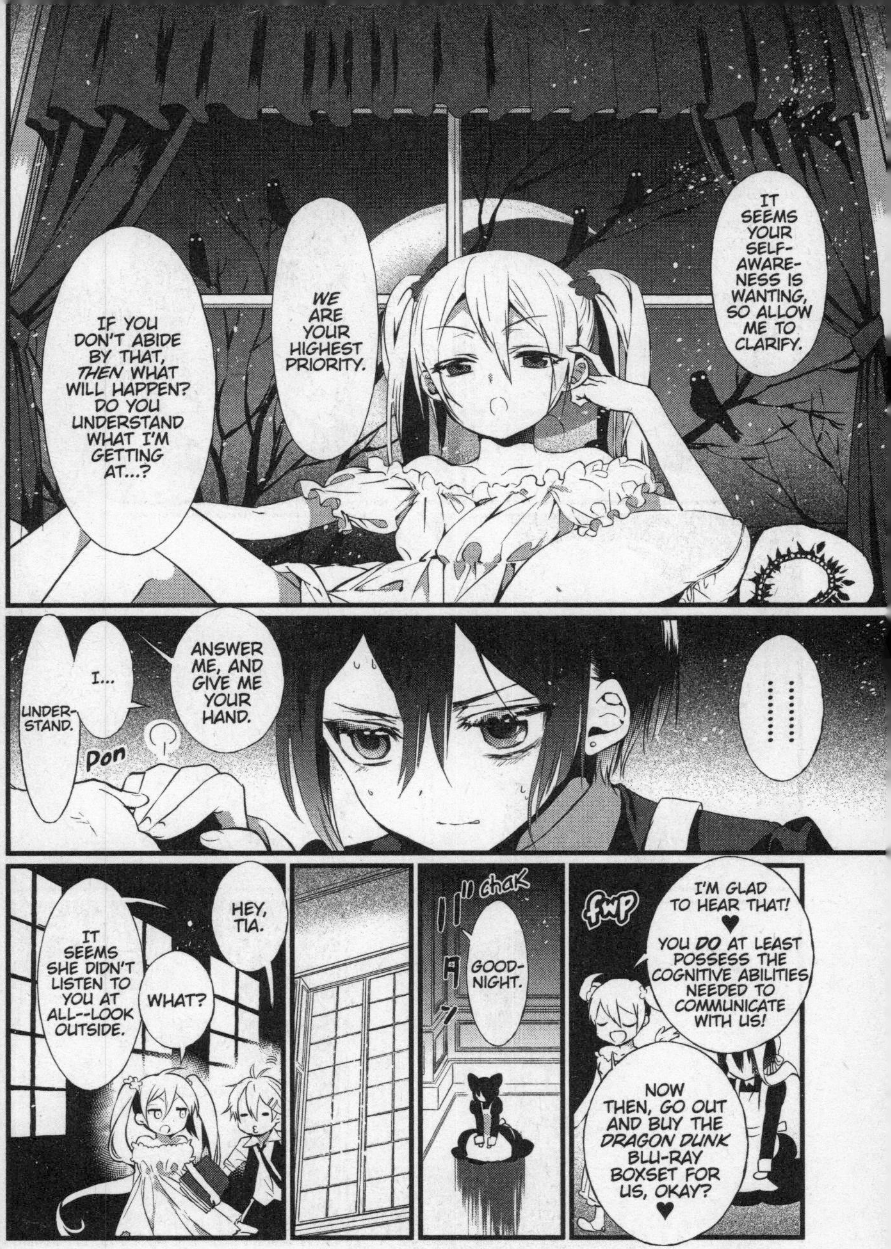
IT SEEMS YOUR SELF-AWARENESS IS WANTING, SO ALLOW ME TO CLARIFY.
WE ARE YOUR HIGHEST PRIORITY.
IF YOU DON'T ABIDE BY THAT, *THEN* WHAT WILL HAPPEN? DO YOU UNDERSTAND WHAT I'M GETTING AT...?
......
ANSWER ME, AND GIVE ME YOUR HAND.
I... UNDERSTAND.
Pon
fwp
I'M GLAD TO HEAR THAT! ♥ YOU *DO* AT LEAST POSSESS THE COGNITIVE ABILITIES NEEDED TO COMMUNICATE WITH US!
NOW THEN, GO OUT AND BUY THE *DRAGON DUNK* BLU-RAY BOXSET FOR US, OKAY? ♥
chaK
GOOD-NIGHT.
HEY, TIA.
WHAT?
IT SEEMS SHE DIDN'T LISTEN TO YOU AT ALL--LOOK OUTSIDE.

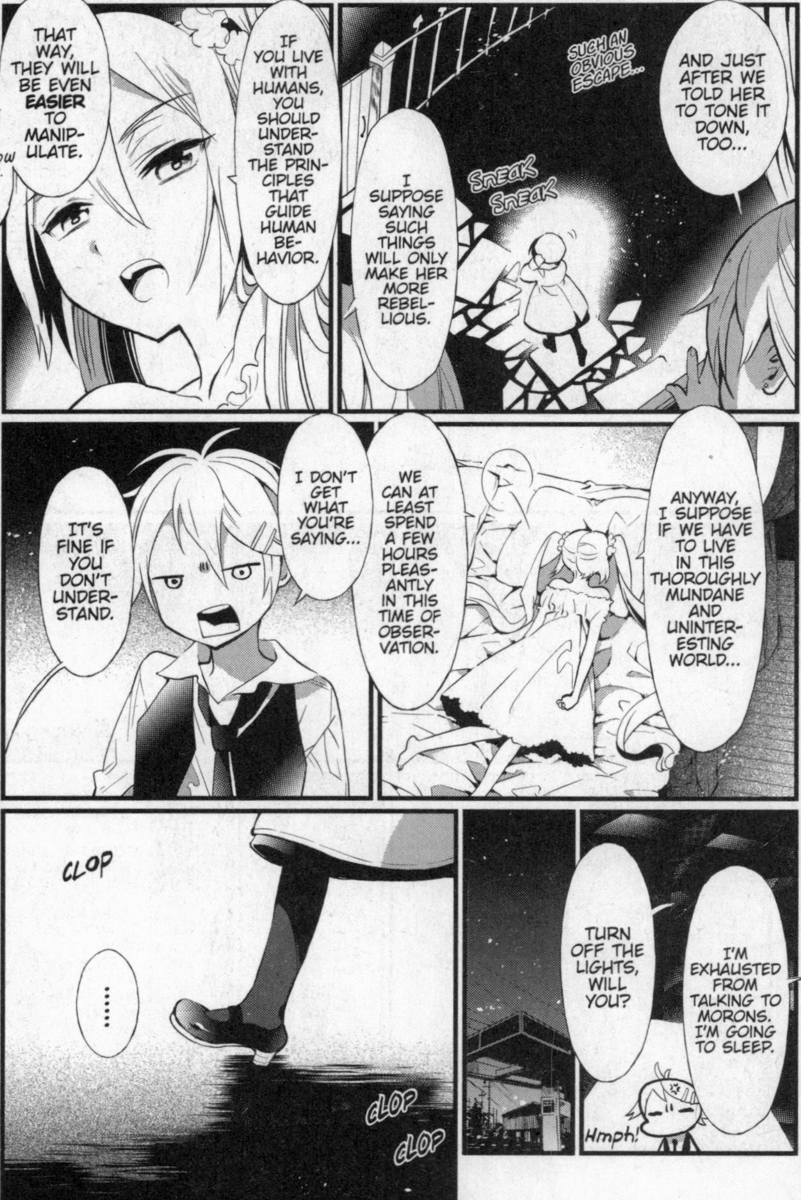
AND JUST AFTER WE TOLD HER TO TONE IT DOWN, TOO...
SUCH AN OBVIOUS ESCAPE...
SNEAK SNEAK
I SUPPOSE SAYING SUCH THINGS WILL ONLY MAKE HER MORE REBELLIOUS.
IF YOU LIVE WITH HUMANS, YOU SHOULD UNDERSTAND THE PRINCIPLES THAT GUIDE HUMAN BEHAVIOR.
THAT WAY, THEY WILL BE EVEN EASIER TO MANIPULATE.
WE'LL HAVE THE CAT FOLLOW HER.
ANYWAY, I SUPPOSE IF WE HAVE TO LIVE IN THIS THOROUGHLY MUNDANE AND UNINTERESTING WORLD...
WE CAN AT LEAST SPEND A FEW HOURS PLEASANTLY IN THIS TIME OF OBSERVATION.
I DON'T GET WHAT YOU'RE SAYING...
IT'S FINE IF YOU DON'T UNDERSTAND.
I'M EXHAUSTED FROM TALKING TO MORONS. I'M GOING TO SLEEP.
TURN OFF THE LIGHTS, WILL YOU?
Hmph!
CLOP
......
CLOP
CLOP

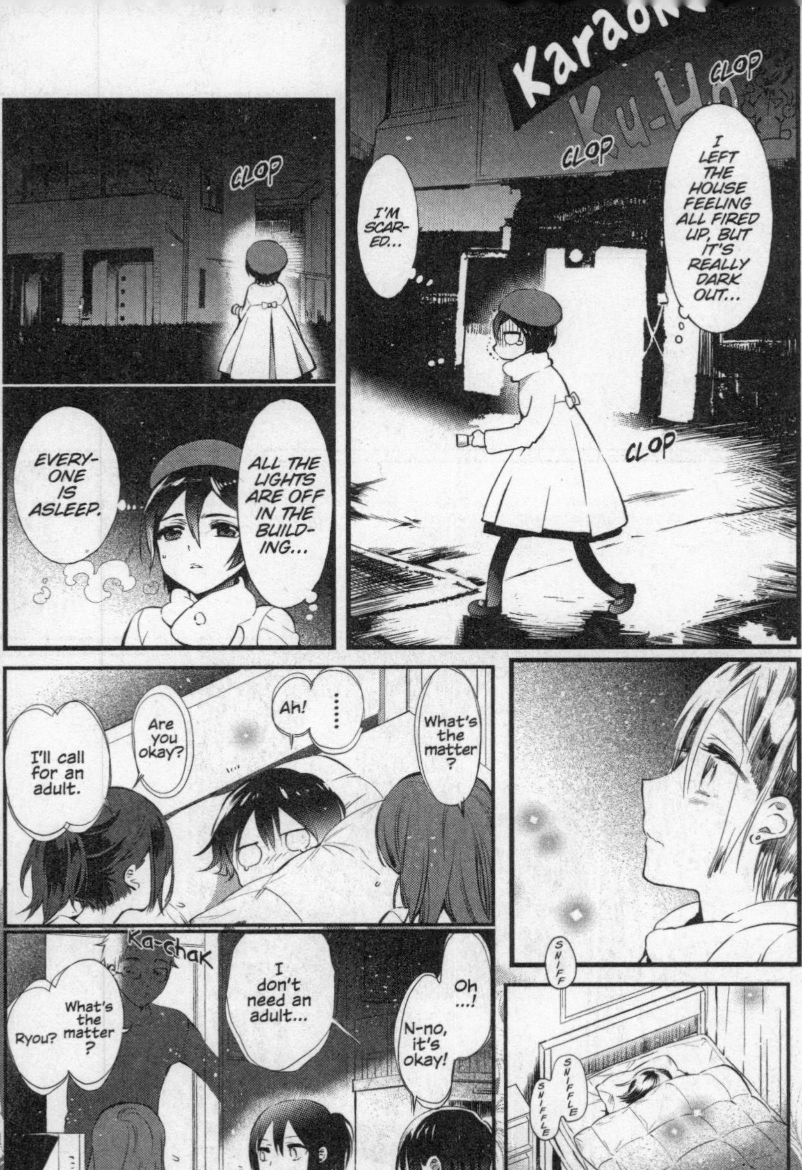
CLOP
CLOP
I LEFT THE HOUSE FEELING ALL FIRED UP, BUT IT'S REALLY DARK OUT...
I'M SCARED...
CLOP
CLOP
ALL THE LIGHTS ARE OFF IN THE BUILDING...
EVERYONE IS ASLEEP.
SNIFF
SNIFFLE SNIFFLE
What's the matter?
Ah!
......
Are you okay?
I'll call for an adult.
Ka-chak
Oh...!
N-no, it's okay!
I don't need an adult...
What's the matter Ryou?

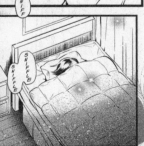

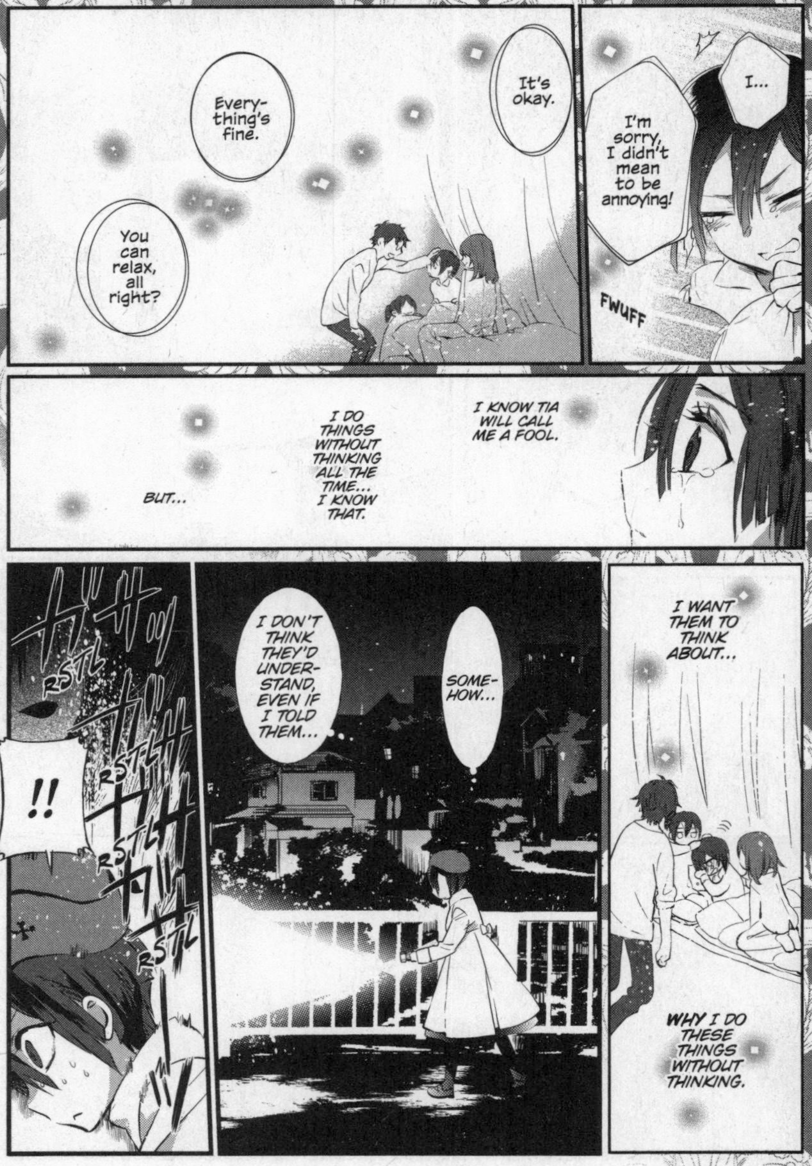
I...
I'm sorry, I didn't mean to be annoying!
FWUFF
It's okay.
Every-thing's fine.
You can relax, all right?
I KNOW TIA WILL CALL ME A FOOL.
I DO THINGS WITHOUT THINKING ALL THE TIME... I KNOW THAT.
BUT...
I WANT THEM TO THINK ABOUT...
WHY I DO THESE THINGS WITHOUT THINKING.
SOME-HOW...
I DON'T THINK THEY'D UNDER-STAND, EVEN IF I TOLD THEM...
RSTL
RSTL
RSTL
RSTL
!!

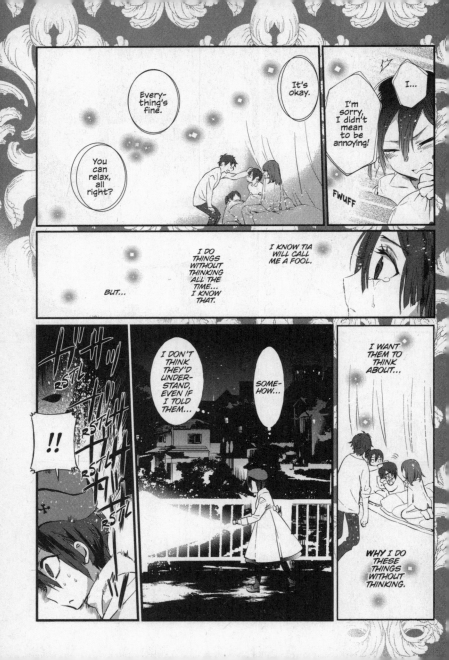

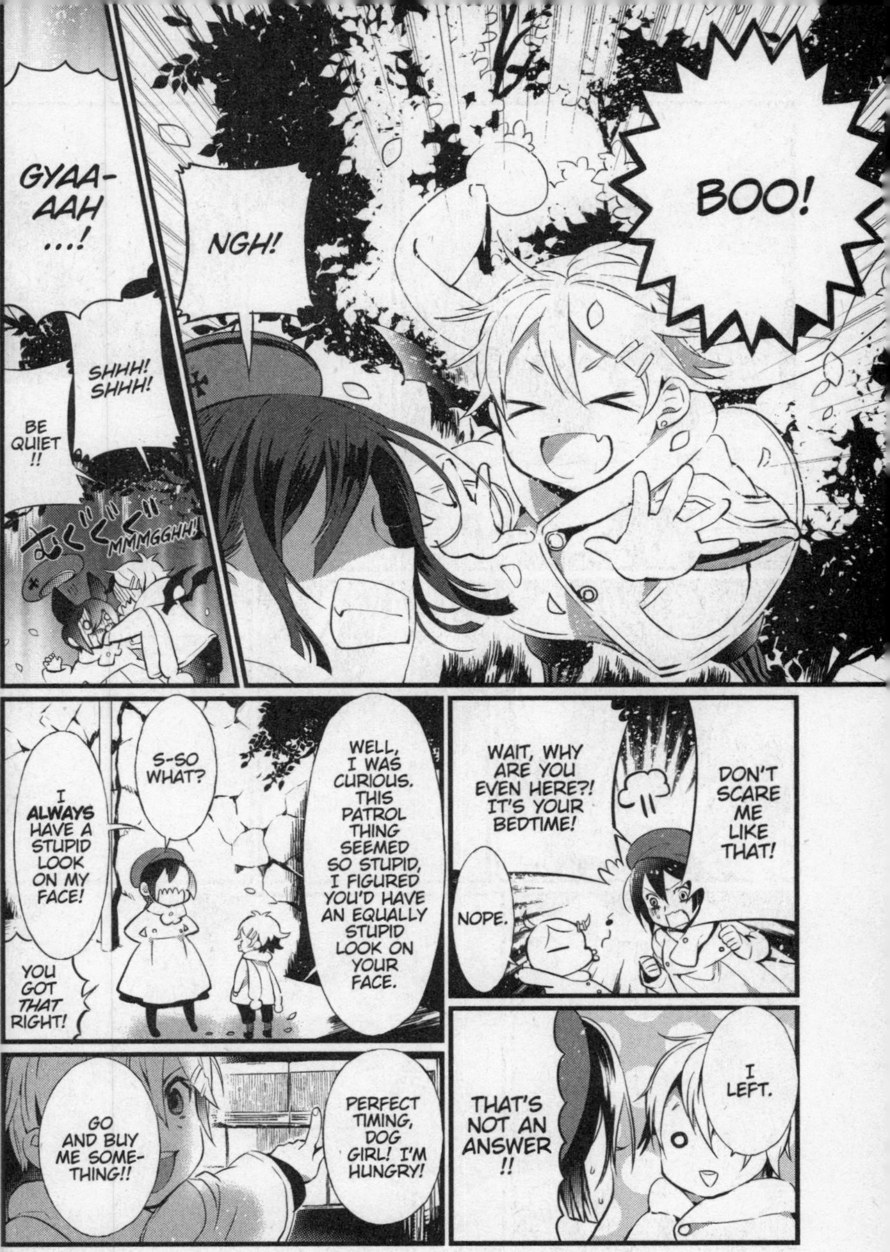
BOO!
NGH!
GYAAA-AAH...!
SHHH! SHHH!
BE QUIET!!
むぐぐぐ MMMGGHH!
DON'T SCARE ME LIKE THAT!
WAIT, WHY ARE YOU EVEN HERE?! IT'S YOUR BEDTIME!
NOPE.
WELL, I WAS CURIOUS. THIS PATROL THING SEEMED SO STUPID, I FIGURED YOU'D HAVE AN EQUALLY STUPID LOOK ON YOUR FACE.
S-SO WHAT?
I **ALWAYS** HAVE A STUPID LOOK ON MY FACE!
YOU GOT *THAT* RIGHT!
I LEFT.
THAT'S NOT AN ANSWER!!
PERFECT TIMING, DOG GIRL! I'M HUNGRY!
GO AND BUY ME SOME-THING!!

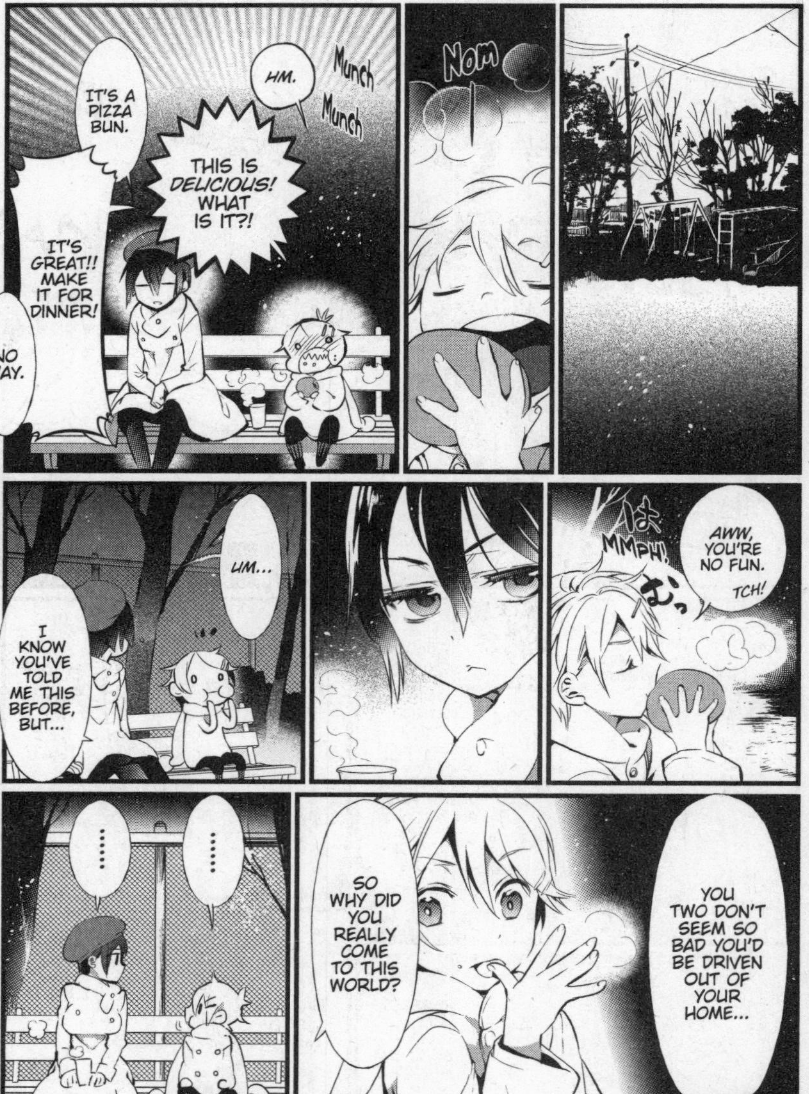
Nom
Munch Munch
HM.
THIS IS DELICIOUS! WHAT IS IT?!
IT'S A PIZZA BUN.
IT'S GREAT!! MAKE IT FOR DINNER!
NO WAY.
は
MMPH!
むっ
AWW, YOU'RE NO FUN.
TCH!
UM...
I KNOW YOU'VE TOLD ME THIS BEFORE, BUT...
YOU TWO DON'T SEEM SO BAD YOU'D BE DRIVEN OUT OF YOUR HOME...
SO WHY DID YOU REALLY COME TO THIS WORLD?
......
......

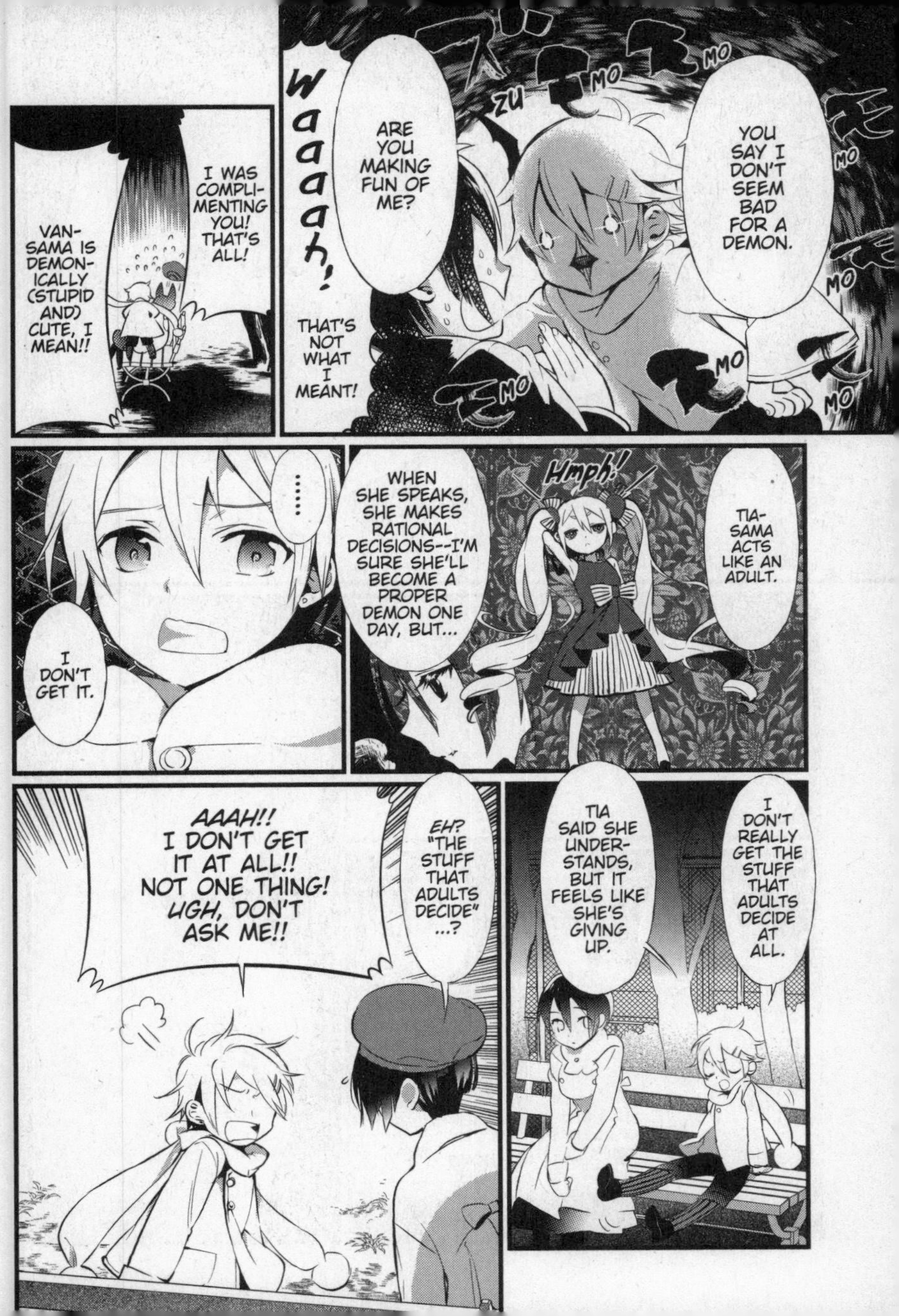
ZU
MO
MO
YOU SAY I DON'T SEEM BAD FOR A DEMON.
MO
MO
MO
MO
MO
ARE YOU MAKING FUN OF ME?
Waaaah!
THAT'S NOT WHAT I MEANT!
I WAS COMPLI-MENTING YOU! THAT'S ALL!
VAN-SAMA IS DEMON-ICALLY (STUPID AND) CUTE, I MEAN!!
Hmph!
TIA-SAMA ACTS LIKE AN ADULT.
WHEN SHE SPEAKS, SHE MAKES RATIONAL DECISIONS--I'M SURE SHE'LL BECOME A PROPER DEMON ONE DAY, BUT...
......
I DON'T GET IT.
I DON'T REALLY GET THE STUFF THAT ADULTS DECIDE AT ALL.
TIA SAID SHE UNDER-STANDS, BUT IT FEELS LIKE SHE'S GIVING UP.
EH? "THE STUFF THAT ADULTS DECIDE" ...?
AAAH!! I DON'T GET IT AT ALL!! NOT ONE THING! UGH, DON'T ASK ME!!

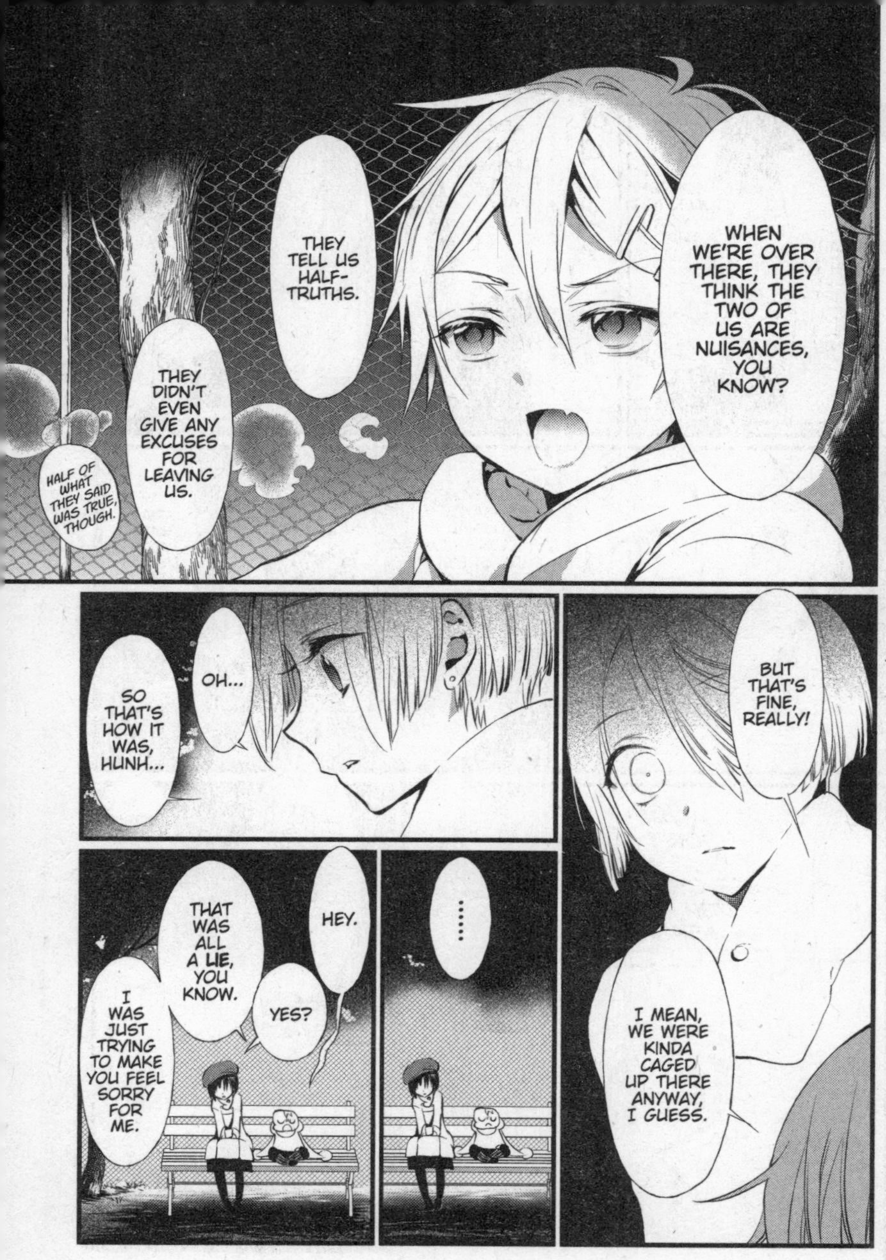
WHEN WE'RE OVER THERE, THEY THINK THE TWO OF US ARE NUISANCES, YOU KNOW?
THEY TELL US HALF-TRUTHS.
THEY DIDN'T EVEN GIVE ANY EXCUSES FOR LEAVING US.
HALF OF WHAT THEY SAID WAS TRUE, THOUGH.
BUT THAT'S FINE, REALLY!
I MEAN, WE WERE KINDA CAGED UP THERE ANYWAY, I GUESS.
OH...
SO THAT'S HOW IT WAS, HUNH...
......
HEY.
YES?
THAT WAS ALL A LIE, YOU KNOW.
I WAS JUST TRYING TO MAKE YOU FEEL SORRY FOR ME.

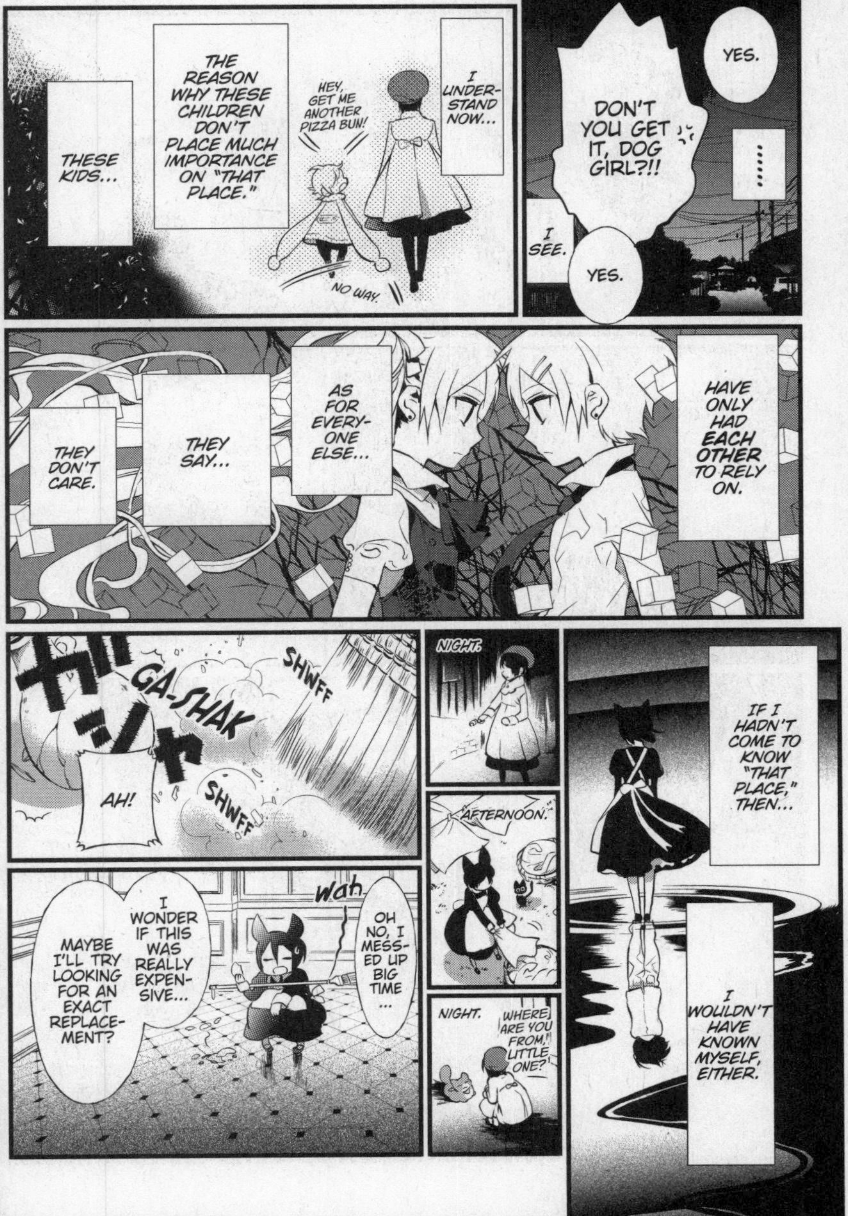
YES.
……
DON'T YOU GET IT, DOG GIRL?!!
I SEE.
YES.
I UNDERSTAND NOW…
HEY, GET ME ANOTHER PIZZA BUN!
THE REASON WHY THESE CHILDREN DON'T PLACE MUCH IMPORTANCE ON "THAT PLACE."
THESE KIDS…
NO WAY.
HAVE ONLY HAD EACH OTHER TO RELY ON.
AS FOR EVERYONE ELSE…
THEY SAY…
THEY DON'T CARE.
IF I HADN'T COME TO KNOW "THAT PLACE," THEN…
I WOULDN'T HAVE KNOWN MYSELF, EITHER.
NIGHT.
AFTERNOON.
NIGHT.
WHERE ARE YOU FROM, LITTLE ONE?
SHWFF
GA-SHAK
AH!
SHWFF
wah
OH NO, I MESSED UP BIG TIME…
I WONDER IF THIS WAS REALLY EXPENSIVE…
MAYBE I'LL TRY LOOKING FOR AN EXACT REPLACEMENT?

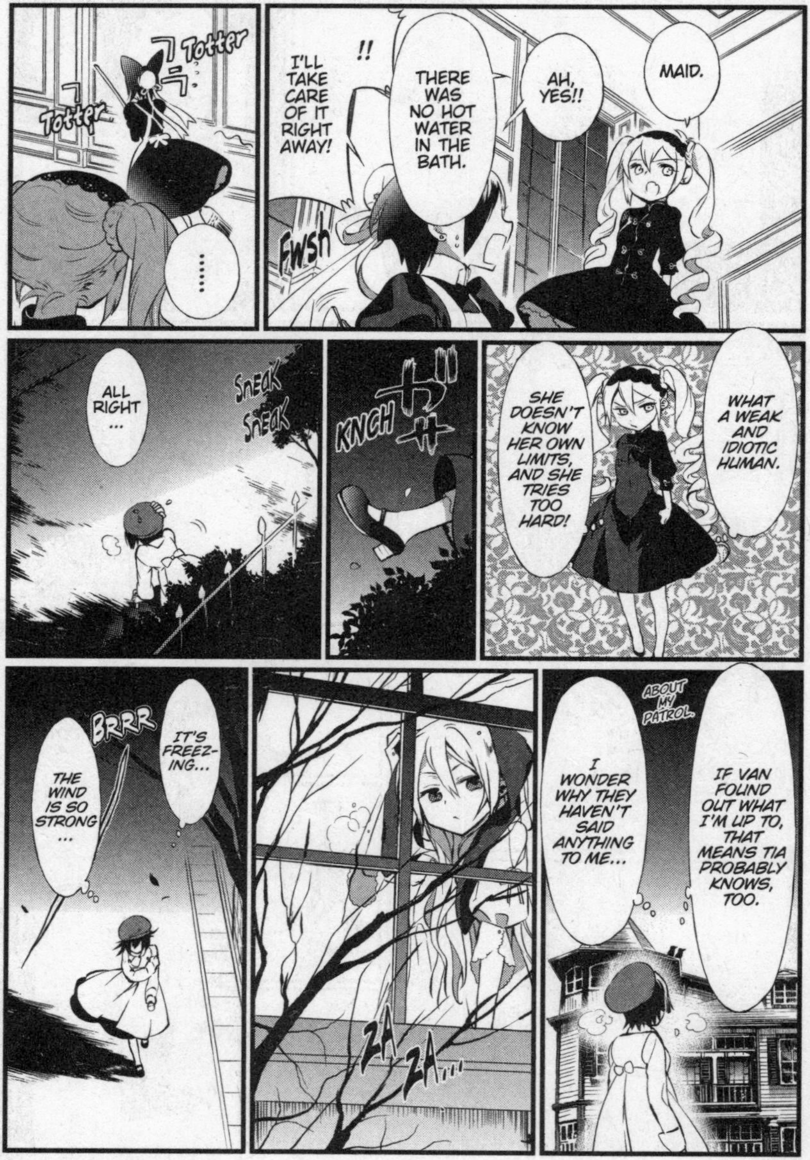
MAID.
AH, YES!!
THERE WAS NO HOT WATER IN THE BATH.
!!
I'LL TAKE CARE OF IT RIGHT AWAY!
Fwsh
Totter
Totter
......
WHAT A WEAK AND IDIOTIC HUMAN.
SHE DOESN'T KNOW HER OWN LIMITS, AND SHE TRIES TOO HARD!
KNCH
Sneak Sneak
ALL RIGHT...
IF VAN FOUND OUT WHAT I'M UP TO, THAT MEANS TIA PROBABLY KNOWS, TOO.
I WONDER WHY THEY HAVEN'T SAID ANYTHING TO ME...
ABOUT MY PATROL.
ZA ZA...
IT'S FREEZING...
BRRR
THE WIND IS SO STRONG...

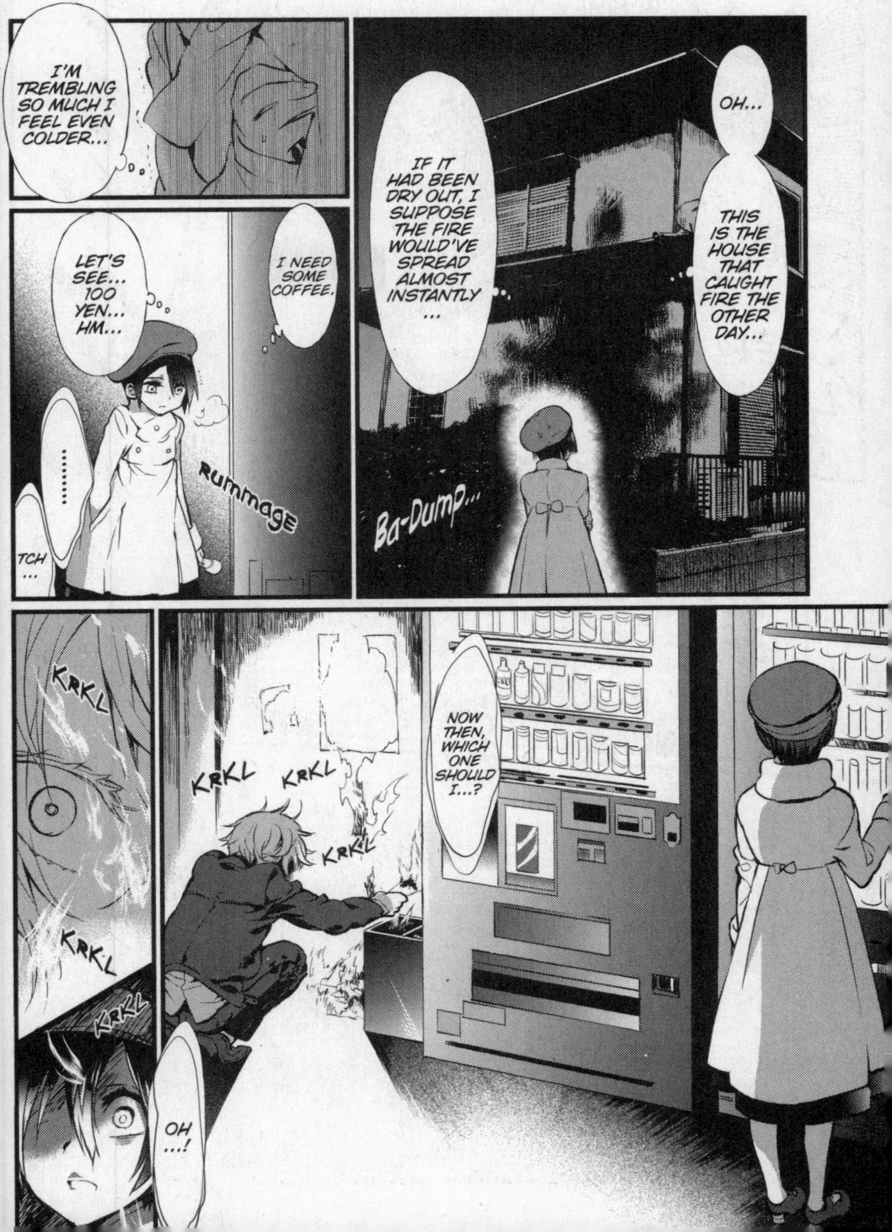
OH...
THIS IS THE HOUSE THAT CAUGHT FIRE THE OTHER DAY...
IF IT HAD BEEN DRY OUT, I SUPPOSE THE FIRE WOULD'VE SPREAD ALMOST INSTANTLY...
Ba-Dump...
I'M TREMBLING SO MUCH I FEEL EVEN COLDER...
I NEED SOME COFFEE.
LET'S SEE... 100 YEN... HM...
Rummage
....
TCH...
NOW THEN, WHICH ONE SHOULD I...?
KRKL
KRKL
KRKL
KRKL
KRKL
KRKL
OH...!

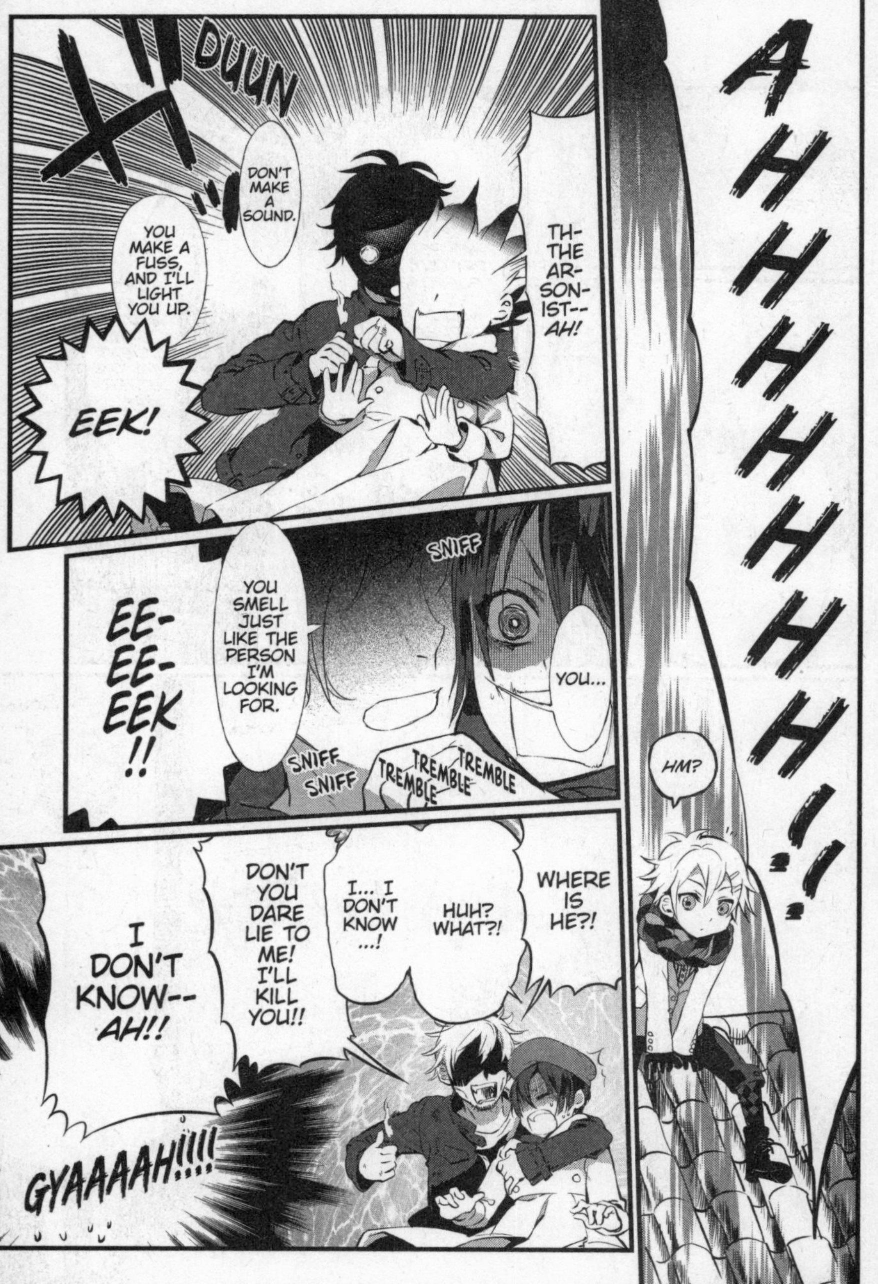
AHHHHHHHH!!!
HM?
DUUN
TH-THE AR-SON-IST--AH!
DON'T MAKE A SOUND.
YOU MAKE A FUSS, AND I'LL LIGHT YOU UP.
EEK!
SNIFF
YOU...
YOU SMELL JUST LIKE THE PERSON I'M LOOKING FOR.
TREMBLE TREMBLE
SNIFF SNIFF
EE-EE-EEK!!
WHERE IS HE?!
HUH? WHAT?!
I... I DON'T KNOW...!
DON'T YOU DARE LIE TO ME! I'LL KILL YOU!!
I DON'T KNOW--AH!!
GYAAAAH!!!!

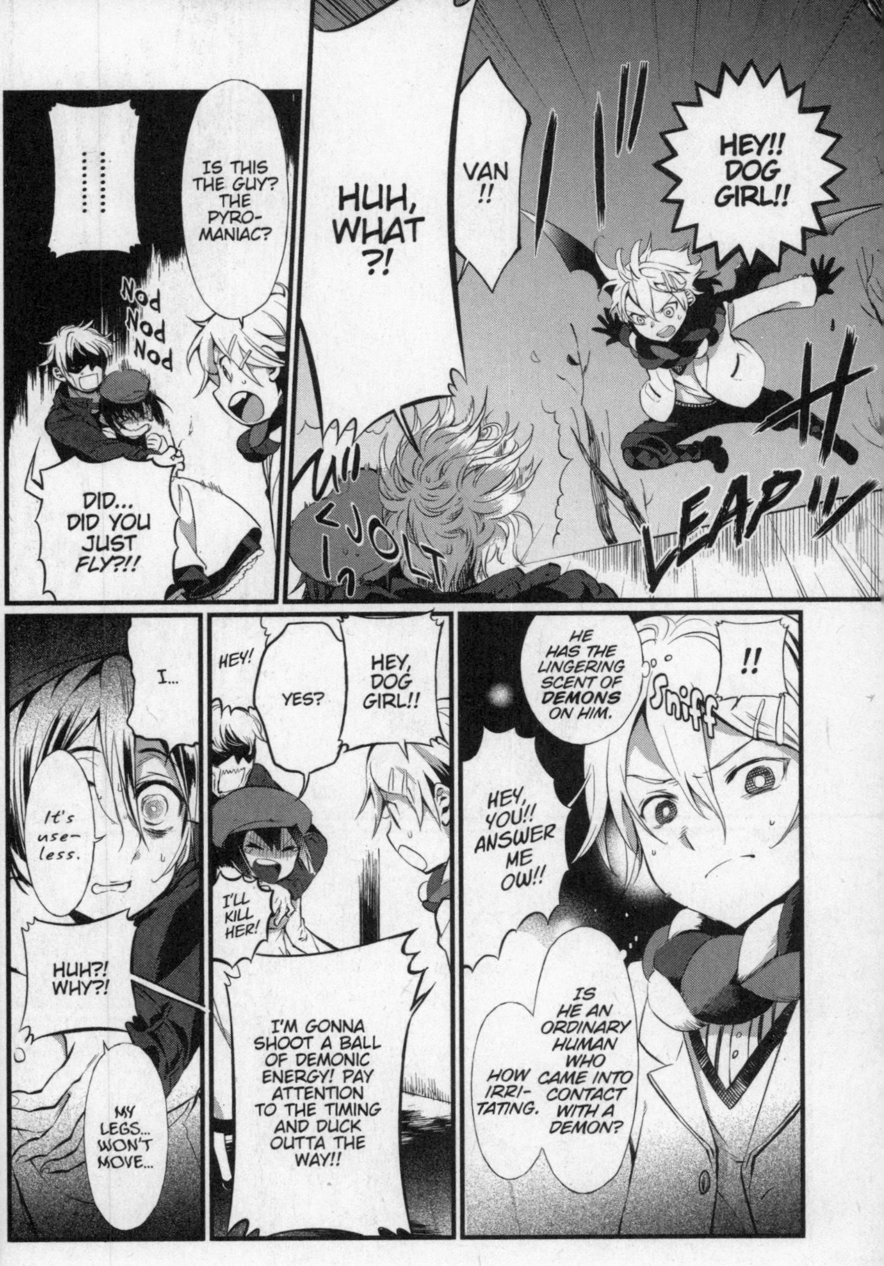
HEY!! DOG GIRL!!
LEAP!!
VAN !!
HUH, WHAT ?!
JOLT
IS THIS THE GUY? THE PYRO-MANIAC?
......
Nod Nod Nod
DID... DID YOU JUST FLY?!!
!!
Sniff
HE HAS THE LINGERING SCENT OF DEMONS ON HIM.
HEY, YOU!! ANSWER ME OW!!
IS HE AN ORDINARY HUMAN WHO CAME INTO CONTACT WITH A DEMON?
HOW IRRI-TATING.
HEY, DOG GIRL!!
YES?
HEY!
I'LL KILL HER!
I'M GONNA SHOOT A BALL OF DEMONIC ENERGY! PAY ATTENTION TO THE TIMING AND DUCK OUTTA THE WAY!!
I...
It's use-less.
HUH?! WHY?!
MY LEGS... WON'T MOVE...

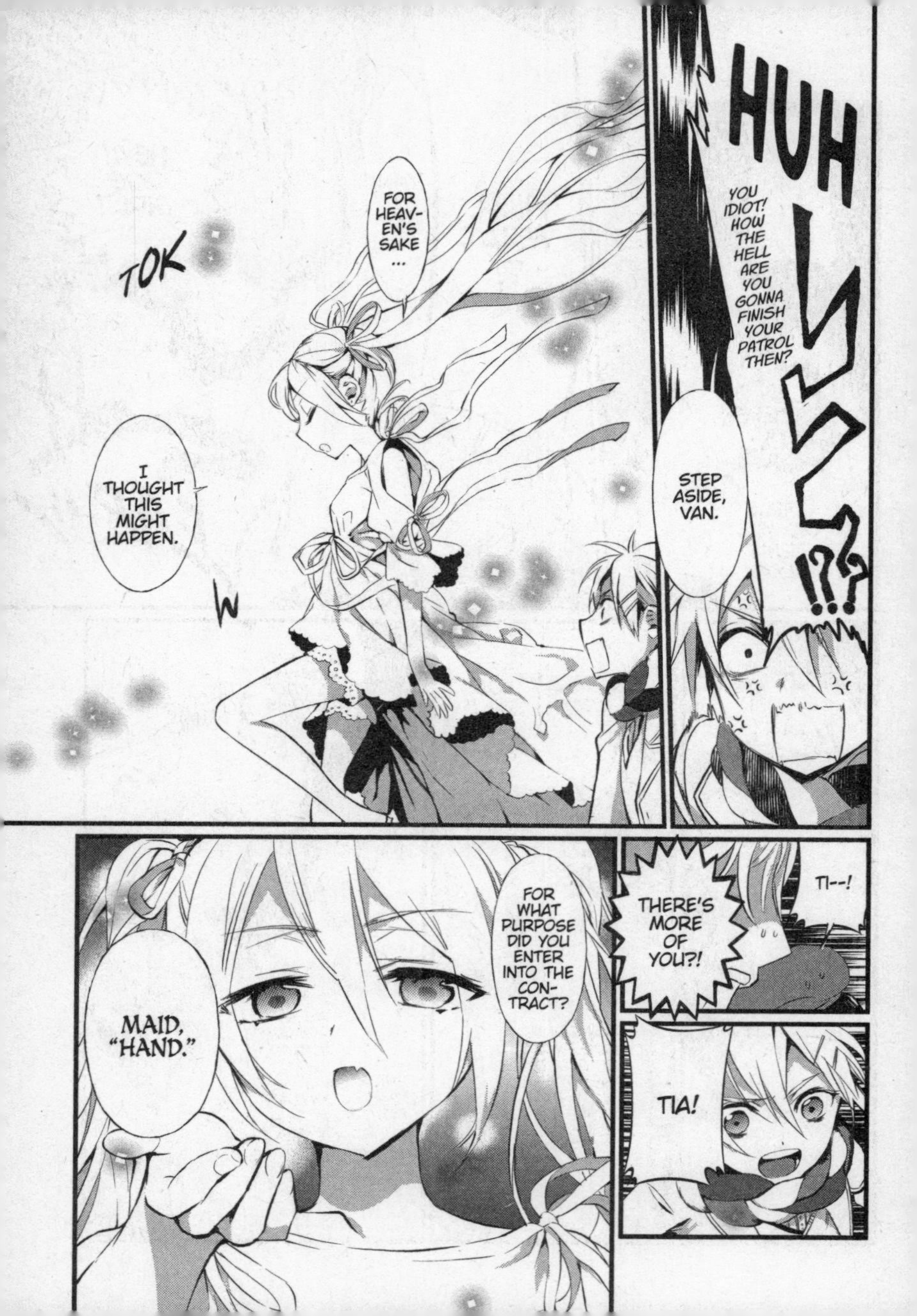
HUH !??!
YOU IDIOT! HOW THE HELL ARE YOU GONNA FINISH YOUR PATROL THEN?
STEP ASIDE, VAN.
FOR HEAV-EN'S SAKE ...
TOK
I THOUGHT THIS MIGHT HAPPEN.
W
TI--!
THERE'S MORE OF YOU?!
TIA!
FOR WHAT PURPOSE DID YOU ENTER INTO THE CON-TRACT?
MAID, "HAND."

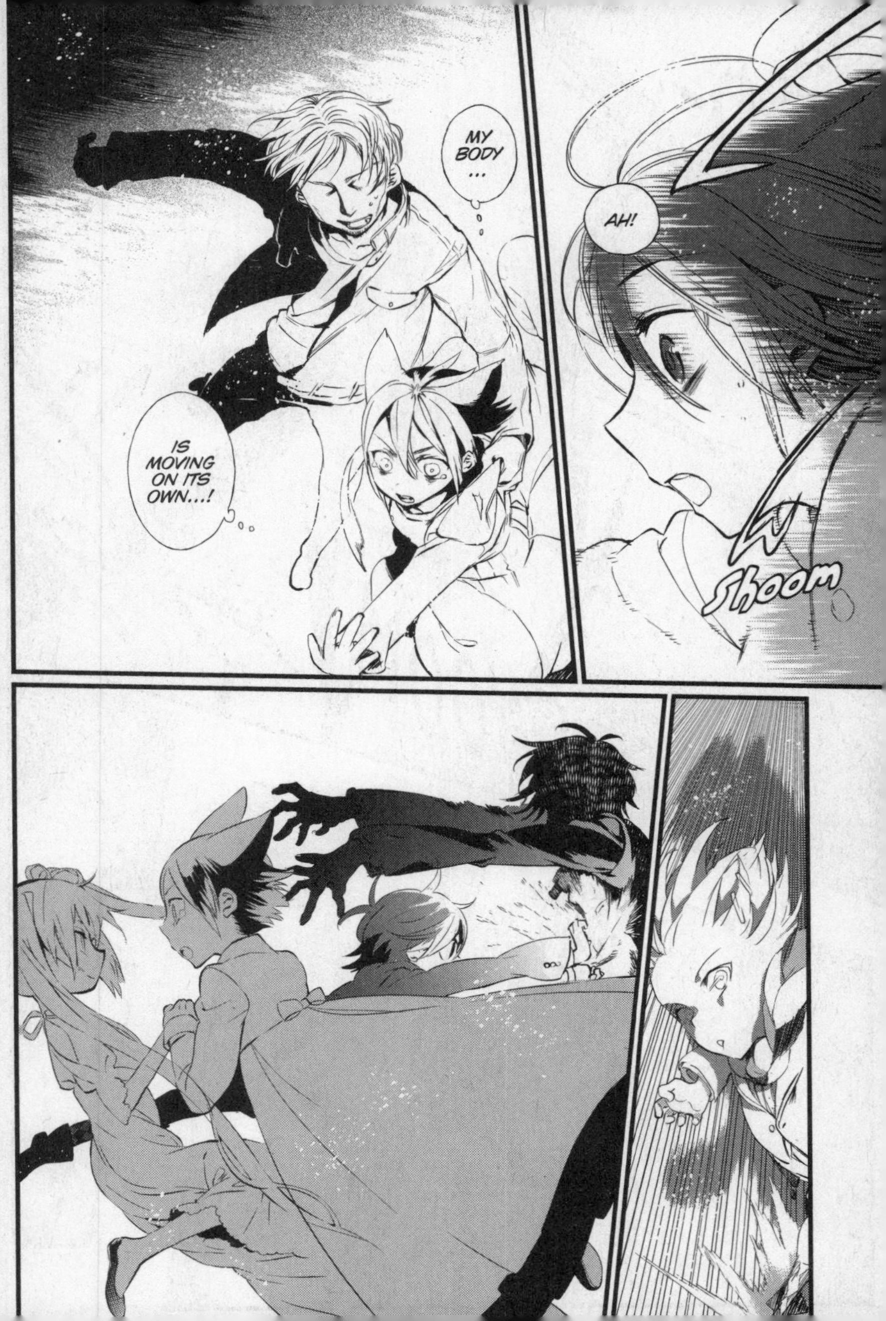
AH!
W
Shoom
MY BODY ...
IS MOVING ON ITS OWN...!

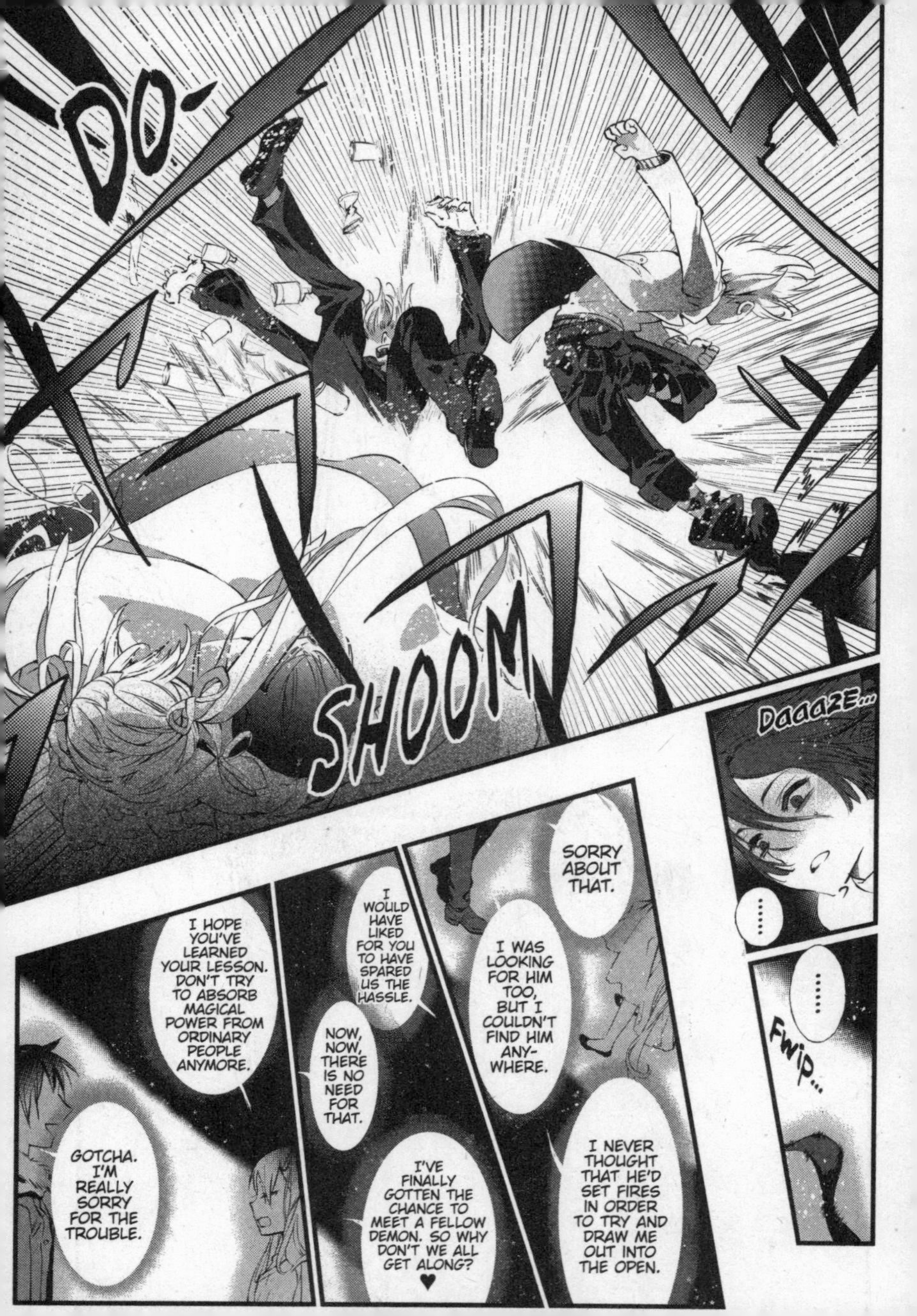
DO-
SHOOM
Daaaze...
......
......
Fwip...
SORRY ABOUT THAT.
I WAS LOOKING FOR HIM TOO, BUT I COULDN'T FIND HIM ANYWHERE.
I NEVER THOUGHT THAT HE'D SET FIRES IN ORDER TO TRY AND DRAW ME OUT INTO THE OPEN.
I WOULD HAVE LIKED FOR YOU TO HAVE SPARED US THE HASSLE.
NOW, NOW, THERE IS NO NEED FOR THAT.
I'VE FINALLY GOTTEN THE CHANCE TO MEET A FELLOW DEMON. SO WHY DON'T WE ALL GET ALONG? ♥
I HOPE YOU'VE LEARNED YOUR LESSON. DON'T TRY TO ABSORB MAGICAL POWER FROM ORDINARY PEOPLE ANYMORE.
GOTCHA. I'M REALLY SORRY FOR THE TROUBLE.

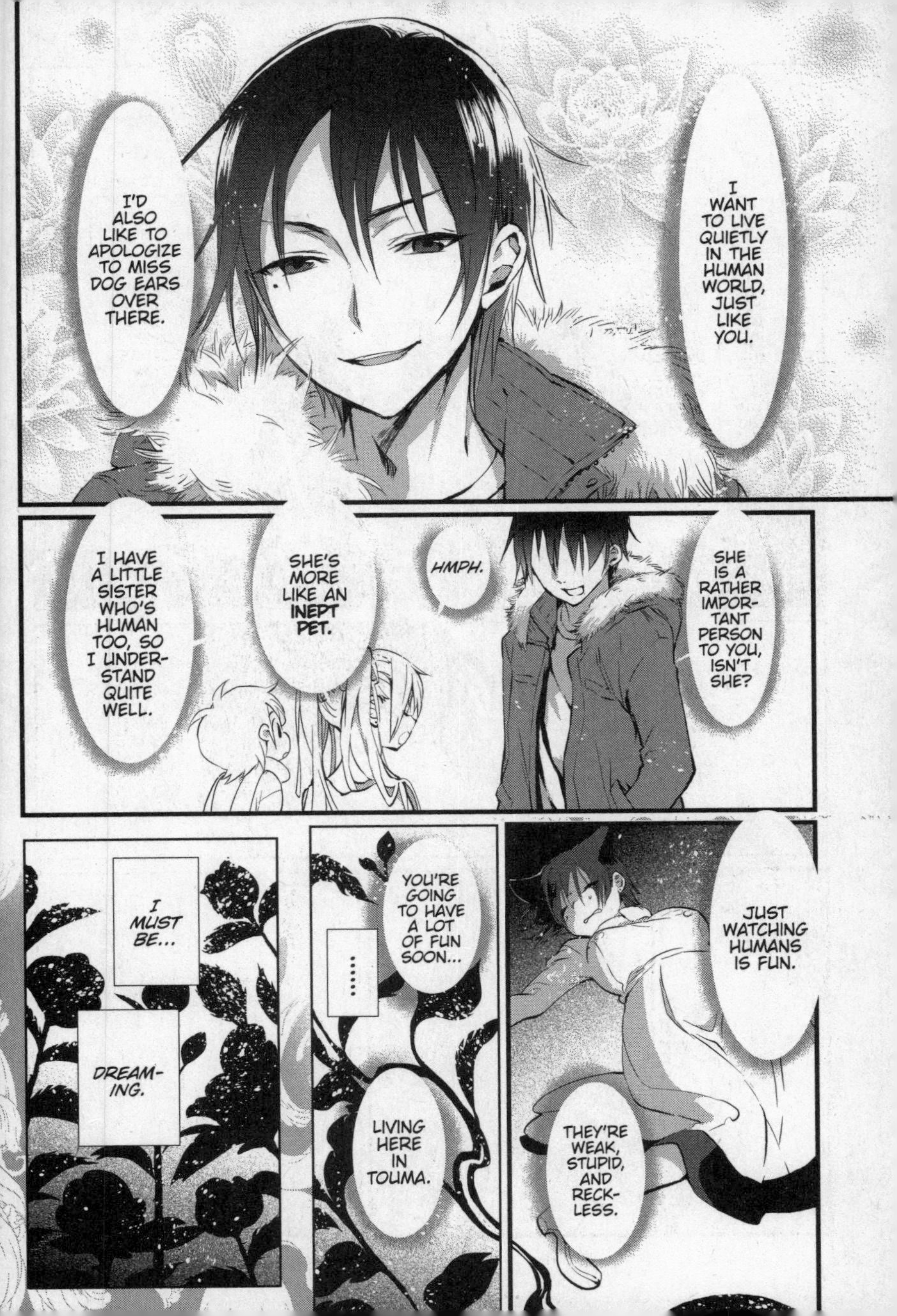
I WANT TO LIVE QUIETLY IN THE HUMAN WORLD, JUST LIKE YOU.
I'D ALSO LIKE TO APOLOGIZE TO MISS DOG EARS OVER THERE.
SHE IS A RATHER IMPORTANT PERSON TO YOU, ISN'T SHE?
HMPH.
SHE'S MORE LIKE AN INEPT PET.
I HAVE A LITTLE SISTER WHO'S HUMAN TOO, SO I UNDERSTAND QUITE WELL.
JUST WATCHING HUMANS IS FUN.
THEY'RE WEAK, STUPID, AND RECKLESS.
YOU'RE GOING TO HAVE A LOT OF FUN SOON...
......
LIVING HERE IN TOUMA.
I MUST BE...
DREAMING.

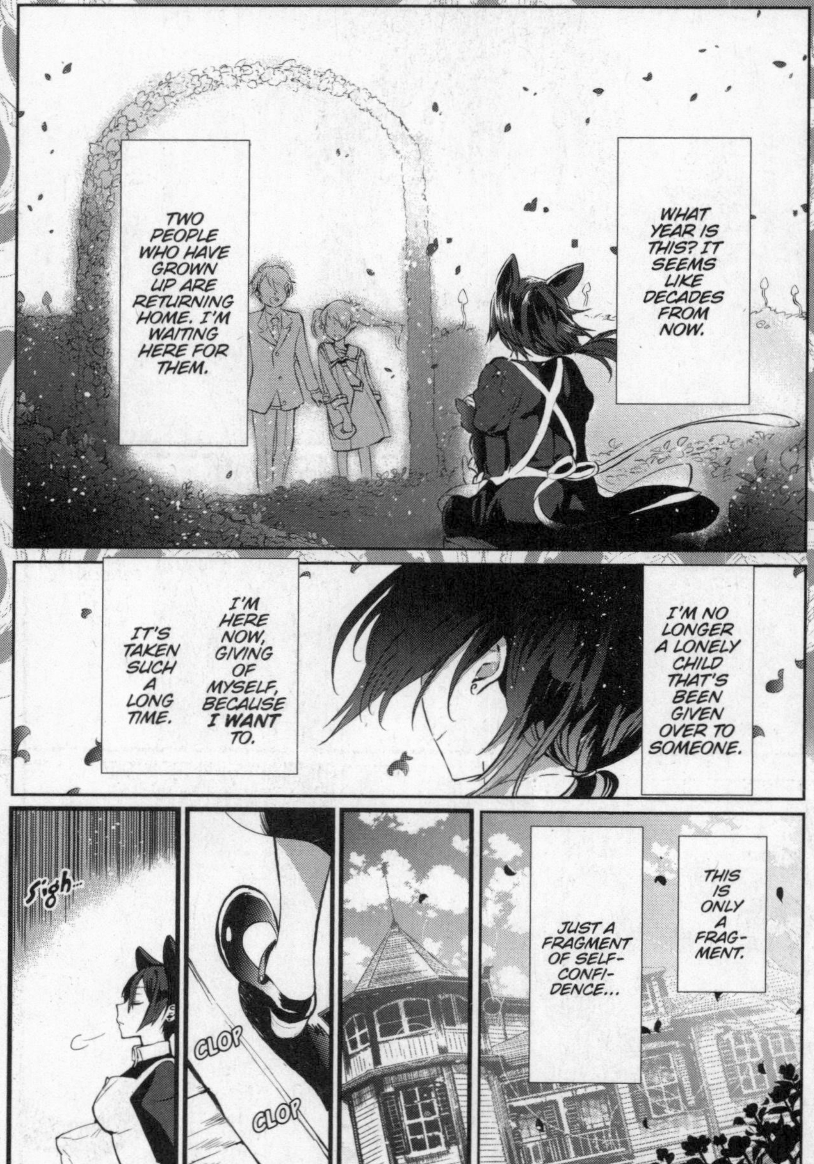
WHAT YEAR IS THIS? IT SEEMS LIKE DECADES FROM NOW.
TWO PEOPLE WHO HAVE GROWN UP ARE RETURNING HOME. I'M WAITING HERE FOR THEM.
I'M NO LONGER A LONELY CHILD THAT'S BEEN GIVEN OVER TO SOMEONE.
I'M HERE NOW, GIVING OF MYSELF, BECAUSE I WANT TO.
IT'S TAKEN SUCH A LONG TIME.
THIS IS ONLY A FRAG-MENT.
JUST A FRAGMENT OF SELF-CONFI-DENCE...
CLOP
CLOP
Sigh...

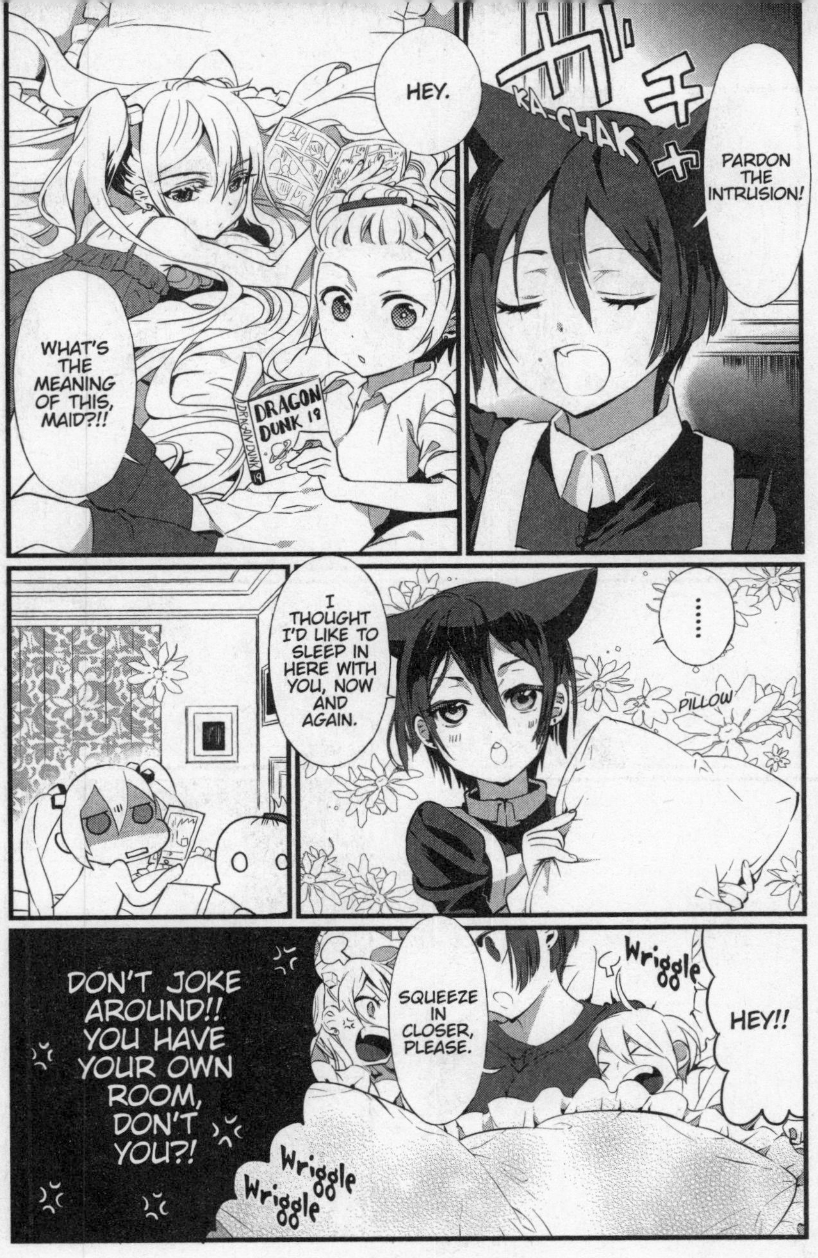
KA-CHAK
PARDON THE INTRUSION!
HEY.
DRAGON DUNK 19
WHAT'S THE MEANING OF THIS, MAID?!!
......
PILLOW
I THOUGHT I'D LIKE TO SLEEP IN HERE WITH YOU, NOW AND AGAIN.
HEY!!
Wriggle
SQUEEZE IN CLOSER, PLEASE.
DON'T JOKE AROUND!! YOU HAVE YOUR OWN ROOM, DON'T YOU?!
Wriggle
Wriggle

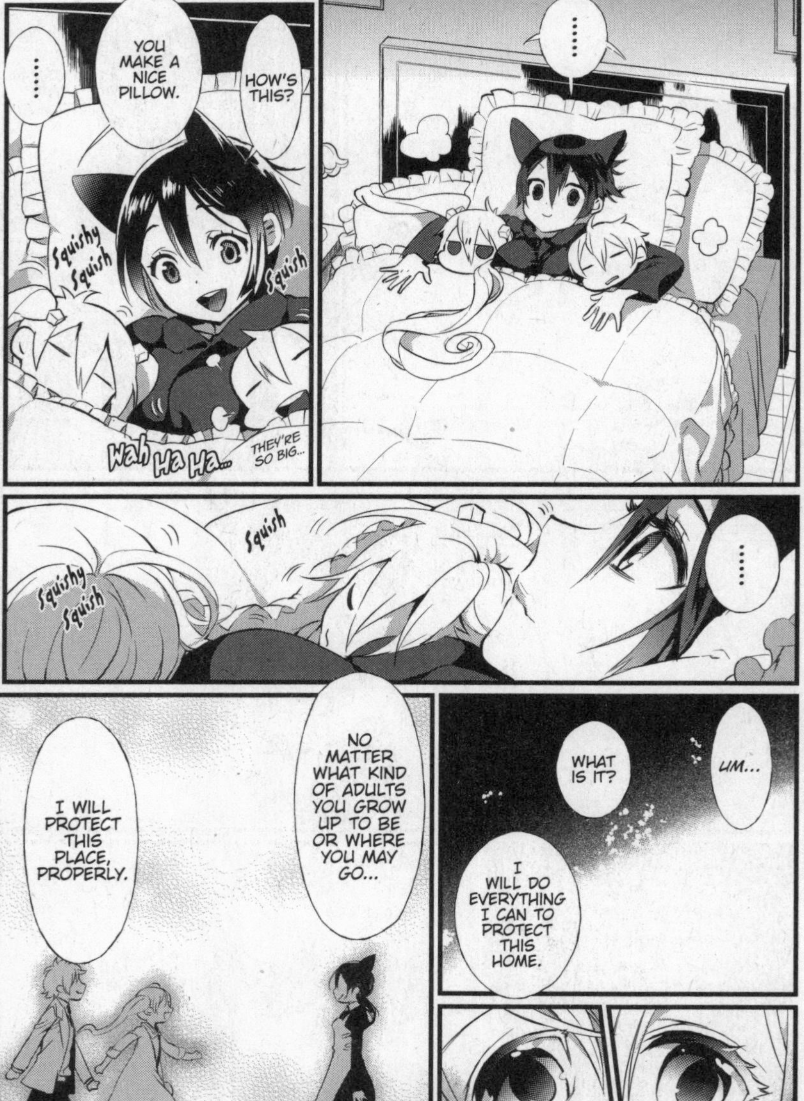
......
HOW'S THIS?
YOU MAKE A NICE PILLOW.
......
Squishy Squish
Squish
Wah Ha Ha...
THEY'RE SO BIG...
......
Squish
Squishy Squish
UM...
WHAT IS IT?
I WILL DO EVERYTHING I CAN TO PROTECT THIS HOME.
NO MATTER WHAT KIND OF ADULTS YOU GROW UP TO BE OR WHERE YOU MAY GO...
I WILL PROTECT THIS PLACE, PROPERLY.

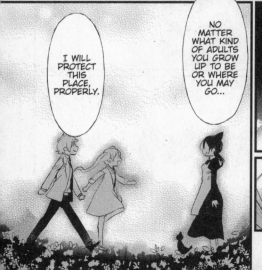

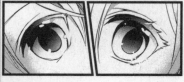

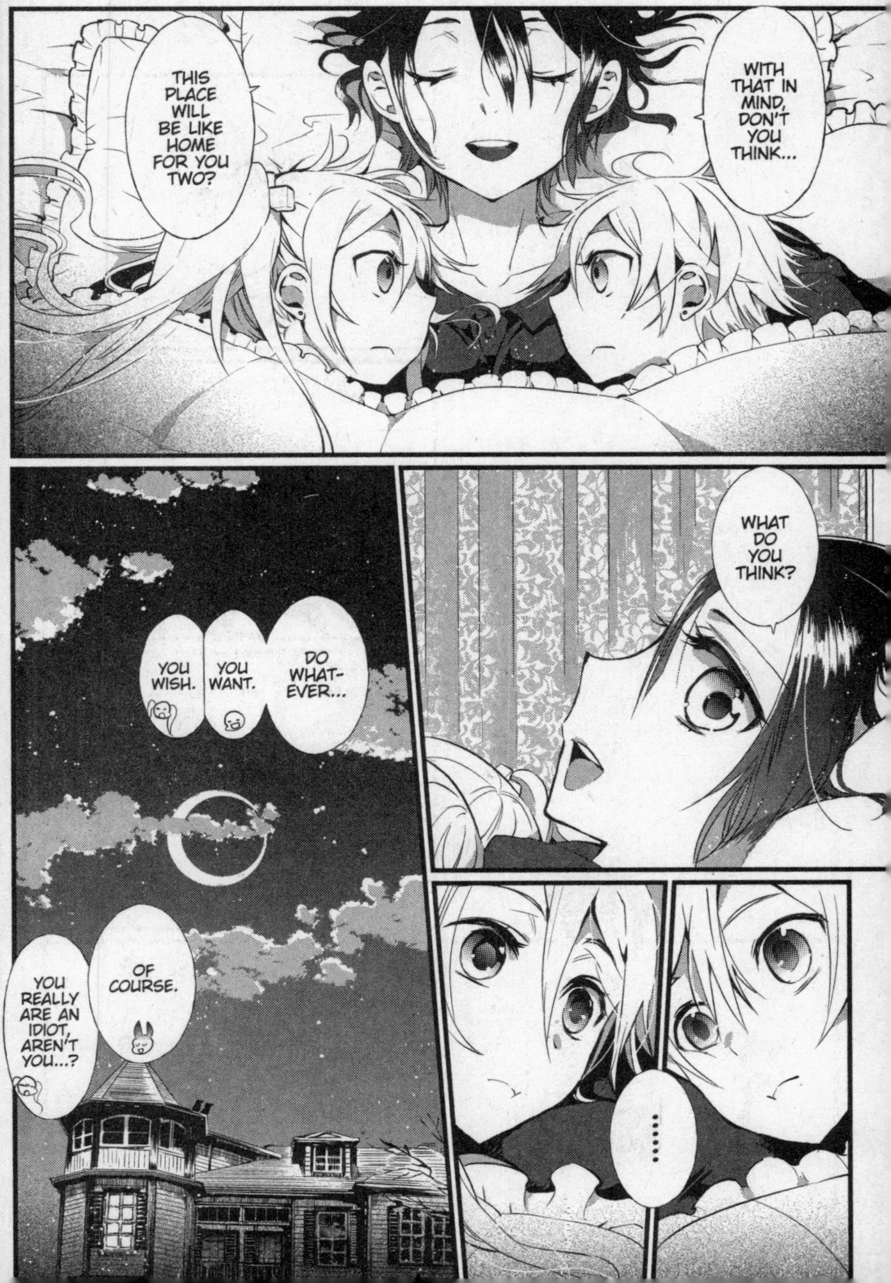
WITH THAT IN MIND, DON'T YOU THINK...
THIS PLACE WILL BE LIKE HOME FOR YOU TWO?
WHAT DO YOU THINK?
......
DO WHAT-EVER...
YOU WANT.
YOU WISH.
OF COURSE.
YOU REALLY ARE AN IDIOT, AREN'T YOU...?

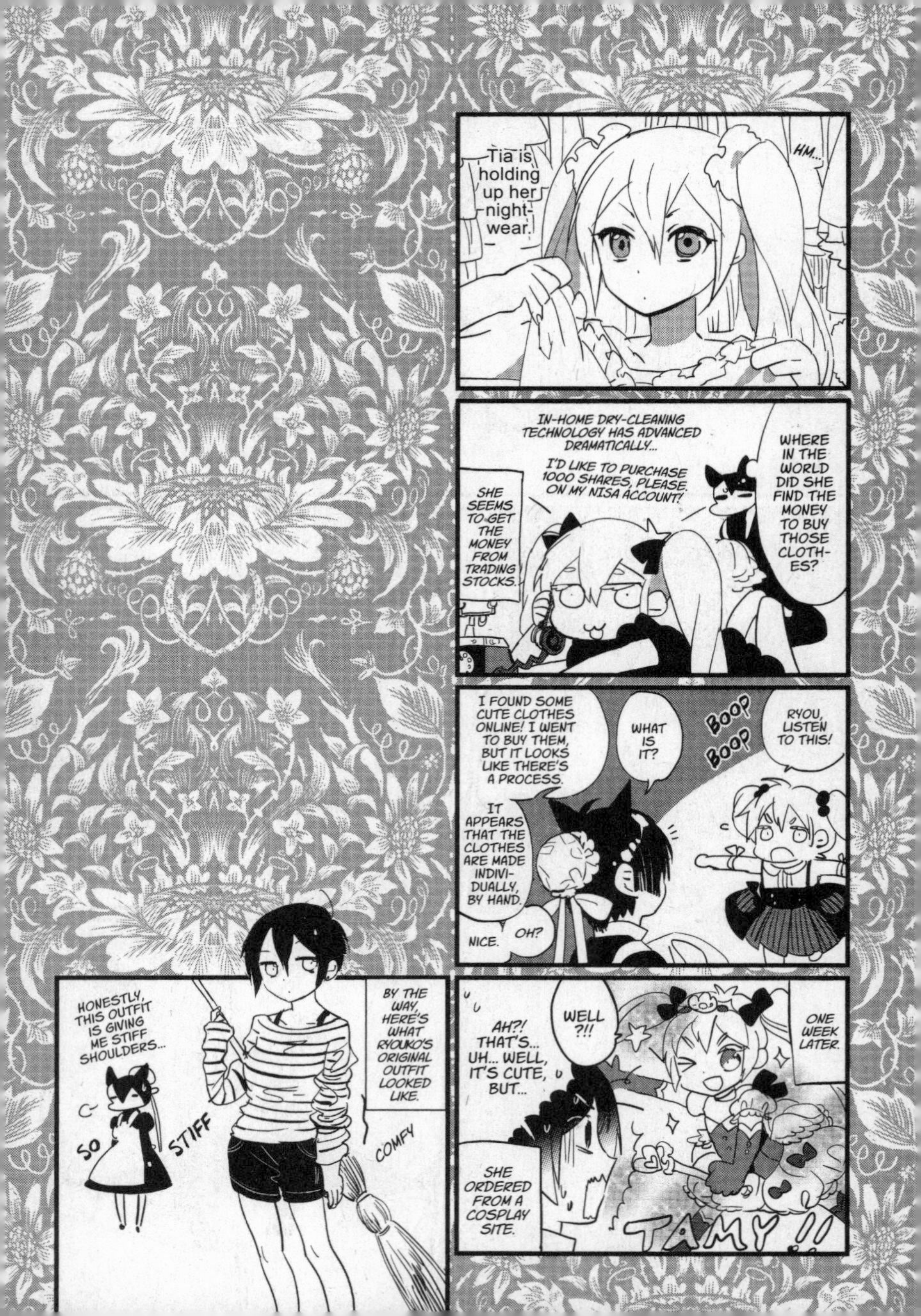
HM...
Tia is holding up her night-wear.
WHERE IN THE WORLD DID SHE FIND THE MONEY TO BUY THOSE CLOTHES?
IN-HOME DRY-CLEANING TECHNOLOGY HAS ADVANCED DRAMATICALLY...
I'D LIKE TO PURCHASE 1000 SHARES, PLEASE, ON MY NISA ACCOUNT!
SHE SEEMS TO GET THE MONEY FROM TRADING STOCKS.
RYOU, LISTEN TO THIS!
Boop Boop
WHAT IS IT?
I FOUND SOME CUTE CLOTHES ONLINE! I WENT TO BUY THEM, BUT IT LOOKS LIKE THERE'S A PROCESS.
IT APPEARS THAT THE CLOTHES ARE MADE INDIVIDUALLY, BY HAND.
OH?
NICE.
ONE WEEK LATER.
WELL ?!!
AH?! THAT'S... UH... WELL, IT'S CUTE, BUT...
SHE ORDERED FROM A COSPLAY SITE.
TAMY !!
BY THE WAY, HERE'S WHAT RYOUKO'S ORIGINAL OUTFIT LOOKED LIKE.
HONESTLY, THIS OUTFIT IS GIVING ME STIFF SHOULDERS...
SO STIFF
COMFY

Generation WITCH

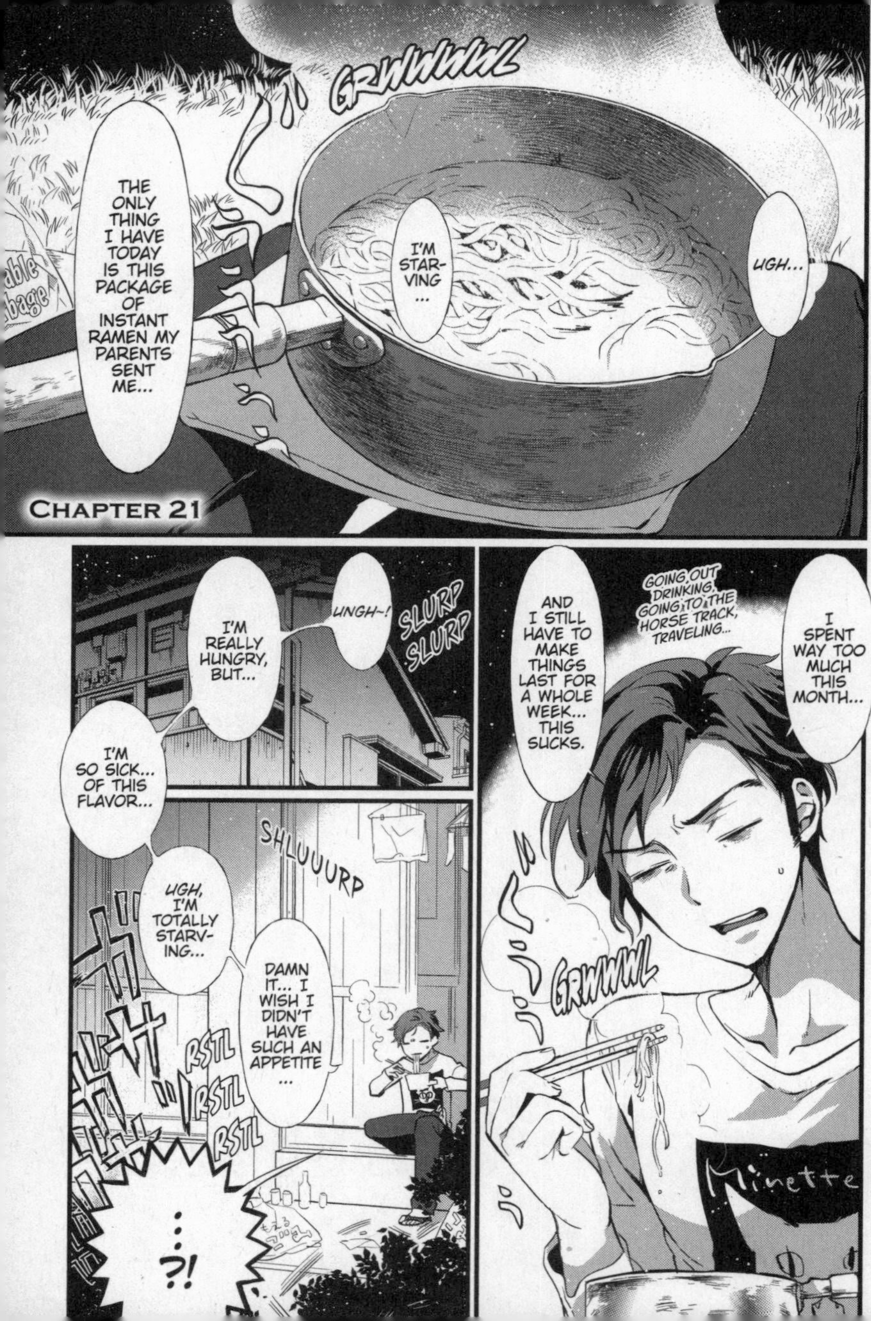
GRWWWWL
UGH...
I'M STARVING...
THE ONLY THING I HAVE TODAY IS THIS PACKAGE OF INSTANT RAMEN MY PARENTS SENT ME...
CHAPTER 21
I SPENT WAY TOO MUCH THIS MONTH...
GOING OUT DRINKING, GOING TO THE HORSE TRACK, TRAVELING...
AND I STILL HAVE TO MAKE THINGS LAST FOR A WHOLE WEEK... THIS SUCKS.
GRWWWL
Minette
UNGH~!
SLURP SLURP
I'M REALLY HUNGRY, BUT...
I'M SO SICK... OF THIS FLAVOR...
SHLUUUURP
UGH, I'M TOTALLY STARVING...
DAMN IT... I WISH I DIDN'T HAVE SUCH AN APPETITE...
RSTL
RSTL
RSTL
...?!

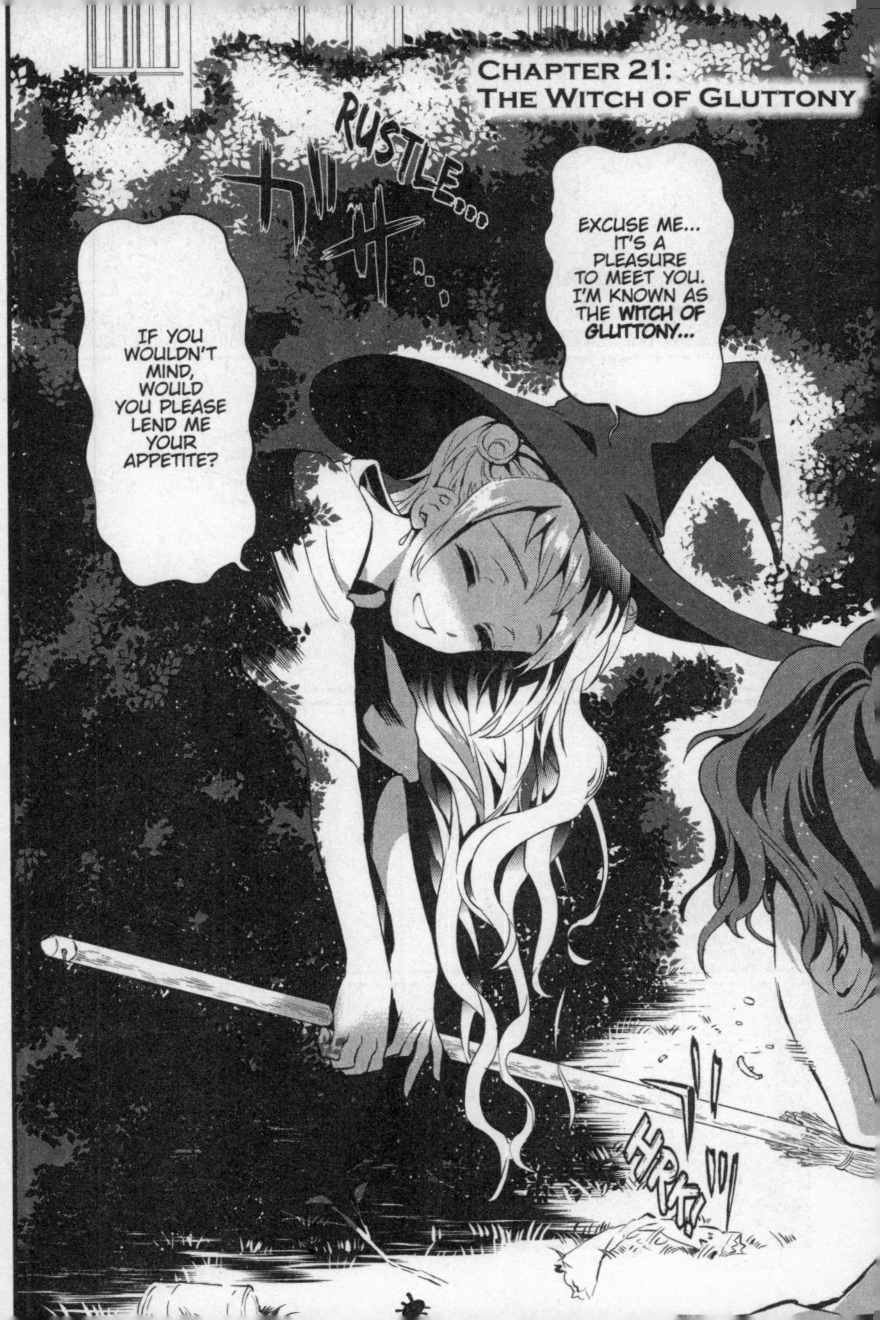
CHAPTER 21: THE WITCH OF GLUTTONY
RUSTLE...
EXCUSE ME... IT'S A PLEASURE TO MEET YOU. I'M KNOWN AS THE WITCH OF GLUTTONY...
IF YOU WOULDN'T MIND, WOULD YOU PLEASE LEND ME YOUR APPETITE?
HRK!!

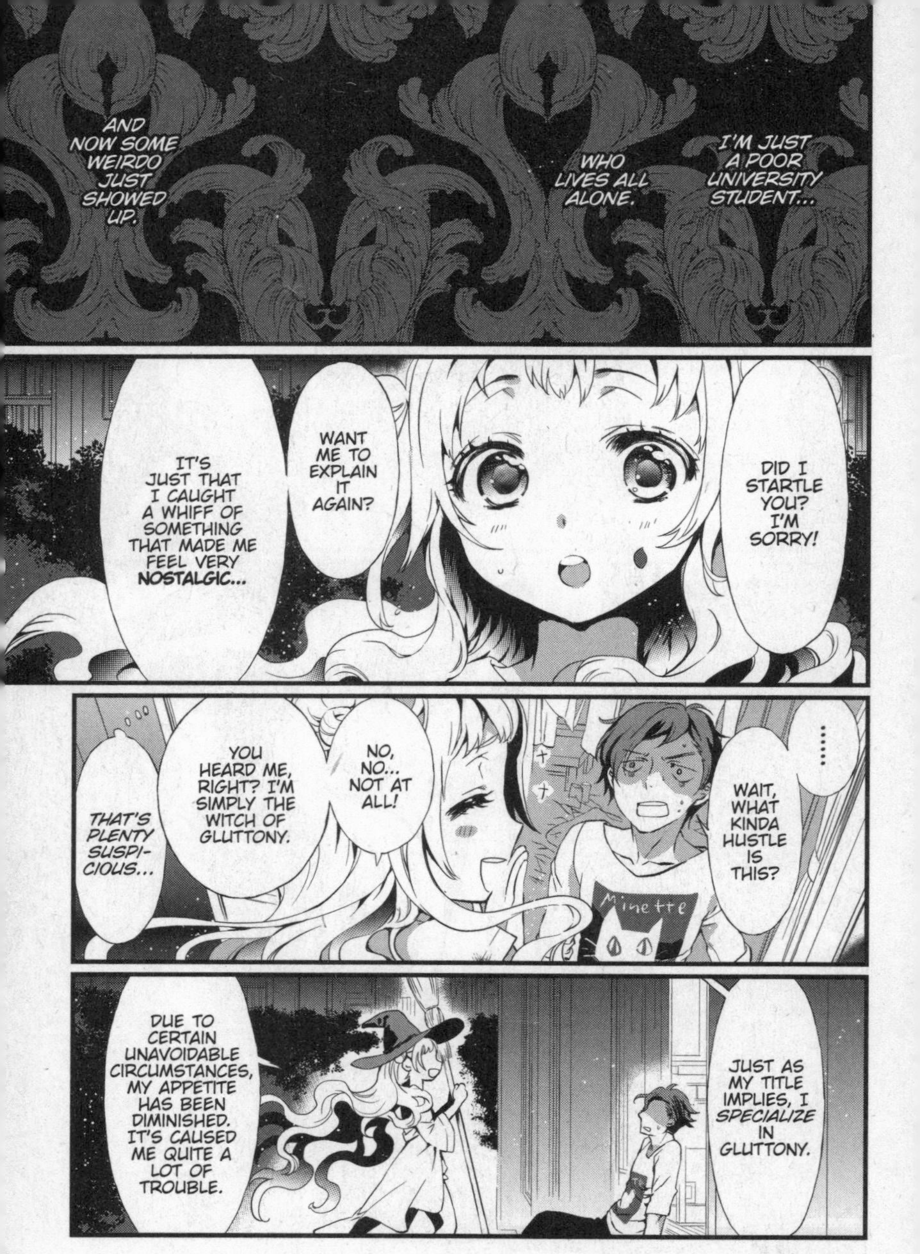
I'M JUST A POOR UNIVERSITY STUDENT...
WHO LIVES ALL ALONE.
AND NOW SOME WEIRDO JUST SHOWED UP.
DID I STARTLE YOU? I'M SORRY!
WANT ME TO EXPLAIN IT AGAIN?
IT'S JUST THAT I CAUGHT A WHIFF OF SOMETHING THAT MADE ME FEEL VERY NOSTALGIC...
......
WAIT, WHAT KINDA HUSTLE IS THIS?
NO, NO... NOT AT ALL!
YOU HEARD ME, RIGHT? I'M SIMPLY THE WITCH OF GLUTTONY.
THAT'S PLENTY SUSPICIOUS...
JUST AS MY TITLE IMPLIES, I SPECIALIZE IN GLUTTONY.
DUE TO CERTAIN UNAVOIDABLE CIRCUMSTANCES, MY APPETITE HAS BEEN DIMINISHED. IT'S CAUSED ME QUITE A LOT OF TROUBLE.

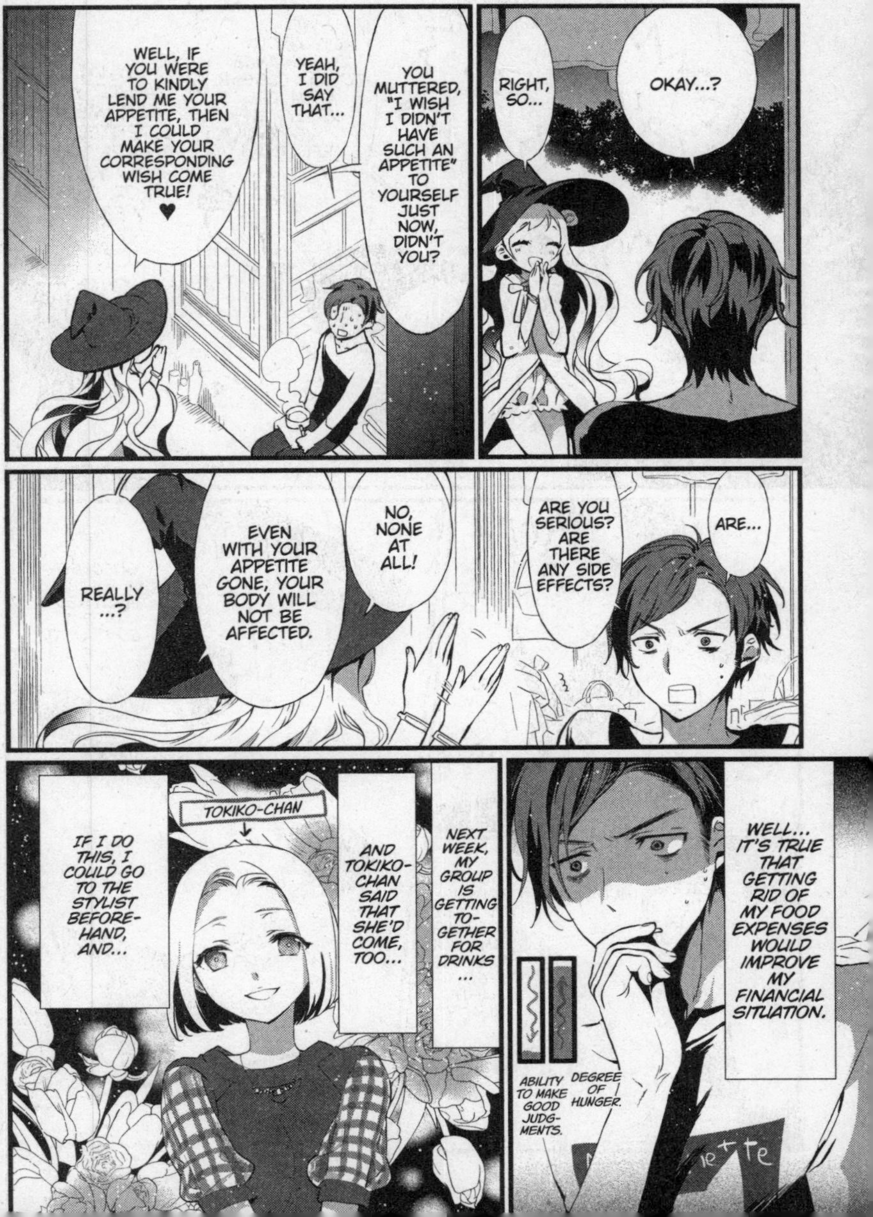
OKAY...?
RIGHT, SO...
YOU MUTTERED, "I WISH I DIDN'T HAVE SUCH AN APPETITE" TO YOURSELF JUST NOW, DIDN'T YOU?
YEAH, I DID SAY THAT...
WELL, IF YOU WERE TO KINDLY LEND ME YOUR APPETITE, THEN I COULD MAKE YOUR CORRESPONDING WISH COME TRUE! ♥
ARE...
ARE YOU SERIOUS? ARE THERE ANY SIDE EFFECTS?
NO, NONE AT ALL!
EVEN WITH YOUR APPETITE GONE, YOUR BODY WILL NOT BE AFFECTED.
REALLY ...?
WELL... IT'S TRUE THAT GETTING RID OF MY FOOD EXPENSES WOULD IMPROVE MY FINANCIAL SITUATION.
DEGREE OF HUNGER.
ABILITY TO MAKE GOOD JUDGMENTS.
NEXT WEEK, MY GROUP IS GETTING TOGETHER FOR DRINKS...
AND TOKIKO-CHAN SAID THAT SHE'D COME, TOO...
TOKIKO-CHAN
IF I DO THIS, I COULD GO TO THE STYLIST BEFOREHAND, AND...

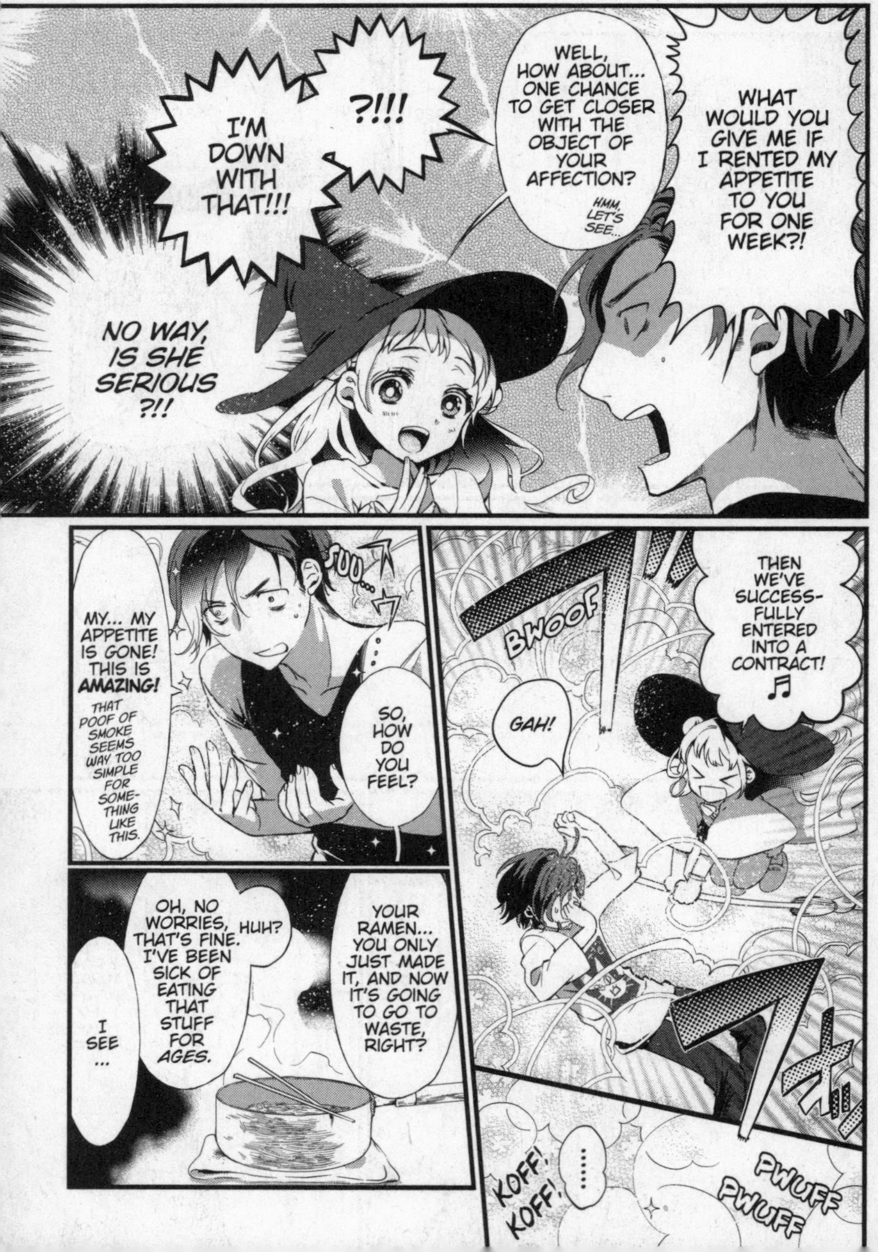
WHAT WOULD YOU GIVE ME IF I RENTED MY APPETITE TO YOU FOR ONE WEEK?!
WELL, HOW ABOUT... ONE CHANCE TO GET CLOSER WITH THE OBJECT OF YOUR AFFECTION?
HMM, LET'S SEE...
?!!!
I'M DOWN WITH THAT!!!
NO WAY, IS SHE SERIOUS ?!!
THEN WE'VE SUCCESS-FULLY ENTERED INTO A CONTRACT! ♬
BWOOF
GAH!
PWUFF PWUFF
KOFF! KOFF!
......
SUU...
SO, HOW DO YOU FEEL?
MY... MY APPETITE IS GONE! THIS IS **AMAZING!**
THAT POOF OF SMOKE SEEMS WAY TOO SIMPLE FOR SOME-THING LIKE THIS.
YOUR RAMEN... YOU ONLY JUST MADE IT, AND NOW IT'S GOING TO GO TO WASTE, RIGHT?
HUH?
OH, NO WORRIES, THAT'S FINE. I'VE BEEN SICK OF EATING THAT STUFF FOR AGES.
I SEE ...

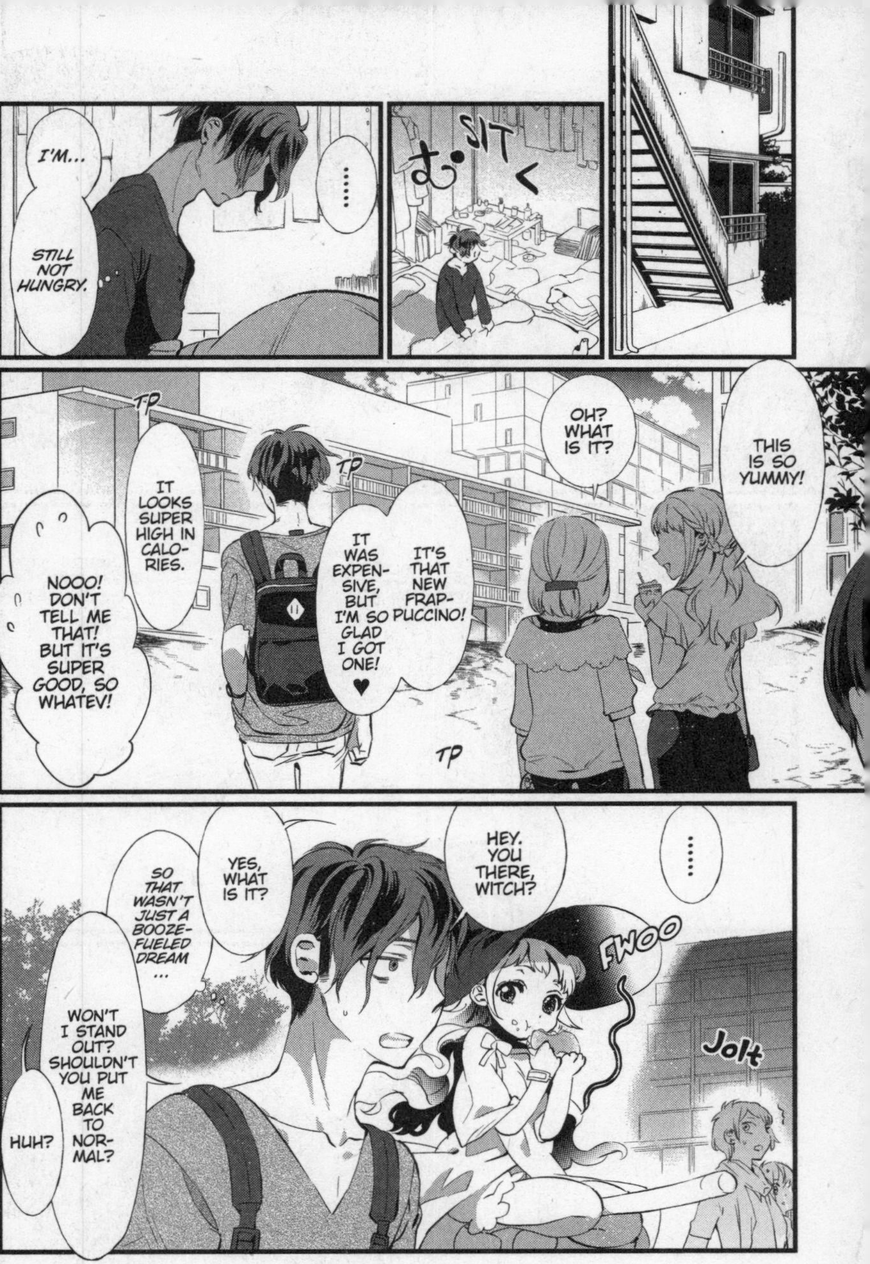

SIT
む く
......
I'M...
STILL NOT HUNGRY.
THIS IS SO YUMMY!
OH? WHAT IS IT?
IT'S THAT NEW FRAPPUCCINO!
IT WAS EXPENSIVE, BUT I'M SO GLAD I GOT ONE! ♥
TP
TP
IT LOOKS SUPER HIGH IN CALORIES.
NOOO! DON'T TELL ME THAT! BUT IT'S SUPER GOOD, SO WHATEV!
TP
......
HEY. YOU THERE, WITCH?
FWOO
YES, WHAT IS IT?
SO THAT WASN'T JUST A BOOZE-FUELED DREAM ...
Jolt
WON'T I STAND OUT? SHOULDN'T YOU PUT ME BACK TO NORMAL?
HUH?

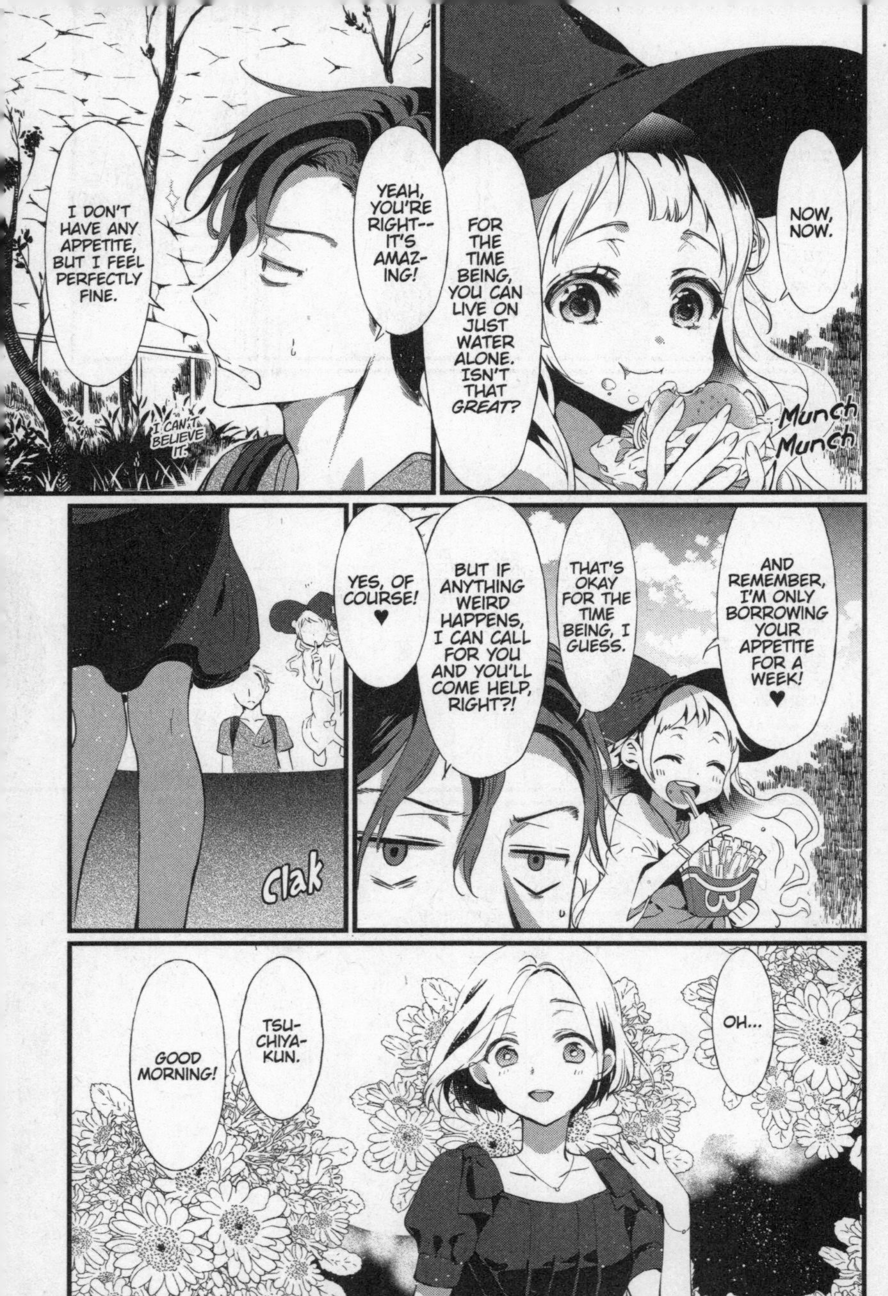
NOW, NOW.
FOR THE TIME BEING, YOU CAN LIVE ON JUST WATER ALONE. ISN'T THAT GREAT?
Munch Munch
YEAH, YOU'RE RIGHT-- IT'S AMAZING!
I DON'T HAVE ANY APPETITE, BUT I FEEL PERFECTLY FINE.
I CAN'T BELIEVE IT.
AND REMEMBER, I'M ONLY BORROWING YOUR APPETITE FOR A WEEK! ♥
THAT'S OKAY FOR THE TIME BEING, I GUESS.
BUT IF ANYTHING WEIRD HAPPENS, I CAN CALL FOR YOU AND YOU'LL COME HELP, RIGHT?!
YES, OF COURSE! ♥
Clak
OH...
TSU-CHIYA-KUN.
GOOD MORNING!

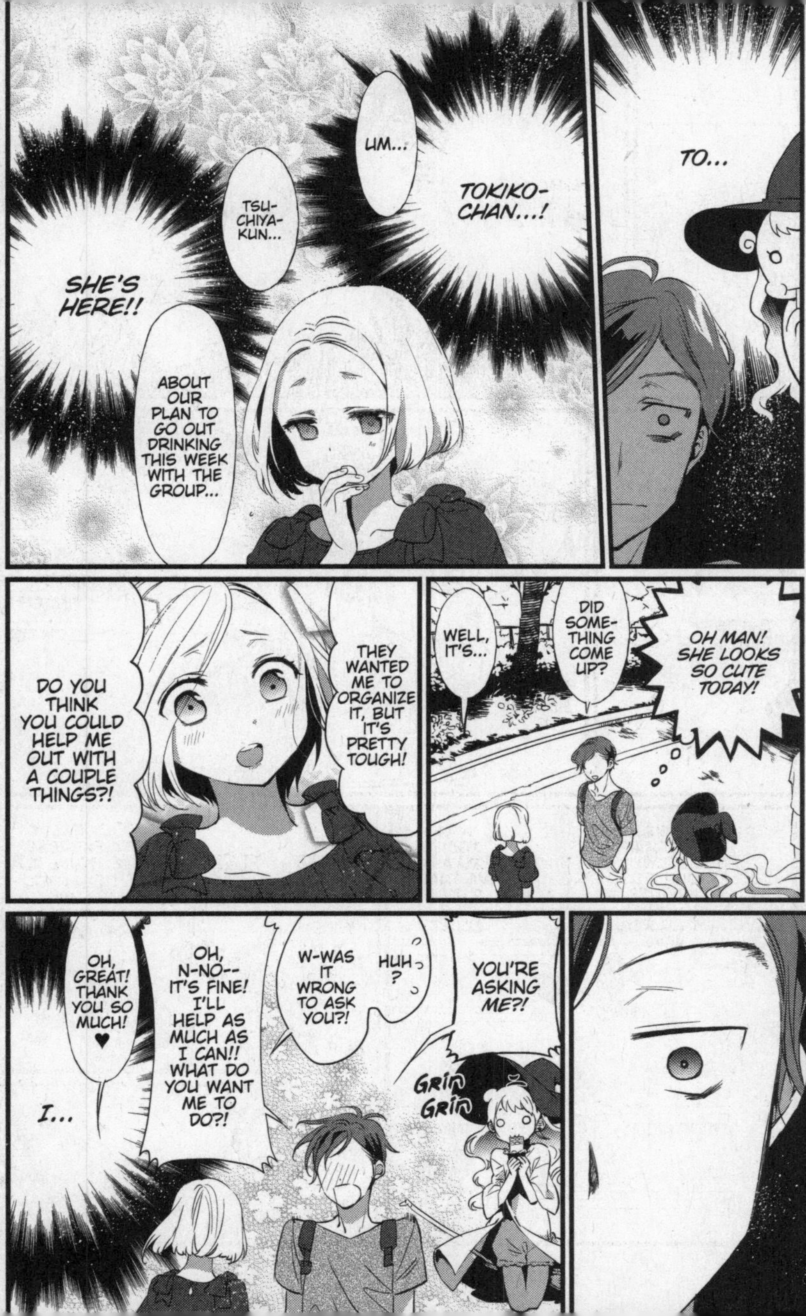
TO...
TOKIKO-CHAN...!
UM...
TSU-CHIYA-KUN...
SHE'S HERE!!
ABOUT OUR PLAN TO GO OUT DRINKING THIS WEEK WITH THE GROUP...
OH MAN! SHE LOOKS SO CUTE TODAY!
DID SOMETHING COME UP?
WELL, IT'S...
THEY WANTED ME TO ORGANIZE IT, BUT IT'S PRETTY TOUGH!
DO YOU THINK YOU COULD HELP ME OUT WITH A COUPLE THINGS?!
YOU'RE ASKING ME?!
HUH?
W-WAS IT WRONG TO ASK YOU?!
OH, N-NO-- IT'S FINE! I'LL HELP AS MUCH AS I CAN!! WHAT DO YOU WANT ME TO DO?!
Grin Grin
OH, GREAT! THANK YOU SO MUCH! ♥
I...

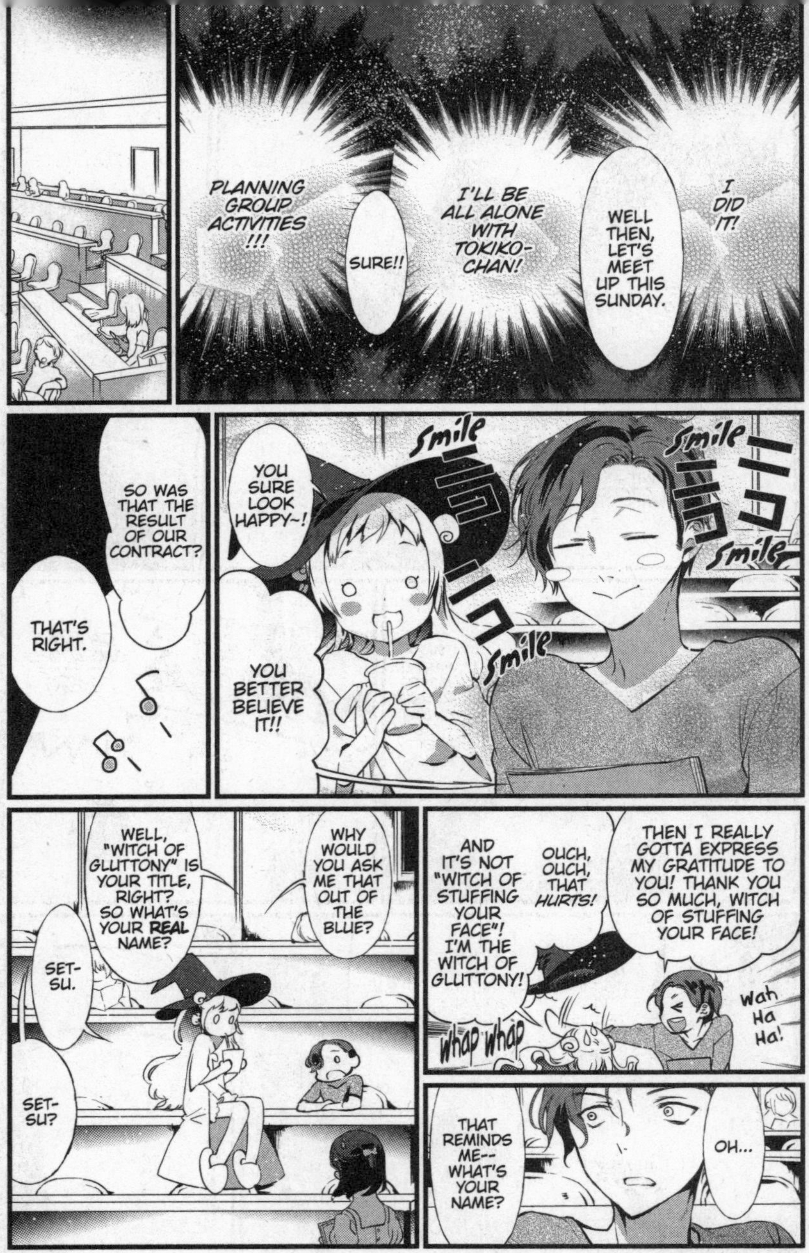
I DID IT!
WELL THEN, LET'S MEET UP THIS SUNDAY.
I'LL BE ALL ALONE WITH TOKIKO-CHAN!
SURE!!
PLANNING GROUP ACTIVITIES!!!
Smile Smile Smile Smile
YOU SURE LOOK HAPPY~!
YOU BETTER BELIEVE IT!!
SO WAS THAT THE RESULT OF OUR CONTRACT?
THAT'S RIGHT.
THEN I REALLY GOTTA EXPRESS MY GRATITUDE TO YOU! THANK YOU SO MUCH, WITCH OF STUFFING YOUR FACE!
OUCH, OUCH, THAT HURTS!
AND IT'S NOT "WITCH OF STUFFING YOUR FACE"! I'M THE WITCH OF GLUTTONY!
Wah Ha Ha!
whap whap
OH...
THAT REMINDS ME-- WHAT'S YOUR NAME?
WHY WOULD YOU ASK ME THAT OUT OF THE BLUE?
WELL, "WITCH OF GLUTTONY" IS YOUR TITLE, RIGHT? SO WHAT'S YOUR REAL NAME?
SET-SU.
SET-SU?

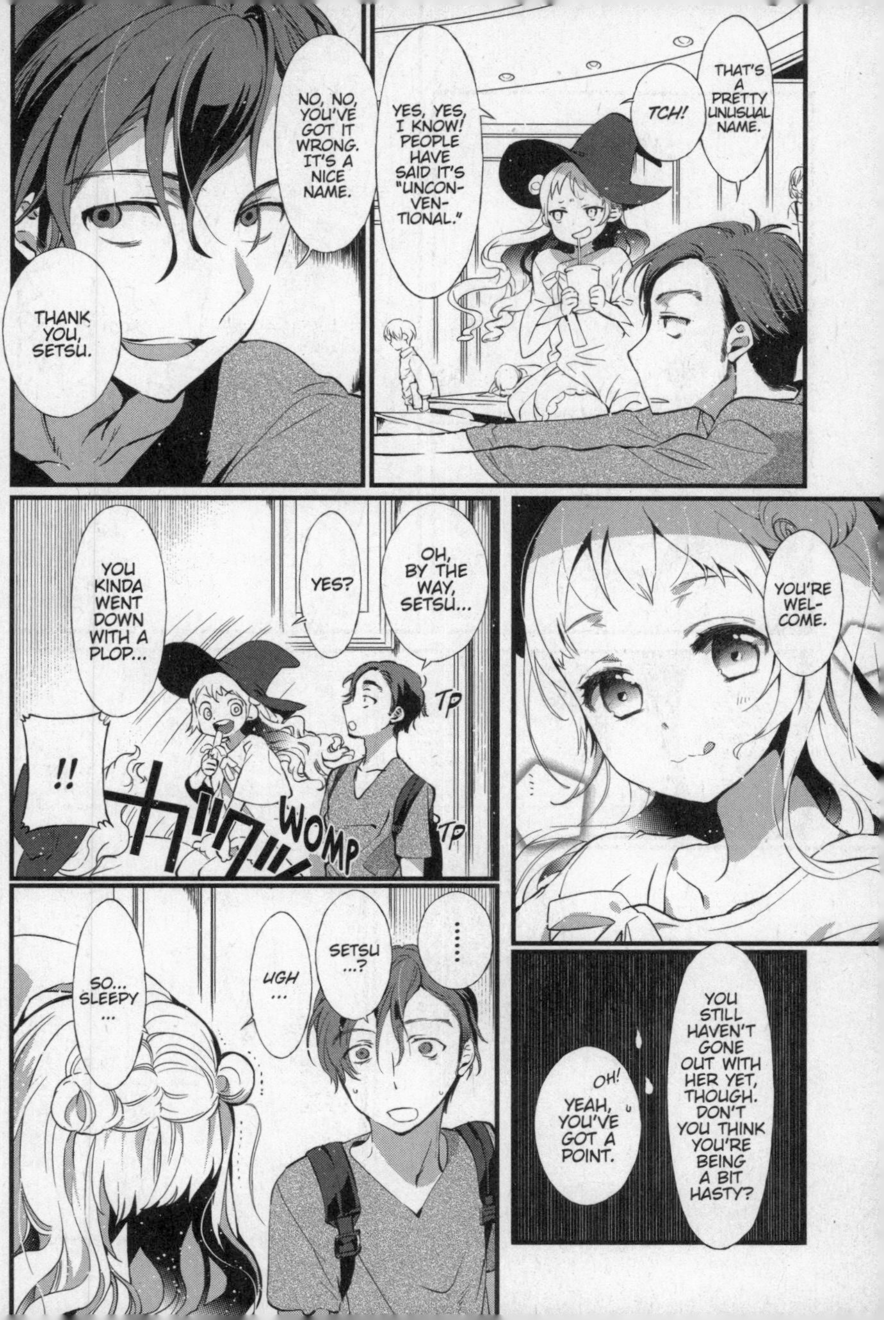
THAT'S A PRETTY UNUSUAL NAME.
TCH!
YES, YES, I KNOW! PEOPLE HAVE SAID IT'S "UNCONVENTIONAL."
NO, NO, YOU'VE GOT IT WRONG. IT'S A NICE NAME.
THANK YOU, SETSU.
YOU'RE WELCOME.
OH, BY THE WAY, SETSU...
YES?
YOU KINDA WENT DOWN WITH A PLOP...
!!
TP
TP
WOMP
YOU STILL HAVEN'T GONE OUT WITH HER YET, THOUGH. DON'T YOU THINK YOU'RE BEING A BIT HASTY?
OH! YEAH, YOU'VE GOT A POINT.
......
SETSU ...?
UGH ...
SO... SLEEPY ...

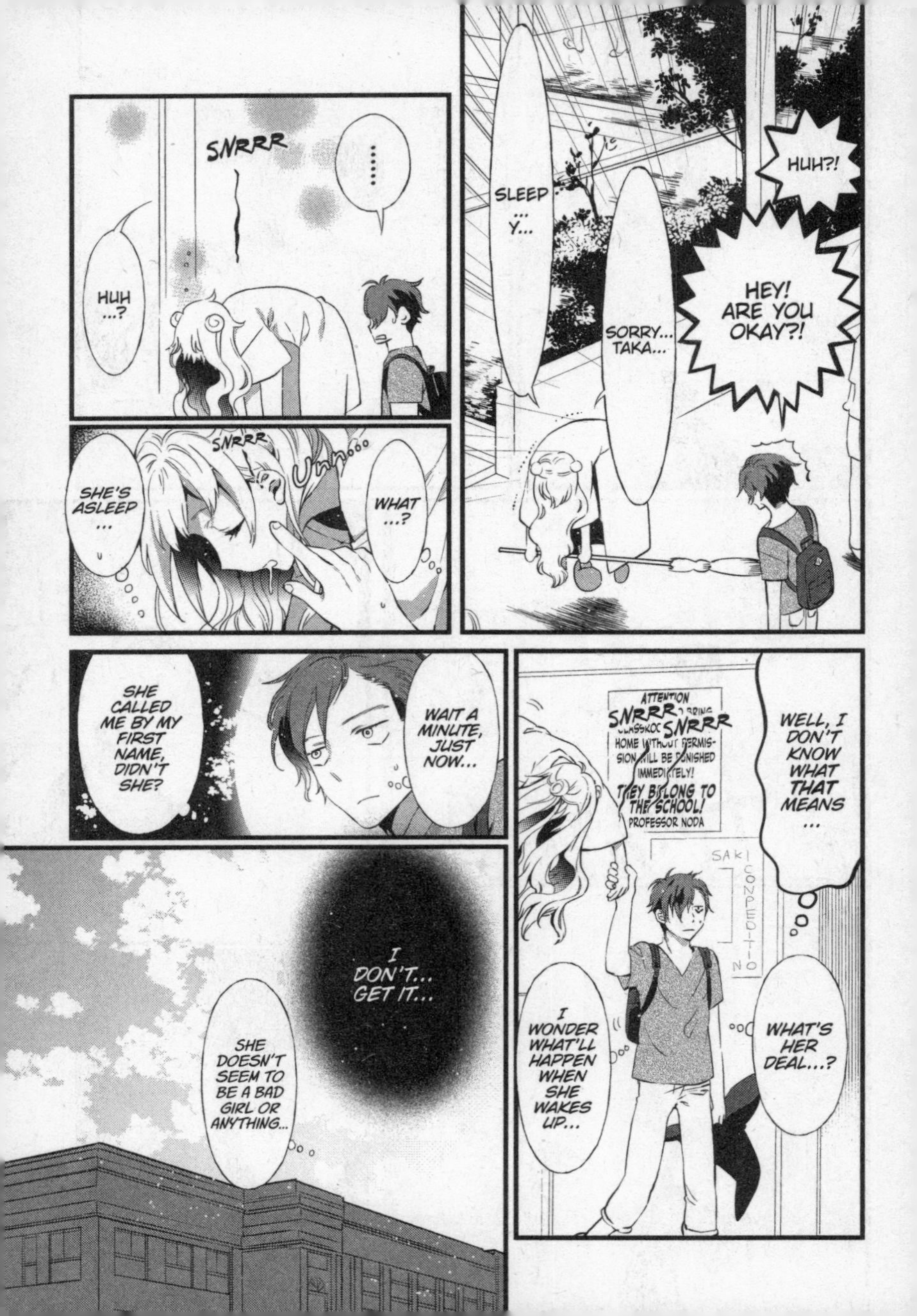
HUH?!
HEY! ARE YOU OKAY?!
SLEEP... Y...
SORRY... TAKA...
......
SNRRR
HUH...?
WHAT...?
SNRRR
Unnooo
SHE'S ASLEEP...
WELL, I DON'T KNOW WHAT THAT MEANS...
ATTENTION
SNRRR SNRRR
HOME WITHOUT PERMISSION WILL BE PUNISHED IMMEDIATELY!
THEY BELONG TO THE SCHOOL!
PROFESSOR NODA
SAKI
CONPEDITION
WHAT'S HER DEAL...?
I WONDER WHAT'LL HAPPEN WHEN SHE WAKES UP...
WAIT A MINUTE, JUST NOW...
SHE CALLED ME BY MY FIRST NAME, DIDN'T SHE?
I DON'T... GET IT...
SHE DOESN'T SEEM TO BE A BAD GIRL OR ANYTHING...

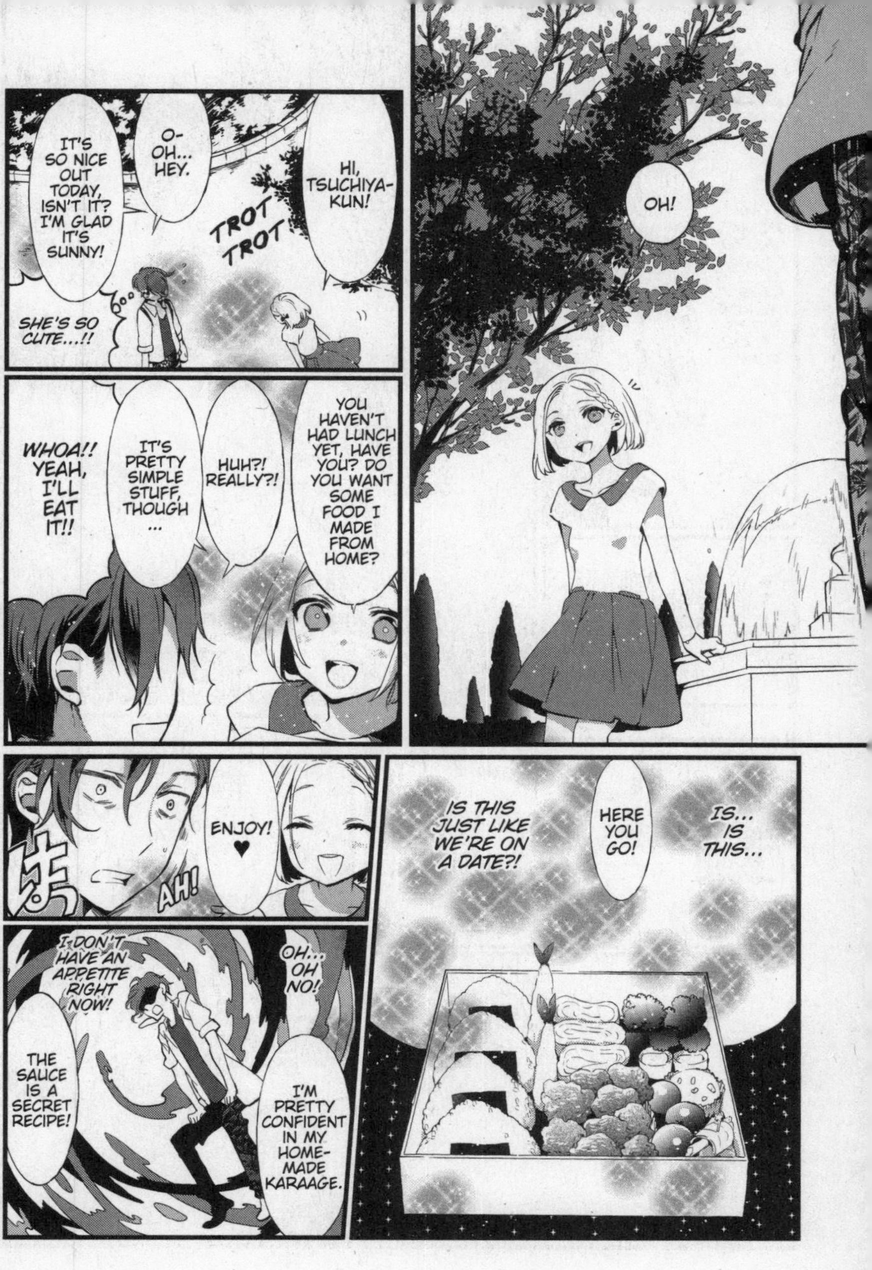
OH!
HI, TSUCHIYA-KUN!
TROT TROT
O-OH... HEY.
IT'S SO NICE OUT TODAY, ISN'T IT? I'M GLAD IT'S SUNNY!
SHE'S SO CUTE...!!
YOU HAVEN'T HAD LUNCH YET, HAVE YOU? DO YOU WANT SOME FOOD I MADE FROM HOME?
HUH?! REALLY?!
IT'S PRETTY SIMPLE STUFF, THOUGH...
WHOA!! YEAH, I'LL EAT IT!!
IS... IS THIS...
HERE YOU GO!
IS THIS JUST LIKE WE'RE ON A DATE?!
ENJOY! ♥
AH!
I'M PRETTY CONFIDENT IN MY HOME-MADE KARAAGE.
THE SAUCE IS A SECRET RECIPE!
OH... OH NO!
I DON'T HAVE AN APPETITE RIGHT NOW!

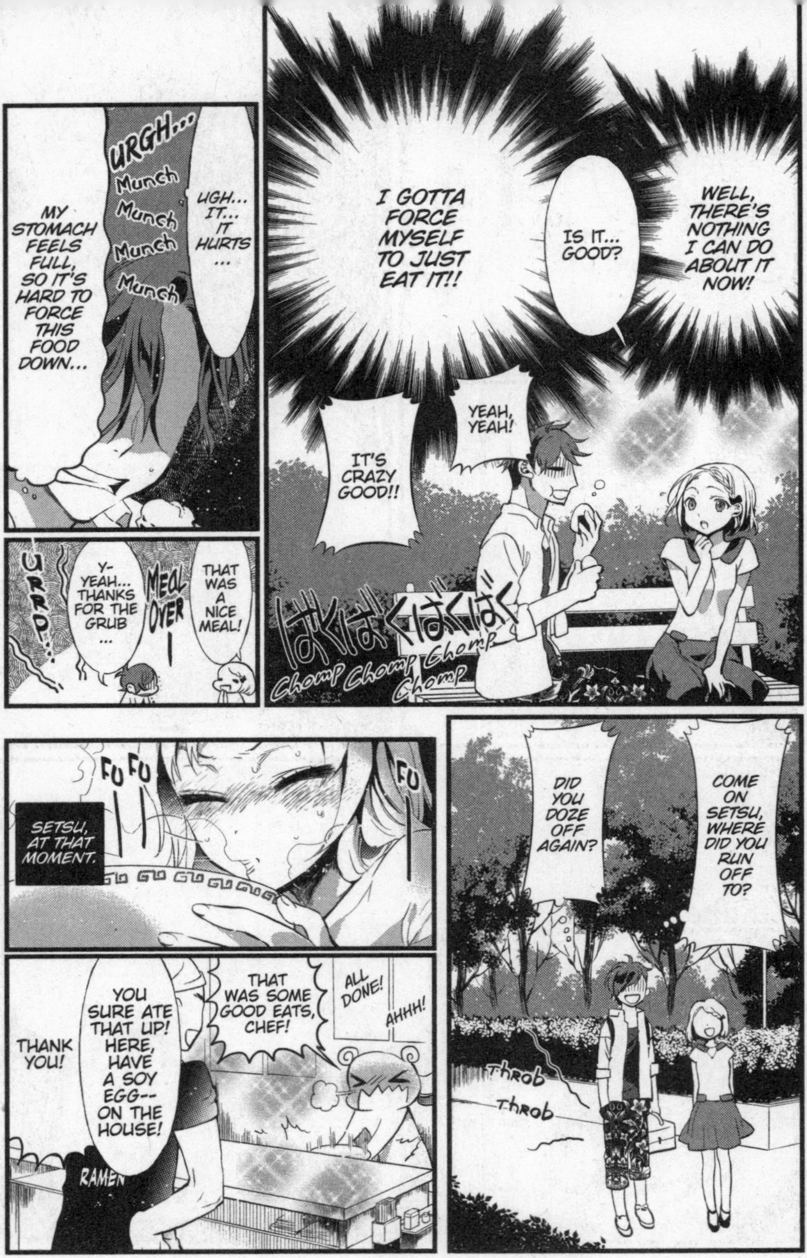
WELL, THERE'S NOTHING I CAN DO ABOUT IT NOW!
IS IT... GOOD?
I GOTTA FORCE MYSELF TO JUST EAT IT!!
YEAH, YEAH!
IT'S CRAZY GOOD!!
ぱくぱくぱくぱく
Chomp Chomp Chomp Chomp
UGH... IT... IT HURTS...
URGH...
Munch Munch Munch Munch
MY STOMACH FEELS FULL, SO IT'S HARD TO FORCE THIS FOOD DOWN...
THAT WAS A NICE MEAL!
MEAL OVER
Y-YEAH... THANKS FOR THE GRUB...
URRP...
COME ON SETSU, WHERE DID YOU RUN OFF TO?
DID YOU DOZE OFF AGAIN?
Throb
Throb
FU
FU FU
SETSU, AT THAT MOMENT.
AHHH!
ALL DONE!
THAT WAS SOME GOOD EATS, CHEF!
YOU SURE ATE THAT UP! HERE, HAVE A SOY EGG-- ON THE HOUSE!
THANK YOU!
RAMEN

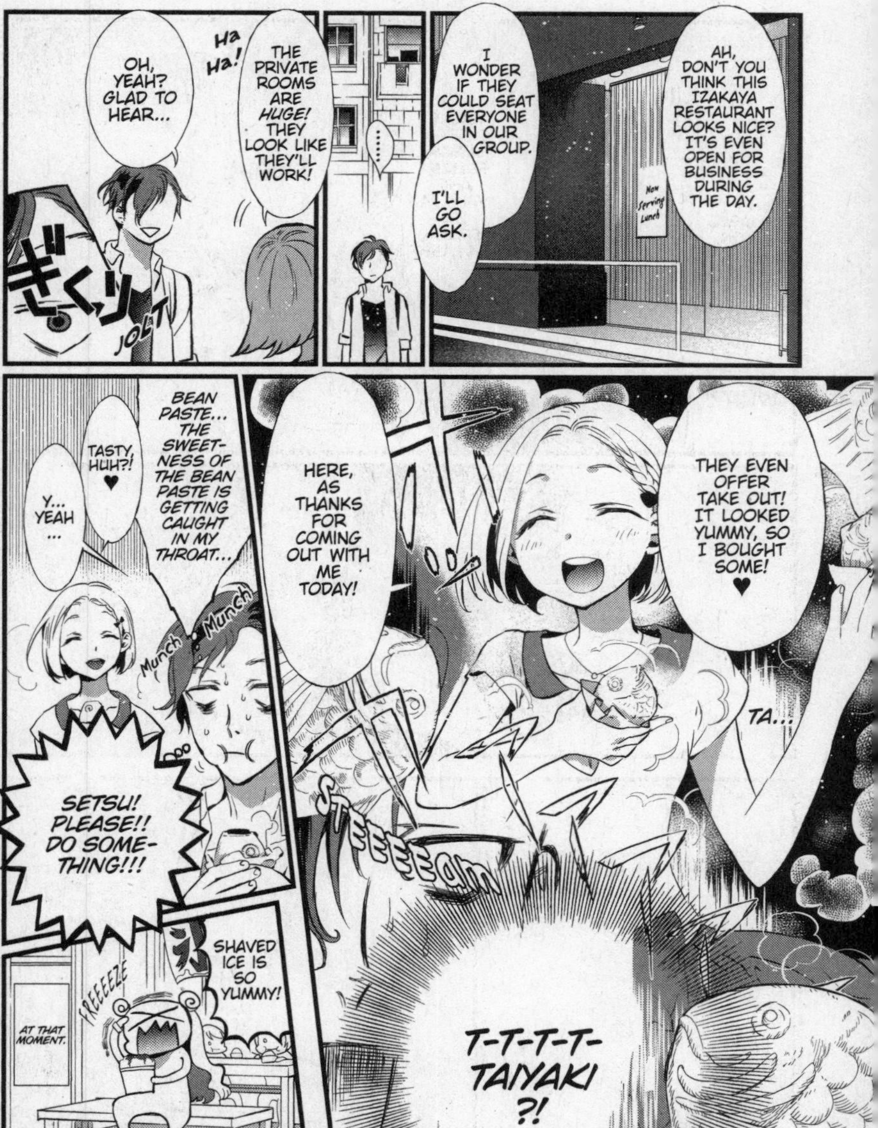
AH, DON'T YOU THINK THIS IZAKAYA RESTAURANT LOOKS NICE? IT'S EVEN OPEN FOR BUSINESS DURING THE DAY.
Now Serving Lunch
I WONDER IF THEY COULD SEAT EVERYONE IN OUR GROUP.
I'LL GO ASK.
......
THE PRIVATE ROOMS ARE HUGE! THEY LOOK LIKE THEY'LL WORK!
Ha Ha!
OH, YEAH? GLAD TO HEAR...
ぎくッ
JOLT
THEY EVEN OFFER TAKE OUT! IT LOOKED YUMMY, SO I BOUGHT SOME! ♥
HERE, AS THANKS FOR COMING OUT WITH ME TODAY!
TA...
STEEEEAM
T-T-T-T-TAIYAKI ?!
BEAN PASTE... THE SWEETNESS OF THE BEAN PASTE IS GETTING CAUGHT IN MY THROAT...
TASTY, HUH?! ♥
Y... YEAH ...
Munch Munch
SETSU! PLEASE!! DO SOME-THING!!!
SHAVED ICE IS SO YUMMY!
FREEEEZE
AT THAT MOMENT.

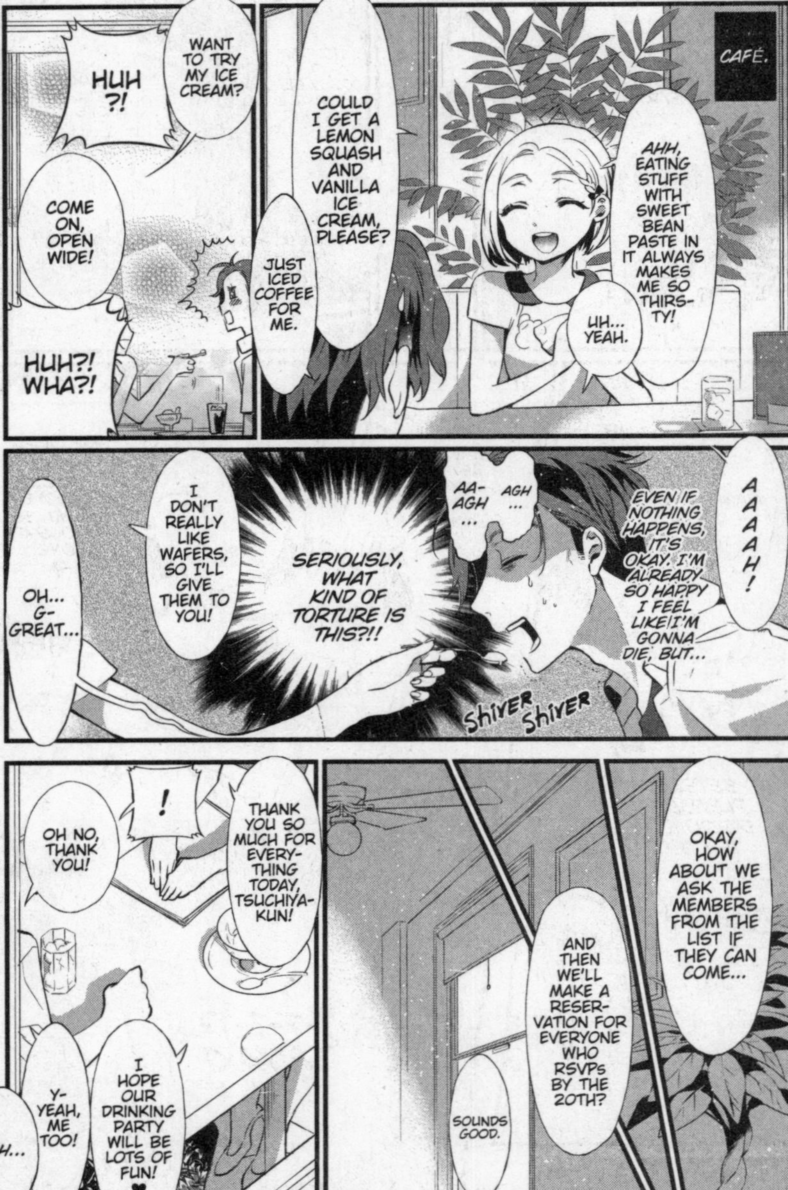
CAFÉ.
AHH, EATING STUFF WITH SWEET BEAN PASTE IN IT ALWAYS MAKES ME SO THIRSTY!
UH... YEAH.
COULD I GET A LEMON SQUASH AND VANILLA ICE CREAM, PLEASE?
JUST ICED COFFEE FOR ME.
WANT TO TRY MY ICE CREAM?
HUH ?!
COME ON, OPEN WIDE!
HUH?! WHA?!
AAAAAH!
EVEN IF NOTHING HAPPENS, IT'S OKAY. I'M ALREADY SO HAPPY I FEEL LIKE I'M GONNA DIE, BUT...
AGH...
AA-AGH...
SERIOUSLY, WHAT KIND OF TORTURE IS THIS?!!
I DON'T REALLY LIKE WAFERS, SO I'LL GIVE THEM TO YOU!
OH... G-GREAT...
Shiver Shiver
OKAY, HOW ABOUT WE ASK THE MEMBERS FROM THE LIST IF THEY CAN COME...
AND THEN WE'LL MAKE A RESERVATION FOR EVERYONE WHO RSVPs BY THE 20TH?
SOUNDS GOOD.
THANK YOU SO MUCH FOR EVERYTHING TODAY, TSUCHIYA-KUN!
!
OH NO, THANK YOU!
I HOPE OUR DRINKING PARTY WILL BE LOTS OF FUN! ♥
Y-YEAH, ME TOO!
OOH...

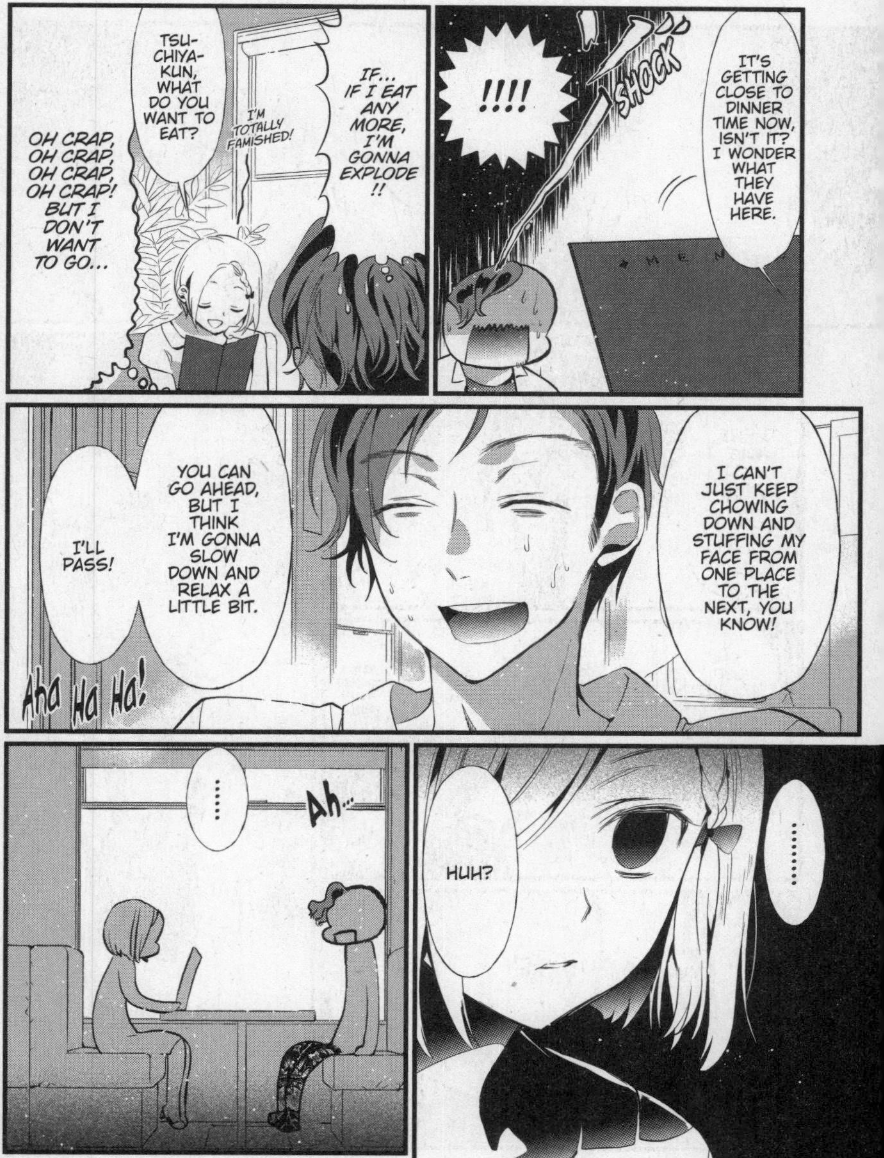
IT'S GETTING CLOSE TO DINNER TIME NOW, ISN'T IT? I WONDER WHAT THEY HAVE HERE.
SHOCK
!!!!
IF... IF I EAT ANY MORE, I'M GONNA EXPLODE !!
I'M TOTALLY FAMISHED!
TSU-CHIYA-KUN, WHAT DO YOU WANT TO EAT?
OH CRAP, OH CRAP, OH CRAP, OH CRAP! BUT I DON'T WANT TO GO...
I CAN'T JUST KEEP CHOWING DOWN AND STUFFING MY FACE FROM ONE PLACE TO THE NEXT, YOU KNOW!
YOU CAN GO AHEAD, BUT I THINK I'M GONNA SLOW DOWN AND RELAX A LITTLE BIT.
I'LL PASS!
Aha Ha Ha!
......
HUH?
Ah...
......

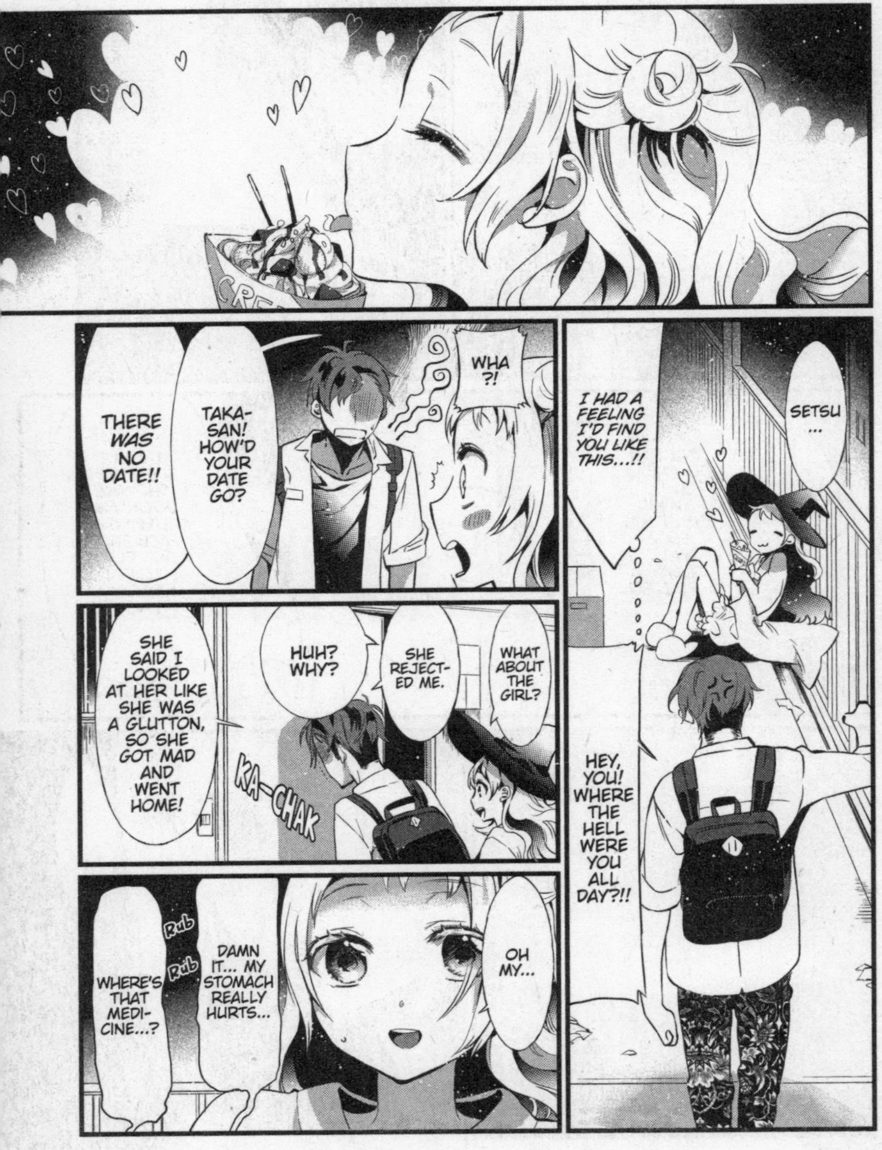
SETSU...
I HAD A FEELING I'D FIND YOU LIKE THIS...!!
HEY, YOU! WHERE THE HELL WERE YOU ALL DAY?!!
WHA?!
TAKA-SAN! HOW'D YOUR DATE GO?
THERE WAS NO DATE!!
WHAT ABOUT THE GIRL?
SHE REJECTED ME.
HUH? WHY?
SHE SAID I LOOKED AT HER LIKE SHE WAS A GLUTTON, SO SHE GOT MAD AND WENT HOME!
KA-CHAK
OH MY...
DAMN IT... MY STOMACH REALLY HURTS...
Rub Rub
WHERE'S THAT MEDICINE...?

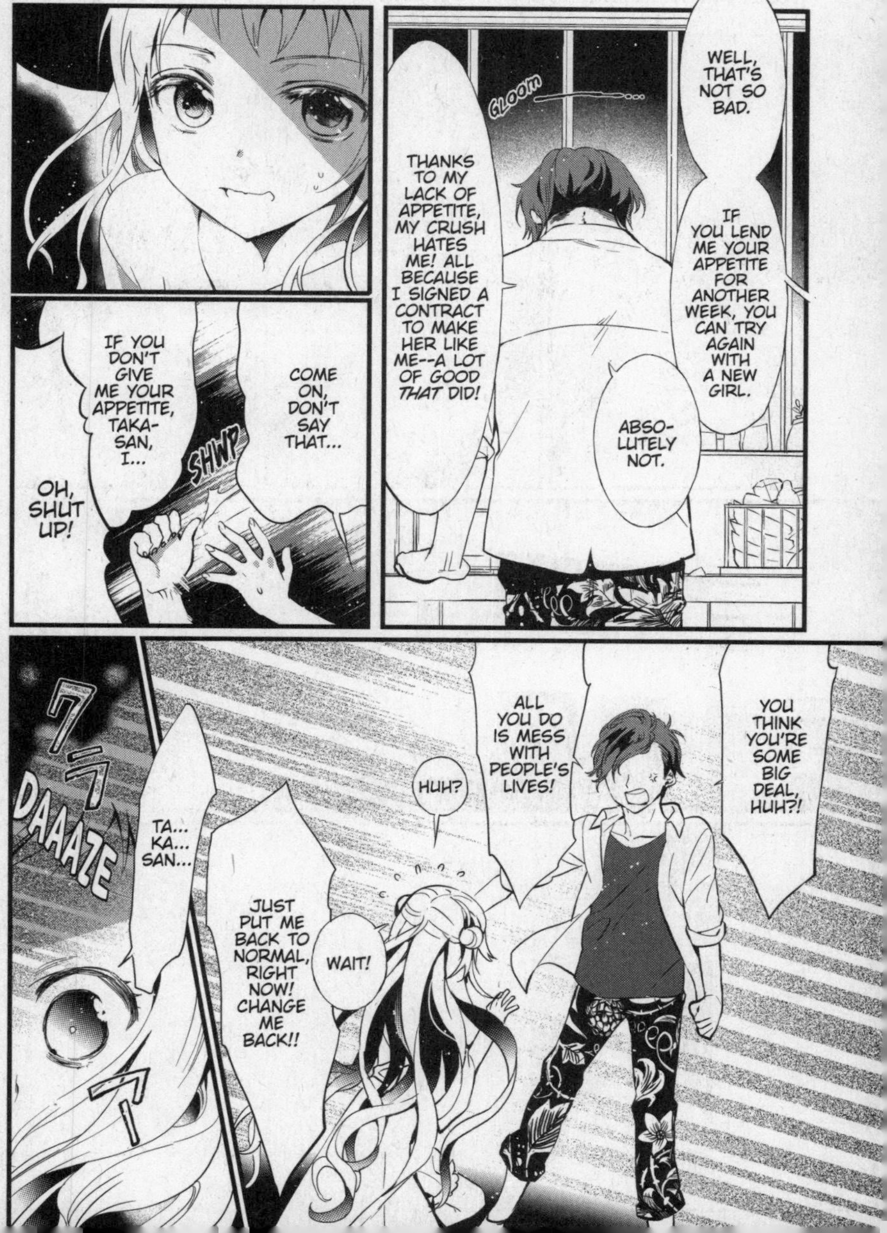
WELL, THAT'S NOT SO BAD.
IF YOU LEND ME YOUR APPETITE FOR ANOTHER WEEK, YOU CAN TRY AGAIN WITH A NEW GIRL.
GLOOM
THANKS TO MY LACK OF APPETITE, MY CRUSH HATES ME! ALL BECAUSE I SIGNED A CONTRACT TO MAKE HER LIKE ME--A LOT OF GOOD *THAT* DID!
ABSO-LUTELY NOT.
COME ON, DON'T SAY THAT...
IF YOU DON'T GIVE ME YOUR APPETITE, TAKA-SAN, I...
SHWP
OH, SHUT UP!
YOU THINK YOU'RE SOME BIG DEAL, HUH?!
ALL YOU DO IS MESS WITH PEOPLE'S LIVES!
HUH?
TA... KA... SAN...
WAIT!
JUST PUT ME BACK TO NORMAL, RIGHT NOW! CHANGE ME BACK!!
DAAAZE

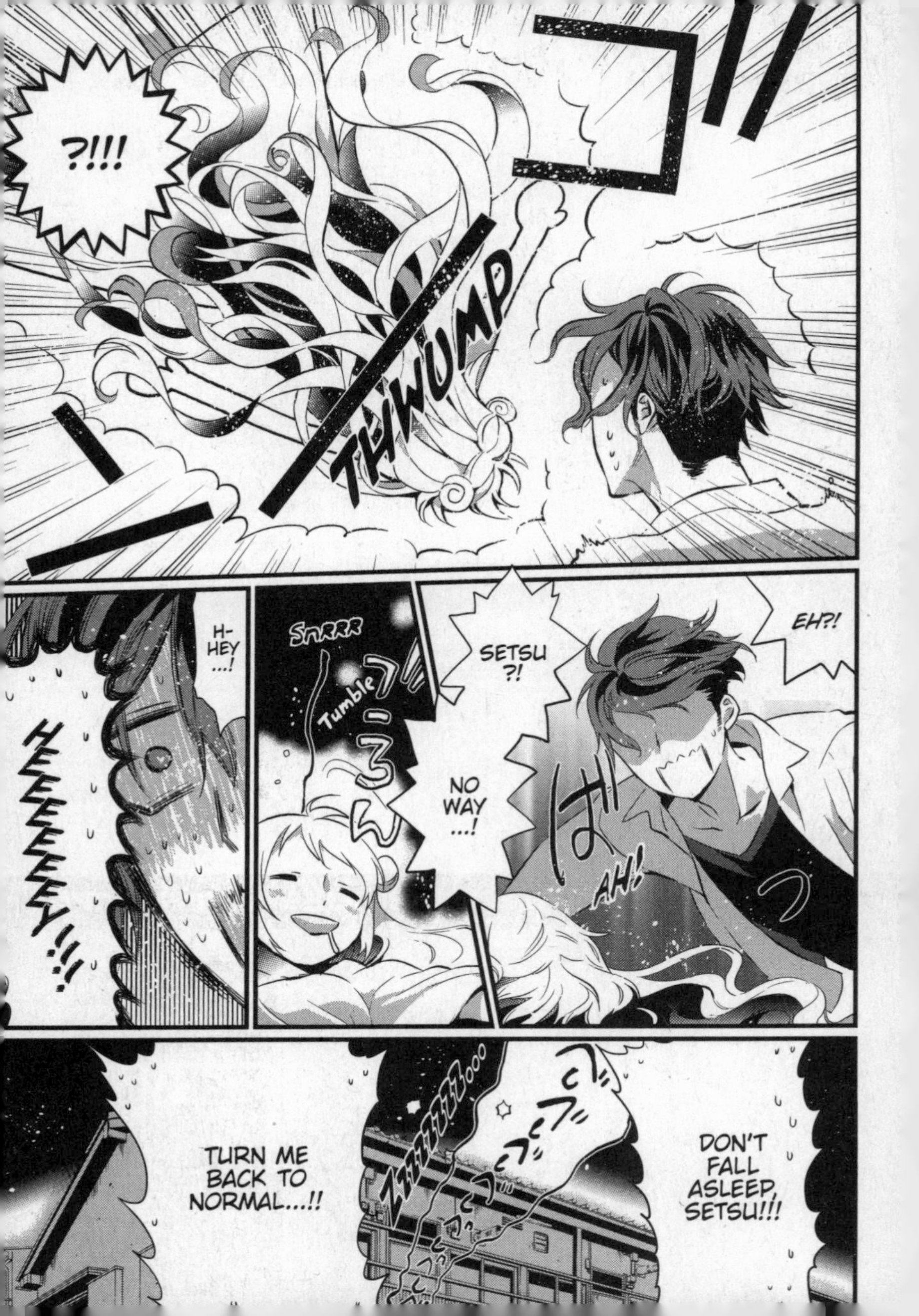
?!!!
THWUMP
EH?!
SETSU ?!
AH!
NO WAY ...!
Snrrr
Tumble
H-HEY ...!
HEEEEEEY!!!!
DON'T FALL ASLEEP, SETSU!!!
ZZZZZZZZZooo
TURN ME BACK TO NORMAL...!!

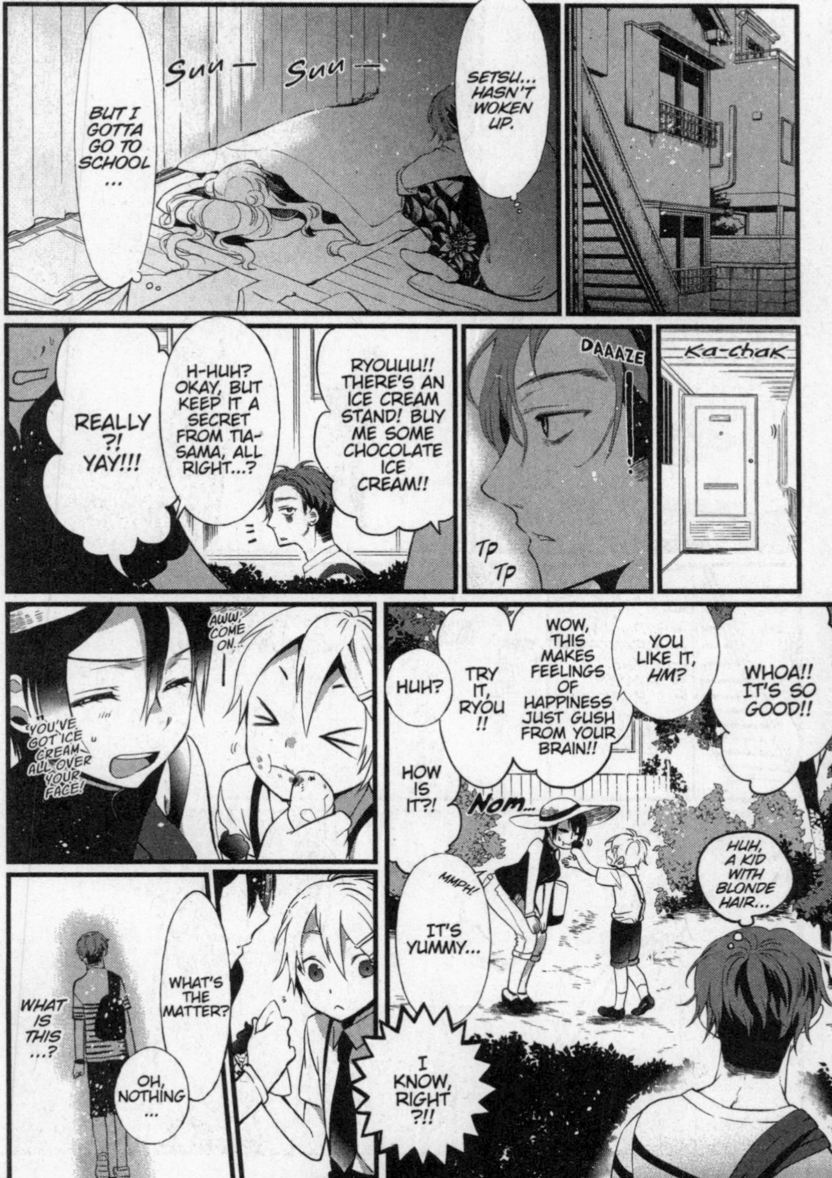
SETSU... HASN'T WOKEN UP.
Suu— Suu—
BUT I GOTTA GO TO SCHOOL...
Ka-chaK
DAAAZE
Tp Tp
RYOUUU!! THERE'S AN ICE CREAM STAND! BUY ME SOME CHOCOLATE ICE CREAM!!
H-HUH? OKAY, BUT KEEP IT A SECRET FROM TIA-SAMA, ALL RIGHT...?
REALLY?! YAY!!!
WHOA!! IT'S SO GOOD!!
YOU LIKE IT, HM?
WOW, THIS MAKES FEELINGS OF HAPPINESS JUST GUSH FROM YOUR BRAIN!!
TRY IT, RYOU!!
HUH?
HOW IS IT?!
Nom...
HUH, A KID WITH BLONDE HAIR...
MMPH!
IT'S YUMMY...
I KNOW, RIGHT?!!
AWW, COME ON...
YOU'VE GOT ICE CREAM ALL OVER YOUR FACE!
WHAT'S THE MATTER?
OH, NOTHING...
WHAT IS THIS...?

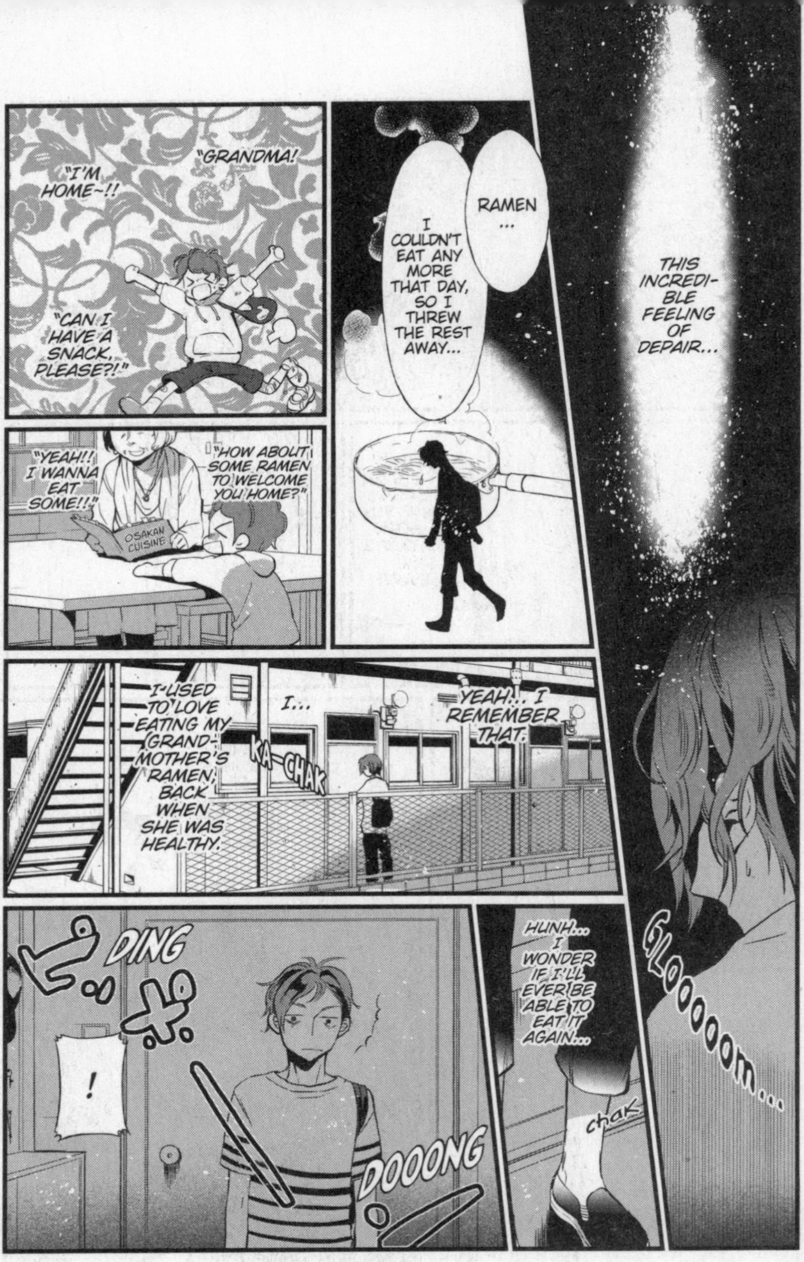
RAMEN ...
I COULDN'T EAT ANY MORE THAT DAY, SO I THREW THE REST AWAY...
THIS INCREDIBLE FEELING OF DEPAIR...
"GRANDMA!
"I'M HOME~!!
"CAN I HAVE A SNACK, PLEASE?!"
"HOW ABOUT SOME RAMEN TO WELCOME YOU HOME?"
"YEAH!! I WANNA EAT SOME!!"
OSAKAN CUISINE
YEAH... I REMEMBER THAT.
I...
I USED TO LOVE EATING MY GRAND-MOTHER'S RAMEN, BACK WHEN SHE WAS HEALTHY.
KA-CHAK
HUNH... I WONDER IF I'LL EVER BE ABLE TO EAT IT AGAIN...
chak
GLOOOOOOM...
DING
!
DOOONG

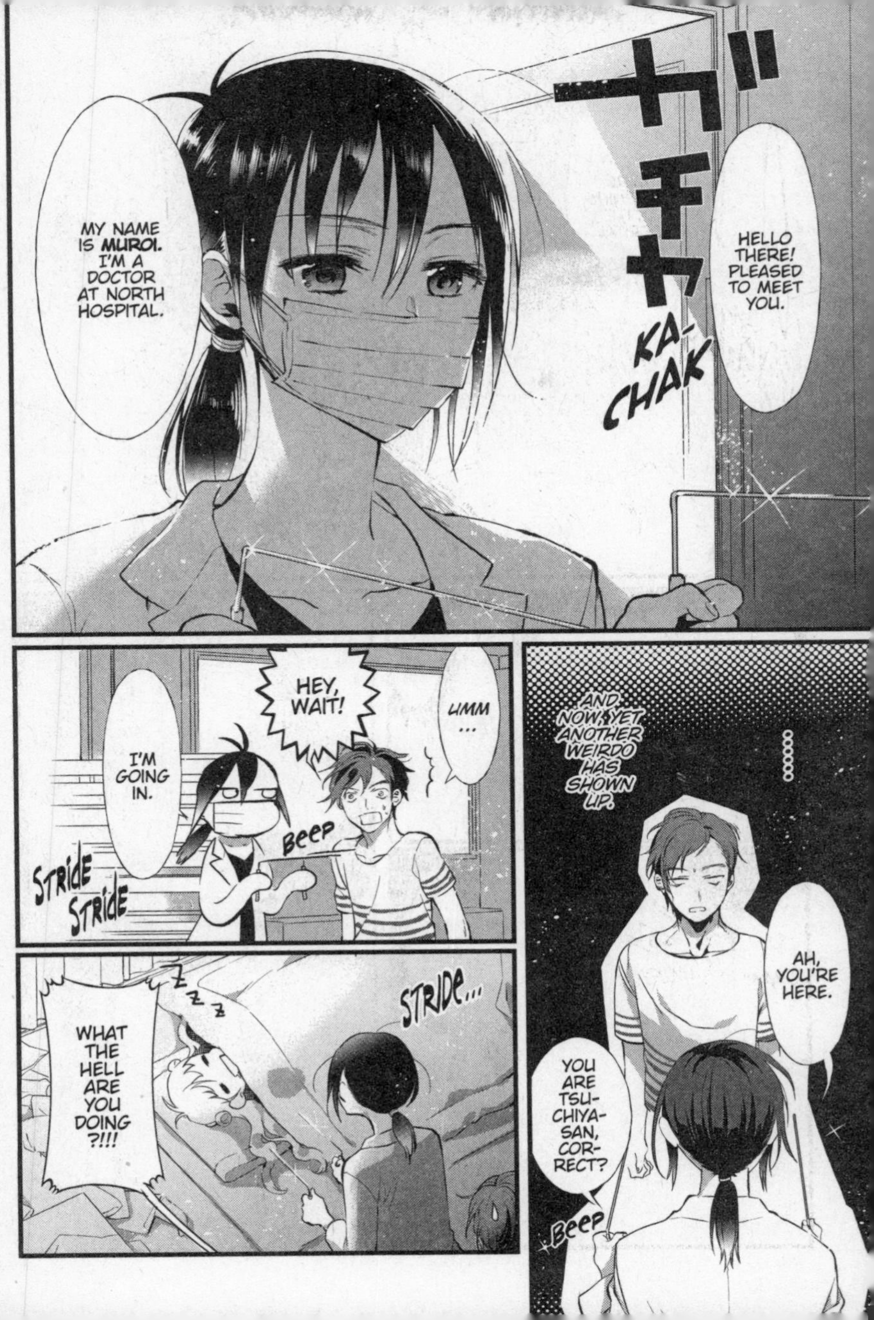
ガチャ
KA-CHAK
HELLO THERE! PLEASED TO MEET YOU.
MY NAME IS MUROI. I'M A DOCTOR AT NORTH HOSPITAL.
AND NOW, YET ANOTHER WEIRDO HAS SHOWN UP.
......
AH, YOU'RE HERE.
YOU ARE TSU-CHIYA-SAN, COR-RECT?
Beep
UMM...
HEY, WAIT!
I'M GOING IN.
Beep
STRIDE STRIDE
STRIDE...
Z Z Z
WHAT THE HELL ARE YOU DOING?!!!

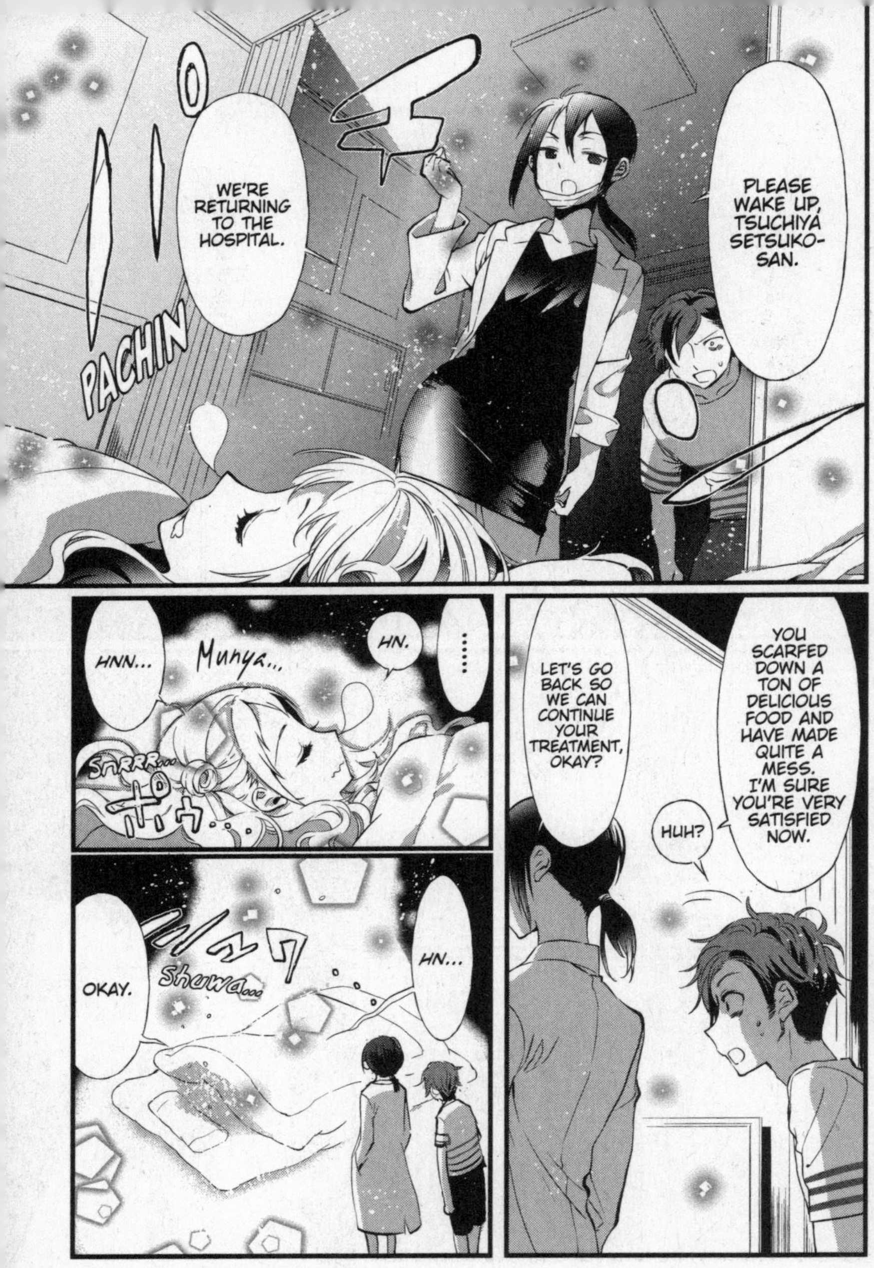
PLEASE WAKE UP, TSUCHIYA SETSUKO-SAN.
WE'RE RETURNING TO THE HOSPITAL.
PACHIN
YOU SCARFED DOWN A TON OF DELICIOUS FOOD AND HAVE MADE QUITE A MESS. I'M SURE YOU'RE VERY SATISFIED NOW.
HUH?
LET'S GO BACK SO WE CAN CONTINUE YOUR TREATMENT, OKAY?
......
HN.
Munya...
HNN...
Snrrr...
HN...
Shuwa...
OKAY.

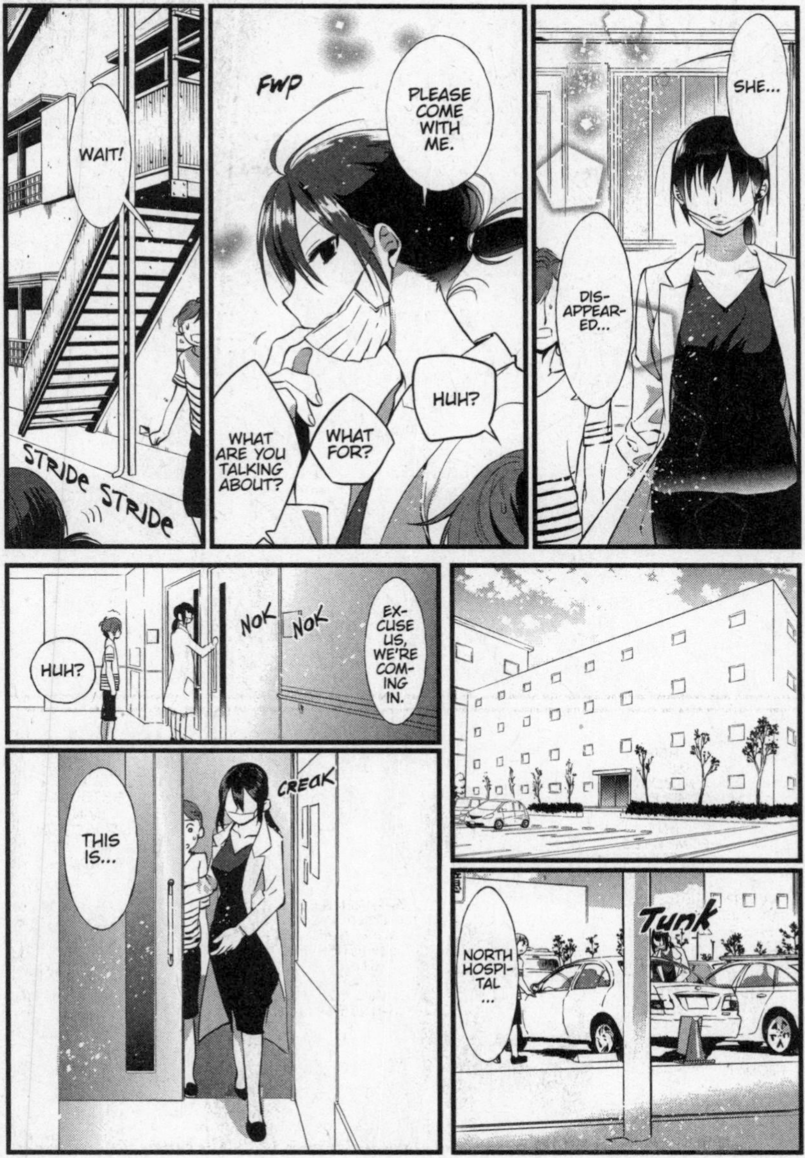
SHE...
DIS-APPEARED...
FWP
PLEASE COME WITH ME.
HUH?
WHAT FOR?
WHAT ARE YOU TALKING ABOUT?
WAIT!
STRIDE STRIDE
Tunk
NORTH HOSPITAL...
NOK NOK
EXCUSE US, WE'RE COMING IN.
HUH?
CREAK
THIS IS...

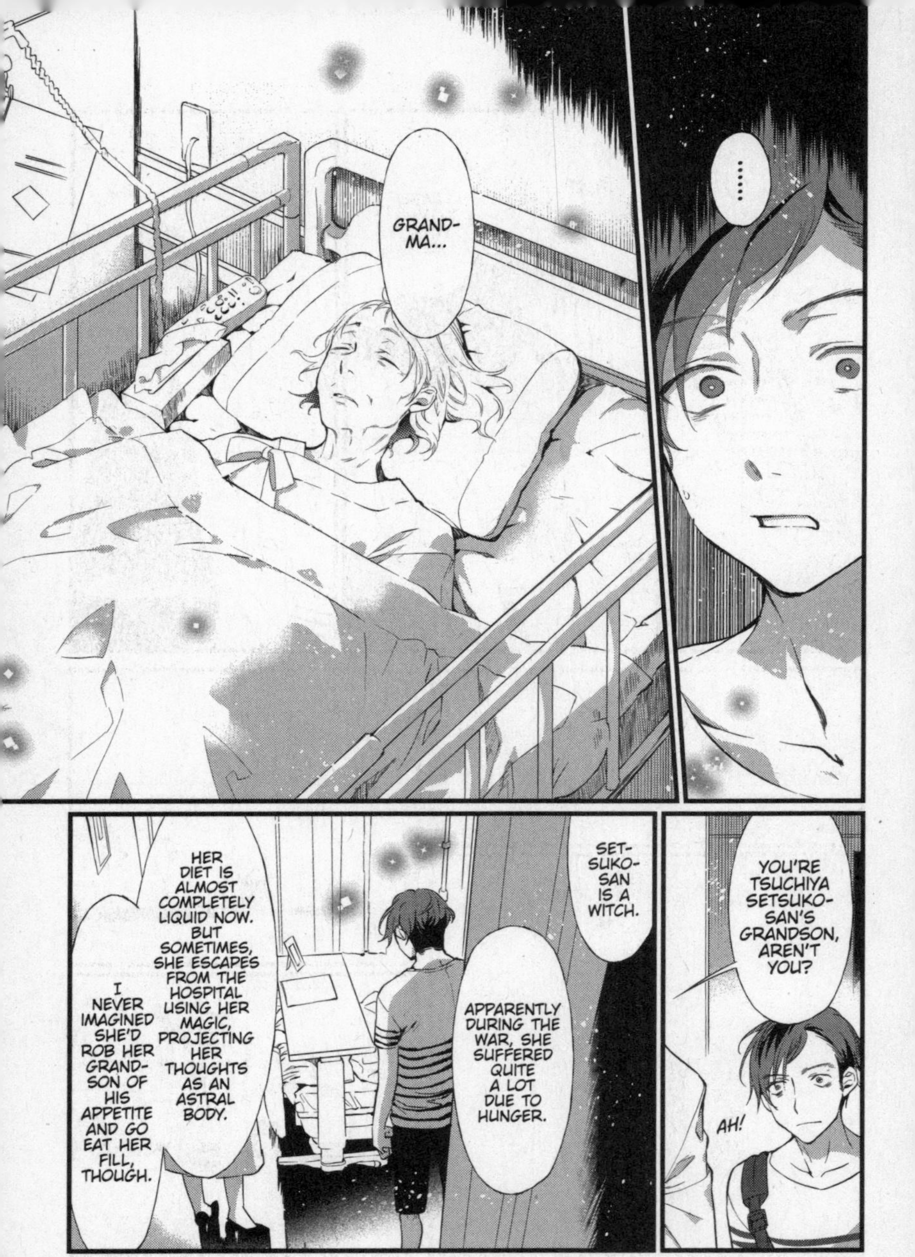
......
GRAND-MA...
YOU'RE TSUCHIYA SETSUKO-SAN'S GRANDSON, AREN'T YOU?
AH!
SET-SUKO-SAN IS A WITCH.
APPARENTLY DURING THE WAR, SHE SUFFERED QUITE A LOT DUE TO HUNGER.
HER DIET IS ALMOST COMPLETELY LIQUID NOW. BUT SOMETIMES, SHE ESCAPES FROM THE HOSPITAL USING HER MAGIC, PROJECTING HER THOUGHTS AS AN ASTRAL BODY.
I NEVER IMAGINED SHE'D ROB HER GRAND-SON OF HIS APPETITE AND GO EAT HER FILL, THOUGH.

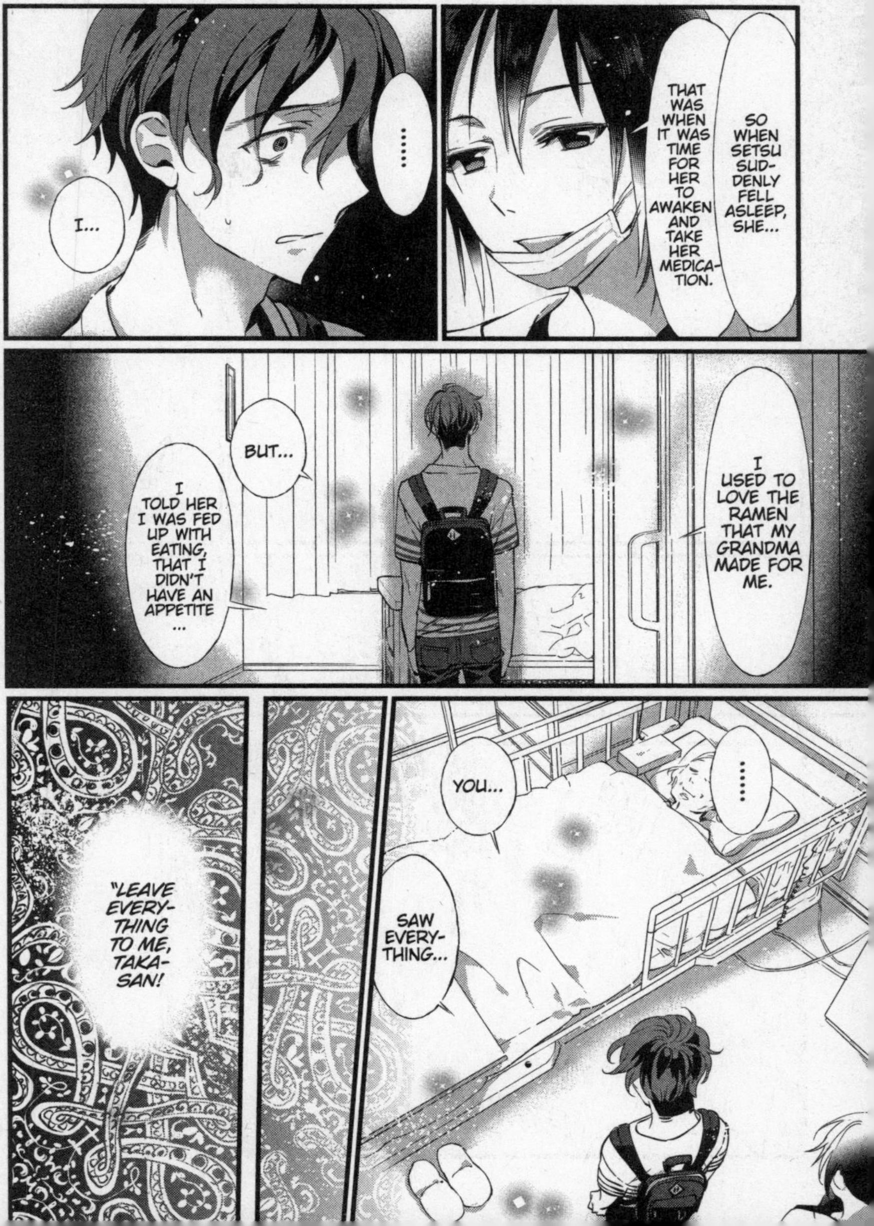
SO WHEN SETSU SUDDENLY FELL ASLEEP, SHE...
THAT WAS WHEN IT WAS TIME FOR HER TO AWAKEN AND TAKE HER MEDICATION.
......
I...
I USED TO LOVE THE RAMEN THAT MY GRANDMA MADE FOR ME.
BUT...
I TOLD HER I WAS FED UP WITH EATING, THAT I DIDN'T HAVE AN APPETITE...
......
YOU...
SAW EVERYTHING...
"LEAVE EVERYTHING TO ME, TAKA-SAN!

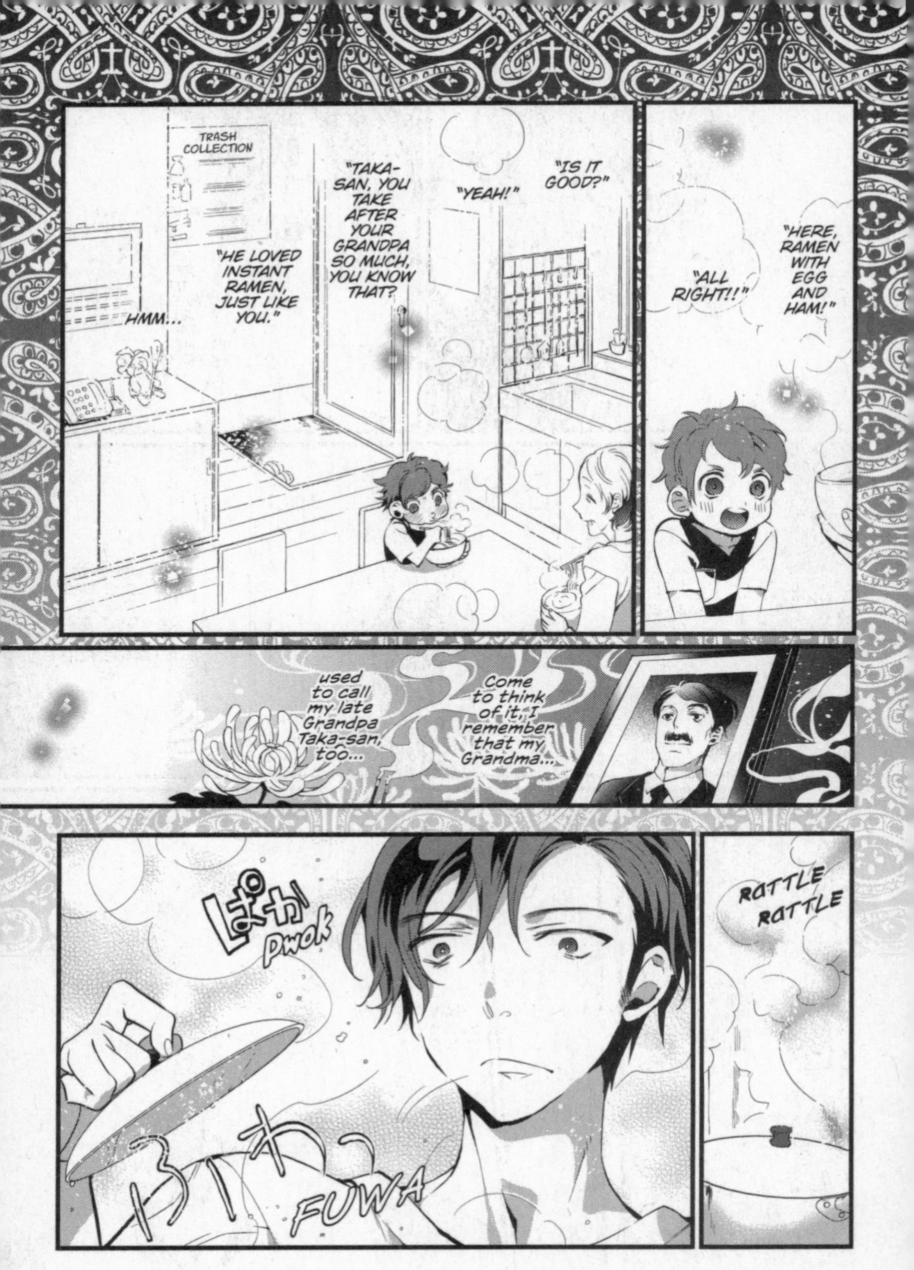
"HERE, RAMEN WITH EGG AND HAM!"
"ALL RIGHT!!"
"IS IT GOOD?"
"YEAH!"
"TAKA-SAN, YOU TAKE AFTER YOUR GRANDPA SO MUCH, YOU KNOW THAT?
TRASH COLLECTION
"HE LOVED INSTANT RAMEN, JUST LIKE YOU."
HMM...
Come to think of it, I remember that my Grandma...
used to call my late Grandpa Taka-san, too...
RATTLE RATTLE
ぱか
pwok
ふわ
FUWA

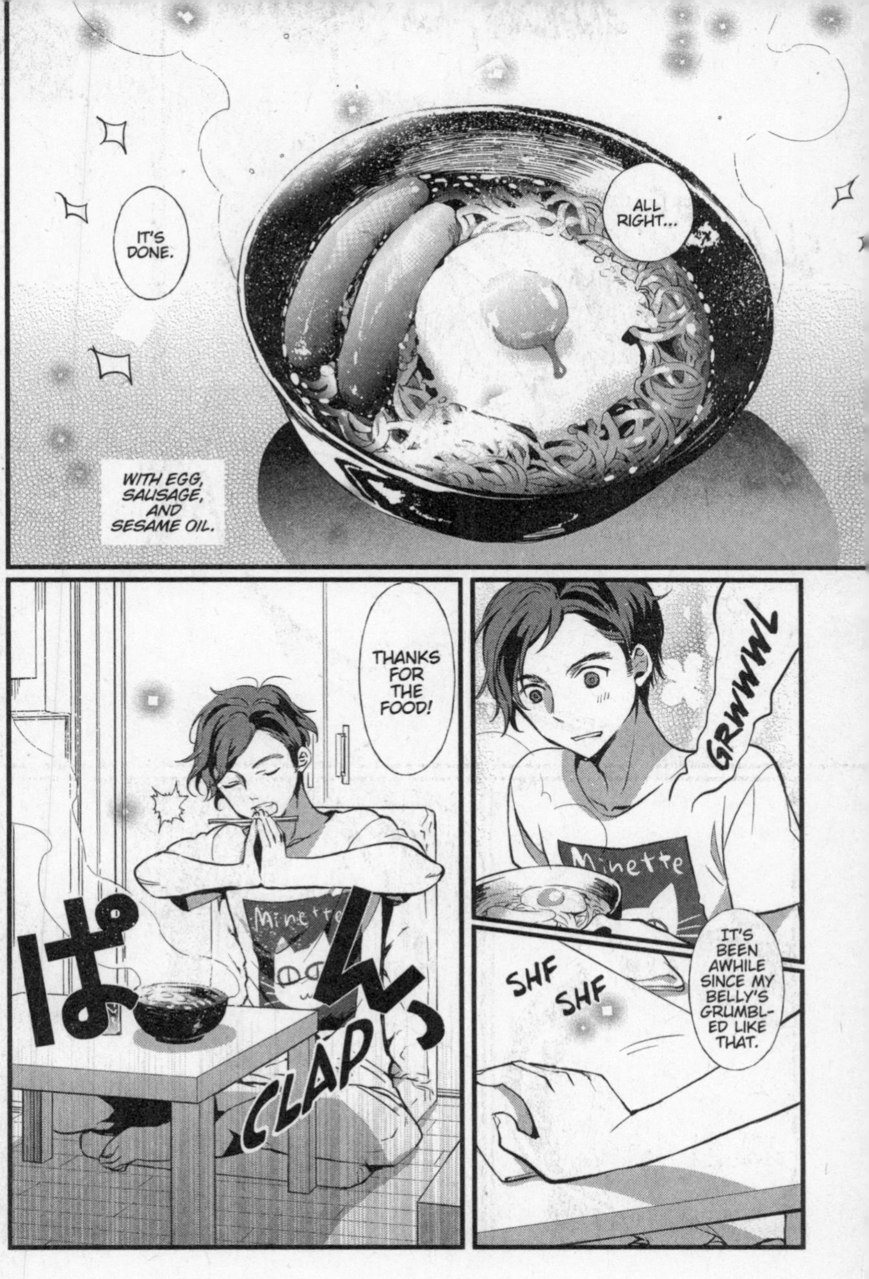
ALL RIGHT...
IT'S DONE.
WITH EGG, SAUSAGE, AND SESAME OIL.
GRWWWL
IT'S BEEN AWHILE SINCE MY BELLY'S GRUMBLED LIKE THAT.
SHF SHF
THANKS FOR THE FOOD!
ぱんっ
CLAP

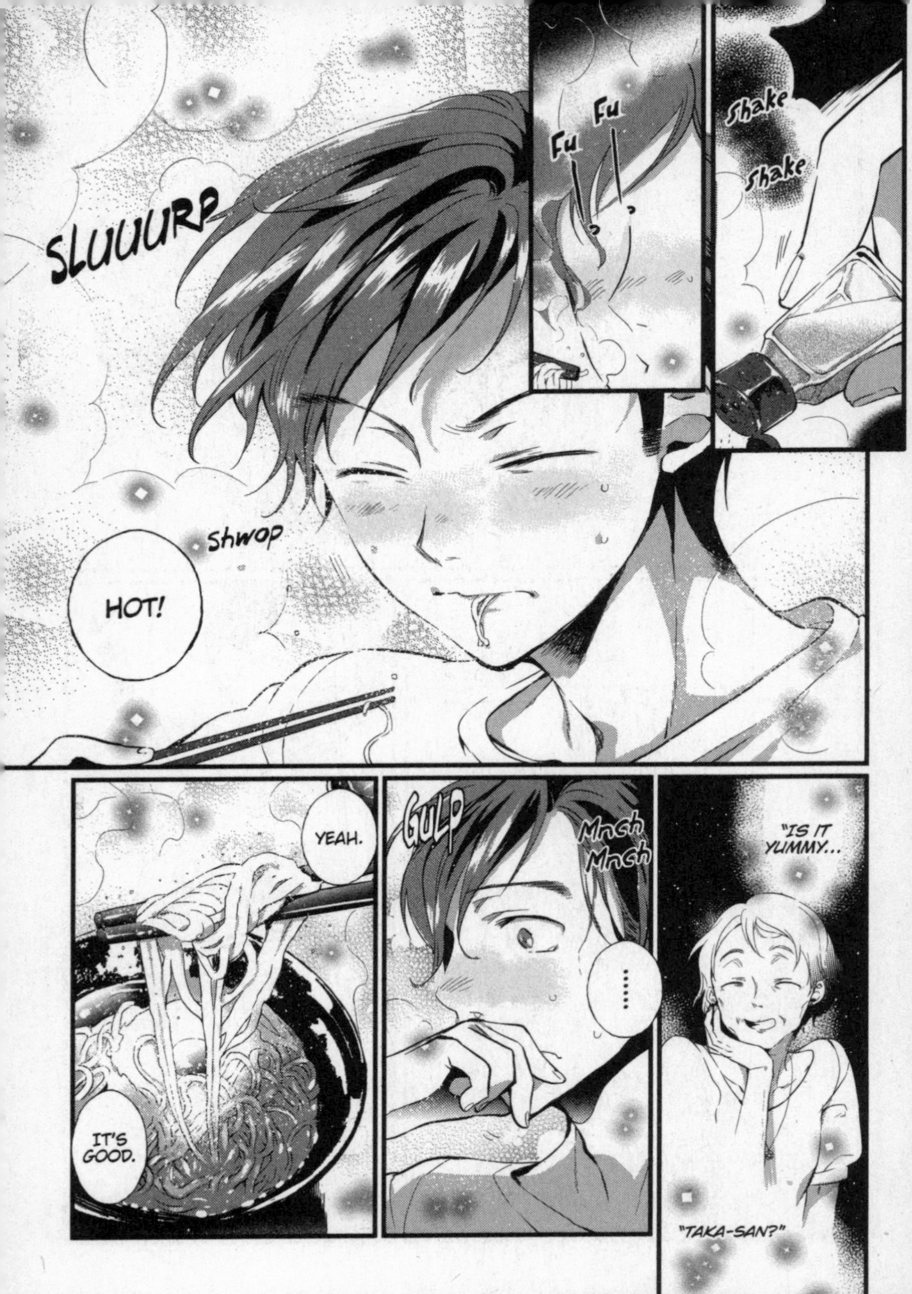
Shake
Shake
Fu
Fu
SLUUURP
Shwop
HOT!
"IS IT YUMMY...
"TAKA-SAN?"
GULP
Mnch
Mnch
......
YEAH.
IT'S GOOD.

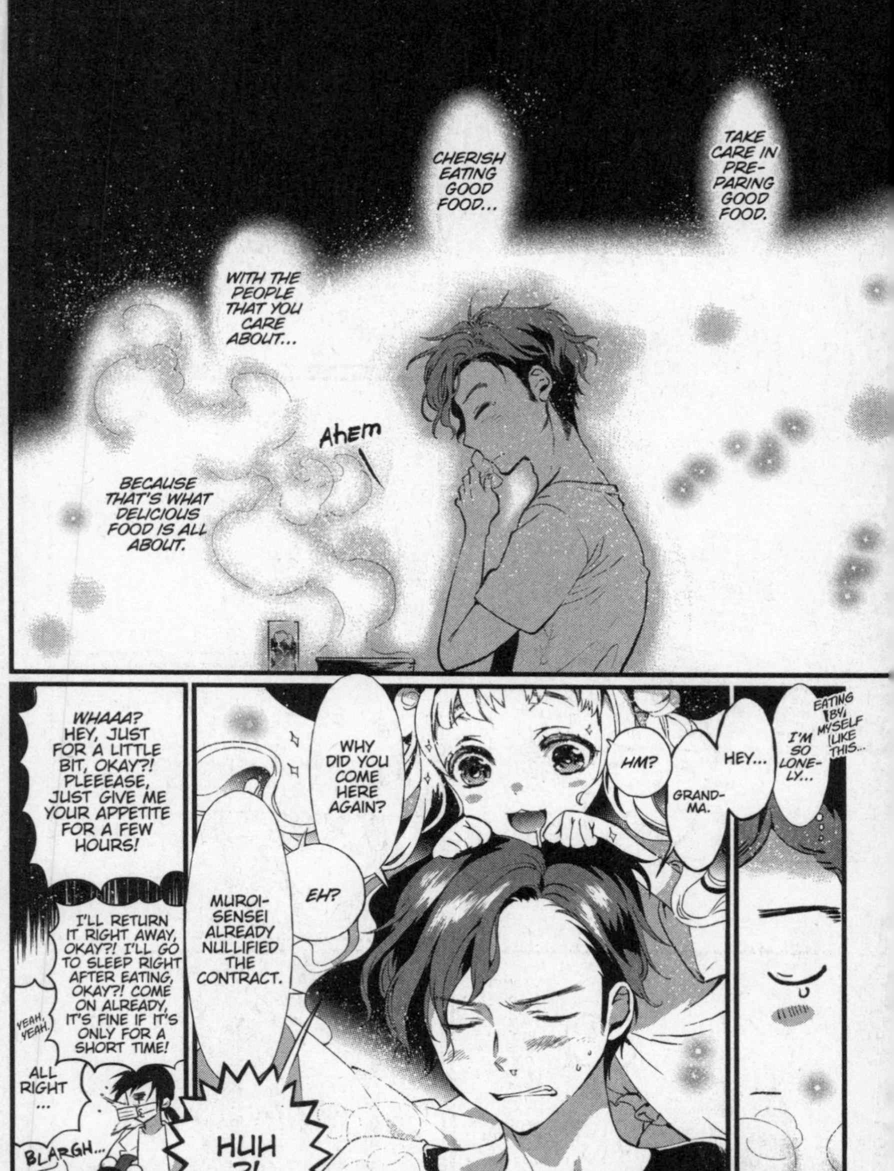
TAKE CARE IN PRE-PARING GOOD FOOD.
CHERISH EATING GOOD FOOD...
WITH THE PEOPLE THAT YOU CARE ABOUT...
Ahem
BECAUSE THAT'S WHAT DELICIOUS FOOD IS ALL ABOUT.
EATING BY MYSELF LIKE THIS...
I'M SO LONE-LY...
HEY...
GRAND-MA.
HM?
WHY DID YOU COME HERE AGAIN?
EH?
MUROI-SENSEI ALREADY NULLIFIED THE CONTRACT.
HUH?!
WHAAAA? HEY, JUST FOR A LITTLE BIT, OKAY?! PLEEEASE, JUST GIVE ME YOUR APPETITE FOR A FEW HOURS!
I'LL RETURN IT RIGHT AWAY, OKAY?! I'LL GO TO SLEEP RIGHT AFTER EATING, OKAY?! COME ON ALREADY, IT'S FINE IF IT'S ONLY FOR A SHORT TIME!
YEAH, YEAH.
ALL RIGHT ...
BLARGH...
Repeat....

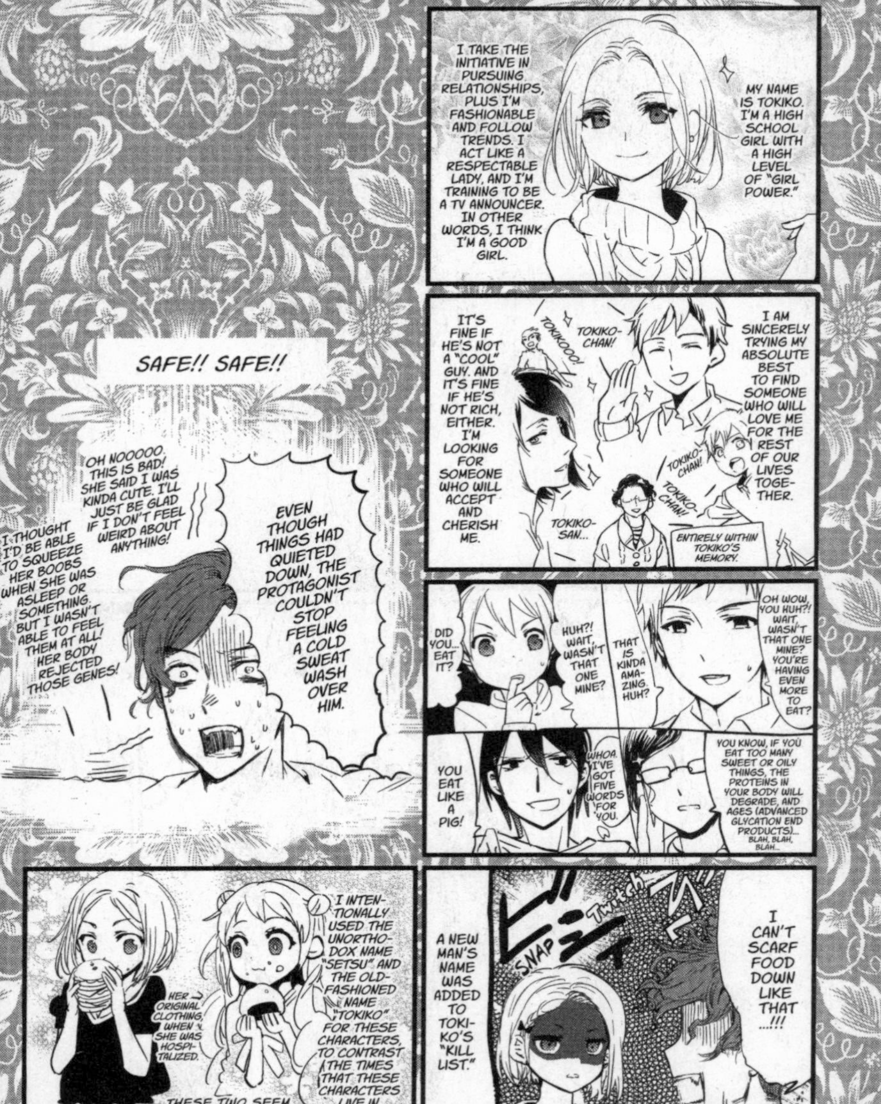
MY NAME IS TOKIKO. I'M A HIGH SCHOOL GIRL WITH A HIGH LEVEL OF "GIRL POWER."
I TAKE THE INITIATIVE IN PURSUING RELATIONSHIPS, PLUS I'M FASHIONABLE AND FOLLOW TRENDS. I ACT LIKE A RESPECTABLE LADY, AND I'M TRAINING TO BE A TV ANNOUNCER. IN OTHER WORDS, I THINK I'M A GOOD GIRL.
I AM SINCERELY TRYING MY ABSOLUTE BEST TO FIND SOMEONE WHO WILL LOVE ME FOR THE REST OF OUR LIVES TOGE-THER.
TOKIKO-CHAN!
TOKIKOOO!
TOKIKO-CHAN!
TOKIKO-CHAN!
TOKIKO-SAN...
IT'S FINE IF HE'S NOT A "COOL" GUY. AND IT'S FINE IF HE'S NOT RICH, EITHER. I'M LOOKING FOR SOMEONE WHO WILL ACCEPT AND CHERISH ME.
ENTIRELY WITHIN TOKIKO'S MEMORY.
OH WOW, YOU HUH?! WAIT, WASN'T THAT ONE MINE? YOU'RE HAVING EVEN MORE TO EAT?
THAT IS KINDA AMA-ZING. HUH?
HUH?! WAIT, WASN'T THAT ONE MINE?
DID YOU... EAT IT?
YOU KNOW, IF YOU EAT TOO MANY SWEET OR OILY THINGS, THE PROTEINS IN YOUR BODY WILL DEGRADE, AND AGES (ADVANCED GLYCATION END PRODUCTS)... BLAH, BLAH, BLAH...
WHOA. I'VE GOT FIVE WORDS FOR YOU.
YOU EAT LIKE A PIG!
I CAN'T SCARF FOOD DOWN LIKE THAT...!!!
Twitch
SNAP
A NEW MAN'S NAME WAS ADDED TO TOKI-KO'S "KILL LIST."
SAFE!! SAFE!!
EVEN THOUGH THINGS HAD QUIETED DOWN, THE PROTAGONIST COULDN'T STOP FEELING A COLD SWEAT WASH OVER HIM.
OH NOOOOO, THIS IS BAD! SHE SAID I WAS KINDA CUTE. I'LL JUST BE GLAD IF I DON'T FEEL WEIRD ABOUT ANYTHING!
I THOUGHT I'D BE ABLE TO SQUEEZE HER BOOBS WHEN SHE WAS ASLEEP OR SOMETHING. BUT I WASN'T ABLE TO FEEL THEM AT ALL! HER BODY REJECTED THOSE GENES!
I INTEN-TIONALLY USED THE UNORTHO-DOX NAME "SETSU" AND THE OLD-FASHIONED NAME "TOKIKO" FOR THESE CHARACTERS, TO CONTRAST THE TIMES THAT THESE CHARACTERS LIVE IN.
HER ORIGINAL CLOTHING, WHEN SHE WAS HOSPI-TALIZED.
THESE TWO SEEM LIKE THEY'D GET ALONG REALLY WELL.

Generation WITCH

CHAPTER 22

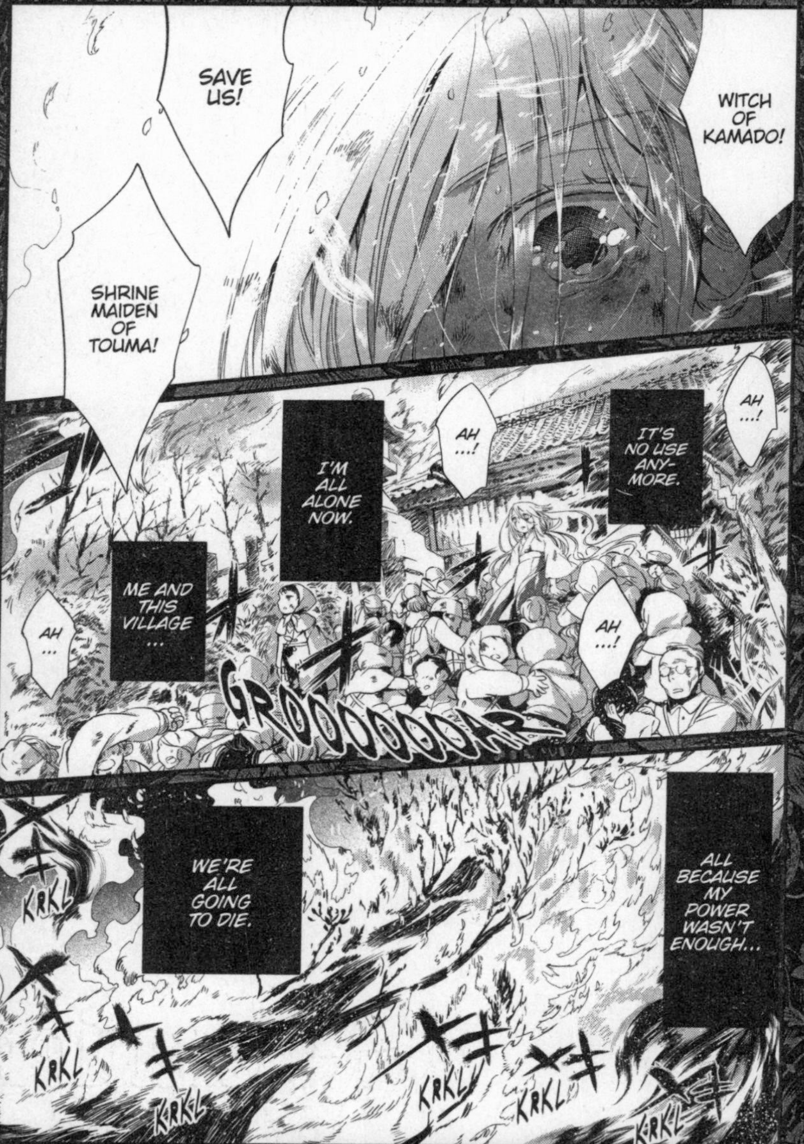
WITCH OF KAMADO!
SAVE US!
SHRINE MAIDEN OF TOUMA!
AH ...!
IT'S NO USE ANYMORE.
AH ...!
I'M ALL ALONE NOW.
ME AND THIS VILLAGE ...
AH ...!
AH ...
GROOOOOOOAR!
ALL BECAUSE MY POWER WASN'T ENOUGH...
WE'RE ALL GOING TO DIE.
KRKL
KRKL
KRKL
KRKL
KRKL
KRKL
KRKL

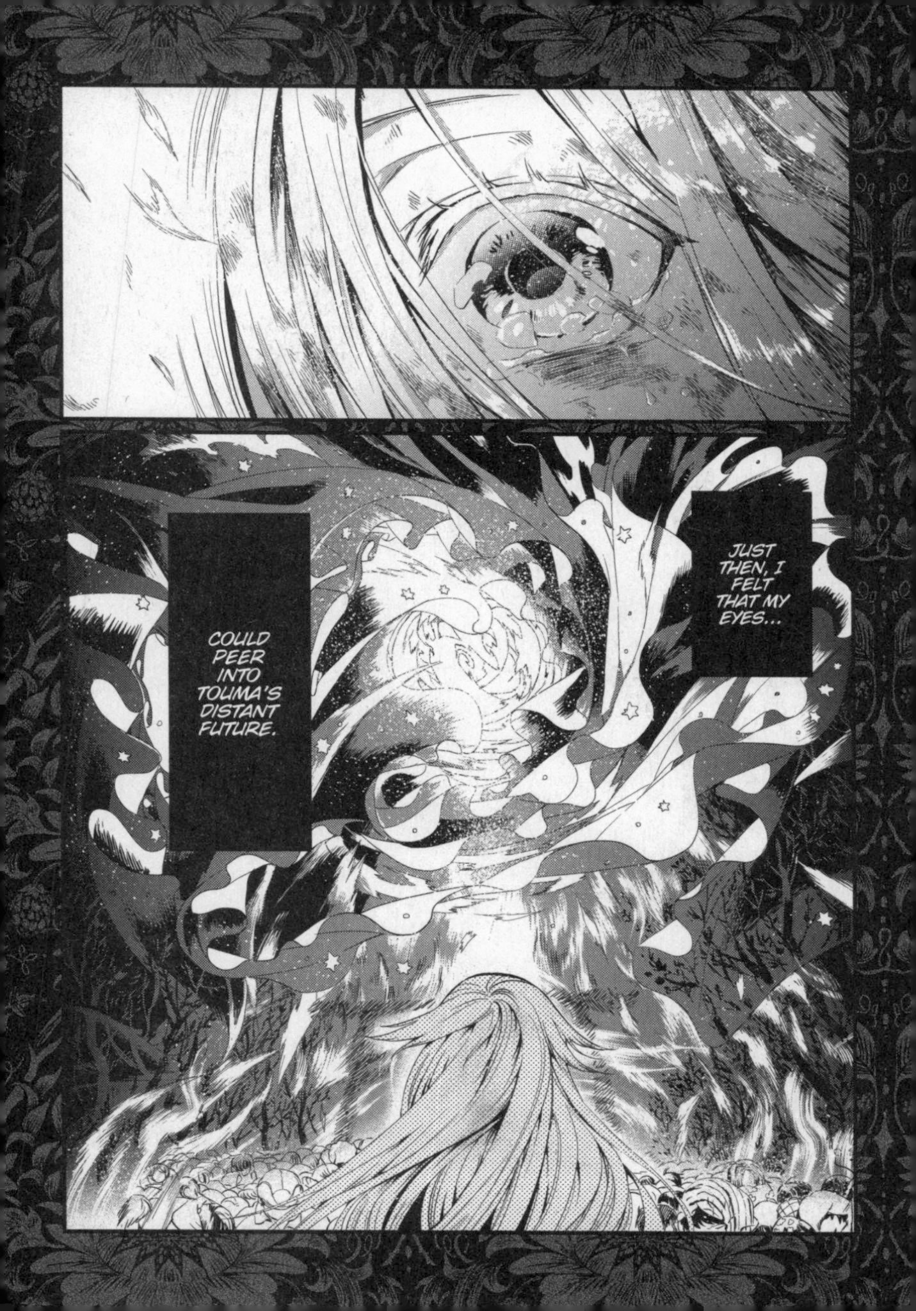
JUST THEN, I FELT THAT MY EYES...
COULD PEER INTO TOUMA'S DISTANT FUTURE.

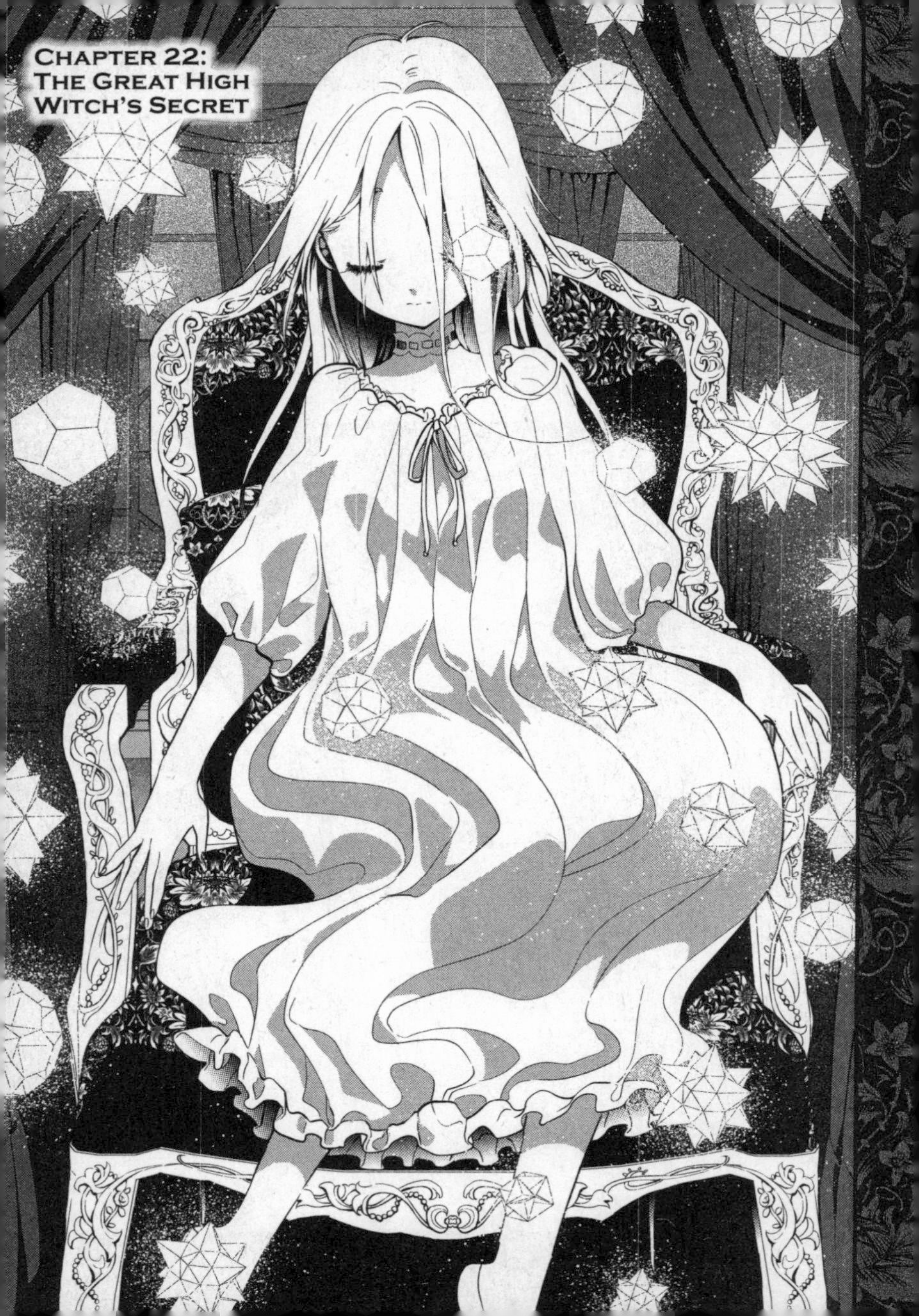
Chapter 22:
The Great High
Witch's Secret

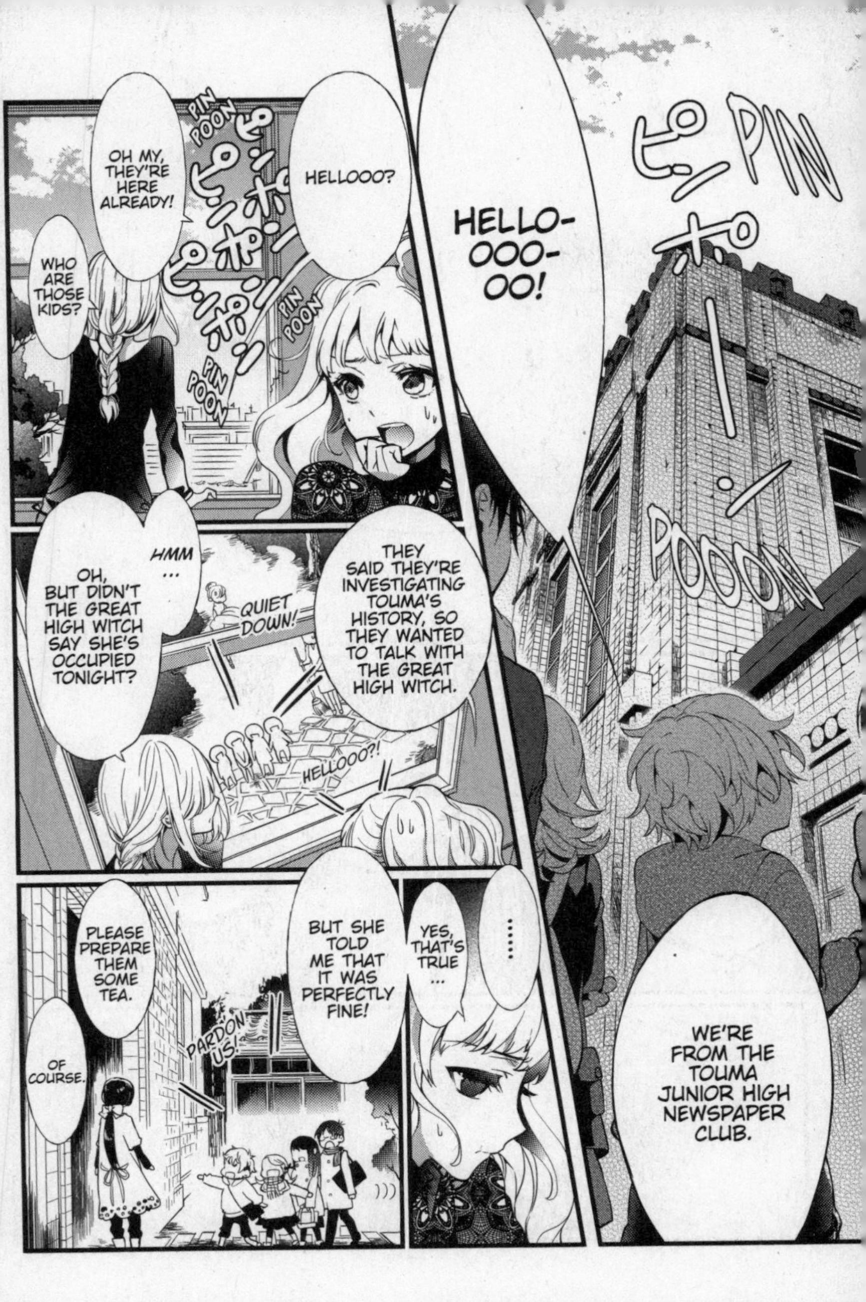
PIN
POOON
HELLO-OOO-OO!
WE'RE FROM THE TOUMA JUNIOR HIGH NEWSPAPER CLUB.
HELLOOO?
PIN POON
PIN POON
PIN POON
OH MY, THEY'RE HERE ALREADY!
WHO ARE THOSE KIDS?
THEY SAID THEY'RE INVESTIGATING TOUMA'S HISTORY, SO THEY WANTED TO TALK WITH THE GREAT HIGH WITCH.
HMM...
OH, BUT DIDN'T THE GREAT HIGH WITCH SAY SHE'S OCCUPIED TONIGHT?
QUIET DOWN!
HELLOOO?!
......
YES, THAT'S TRUE...
BUT SHE TOLD ME THAT IT WAS PERFECTLY FINE!
PLEASE PREPARE THEM SOME TEA.
PARDON US!
OF COURSE.

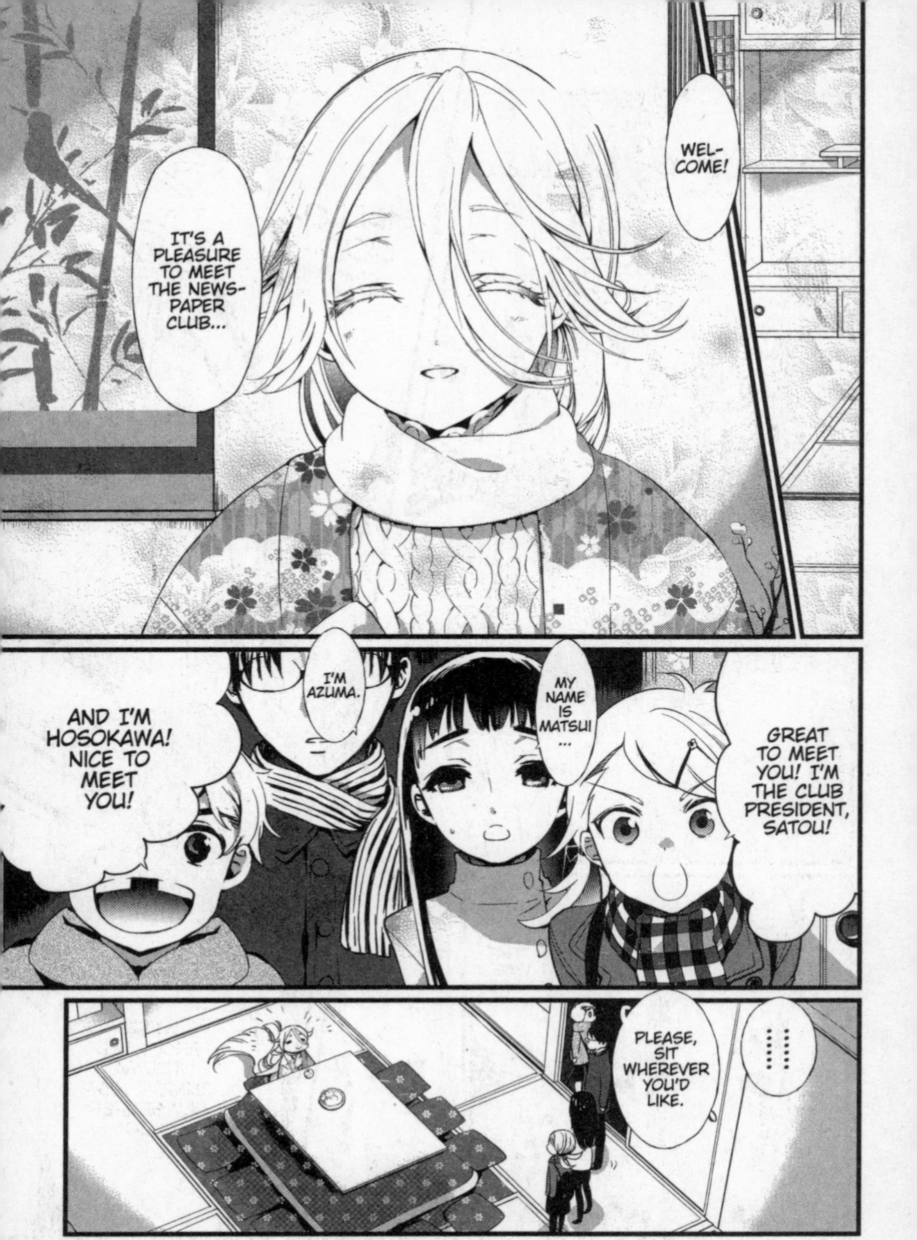
WEL-COME!
IT'S A PLEASURE TO MEET THE NEWS-PAPER CLUB...
GREAT TO MEET YOU! I'M THE CLUB PRESIDENT, SATOU!
MY NAME IS MATSUI ...
I'M AZUMA.
AND I'M HOSOKAWA! NICE TO MEET YOU!
......
PLEASE, SIT WHEREVER YOU'D LIKE.

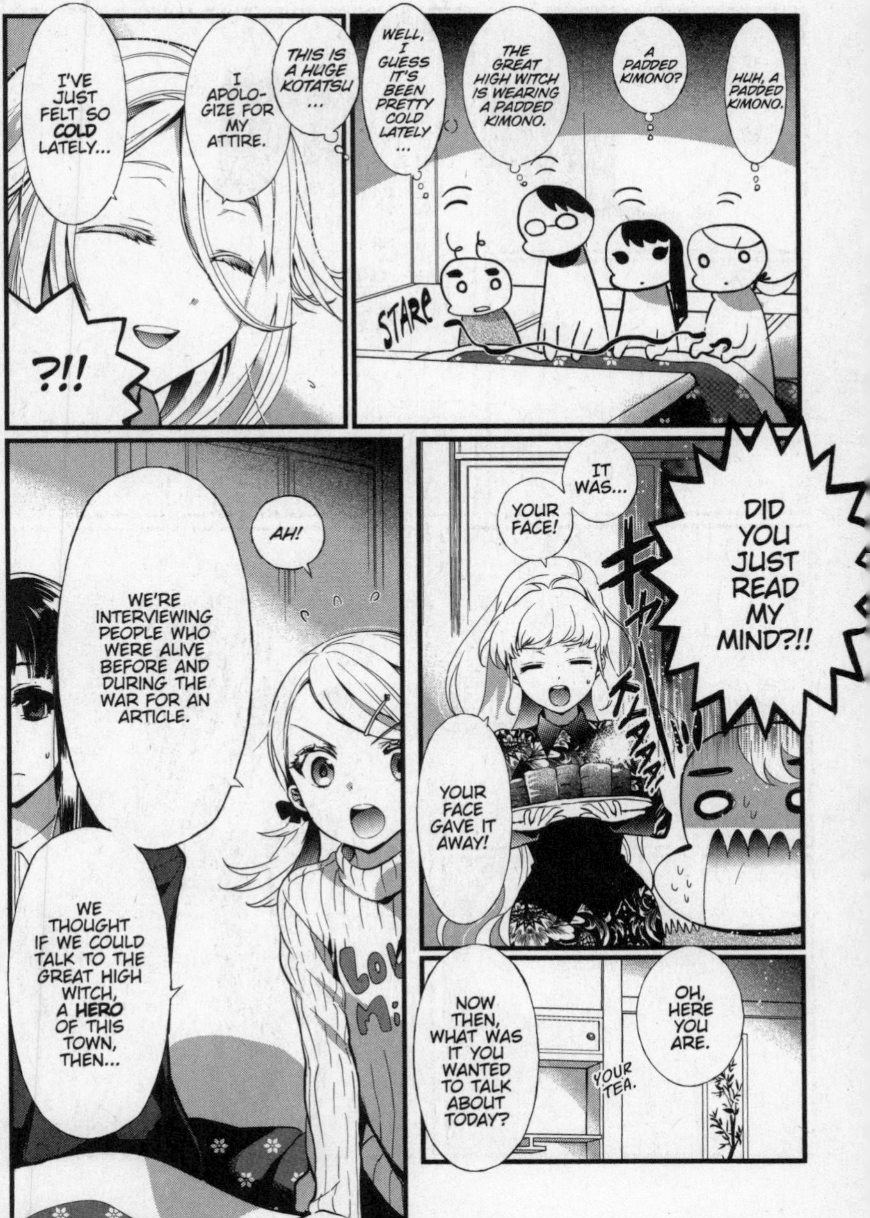
HUH, A PADDED KIMONO.
A PADDED KIMONO?
THE GREAT HIGH WITCH IS WEARING A PADDED KIMONO.
WELL, I GUESS IT'S BEEN PRETTY COLD LATELY...
STARE
THIS IS A HUGE KOTATSU...
I APOLOGIZE FOR MY ATTIRE.
I'VE JUST FELT SO COLD LATELY...
?!!
DID YOU JUST READ MY MIND?!!
IT WAS...
YOUR FACE!
KYAAA!
YOUR FACE GAVE IT AWAY!
OH, HERE YOU ARE.
YOUR TEA.
NOW THEN, WHAT WAS IT YOU WANTED TO TALK ABOUT TODAY?
AH!
WE'RE INTERVIEWING PEOPLE WHO WERE ALIVE BEFORE AND DURING THE WAR FOR AN ARTICLE.
WE THOUGHT IF WE COULD TALK TO THE GREAT HIGH WITCH, A HERO OF THIS TOWN, THEN...

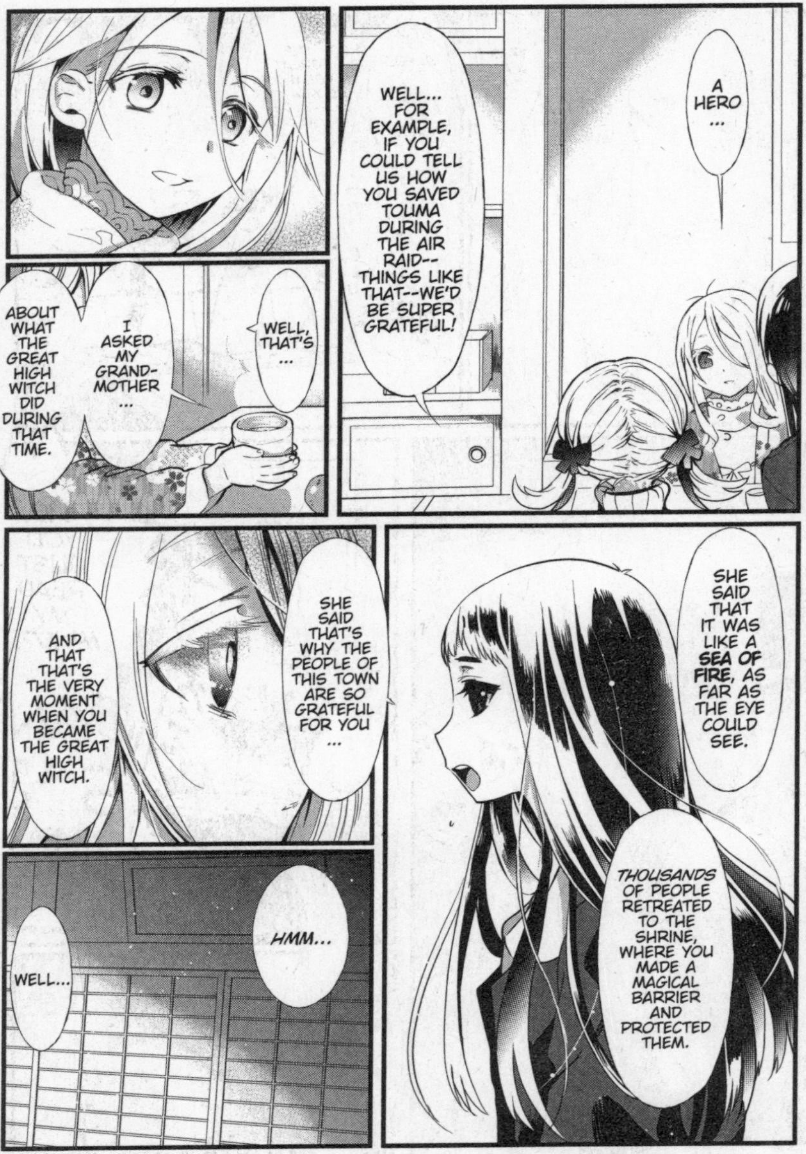
A HERO ...
WELL... FOR EXAMPLE, IF YOU COULD TELL US HOW YOU SAVED TOUMA DURING THE AIR RAID--THINGS LIKE THAT--WE'D BE SUPER GRATEFUL!
WELL, THAT'S ...
I ASKED MY GRAND-MOTHER ...
ABOUT WHAT THE GREAT HIGH WITCH DID DURING THAT TIME.
SHE SAID THAT IT WAS LIKE A **SEA OF FIRE**, AS FAR AS THE EYE COULD SEE.
THOUSANDS OF PEOPLE RETREATED TO THE SHRINE, WHERE YOU MADE A MAGICAL BARRIER AND PROTECTED THEM.
SHE SAID THAT'S WHY THE PEOPLE OF THIS TOWN ARE SO GRATEFUL FOR YOU ...
AND THAT THAT'S THE VERY MOMENT WHEN YOU BECAME THE GREAT HIGH WITCH.
HMM...
WELL...

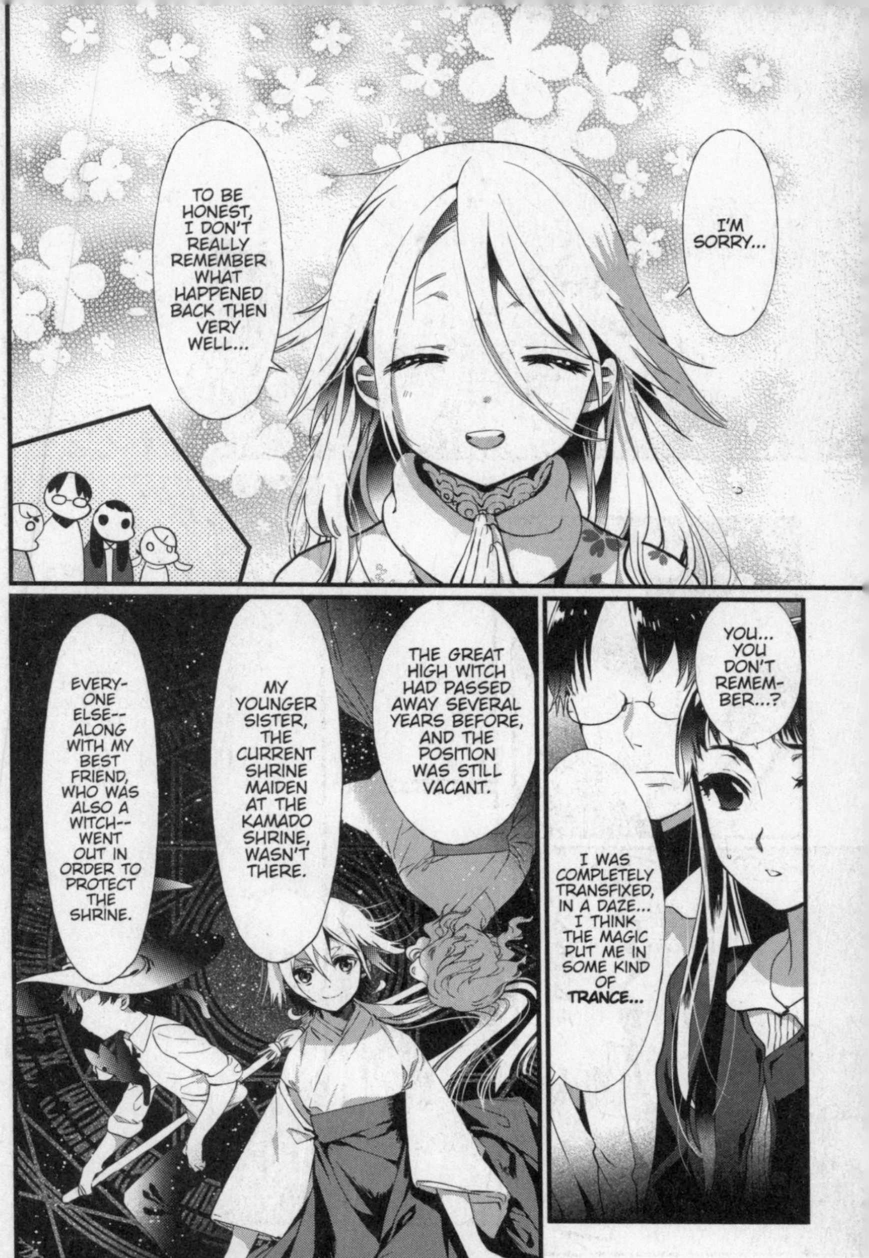
I'M SORRY...
TO BE HONEST, I DON'T REALLY REMEMBER WHAT HAPPENED BACK THEN VERY WELL...
YOU... YOU DON'T REMEMBER...?
I WAS COMPLETELY TRANSFIXED, IN A DAZE... I THINK THE MAGIC PUT ME IN SOME KIND OF TRANCE...
THE GREAT HIGH WITCH HAD PASSED AWAY SEVERAL YEARS BEFORE, AND THE POSITION WAS STILL VACANT.
MY YOUNGER SISTER, THE CURRENT SHRINE MAIDEN AT THE KAMADO SHRINE, WASN'T THERE.
EVERYONE ELSE--ALONG WITH MY BEST FRIEND, WHO WAS ALSO A WITCH--WENT OUT IN ORDER TO PROTECT THE SHRINE.

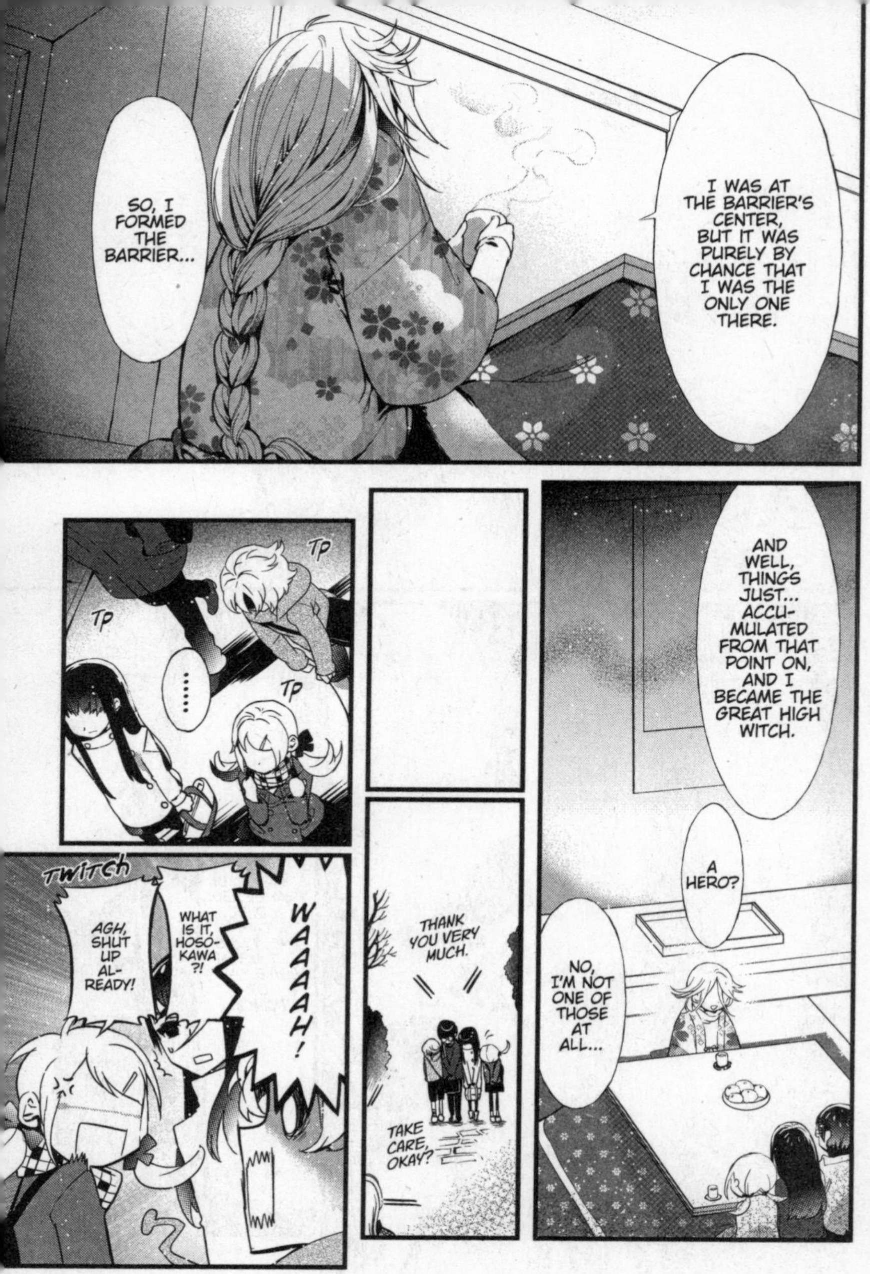
I WAS AT THE BARRIER'S CENTER, BUT IT WAS PURELY BY CHANCE THAT I WAS THE ONLY ONE THERE.
SO, I FORMED THE BARRIER...
AND WELL, THINGS JUST... ACCU-MULATED FROM THAT POINT ON, AND I BECAME THE GREAT HIGH WITCH.
A HERO?
NO, I'M NOT ONE OF THOSE AT ALL...
THANK YOU VERY MUCH.
TAKE CARE, OKAY?
Tp
Tp
......
Tp
WAAAAAH!
WHAT IS IT, HOSO-KAWA?!
AGH, SHUT UP AL-READY!
TWITCH

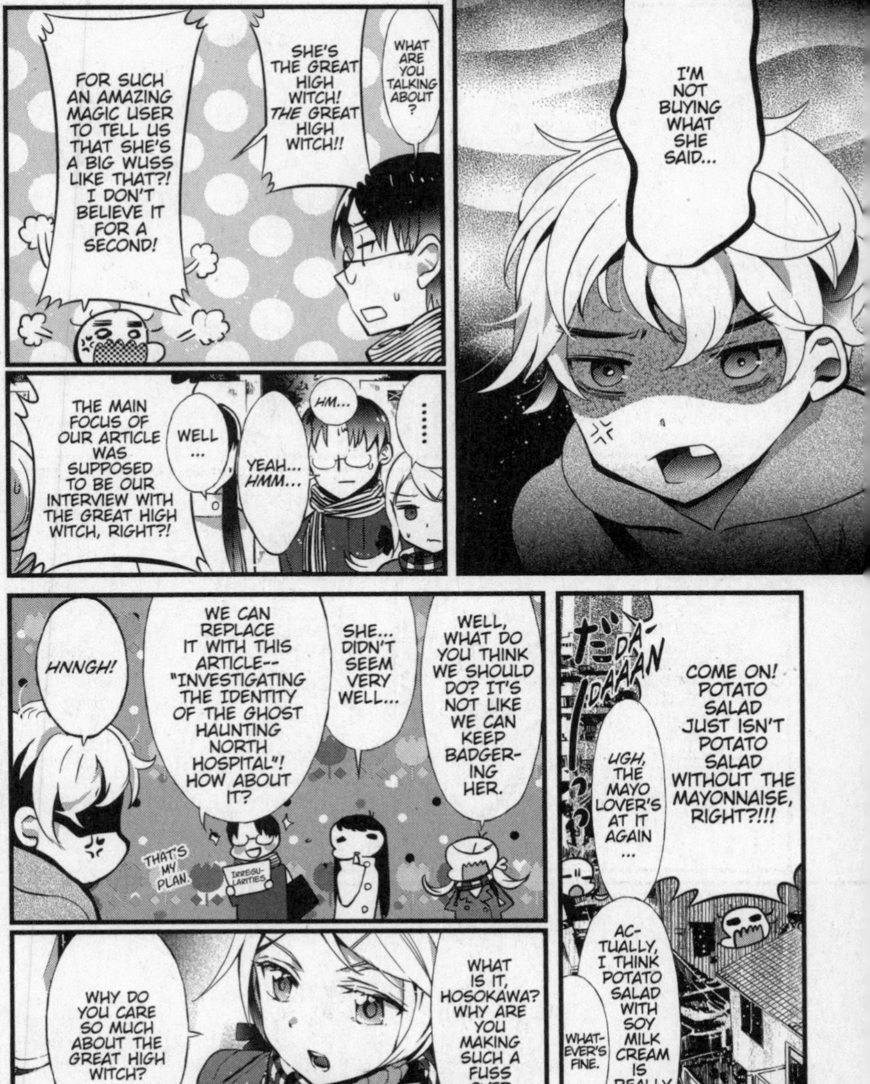
I'M NOT BUYING WHAT SHE SAID...
WHAT ARE YOU TALKING ABOUT?
SHE'S THE GREAT HIGH WITCH! THE GREAT HIGH WITCH!!
FOR SUCH AN AMAZING MAGIC USER TO TELL US THAT SHE'S A BIG WUSS LIKE THAT?! I DON'T BELIEVE IT FOR A SECOND!
......
HM...
YEAH... HMM...
WELL...
THE MAIN FOCUS OF OUR ARTICLE WAS SUPPOSED TO BE OUR INTERVIEW WITH THE GREAT HIGH WITCH, RIGHT?!
DA DAAAN
COME ON! POTATO SALAD JUST ISN'T POTATO SALAD WITHOUT THE MAYONNAISE, RIGHT?!!!
UGH, THE MAYO LOVER'S AT IT AGAIN...
ACTUALLY, I THINK POTATO SALAD WITH SOY MILK CREAM IS REALLY GOOD, TOO! ♥
WHATEVER'S FINE.
WELL, WHAT DO YOU THINK WE SHOULD DO? IT'S NOT LIKE WE CAN KEEP BADGERING HER.
SHE... DIDN'T SEEM VERY WELL...
WE CAN REPLACE IT WITH THIS ARTICLE-- "INVESTIGATING THE IDENTITY OF THE GHOST HAUNTING NORTH HOSPITAL"! HOW ABOUT IT?
HNNGH!
THAT'S MY PLAN.
IRREGULARITIES
WHAT IS IT, HOSOKAWA? WHY ARE YOU MAKING SUCH A FUSS OVER THIS?
WHY DO YOU CARE SO MUCH ABOUT THE GREAT HIGH WITCH?

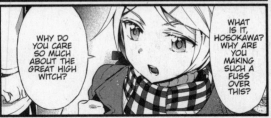

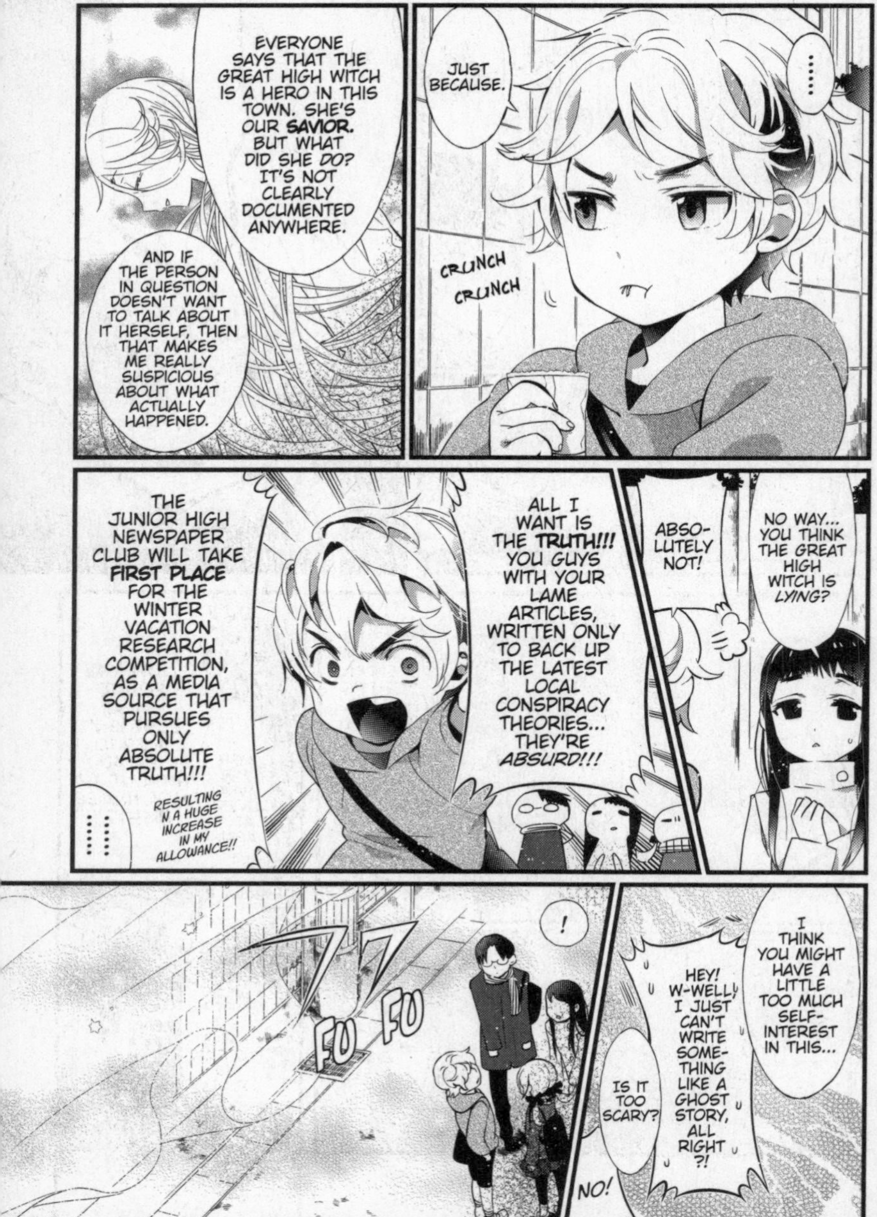

JUST BECAUSE.
......
CRUNCH
CRUNCH
EVERYONE SAYS THAT THE GREAT HIGH WITCH IS A HERO IN THIS TOWN. SHE'S OUR **SAVIOR.** BUT WHAT DID SHE *DO?* IT'S NOT CLEARLY DOCUMENTED ANYWHERE.
AND IF THE PERSON IN QUESTION DOESN'T WANT TO TALK ABOUT IT HERSELF, THEN THAT MAKES ME REALLY SUSPICIOUS ABOUT WHAT ACTUALLY HAPPENED.
NO WAY... YOU THINK THE GREAT HIGH WITCH IS *LYING?*
ABSO-LUTELY NOT!
ALL I WANT IS THE **TRUTH!!!** YOU GUYS WITH YOUR LAME ARTICLES, WRITTEN ONLY TO BACK UP THE LATEST LOCAL CONSPIRACY THEORIES... THEY'RE *ABSURD!!!*
THE JUNIOR HIGH NEWSPAPER CLUB WILL TAKE **FIRST PLACE** FOR THE WINTER VACATION RESEARCH COMPETITION, AS A MEDIA SOURCE THAT PURSUES ONLY ABSOLUTE TRUTH!!!
RESULTING N A HUGE INCREASE IN MY ALLOWANCE!!
......
I THINK YOU MIGHT HAVE A LITTLE TOO MUCH SELF-INTEREST IN THIS...
HEY! W-WELL, I JUST CAN'T WRITE SOME-THING LIKE A GHOST STORY, ALL RIGHT ?!
IS IT TOO SCARY?
NO!
!
FU FU

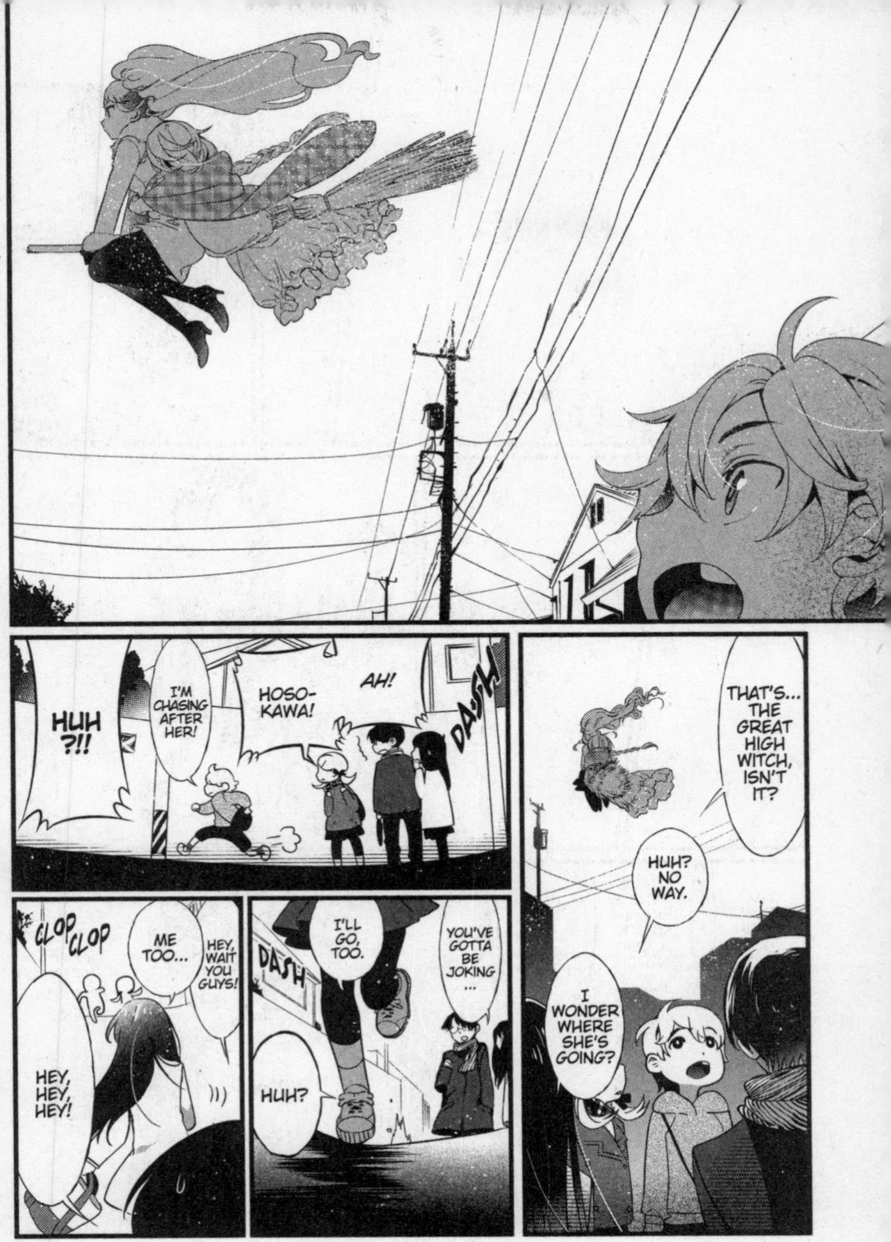
THAT'S... THE GREAT HIGH WITCH, ISN'T IT?
HUH? NO WAY.
I WONDER WHERE SHE'S GOING?
DASH
AH!
HOSO-KAWA!
I'M CHASING AFTER HER!
HUH ?!!
YOU'VE GOTTA BE JOKING ...
I'LL GO, TOO.
DASH
HUH?
HEY, WAIT YOU GUYS!
ME TOO...
CLOP CLOP
HEY, HEY, HEY!

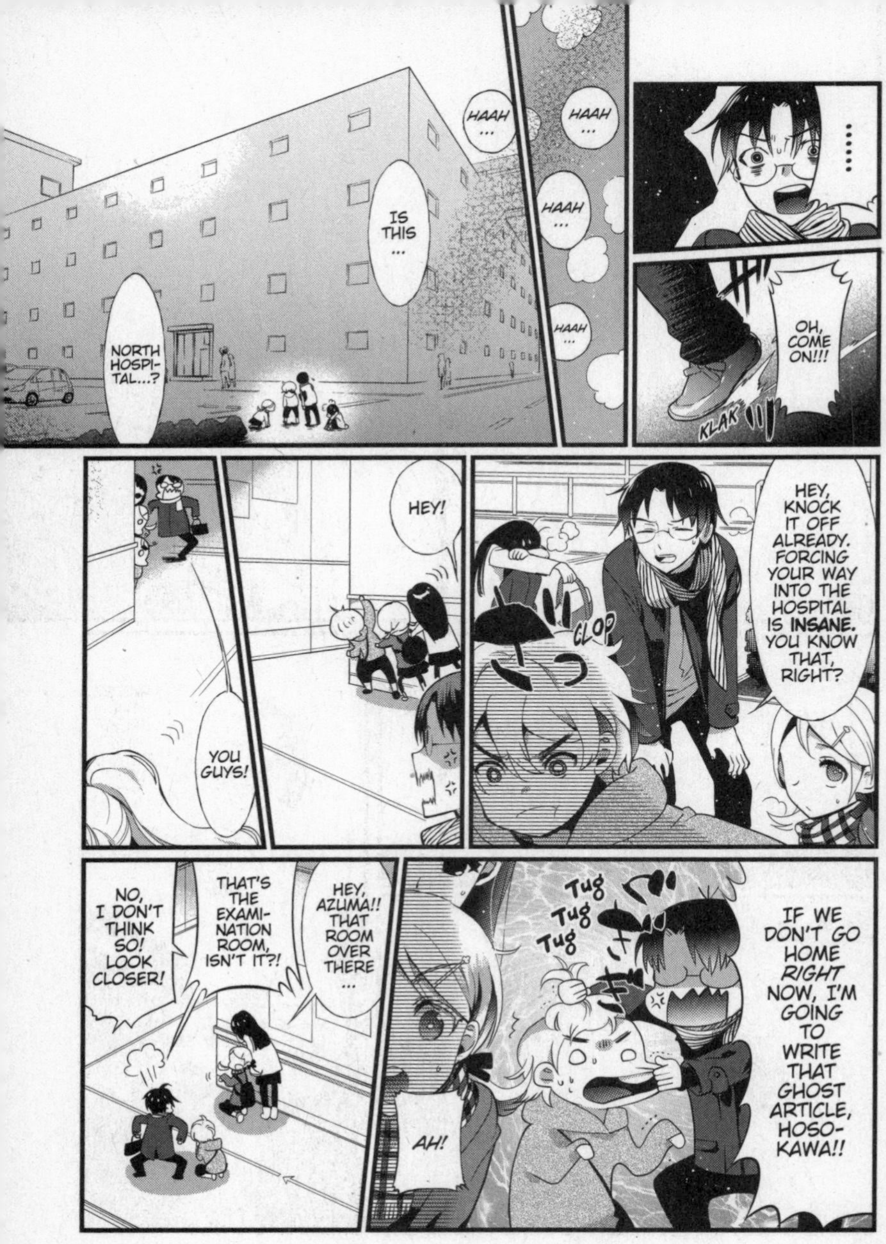
......
OH, COME ON!!!
KLAK
HAAH ...
HAAH ...
HAAH ...
HAAH ...
IS THIS ...
NORTH HOSPITAL...?
HEY, KNOCK IT OFF ALREADY. FORCING YOUR WAY INTO THE HOSPITAL IS **INSANE.** YOU KNOW THAT, RIGHT?
CLOP
HEY!
YOU GUYS!
IF WE DON'T GO HOME *RIGHT* NOW, I'M GOING TO WRITE THAT GHOST ARTICLE, HOSOKAWA!!
Tug
Tug
Tug
AH!
HEY, AZUMA!! THAT ROOM OVER THERE ...
THAT'S THE EXAMINATION ROOM, ISN'T IT?!
NO, I DON'T THINK SO! LOOK CLOSER!

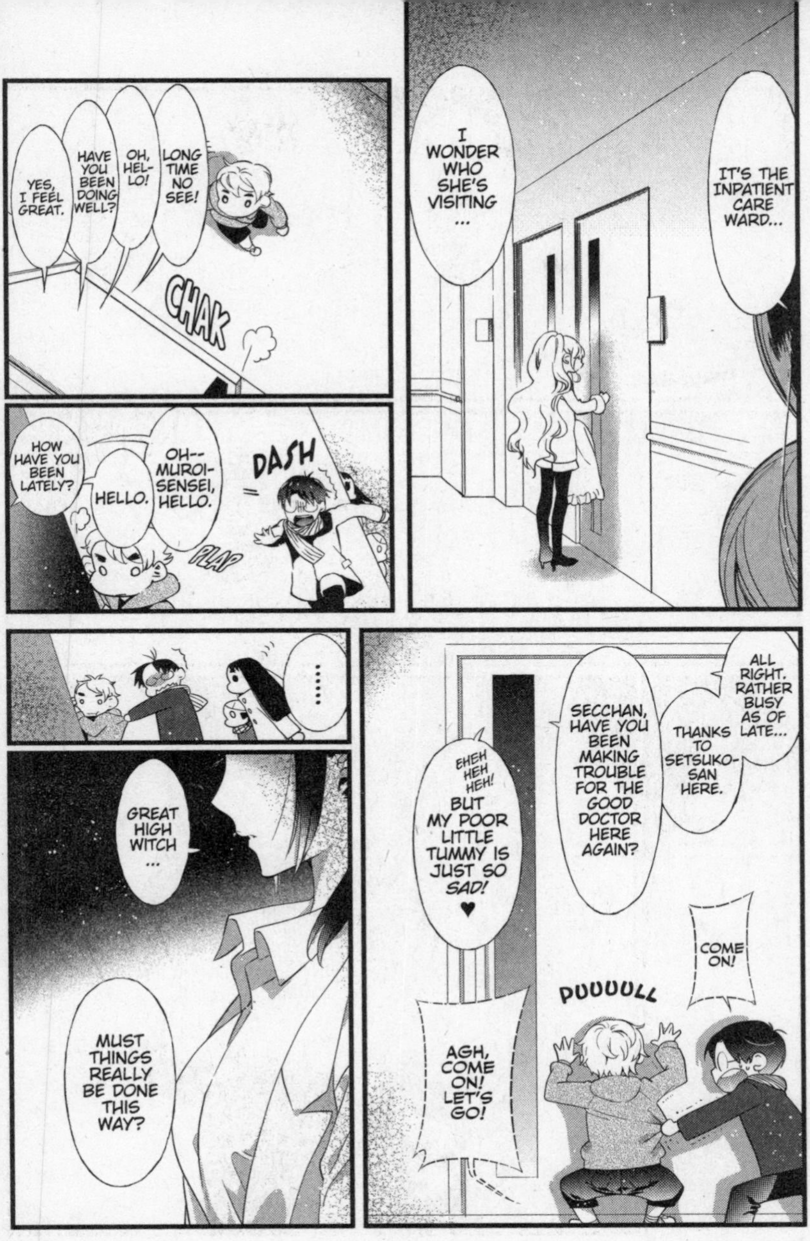
IT'S THE INPATIENT CARE WARD...
I WONDER WHO SHE'S VISITING...
LONG TIME NO SEE!
OH, HEL-LO!
HAVE YOU BEEN DOING WELL?
YES, I FEEL GREAT.
CHAK
DASH
OH-- MUROI-SENSEI, HELLO.
HELLO.
HOW HAVE YOU BEEN LATELY?
PLAP
ALL RIGHT. RATHER BUSY AS OF LATE...
THANKS TO SETSUKO-SAN HERE.
SECCHAN, HAVE YOU BEEN MAKING TROUBLE FOR THE GOOD DOCTOR HERE AGAIN?
EHEH HEH HEH! BUT MY POOR LITTLE TUMMY IS JUST SO SAD! ♥
COME ON!
PUUUULL
AGH, COME ON! LET'S GO!
......
GREAT HIGH WITCH...
MUST THINGS REALLY BE DONE THIS WAY?

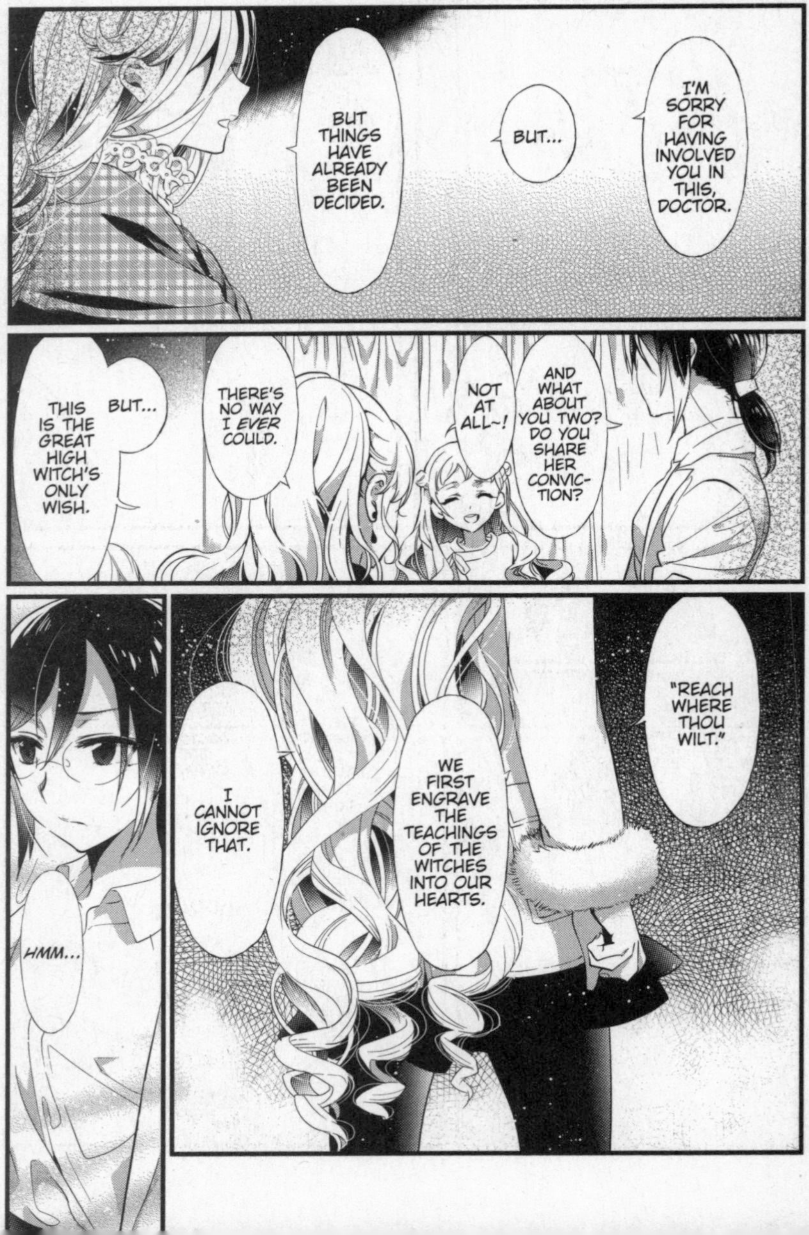
I'M SORRY FOR HAVING INVOLVED YOU IN THIS, DOCTOR.
BUT...
BUT THINGS HAVE ALREADY BEEN DECIDED.
AND WHAT ABOUT YOU TWO? DO YOU SHARE HER CONVICTION?
NOT AT ALL~!
THERE'S NO WAY I *EVER* COULD.
BUT... THIS IS THE GREAT HIGH WITCH'S ONLY WISH.
"REACH WHERE THOU WILT."
WE FIRST ENGRAVE THE TEACHINGS OF THE WITCHES INTO OUR HEARTS.
I CANNOT IGNORE THAT.
HMM...

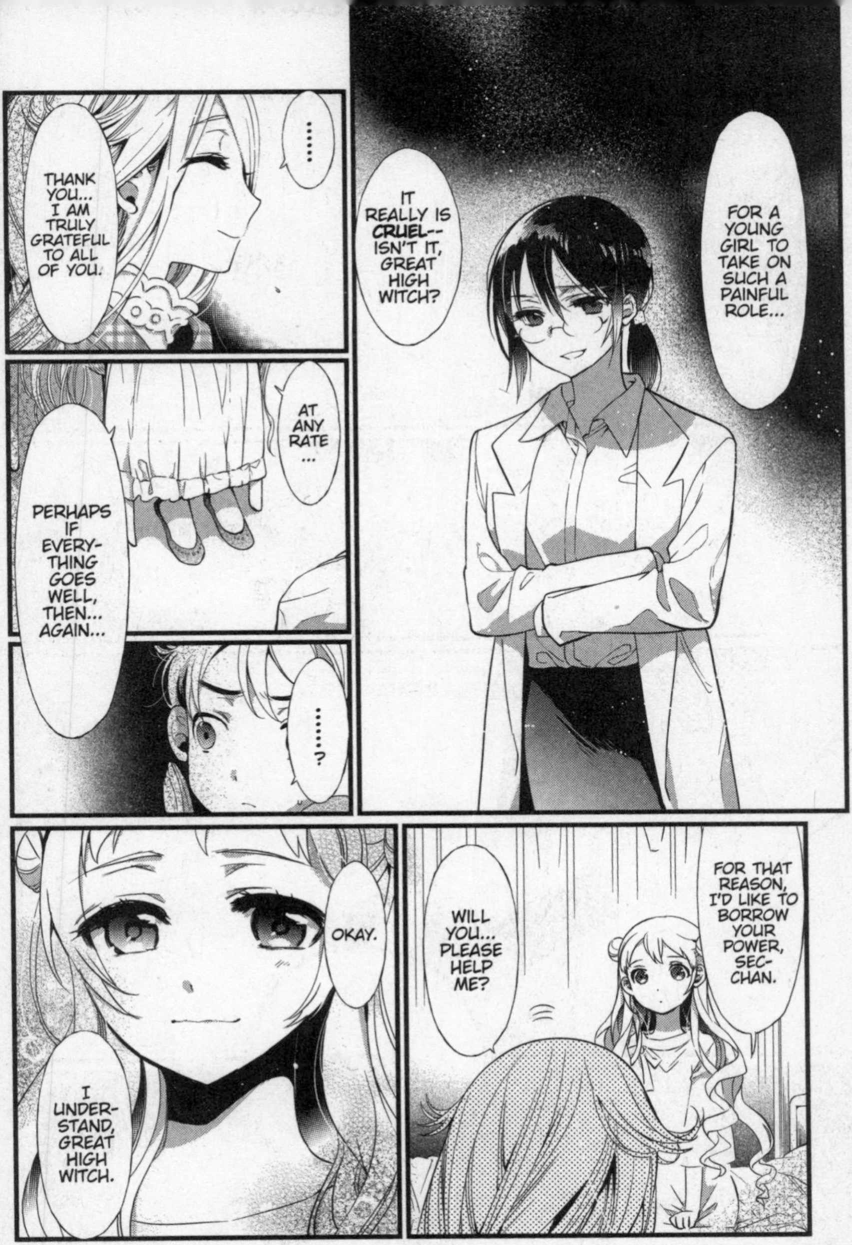
FOR A YOUNG GIRL TO TAKE ON SUCH A PAINFUL ROLE...
IT REALLY IS CRUEL-- ISN'T IT, GREAT HIGH WITCH?
......
THANK YOU... I AM TRULY GRATEFUL TO ALL OF YOU.
AT ANY RATE ...
PERHAPS IF EVERY-THING GOES WELL, THEN... AGAIN...
......?
FOR THAT REASON, I'D LIKE TO BORROW YOUR POWER, SEC-CHAN.
WILL YOU... PLEASE HELP ME?
OKAY.
I UNDER-STAND, GREAT HIGH WITCH.

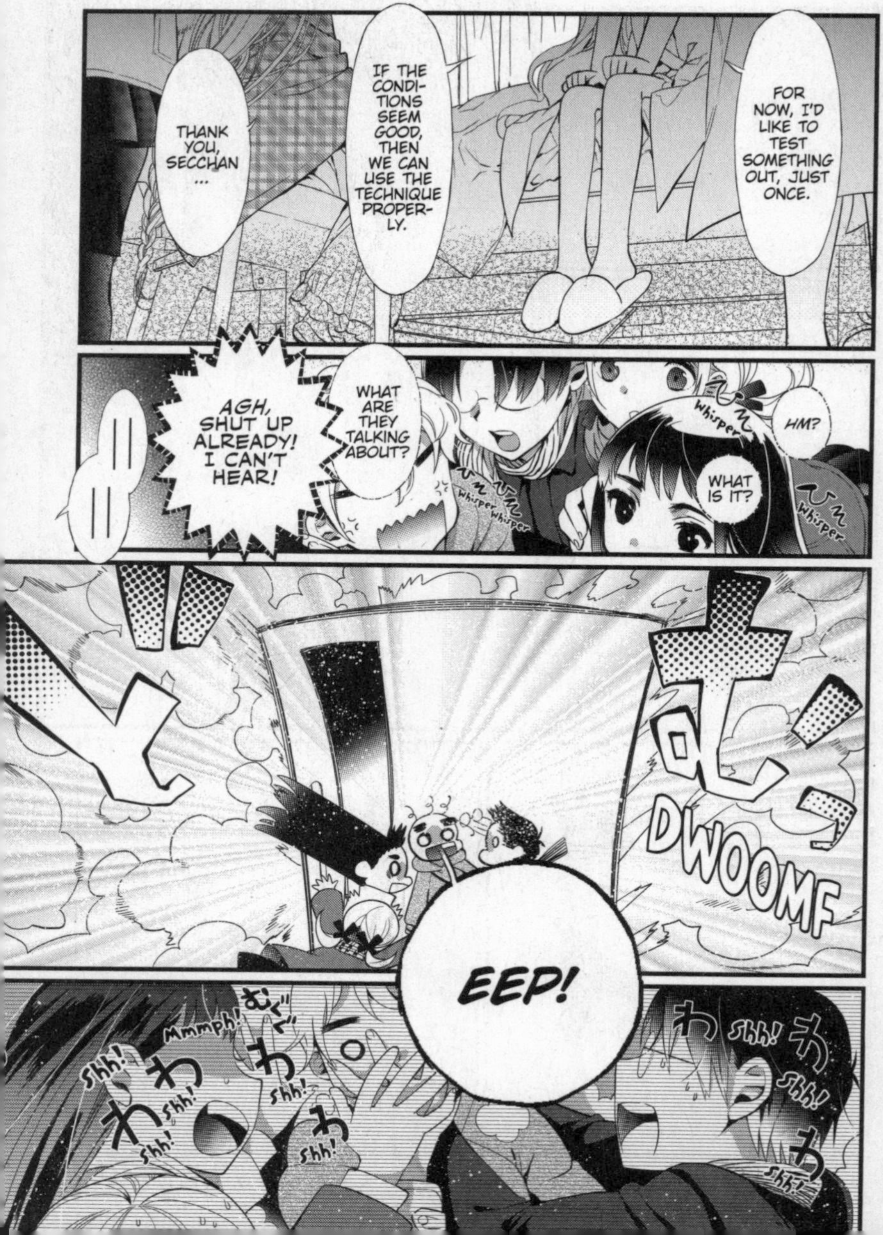
FOR NOW, I'D LIKE TO TEST SOMETHING OUT, JUST ONCE.
IF THE CONDITIONS SEEM GOOD, THEN WE CAN USE THE TECHNIQUE PROPERLY.
THANK YOU, SECCHAN...
HM?
WHAT IS IT?
Whisper
Whisper
WHAT ARE THEY TALKING ABOUT?
Whisper Whisper
AGH, SHUT UP ALREADY! I CAN'T HEAR!
!!
DWOOMF
EEP!
Shh!
Shh!
Shh!
Mmmph!
Shh!
Shh!
Shh!
Shh!
Shh!
Shh!

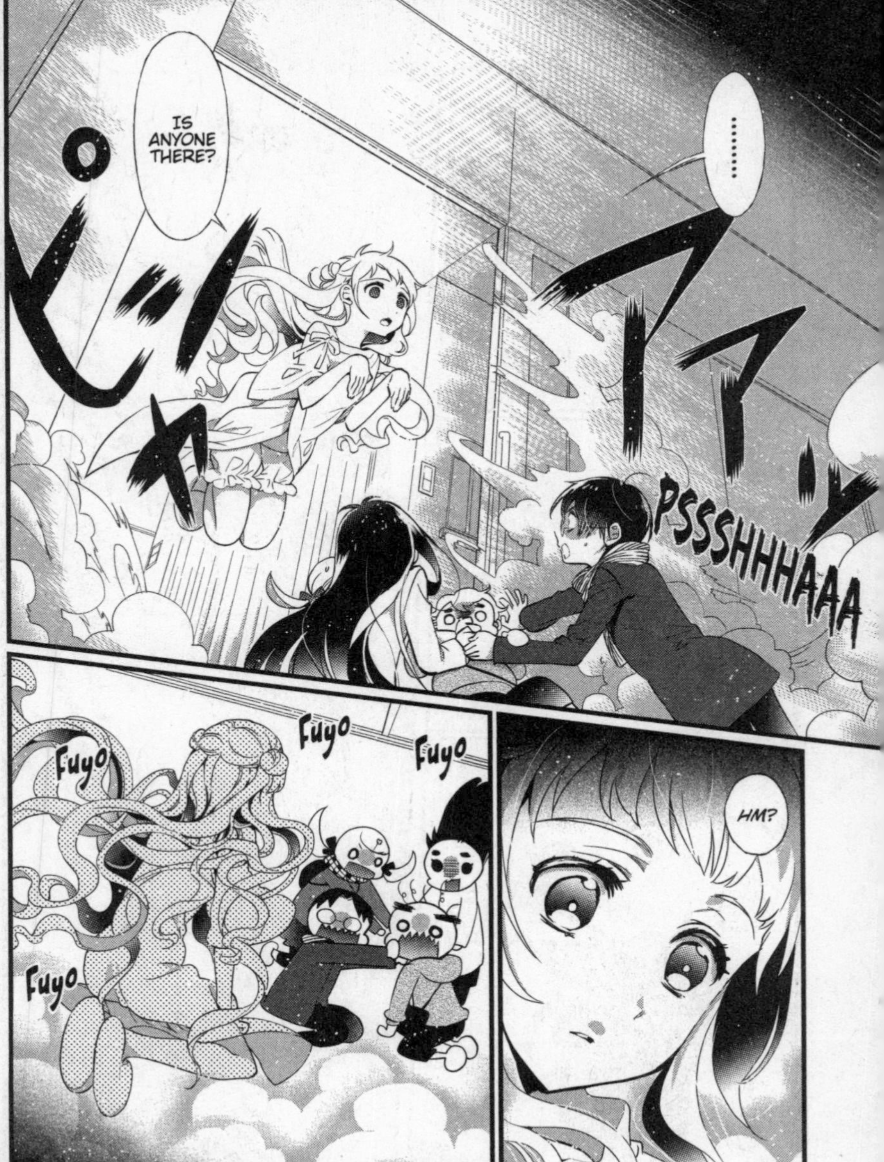
......
IS ANYONE THERE?
PSSSHHHAAA
HM?
Fuyo
Fuyo
Fuyo
Fuyo

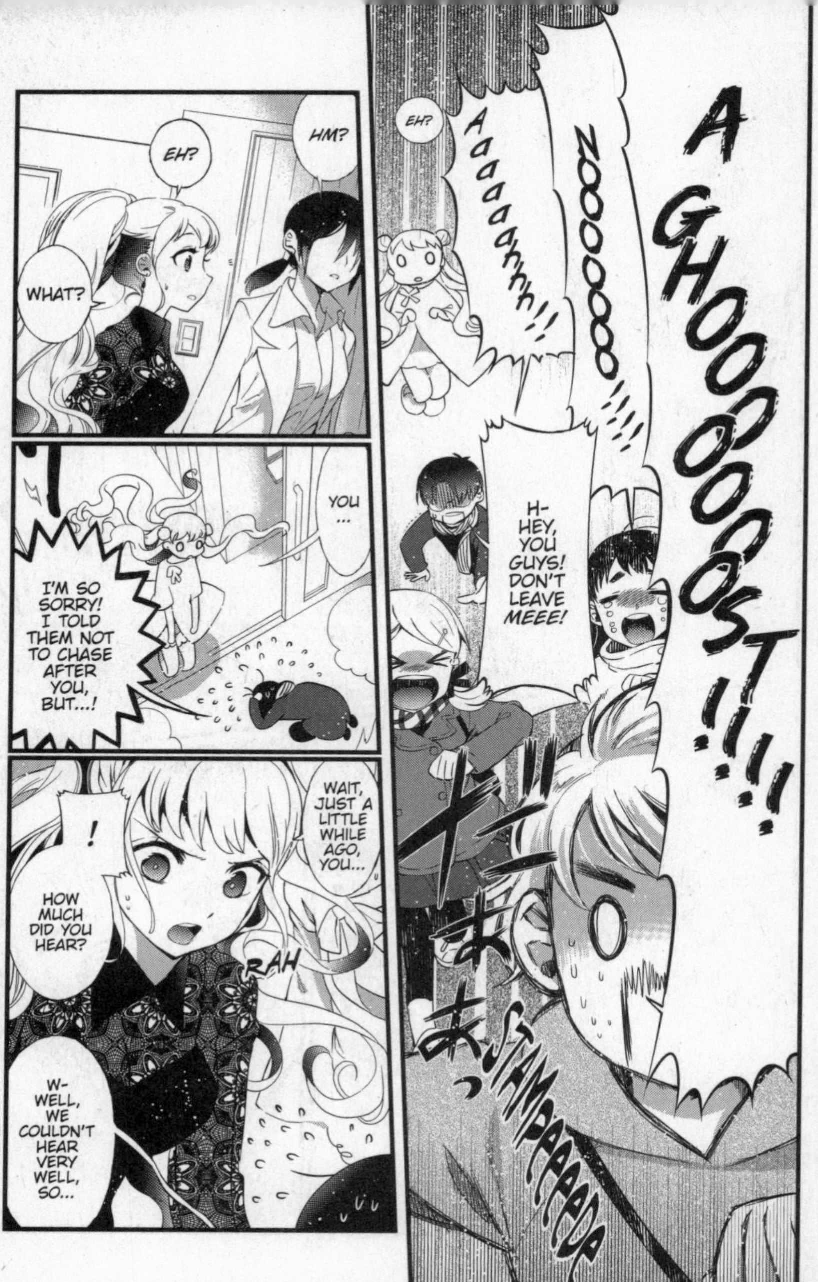
A GHOOOOOOOOST!!!!!
NOOOOOOOO!!!!
AAAAAAAAHHH!!!
EH?
H-HEY, YOU GUYS! DON'T LEAVE MEEE!
STAMPAAAAAP
HM?
EH?
WHAT?
YOU ...
I'M SO SORRY! I TOLD THEM NOT TO CHASE AFTER YOU, BUT...!
WAIT, JUST A LITTLE WHILE AGO, YOU...
!
HOW MUCH DID YOU HEAR?
RAH
W-WELL, WE COULDN'T HEAR VERY WELL, SO...

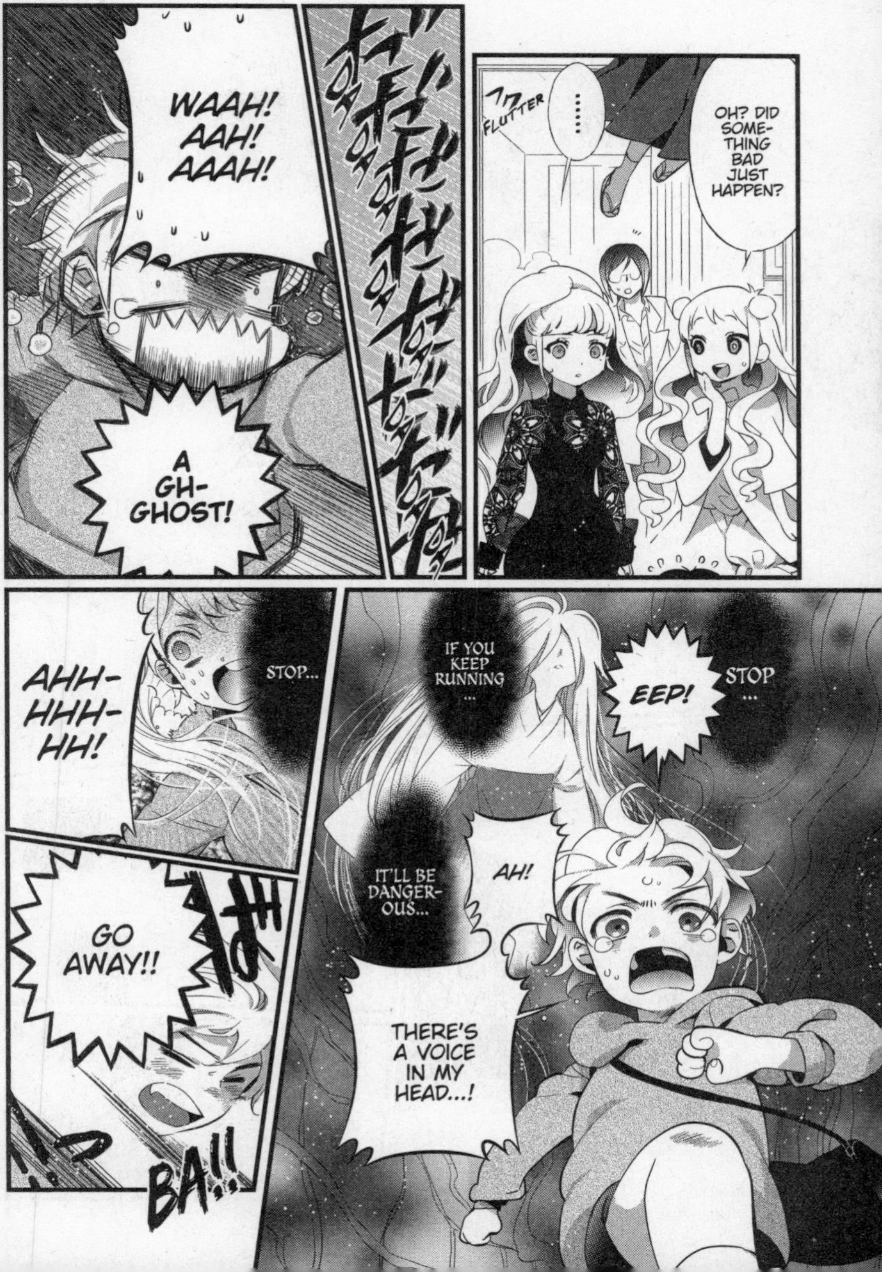
OH? DID SOME-THING BAD JUST HAPPEN?
......
FLUTTER
WAAH! AAH! AAAH!
A GH-GHOST!
STOP ...
EEP!
IF YOU KEEP RUNNING ...
AH!
IT'LL BE DANGER-OUS...
THERE'S A VOICE IN MY HEAD...!
STOP...
AHH-HHH-HH!
GO AWAY!!
BA!!

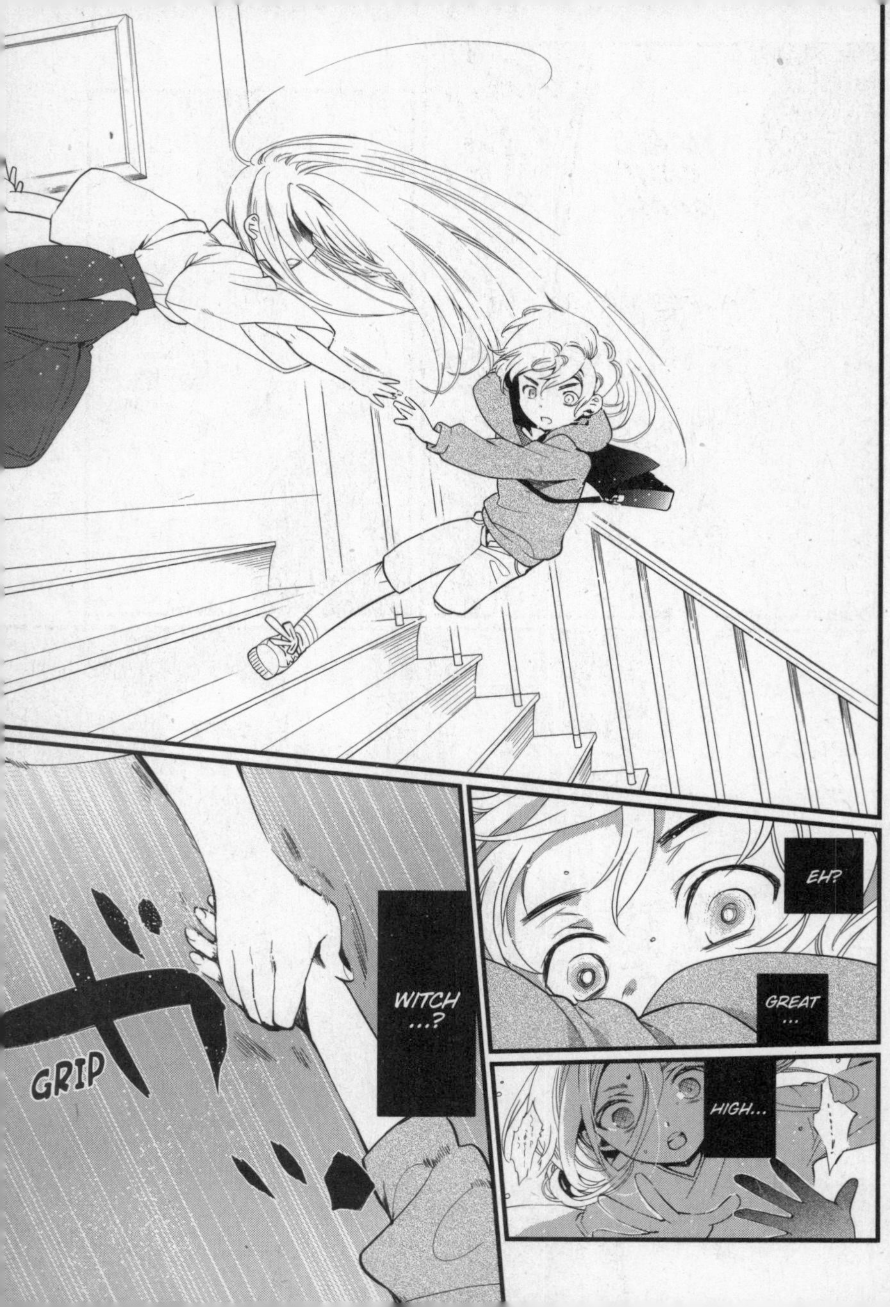
EH?
GREAT ...
HIGH...
WITCH ...?
GRIP

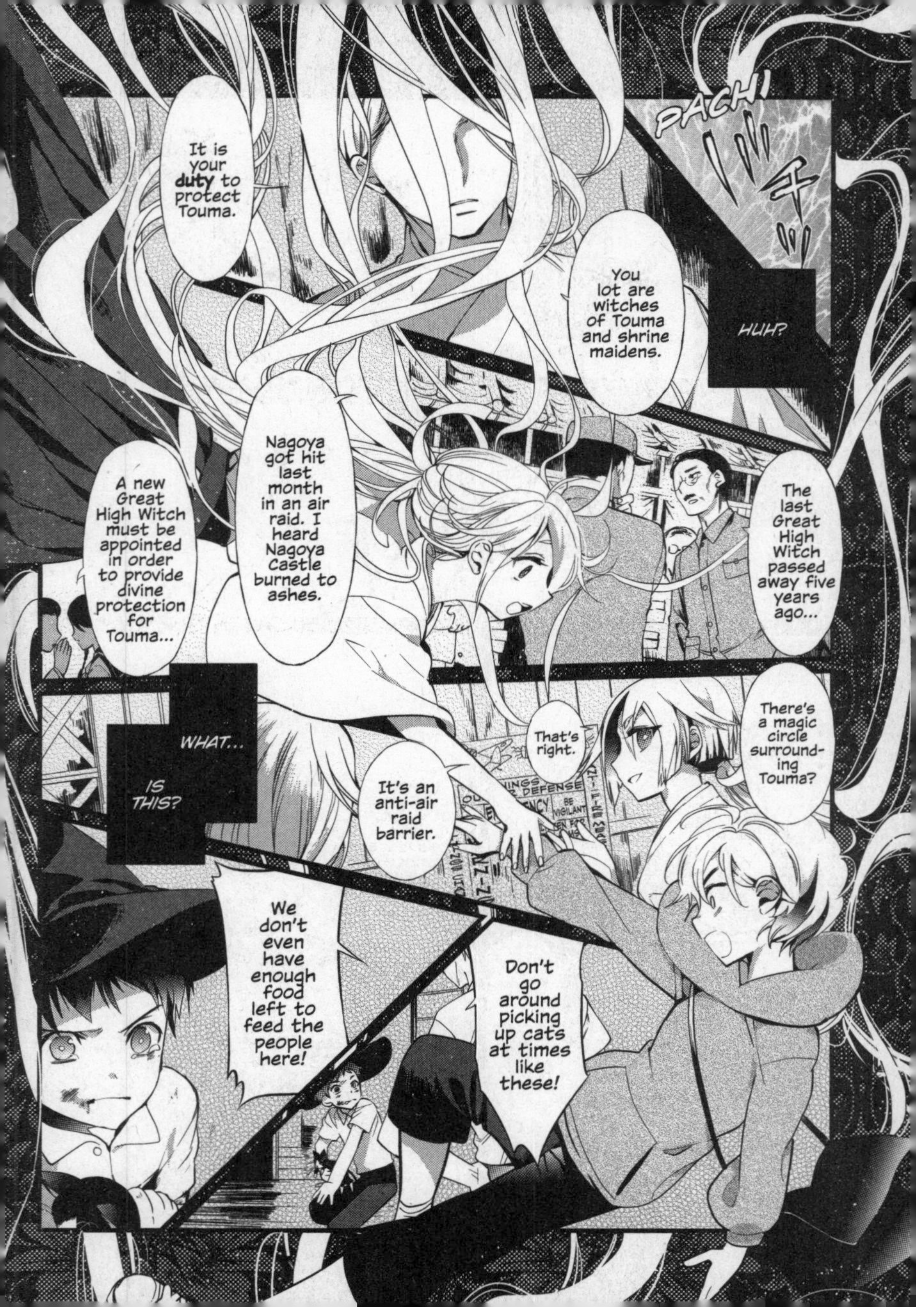
PACHI
HUH?
You lot are witches of Touma and shrine maidens.
It is your **duty** to protect Touma.
The last Great High Witch passed away five years ago...
Nagoya got hit last month in an air raid. I heard Nagoya Castle burned to ashes.
A new Great High Witch must be appointed in order to provide divine protection for Touma...
There's a magic circle surrounding Touma?
That's right.
It's an anti-air raid barrier.
WHAT...
IS THIS?
Don't go around picking up cats at times like these!
We don't even have enough food left to feed the people here!

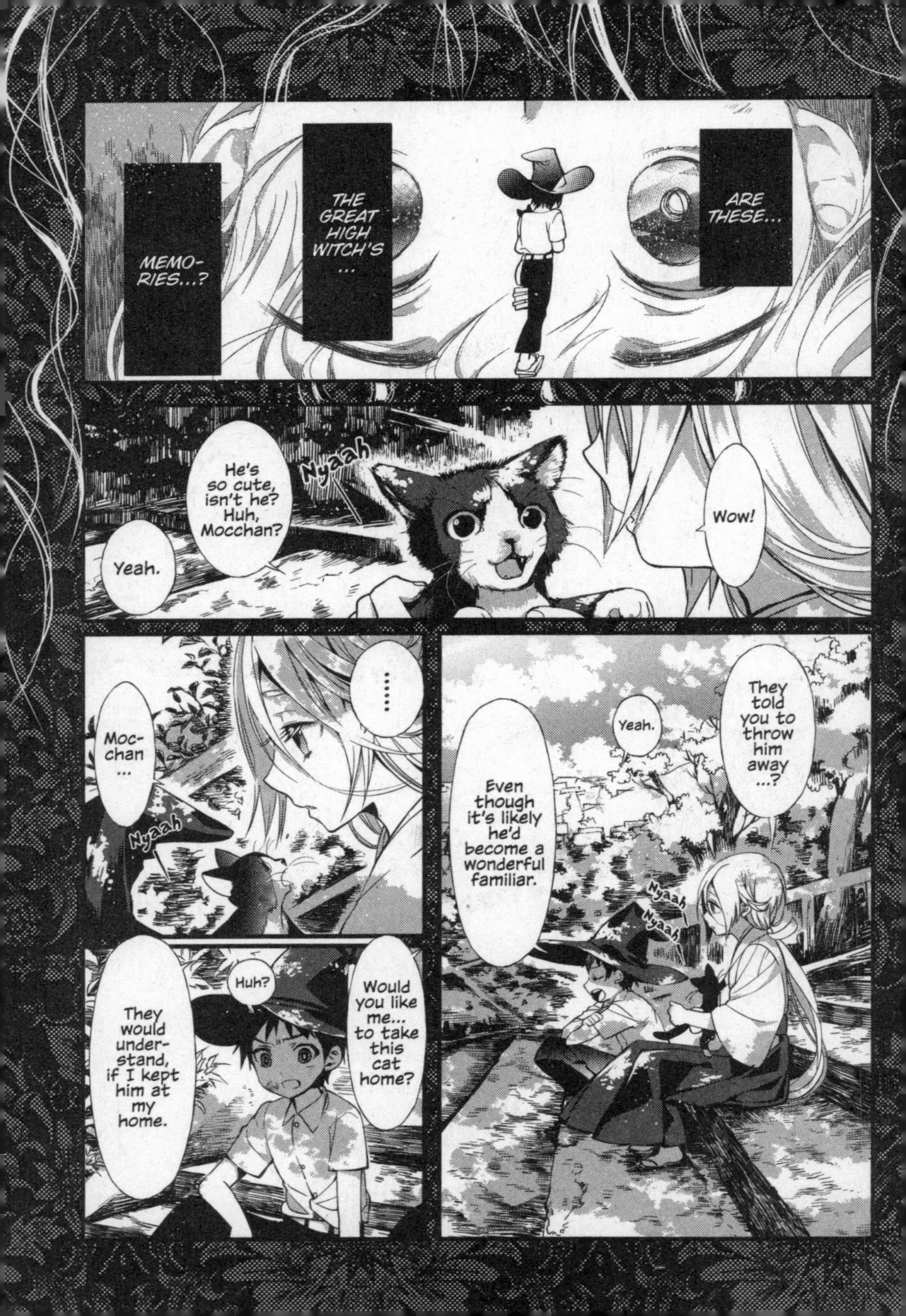
ARE THESE...
THE GREAT HIGH WITCH'S ...
MEMO-RIES...?
Wow!
Nyaah
He's so cute, isn't he? Huh, Mocchan?
Yeah.
They told you to throw him away ...?
Yeah.
Even though it's likely he'd become a wonderful familiar.
Nyaah
Nyaah
......
Moc-chan ...
Nyaah
Would you like me... to take this cat home?
Huh?
They would under-stand, if I kept him at my home.

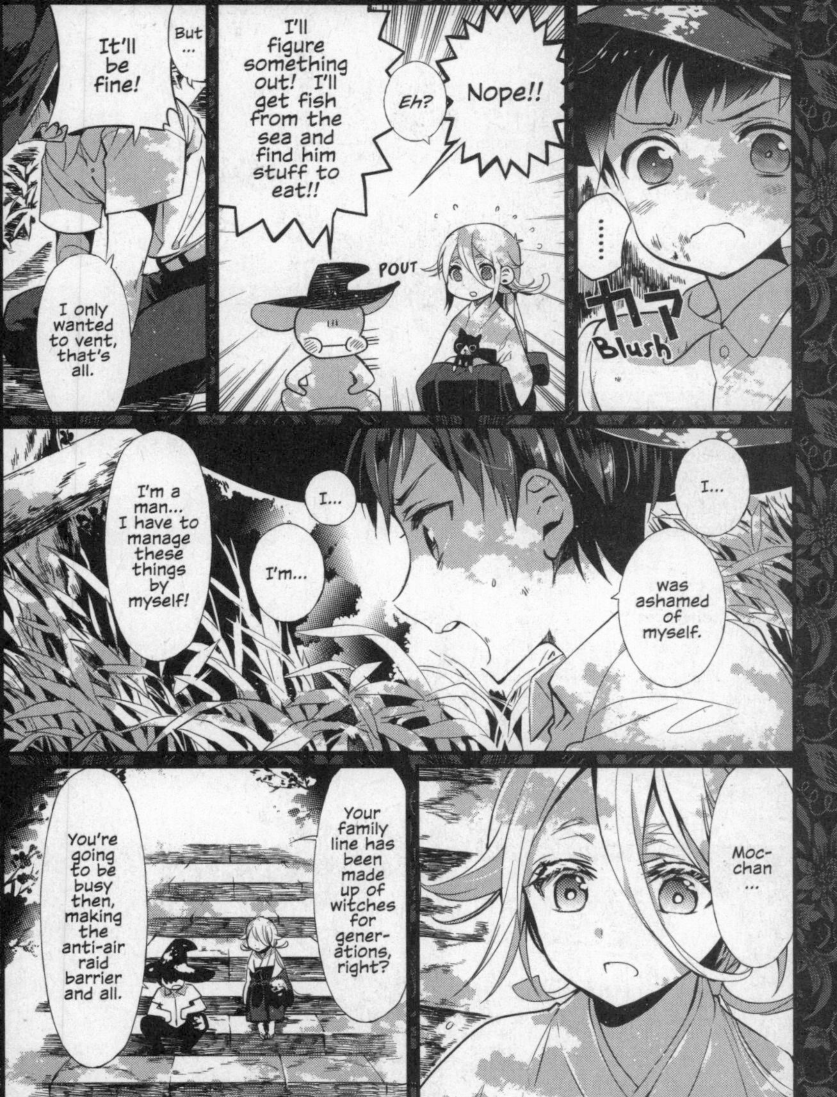
......
カア
Blush
Nope!!
Eh?
I'll figure something out! I'll get fish from the sea and find him stuff to eat!!
POUT
But ...
It'll be fine!
I only wanted to vent, that's all.
I...
was ashamed of myself.
I...
I'm...
I'm a man... I have to manage these things by myself!
Moc-chan ...
Your family line has been made up of witches for generations, right?
You're going to be busy then, making the anti-air raid barrier and all.

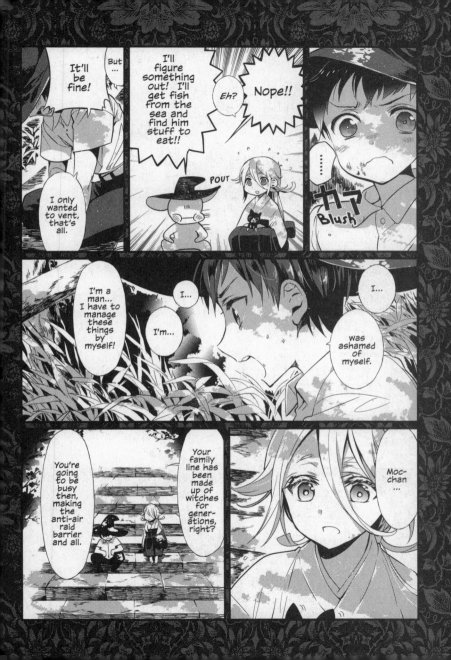

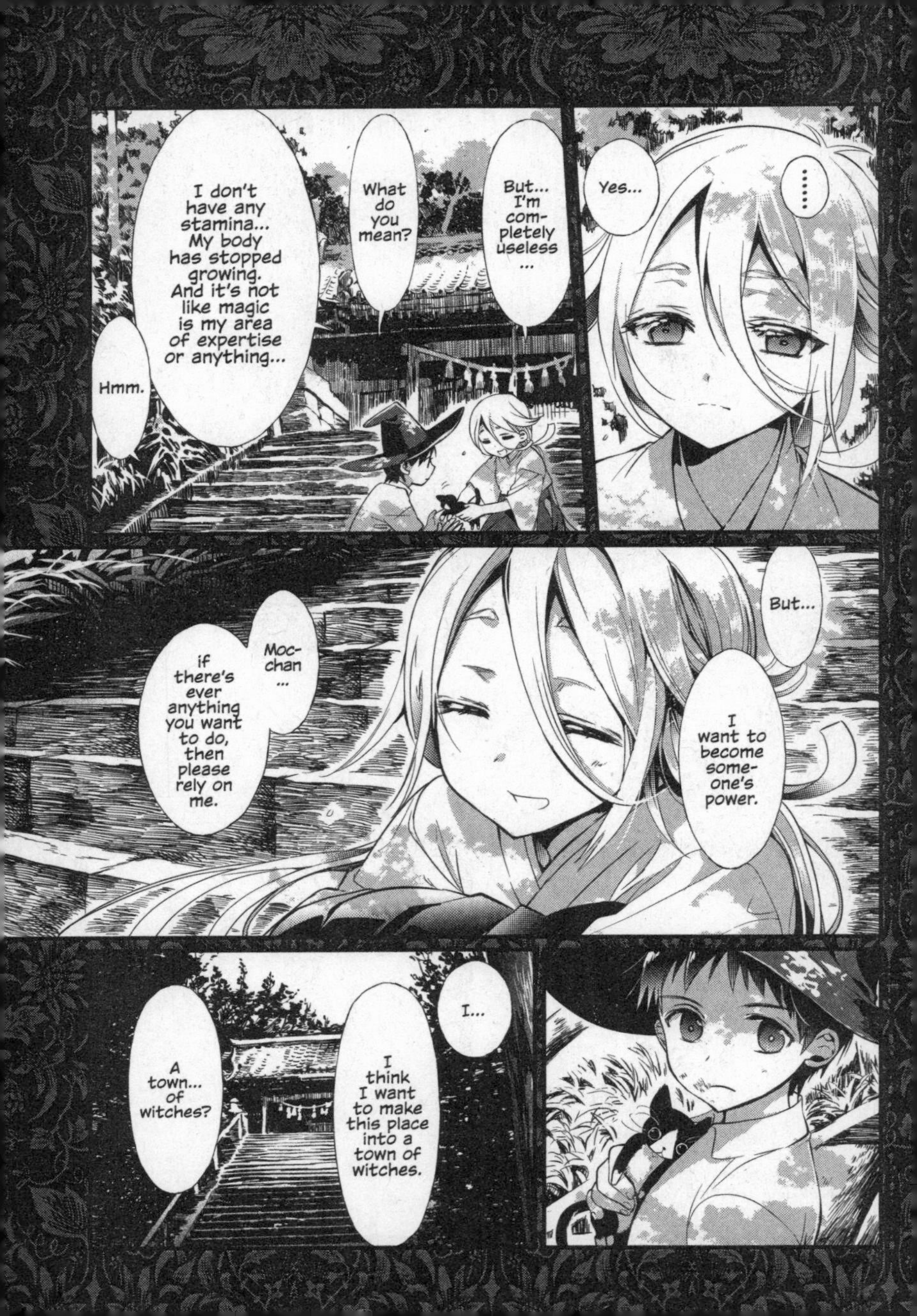
......
Yes...
But... I'm completely useless...
What do you mean?
I don't have any stamina... My body has stopped growing. And it's not like magic is my area of expertise or anything...
Hmm.
But...
I want to become someone's power.
Moc-chan...
if there's ever anything you want to do, then please rely on me.
I...
I think I want to make this place into a town of witches.
A town... of witches?

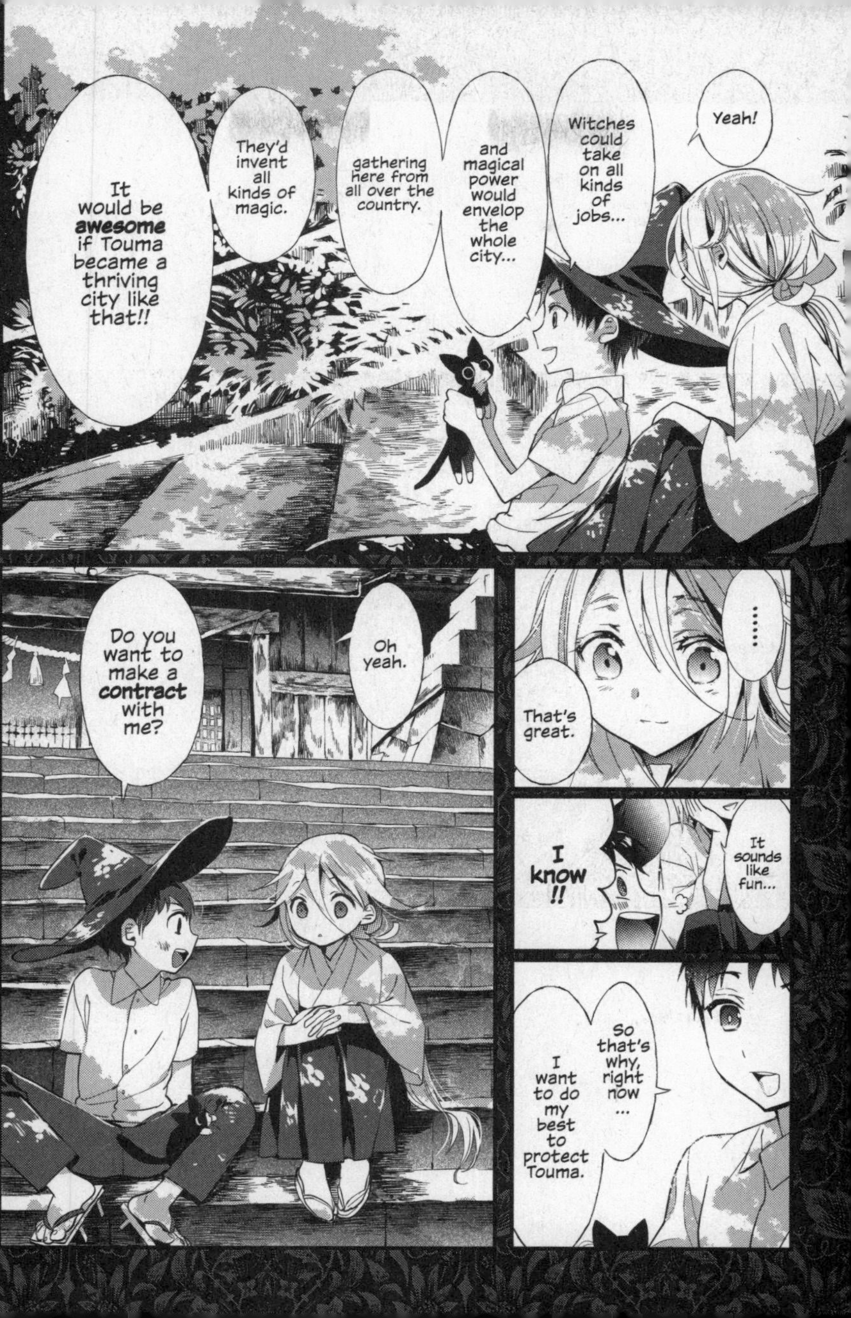

Yeah!
Witches could take on all kinds of jobs...
and magical power would envelop the whole city...
gathering here from all over the country.
They'd invent all kinds of magic.
It would be **awesome** if Touma became a thriving city like that!!
......
That's great.
It sounds like fun...
I know!!
So that's why, right now...
I want to do my best to protect Touma.
Oh yeah.
Do you want to make a **contract** with me?

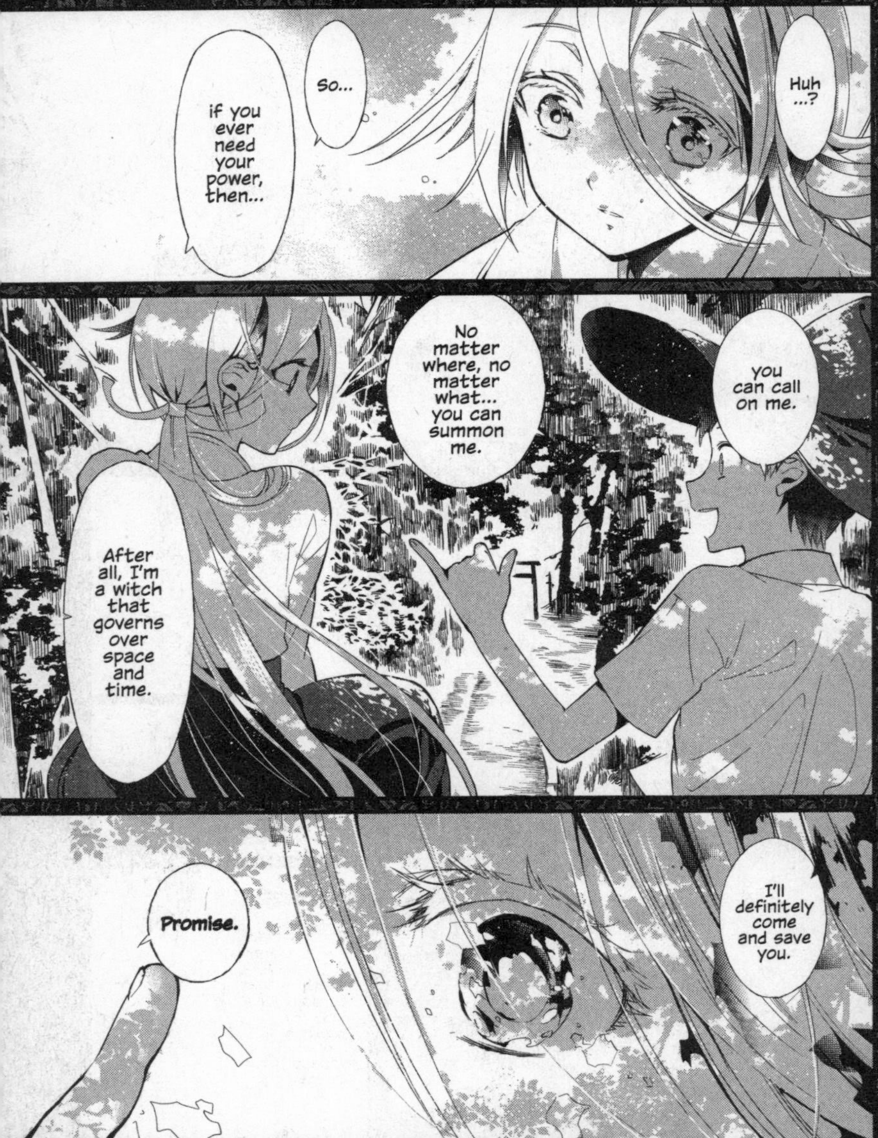
Huh ...?
So...
if you ever need your power, then...
you can call on me.
No matter where, no matter what... you can summon me.
After all, I'm a witch that governs over space and time.
I'll definitely come and save you.
Promise.

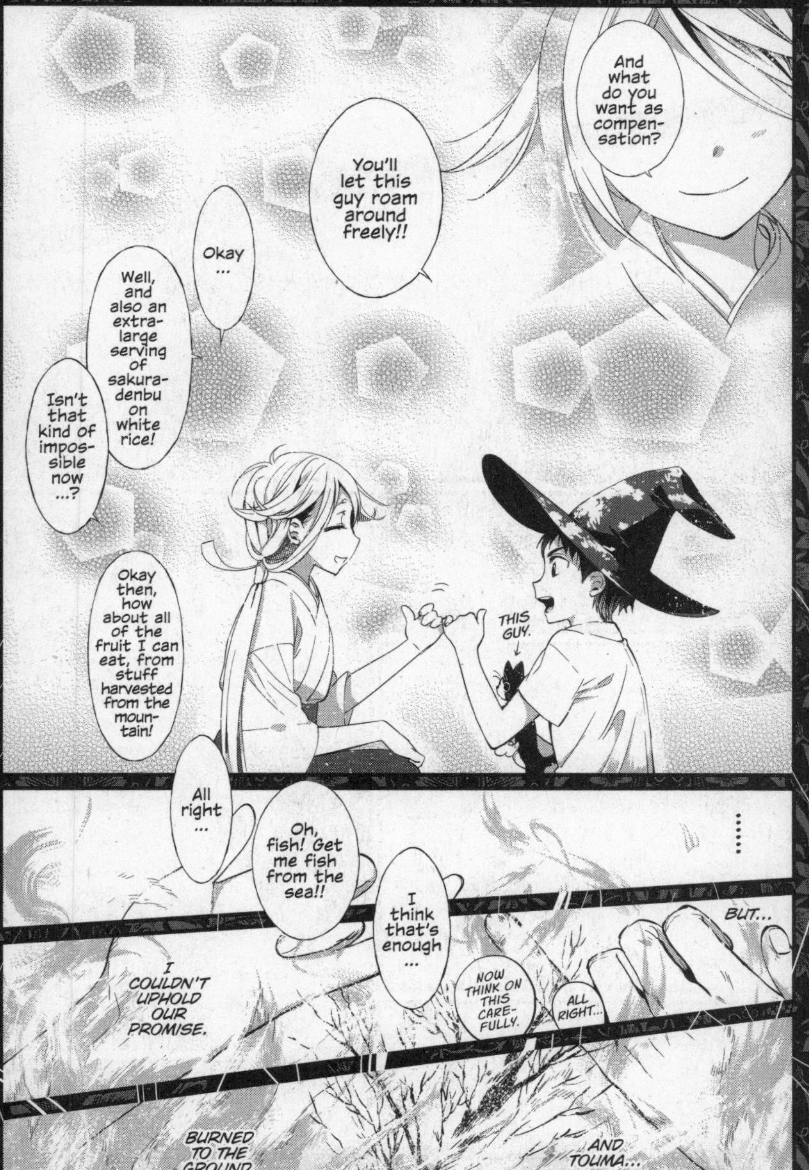
And what do you want as compensation?
You'll let this guy roam around freely!!
Okay ...
Well, and also an extra-large serving of sakura-denbu on white rice!
Isn't that kind of impossible now ...?
Okay then, how about all of the fruit I can eat, from stuff harvested from the mountain!
THIS GUY.
......
All right ...
Oh, fish! Get me fish from the sea!!
I think that's enough ...
BUT...
ALL RIGHT...
NOW THINK ON THIS CAREFULLY.
I COULDN'T UPHOLD OUR PROMISE.
AND TOUMA...
BURNED TO THE GROUND.

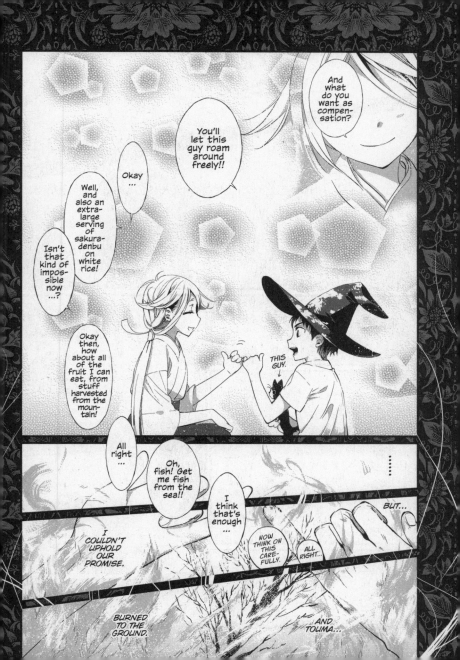

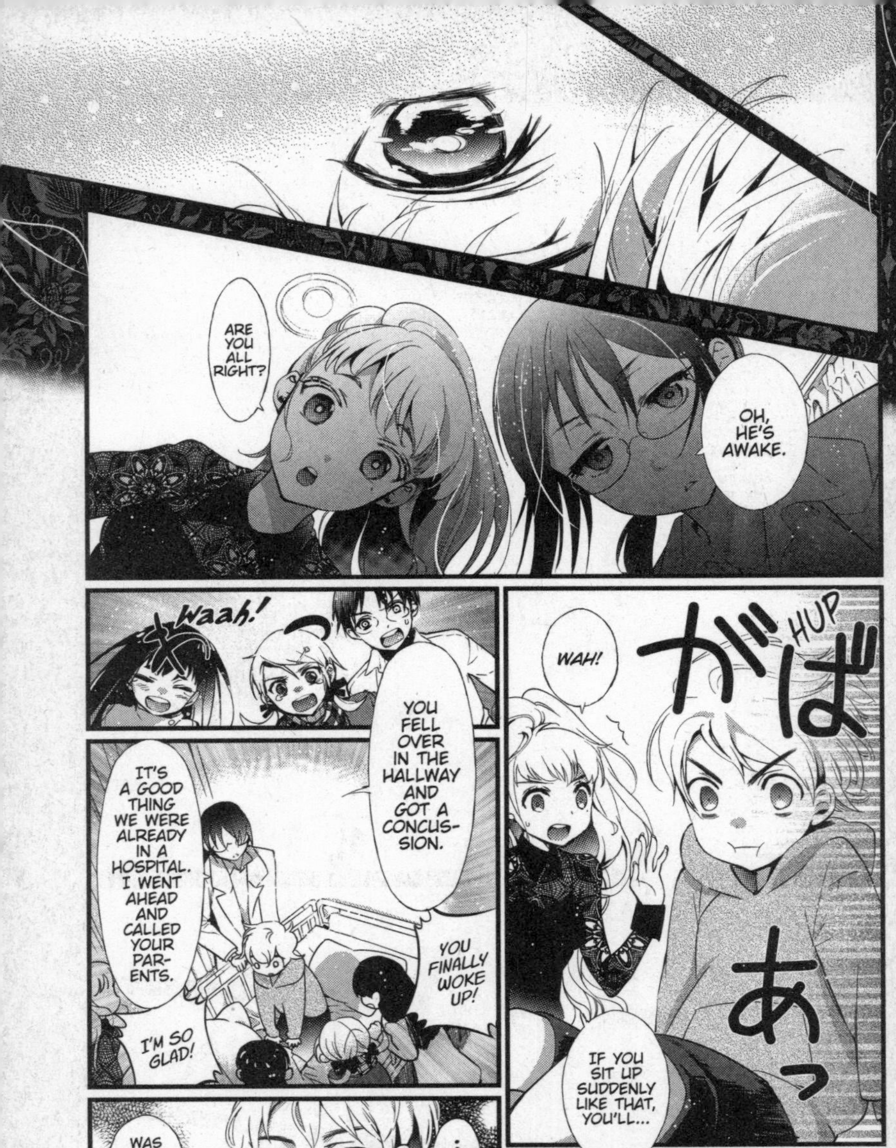
OH, HE'S AWAKE.
ARE YOU ALL RIGHT?
HUP
がばっ
WAH!
IF YOU SIT UP SUDDENLY LIKE THAT, YOU'LL...
Waah!
YOU FELL OVER IN THE HALLWAY AND GOT A CONCUSSION.
YOU FINALLY WOKE UP!
IT'S A GOOD THING WE WERE ALREADY IN A HOSPITAL. I WENT AHEAD AND CALLED YOUR PARENTS.
I'M SO GLAD!
DAAAZE
ぐわん
THAT'LL HAPPEN.
......
WAS THAT A DREAM ...?

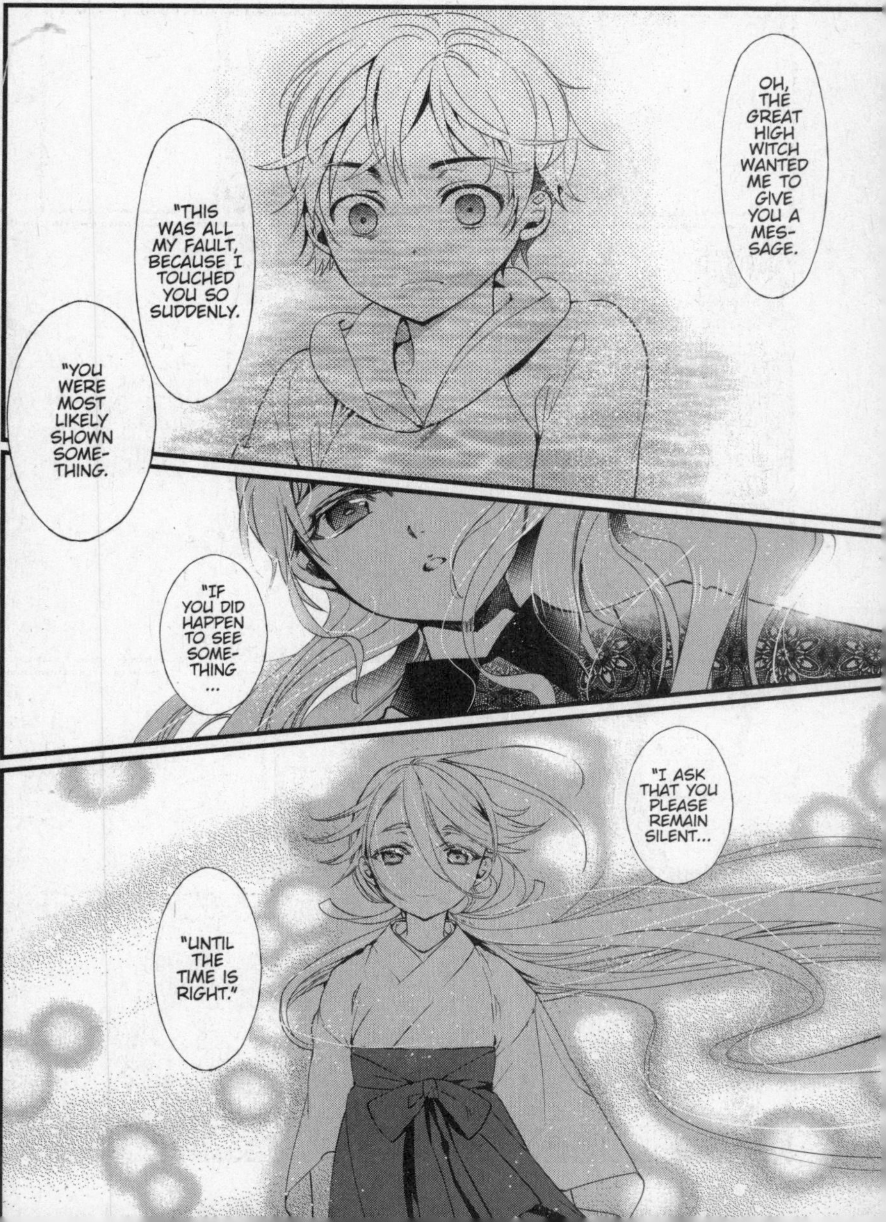
OH, THE GREAT HIGH WITCH WANTED ME TO GIVE YOU A MES-SAGE.
"THIS WAS ALL MY FAULT, BECAUSE I TOUCHED YOU SO SUDDENLY.
"YOU WERE MOST LIKELY SHOWN SOME-THING.
"IF YOU DID HAPPEN TO SEE SOME-THING ...
"I ASK THAT YOU PLEASE REMAIN SILENT...
"UNTIL THE TIME IS RIGHT."

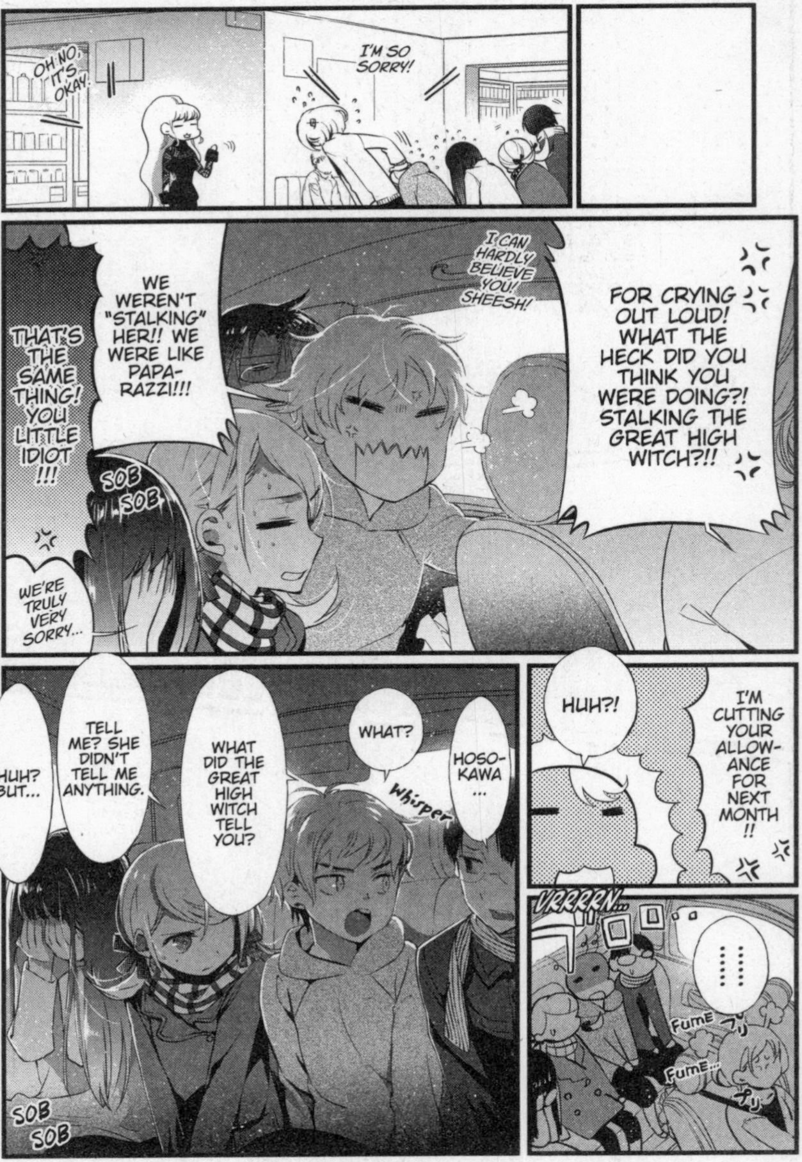
I'M SO SORRY!
OH NO, IT'S OKAY.
FOR CRYING OUT LOUD! WHAT THE HECK DID YOU THINK YOU WERE DOING?! STALKING THE GREAT HIGH WITCH?!!
I CAN HARDLY BELIEVE YOU! SHEESH!
WE WEREN'T "STALKING" HER!! WE WERE LIKE PAPA-RAZZI!!!
THAT'S THE SAME THING! YOU LITTLE IDIOT!!!
SOB SOB
WE'RE TRULY VERY SORRY...
I'M CUTTING YOUR ALLOWANCE FOR NEXT MONTH!!
HUH?!
VRRRRN...
......
Fume プリ
Fume... プリ
HOSO-KAWA...
Whisper
WHAT?
WHAT DID THE GREAT HIGH WITCH TELL YOU?
TELL ME? SHE DIDN'T TELL ME ANYTHING.
HUH? BUT...
SOB SOB

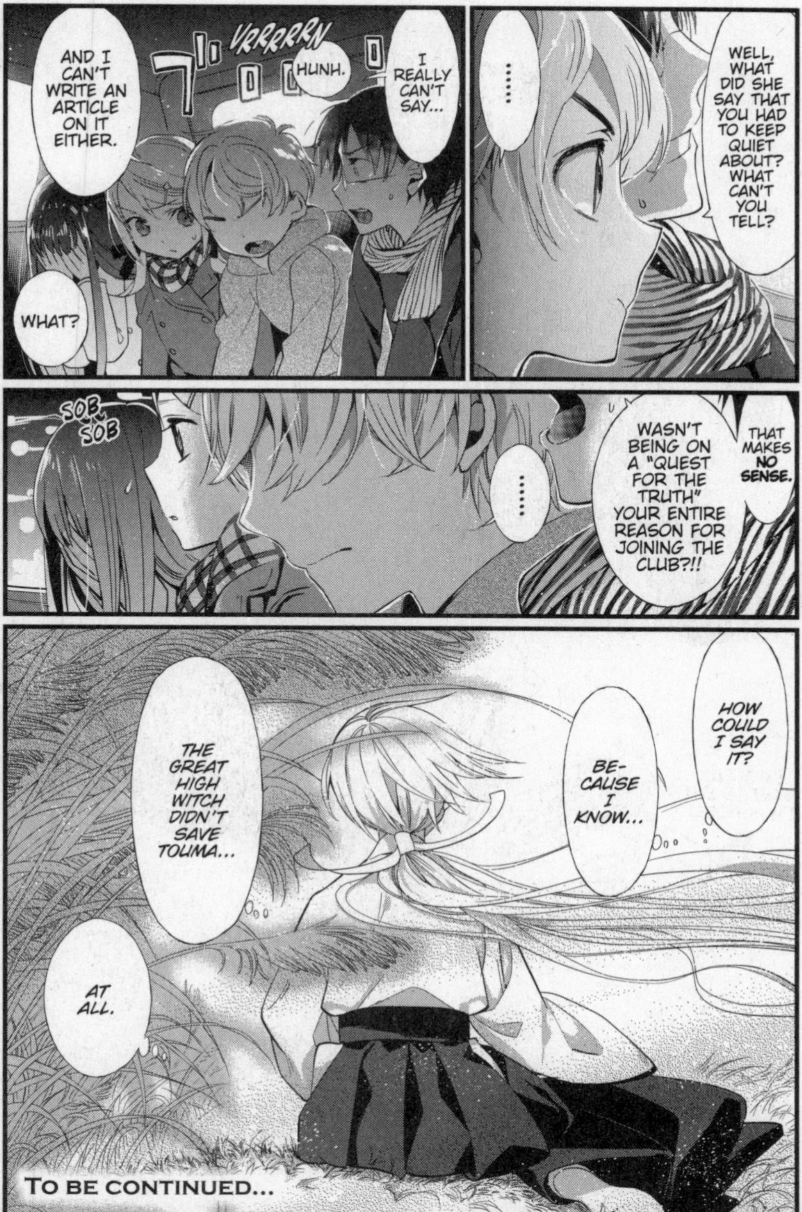
WELL, WHAT DID SHE SAY THAT YOU HAD TO KEEP QUIET ABOUT? WHAT CAN'T YOU TELL?
......
I REALLY CAN'T SAY...
HUNH.
VRRRRRN
AND I CAN'T WRITE AN ARTICLE ON IT EITHER.
WHAT?
THAT MAKES **NO SENSE.**
WASN'T BEING ON A "QUEST FOR THE TRUTH" YOUR ENTIRE REASON FOR JOINING THE CLUB?!!
......
SOB SOB
HOW COULD I SAY IT?
BE-CAUSE I KNOW...
THE GREAT HIGH WITCH DIDN'T SAVE TOUMA...
AT ALL.
TO BE CONTINUED...